Family Therapy

Complementary Frameworks of
Theory and Practice

Volume 1

Family Therapy

Complementary Frameworks of Theory and Practice

Volume 1

edited by

Arnon Bentovim

Gill Gorell Barnes

Alan Cooklin

1982

published for

The Institute of Family Therapy (London)
43 New Cavendish St, London W1

by

ACADEMIC PRESS London Paris San Diego São Paulo Sydney Tokyo Toronto
GRUNE & STRATTON New York San Francisco

ACADEMIC PRESS INC. (LONDON) LTD.
24/28 Oval Road, London NW1 7DX

United States Edition published by
GRUNE & STRATTON INC.
111 Fifth Avenue, New York, New York, 10003

British Library Cataloguing in Publication Data

Family therapy.
 Vol. 1
 1. Family psychotherapy
 I. Bentovim, A.   II. Gorell Barnes, G.
 III. Cooklin, A.
 616.89'156   RC488.5

 ISBN (Academic Press) 0-12-790545-6
 ISBN (Grune & Stratton) 0-8089-1479-0

Phototypeset in Great Britain by Dobbie Typesetting Service, Plymouth
Printed in Great Britain by T. J. Press (Padstow) Ltd.

Contributors

ARNON BENTOVIM *Department of Psychological Medicine, The Hospital for Sick Children, Department for Children and Parents, The Tavistock Clinic and The Institute of Family Therapy, London*

DORA BLACK *Edgware General Hospital and The Hospital for Sick Children and The Institute of Family Therapy, London*

TERRY BRUCE *St. Bartholomew's Hospital and The Institute of Family Therapy, London*

JOHN BYNG-HALL *Department for Children and Parents, The Tavistock Clinic and The Institute of Family Therapy, London*

DAVID CAMPBELL *Department for Children and Parents, The Tavistock Clinic, Uxbridge Child Guidance Clinic and The Institute of Family Therapy, London*

ALAN COOKLIN *Marlborough Hospital and The Institute of Family Therapy, London*

MICHAEL CROWE *Children's Department, Bethlem Royal and Maudsley Hospitals and The Institute of Family Therapy, London*

CHRISTOPHER DARE *Children's Department, Bethlem Royal and Maudsley Hospitals and The Institute of Family Therapy, London*

ANNE ELTON *Department of Psychological Medicine, The Hospital for Sick Children and The Institute of Family Therapy, London*

GILL GORELL BARNES *Department for Children and Parents, The Tavistock Clinic and The Institute of Family Therapy, London*

BRYAN LASK *Department of Psychological Medicine, The Hospital for Sick Children and The Institute of Family Therapy, London*

STUART LIEBERMAN *St. George's Hospital Medical School and The Institute of Family Therapy, London*

WINIFRED ROBERTS *Marlborough Hospital and The Institute of Family Therapy, London*

MARGARET ROBINSON *Chelsea College and The Institute of Family Therapy, London*

ROBIN SKYNNER *Institute of Psychiatry and The Institute of Family Therapy, London*

Acknowledgements

We would like to thank the many colleagues including secretaries and librarians from our institutions whose assistance has played such an important part in the writing and preparations of the contributions for this book. We would also like to thank Sylvia Donald and Linda Collins of the Institute of Family Therapy for their assistance in the final production.

Preface

The year 1982 sees seven years development of a professional association for Family Therapy in Britain (AFT), a flourishing journal, and signs of accelerating interest in the field. Practitioners, theories and practices abound. The aim of this book is to try and place some of these developments in context and to examine the relationship between some of these apparently diverse ideas and approaches. As editors, we have been privileged to have a ready-made group of authors who have shared some basic assumptions, and some common professional history, while representing specific points of view in their own right. This group is the Institute of Family Therapy (London), and the authors are its members. We hope this work will provide a useful milestone in the rapid development of the field, as its production has been in the development of the Institute.

The group was conceived in 1973 when Robin Skynner convened teachers to run the one year Family and Marital course under the auspices of the Institute of Group Analysis. Thus began what he has called an "open systems" method of training in Family Therapy. One of its great strengths was that it brought together teachers of different disciplines and orientations who were prepared to unlearn some aspects of their old allegiances—sufficient to create something new as a group. After three years, the group of teachers felt that there was a need for a setting from which the work could develop further, and in 1977 the Institute of Family Therapy was established with the aims of furthering teaching, practice and research in Family Therapy. The open systems nature of Robin Skynner's original concept has in many respects continued. This is reflected both in the variety of disciplines, settings and theoretical views held by the contributors to these volumes, as well as the fact that they hang together as a whole.

Our title indicates that we are concerned with a variety of complementary frameworks to view the theory and practice of Family Therapy. We are not concerned with the exposition of one "right" way of conceptualizing the work or practising it, but of trying to present a set of usable frameworks for practitioners. A set of models has been described which are helpful in thinking about families, in the practice of Family Therapy, and in particular for the application of such notions to the wide variety of settings where Family Therapy can be, and is, now practised. Throughout, the emphasis is on the encounter between the therapist and the family, and we have asked contributors where possible to bring their own experience, their own case material and, if possible, the blow-by-blow account of work which can convey more than description alone. Thus we have aimed the book at the beginning practitioner who needs a compass on a new and uncharted sea, as well as the experienced old salts who have taken and steered a particular course. We hope that the work will provide a helpful background for the development of the ideas of this latter group.

The work has been divided into two volumes: Volume 1 and Volume 2. The first section of Volume 1 is introduced by Robin Skynner. He has written a chapter on "Frameworks for Viewing the Family as a System", thinking about family functioning in health rather than in dysfunction and ill health. We have asked Robin Skynner to introduce the three basic frameworks for viewing the family which are repeated in a variety of different ways throughout the book. The first section considers the family as a "here-and-now" interacting entity, in which the Systems Communication and Cybernetic models of the family are presented. Robin Skynner then outlines the second basic framework: "The Family as a System Over Time", the family as a unit of reproduction, a growing, living organism with a history of its own that complements its current "here-and-now" patterns of behaviour. These first two frameworks come together with a different perspective in the third section. Describing the "Inner or Experiential Life of the Family", Robin Skynner is concerned with such issues as consciousness and the fragmentation of experience and the way that such fragmentation can occur and becomes healed. He applies some of these ideas to the research on non-clinically labelled families, and introduces the notion of different levels of family functioning by summarizing such work as the "Timberlawn" family studies.

Such theoretical ideas are explored in practice in the second chapter of this section, where a group of contributors: Arnon Bentovim, John Byng-Hall, Alan Cooklin, Gill Gorell Barnes and Robin Skynner, discuss some video-tapes of the interactions of what was considered to be a relatively healthy family. In their observations and interchange about the interactions, they reviewed the issues of what makes for a healthy family and what is ill health in families, again in practice and not just in theory.

By contrast, the second part: "The Family and Therapy", opens with the same group discussing an identified family who presented with a number of problems in the children. Through observing video-taped interaction between the therapist and the family the group begin to identify some of the elements that are involved, not only in dysfunctional patterns in the family, but in interventions to change families. An important aim for us in this book has been to show the way that frameworks for thinking about how families can be changed co-exist, and how different aspects of these frameworks can be integrated by individual practitioners.

Reflecting our basic frameworks, Alan Cooklin in Chapter 4 looks at the framework of changes in "here-and-now" family systems *vs* the framework of change in family systems "over time". By using a variety of metaphors, such as the holograph and the patterns of wave forms, he examines interventions which are aimed at changing the "here-and-now" family system *vs* the deeper, longer-standing rules which govern the family over time. He is concerned with issues of time, the communication process, and the ways in which families themselves speak in terms of the short- and longer-span patterns which affect them. He examines the way that a variety of well-developed therapeutic methods, such as structural and strategic approaches, affect change, and the way that short and long sequence changes can be integrated together in a complementary fashion.

Chapter 5 examines "Dysfunction in the Feeling or Experiential Life of the Family", and John Byng-Hall describes a variety of experiential techniques used in Family Therapy, such as changing boundaries, the use of space and distance, in sculpting and role playing, and again, shows how such notions can be integrated into an attitude towards Family Therapy which is concerned not only with the feeling, experiencing life of the family, but again in relationship to the complementary modes of the structure of family interactions in the light of the systems over time: the family's history.

In Chapter 6, the fourth chapter in this part, Gill Gorell Barnes extends the issues of change and the production of therapeutic change from our three basic frameworks to considering the issues of change which emerge from work adjacent to the field of Family Therapy—from parent/infant and parent/child interactional studies, from child and family development research, from child and adult psychiatric research—and focusses again on the development of patterns within families and the way such patterns are maintained both in the present, and over time, affecting both the individuals development and the feeling state of the family.

The third part of the book is a major section concerned with "Practical Issues in Family Therapy". It is helpful to have a clear, complementary set of frameworks for thinking about families, and thinking about the way that families are changed using a variety of different approaches which can be integrated together. However, there are a variety of practical issues which have to be addressed to ensure that the family is in the room, or that the therapist is in the home with the family, to be able to apply them. We start from the beginning through Win Roberts' chapter on "Preparing the Referral Network", the professional and the family. She is, in particular, concerned with the way in which the very wide variety of agencies who are concerned with families think about and consider the role of Family Therapy and agencies which provide Family Therapy for their clients. She describes the conflicts which can occur both within the referral agency and within the agency practising Family Therapy, and describes ways in which such mixed communications may be recognized and the principles to follow in ensuring a successful referral. She also describes the principles necessary to ensure that the invitation to the family will work in securing attendance, and the preparations to be made in the agency itself to receive the family.

In Chapter 8, Gill Gorell Barnes describes the "Initial Work with the Family". Picking up from the point of receiving the family, she describes possible settings for meeting families, including the home as well as the agency, and is concerned with who comes from the family, and considers the different approaches that can be made to the family in relationship to the therapist's own views of the way in which he wants to promote change, whether by focussing on the "here-and-now" interactions, or through being concerned with long-standing rules over time. She considers the initial moves in the session, defining and formulating the problem and where the therapist might be at the end of an initial meeting in terms of the tasks to be used and the varieties of these which are possible, depending on the therapist's view of his task. Very often the initial enthusiasm of the first meeting can carry the therapist through the first sessions, but maintaining family motivation during treatment becomes an issue in all forms of Family Therapy.

In Chapter 9, Anne Elton describes the factors of "hope for relief", "interest" and "excitement and even enjoyment" which can hold families to the work. However, she is also concerned with describing the resistances and prevention of change, the homeostatic forces which pull the family back to their original shape. She introduces a variety of frameworks, dynamic and systems, to examine the issue of resistance in families, and through a number of examples, describes ways in which such resistances may be tackled and the families' motivation maintained. She describes ways of establishing therapists' authority, creating a focus for work and changing, and a variety of techniques both concerned with the "here-and-now", and with history to be able to maintain the families' and therapists' motivation to work. She describes in detail issues of the families dropping out from therapy, a common experience for all family therapists, and specific ways of dealing with this.

In Chapter 10, John Byng-Hall examines the "Place of Family Myths and Legends". Through examining a legend in his own family, he shows how powerfully shared beliefs can limit the family's view of what actions are possible, and what changes can be made. He shows how such legends and myths can be "re-edited", so freeing the family to be able to choose a different pattern of interaction in the present.

The next two chapters (11 and 12) are concerned more with practical issues for the therapist. Win Roberts examines the "Strengths and Weaknesses of Co-therapy Relationships in Family Therapy". Co-therapy has an honourable tradition in ensuring that Family Therapy practice actually began. It has helped professionals face the unknown of working with the family as a group, rather than with individuals, and has had an enabling role for many. She describes the issues that have to be tackled if co-therapy is to be successful, and these again are concerned both in the individuals and their personal qualities as well as the agency setting where the work takes place. She describes situations such as disadvantaged families where co-therapy can be particularly helpful and developments in co-therapy where, instead of the co-therapist taking a co-equal part, he takes a position as a colleague perhaps behind a one-way screen or within the room taking a clearly different position as far as helping the therapist rather than the family.

In Chapter 12, Stuart Lieberman is concerned with a further exploration for the therapist, and argues that "Going Back to the Therapist's Own Family" both teaches him about the families he is working with, and becomes a resource in his on-going work. He traces the history of the use of "going back to one's own family", and then gives a personal account of his work with his own family, and attempts to relate his experiences to a variety of theoretical frameworks. Again, he pursues the need for complementary frameworks to view one's work and experience rather than a single one. He explores the use of such a technique for Family Therapy generally.

Michael Crowe contributes the last chapter (13) in this section on the "Treatment of Marital and Sexual Problems from the Behavioural Point of View". Although describing the characteristics of behavioural approaches, he shows how such frameworks differ and are similar to those other frameworks described in other sections of the book, such as structural and strategic approaches. He describes the behavioural approaches to marital problems, such as reciprocal negotiation and communication training, and examines the ways in which sexual dysfunction as a presenting problem can be both thought about and approached through a variety of behavioural techniques. He critically reviews the results of such approaches, and puts them in the context of the field in general.

Although many frameworks are described in this volume and are further developed in Volume 2 (Chapters 14-28) including theoretical frameworks for viewing healthy and unhealthy families, frameworks of practical techniques and procedures to work with, engage and motivate families to work, frameworks of the family as having a history reflected in its life-cycle, and frameworks for considering intrusions in this cycle; there will inevitably be omissions and repetitions. Our aim has *not* been to present two totally comprehensive volumes, but to weave together some common threads which have originated in and been applied to different contexts. We hope, therefore, that the frameworks described in these volumes and the way in which they can be seen to be integrated into a set of operational notions from which specific actions can follow, will help the practitioner to think about the frameworks with which he or she finds himself or herself working. He may be able to identify through the therapists who have written chapters in these volumes, and get some ideas about settings where he has to find his own way because none have trodden in that direction before.

London   Arnon Bentovim
March 1982   Gill Gorell Barnes
                                                                      Alan Cooklin

Contents of Volume 1

Contents of Volume 2

xv

PART VI—FAMILY THERAPY AND THE SETTING

Part I

The Healthy Family as a System

Chapter 1

Frameworks for Viewing the Family as a System

R. Skynner

A. THE FAMILY AS A HERE-AND-NOW INTERACTING ENTITY

I. INTRODUCTION: HOMEOSTATIC SYSTEMS

Imagine the situation of primitive man, familiar with fire and able to build a crude hut, who comes upon a modern house, deserted by its occupants, which possesses an efficient central heating system. After exploring the house, the man chooses a room to live in, but finds it a little too cool for his liking. The room is fitted with a fireplace and, recognizing the ashes from previous fires, he gathers sticks, creates a flame by friction between pieces of wood, and lights a fire.

As the flames take hold and throw out heat, he experiences a pleasant warmth. But soon the room is as cool as before. He throws on more wood. Again there is a transient increase in temperature, but away from the direct heat of the fire itself, the room soon feels no warmer. Finally, when the wood is exhausted, the fire dies out. Having found it difficult to generate any warmth in the room even with a large fire, he expects the temperature to drop rapidly now that the fire is no longer providing heat. But even more mysterious, it hardly changes at all!

We know something that he is unaware of: the thermostat in the hall is designed to switch on the central heating boiler at a temperature set on its dial, and to switch off again when the temperature is a few degrees higher. The temperature of the air, at least in the vicinity of the thermostat, will move up and down between those two limits as the boiler is repeatedly switched on and off by the device.

Though the doors and windows to the exterior were shut, the rooms were connected with one another. This being the case, when the visitor lit his fire the warm air in the room gradually passed out into the hallway so that the thermostat exceeded its upper limit and switched the boiler off. Eventually, the more the fire warmed the room, the more the radiators cooled to compensate, keeping the temperature more or less constant. The reverse principle applied when the fire went out.

Here we have a simple, commonly used example of a *system* (in this case a heating system) maintaining *homeostasis* (keeping the temperature more or less constant) through the principle of *negative feedback* (the thermostat informs the boiler about the effects of its performance in achieving this task, in such a way that it *resists* change; i.e. it stops the boiler when the air gets too hot, and starts it when it gets too cold, rather than the reverse). It is able to achieve this throughout the house because the house is an *open system* (the doors are open or partly open, so that temperature changes in individual rooms are communicated through the house over a period of time). Had the *boundaries* defining the parts (rooms) of the whole system (house) been more rigid and closed (i.e. if the doors of the rooms had been shut), it would have been possible to change the temperature of separate rooms without affecting the whole house, and without producing the "negative feedback" effect described.

II. SYSTEMS THINKING AND THERAPY

A. From Individual to Families

Though this type of analogy has been used often enough before, we begin with it here because it emphasizes the essential simplicity of the concepts of systems theory, provided they are properly understood rather than employed as a new jargon substituting for thought. The situation of the therapist who attempts to change one individual, without taking into consideration the effects of any success he may have upon the whole family system, is very similar to that of the man who lights the fire in one room of the centrally heated house. Changes may be achieved, to be sure, but they last a short time only, and are mysteriously reversed by influences invisible to all but the trained eye. The patient improves in hospital (subsystem boundary closed = door to rooms shut), but relapses as soon as he is well enough to go home, or perhaps even deteriorates during the visit of a parent (open boundary = doors to rooms open). Not only is it difficult to change him for the "better", while he remains connected with his family; it is also puzzlingly difficult to make him "worse" while he is part of this system. In short, the widening of our perspective from its earlier focus on the individual, to an awareness of family and community systems, has shown us some clear reasons for the extraordinary difficulty everyone has found in changing individuals separately from their family systems; or in changing families separately from the influence of their neighbourhood communities, as long as they remain in close psychological contact with, and so are deeply affected by, these larger structures in which their lives are led.

But the other side of the coin is as encouraging as the first is depressing. If the man who had tried to warm the room with his fire had understood the function of the central heating system, a slight movement of his fingers, taking less than a second and using scarcely any energy at all, would not only have led to a change in temperature of exactly the order he was seeking through his laborious fire-making efforts, but would have maintained temperature at that level until he chose to change it. Similarly, once we begin to understand the feedback systems which govern the behaviour of families by the way they maintain homeostasis in the repetitive patterns of interaction between the members, we have the possibility of finding crucial points of intervention (like the dial on the thermostat in the heating system) where a small intervention can have a maximum affect of the kind we aim for upon the total functioning. Moreover, once achieved, this is likely to be maintained within a new equilibrium without further efforts on our part.

B. Change and Positive Feedback

The example of the central heating system does not help us to explain the idea of *positive* feedback, for though this could be provided by changing the design of the thermostat so that it turned the boiler on just above the temperature setting, and off just below the setting (that is, the *reverse* of the negative feedback condition), this arrangement would quickly lead to the air in the house rapidly reaching either its maximum or its minimum temperature and remaining there, an arrangement which could serve no useful purpose. But even this makes the point that positive feedback produces *change* rather than stability. An example may be seen in a business enterprise, where some proportion of the profits is fed back into the business itself. Then, the more successful the company, the greater the capital investment and the greater the productive capacity. Given an initial success and stable external conditions, the business will steadily grow with time. Similarly, if the business begins to fail, less money is put into capital investment, output diminishes, and the business shrinks at an increasing rate, leading ultimately to bankruptcy. The principle of positive feedback is thus at the root of *changes* in a system, whether in the form of growth or decay, just as negative feedback is concerned with maintaining the system steady.

Biological systems will usually contain a combination of both negative and positive feedback loops of this kind, which together determine the "balance of nature" at a given moment. Positive feedback alone leads to an exponential increase in whatever the positive feedback loop applies to, such as the screaming of a panicking crowd where the *expression* of the panic through screaming constantly magnifies the panic; or in the failure of the control (negative feedback) mechanisms at the Three Mile Island nuclear reactor.

C. Circular Causality

It will be seen that, in moving towards the systems approach, *causality* becomes *circular* rather than simply *linear*. The model of linear causality with which we grew up no longer suffices as an accurate way of construing the world. This may be typified by the image of the movements of balls on a billiards or snooker table, where once we know the speed and velocity of the initial shock, we can in theory predict the movements of all the balls according to the principles of Newtonian mechanics, and can accurately assess the transmission of energy from one ball to the next as they bounce against each other. Once we introduce the ideas of feedback and of circular causality, the individual billiard balls become equipped with self-steering gear or pre-programmed automatic pilots as it were which ensure that they all fall into the pockets no matter what motion the player gives to the first ball, or alternatively that they all avoid ever falling into the pockets; yet again, that they sometimes do and sometimes don't depending upon the state of the game, etc. If these billiard balls are already beginning to resemble living organisms, that is because, as Bateson (1972) constantly points out, such feedback loops are among the most fundamental characteristics of "life".

D.   The Need for a General Systems Theory

So far we have presented some of the concepts of systems theory in a manner which is in some ways more typical of a pre-systems, reductionist approach to science. That is, we have given examples of "chunks" of the world, and though we have looked at the relationships within their boundaries, we have treated them as if they can be studied in isolation from the rest of the universe. To some extent we can do this, of course, and all science must be based on approximations of this sort if we are to simplify things sufficiently to be able to think about them at all. As von Bertalanffy (1968, pp.18-19) expressed it:

> the system problem is essentially the problem of limitations of analytical pro-
> cedures in science . . . 'Analytical procedure' means that an entity investigated be
> resolved into and hence can be constituted or reconstituted from, the parts put
> together, these procedures being understood both in their material and conceptual
> sense. This is the basic principle of 'classical' science, which can be circumscribed
> in different ways: a resolution into isolable causal trains, seeking for 'atomic' units
> in the various fields of science, etc. The progress of science has shown that these
> principles of classical science — first enunciated by Galileo and Descartes — are
> highly successful in a wide realm of phenomena.
> Application of the analytical procedure depends on two conditions. The first is that
> interactions between 'parts' be non-existent or weak enough to be neglected for
> certain research purposes. . . . The second condition is that the relations describing
> the behaviour of parts be linear; only then is the condition of summativity given,
> i.e., an equation describing the behaviour of the total is of the same form as the
> equations describing the behaviour of the parts; partial processes can be super-
> imposed to obtain the total process, etc.
>   These conditions are not fulfilled in the entities called systems, i.e., consisting
> of parts 'in interaction'. The prototype of their description is a set of simultaneous
> differential equations . . . which are nonlinear in the general case.

If we take these ideas seriously, we can see that we cannot stop at considering discrete parts of the world one at a time, but that, if these "systems" principles are accepted as applying to any one scale or level of organisation, they must apply at all others and indeed to the whole. In the words of von Bertalanffy (1968) again:

> There appear to exist general system laws which apply to any system of a certain
> type, irrespective of the particular properties of the system and of the elements
> involved.
>   These considerations lead to the postulate of a new scientific discipline which we
> call general system theory. It's subject matter is formulation of principles that are

valid for 'systems' in general whatever the nature of their component elements and the relations or forces between them. (p.37)

Thus, not only can the world be seen as made up of systems, but the systems at any level are parts of larger systems still, in the way that a number of fields are part of a farm, a number of farms in turn may be part of a district, the district a part of a county, and so on. To quote von Bertalanffy (1968) again:

> The above considerations pertain particularly to a concept or complex of concepts which indubitably is fundamental in the general theory of systems: that of *hierarchic order*. We presently 'see' the universe as a tremendous hierarchy, from elementary particles to atomic nuclei, to atoms, molecules, high-molecular compounds, to the wealth of structures, electron and light-microscopic between molecules and cells . . . , to cells, organisms and beyond to supra-individual organisations. (p.27)

If we look at human life from this point of view, we may consider any level of organisation as a system. If we are focusing particularly on an individual, and regard that person as the "system", then the larger system of which he is a part (the family) is termed the *"supra-system,"* and the *parts* of the individual are called *sub-systems* (e.g. the nervous system, the circulatory system, the "unconscious"). However, if we are focussing on the *family* as the system, then the individual is the sub-system (one of its parts), and some higher level of social organization such as the extended family or community, is then the supra-system of which the family is a part. The whole of mankind can then be viewed as a series of concentric circles or "chinese boxes", each circle containing smaller ones contained within larger ones. (We hope that readers familiar with these ideas will bear with us while they are presented. A good grasp of them is essential for understanding modern developments in family therapy, and the difficulty in presenting them is somehow to combine an expression of both their profound simplicity and their profound generality. Emphasis on the generality alone tends to make readers shrink before the vast scale to which the ideas are applied, which suggests a daunting complexity; emphasizing the simplicity alone, however, often has the contrary effect of causing the reader to brush the ideas aside as too trivial and obvious to need emphasis.)

III. THE ELEMENTS OF HUMAN SYSTEMS

A. Boundaries

In our image of concentric circles, the circles themselves would represent the *boundaries* of the system (space) they surround, and in human systems, the boundary can be seen as the dividing line between one system and another on the same level, all marking off the system from its supra-system and defining the sub-systems within itself. Nevertheless, the boundary may be easier to define in spatial terms, like the membrane of a living cell, or the skin of a man. The boundary of a family has more to do with distinctions between the special degree of experience and information sharing among family members when they are compared with outsiders, and also a certain centring of movement or communication in space, in a dynamic rather than a static sense. Similarly, the boundary of a family sub-system such as the parental couple is recognized by the special degrees of physical intimacy, privacy and depth of information exchanged, and the degree and duration of commitment in their relationship, differing from the relationships of the spouses to other family members. "Boundary" denotes a point of transition where *differences* can be observed in structure, function, behaviour etc. on either side. Seen from another view-point, the boundary is defined by the rules as to who may participate in certain kinds of interaction and information sharing, and who may not. In technical terms applicable to all systems, Miller (1965) defines the boundary as that region round the exterior of the system "over which there is less transmission of matter/energy and information than there is within the system or within its environment." (p.214).

B. Decider Subsystems

The other vital part of the system is the *decider subsystem:*

> The essential critical sub-system which controls the entire system, causing its sub-systems and components to co-act, without which there is no system [204] . . . Of (the systems) only the decider is essential, in a sense that a system cannot be parasitic or symbiotic with another system for its deciding. A living system does not exist if the decider is displaced upwardly (to the supra-system), downwardly (to the sub-system) or outwardly (to another system i.e. parasitic or symbiotic). (Miller, 1965 p.222)

On different levels, the "decider" may be the chromosomes in a fertilized egg, the nervous system of an animal, the brain of the nervous system, the queen of a colony of bees, the parents of a family, or the government of a country. The decider has the task of co-ordinating the activities of all the parts of the system in the light of what is required of it by events in the outside environment. The co-ordination must concern the welfare of the whole system, since the decider's fate is bound up with it. The decider is *responsible* for the whole system, in the original sense that it must be able to *respond* appropriately to the situation. And for this to be accomplished, it must receive information about the functioning of all the parts of the system, and of events in the environment.

The decider thus ensures the *integrity* of the system, and its continued *differentiation* from the environment. It has a similar function to the boundary, over which it has a varying degree of control, but they each protect the system's integrity in a different way, which as we shall see, has great relevance to the functioning of families and their treatment. In the case of a nation, for example, a looser structure with more freedom to the sub-systems, may be possible if its boundary is relatively impermeable. Such is the case of Britain's tradition of democratic institutions, which owe much to its sea boundary and past naval power; or the similar case of the United States, divided by oceans and comparable power of potentially predatory neighbours. The democratic traditions of Iceland, even more protected by its inhospitable northern waters, are even older. But a powerful unity and identity may be maintained despite a lack of protective boundaries of this kind, through shared values, information-exchange and clear rules regulating insider/outsider status, as in the case of the Jewish diaspora.

C. Hierarchy

In addition to pointing out that a system cannot exist without its decider, Miller (1965) also notes that "If there are multiple parallel deciders, without a hierarchy that has subordinate and superordinate deciders, there is not one system but multiple ones." (p.218) This is obviously of crucial importance to us in considering the division or sharing of power between father and mother in a family. Unless there is a hierarchy with either mother or father dominant, or some satisfactory system to ensure collaboration between the two parents, perhaps with shared decisions, clearly defined separate roles, or alternating dominance, there will not be one family, but two. Chapter 2 describes a family inter-acting in the present day context to illustrate some these issues.

B. THE FAMILY AS A SYSTEM OVER A PERIOD OF TIME

I. INTRODUCTION

Our discussion of systems ideas has used mechanical/electrical examples to illustrate the principles; or, where living organisms were discussed, has focussed more often on short time-spans than on the life-time of an individual. But the one certain fact of "life" is the fact of death. Living organisms are not only vulnerable to irreversible damage from forces in their environment, including other organisms, but are actually programmed to self-destruct after a variable but limited period of time. Life involves continuance only for the group, not for the separate individual member, and to maintain it, new members must repeatedly be created, to replace those who die.

II. TRANSMISSION OF HUMAN STRUCTURE AND FUNCTION

A. The Family as the Unit of Reproduction

If the continuation even of the group is to have any meaning, some *pattern* regarding the structure and function of the members, both as individuals and as a group, must be transmitted from the existing members to the newly-created ones. Much of this process takes place in, and is the *raison d'être* of, the family, the smallest unit within which this process can be fulfilled. As dysfunction is dealt with in other chapters, the focus here will be on *healthy, "optimal"* functioning, the "ideal" rather than the statistically "normal", average or mid-range.

Transmission of the pattern is achieved through a number of routes. The act of sexual intercourse between the parental couple initiates the union of sperm and egg, resulting in a genetic programme different from each parent yet with characteristics of both. Protected at first within the mother's body, and later within the safety of the family boundary, matter/energy is at first absorbed from the mother's blood, then from her milk, later at the high chair and finally the family table. The basic shaping of this material by the chromosomal instructions is further modified by information absorbed by the sense organs from the environment, particularly from other family members. At first the very fact that things exist as they do and where they do; the fact that mother exists, has a certain shape, and gratifies; while at other times seems not to exist, does not gratify, but yet appears again repeatedly; all begin to form within the infant's inner communicational network "a model" or "map" of the outside world. During this early period in particular (say about the first year or so) a certain stability and regularity must obtain in the immediate environment to avoid such a bombardment of new impressions that the infant has no hope of bringing order out of seeming chaos, and is driven to "blinker" itself from the overload. The mother's nurture, both in terms of feeding and of comforting presence, must also be reliable enough to keep *internal* stimulation within manageable limits, avoiding extremes of rage or frustration so that emotional responses may gradually be integrated and mastered. In the early stages, this requires the provision of a protective boundary by the mother while these delicate processes are proceeding, and the mother in turn will need to be looked after herself and to have the family boundary guarded by others, particularly the father or the grandparents, while she gives attention to her immediate task.

B.   The Discovery of Boundaries

During this period, the infant will be discovering that *not everything is itself*, that it has an *edge* (boundary), beyond which its wishes and fantasies have less effect than they do within that edge (a task not helped by the fact that it discovers it does not have very much more control even *within* that edge). It is not so much that the infant *thinks* he *is* the world, that he desires to be omnipotent and omnipresent, but rather that there is no reason to be aware that there *is* anything else, anything other than self, until the "not-self" makes its presence felt. The infant is necessarily "all", "everything", indeed "God", until it discovers otherwise. If its needs could be anticipated and met in every detail, it would perhaps have no reason to suspect that it was in any way separate from the rest of the universe. It is the *failure* of the environment to behave as if it is part of the infant's self that shows where the edge or boundary is, thereby providing the beginning sense of identity of self and difference from others (though as already suggested, this failure must be carefully graded to what the infant can tolerate if it is to endure the painful realization that it is *not* God, that indeed it is almost helpless and dependent on another being with a life of her own). Winnicott (1958) has developed this issue particularly clearly.

C. Learning about the Insides and Outsides of the System

Klein (1932) and her followers have emphasized how one aspect of this increasing discrimination between inside and outside, self and other, is an increasing ability to experience feeling-states as contained within that boundary, rather than pervading its view of the external world and distorting the infant's perception of it. And this process is accompanied by a similar integration of perceptions, both internal and external, whereby love and hate, and the gratifying or frustrating behaviour of the care-giving person to which these two states are related, are integrated instead of being kept separate. "Good mother" and "bad mother" become one mother, who is sometimes there and sometimes not. Pure love and pure hate, both overwhelming, become fused to form manageable ambivalence, sufficiently variable through the balance of its positive or negative components to permit management of attachment and rejecting behaviour. The infant is then capable of functioning in what Klein calls the *depressive position.* But poor handling of this developmental process, with excessive frustration in comparison to gratification, does not permit the infant to move beyond the *paranoid-schizoid position,* with consequent failure of integration and discrimination demonstrated by *part-object* relationships (failure to perceive others as separate whole persons) *splitting* (inability to integrate positive and negative aspects of external reality or of internal responses to them) and *projection* (the attribution to persons or events, outside the self, of unacceptable aspects too painful to contain within it). Even where depressive position functioning has been to some extent achieved but is only precariously established, stressful situations, leading to frustration too painful to bear, may cause a regression to paranoid-schizoid position functioning (as with a badly handled hospitalization).

D. The Need for Adequate Parental Boundaries

If these tasks characteristic of the first year of the infant's life are to be accomplished, one requirement which is perhaps not always sufficiently emphasized is that the parental figures should be clear about their own boundaries. If the primary care-giving figure (usually the mother) is not clear and secure about her own personal boundary, she will be unable to help the infant to find its own boundary. Marking the border defining the northern boundary of England, automatically defines the southern edge of Scotland as well. In similar fashion, parents who are clear about their own boundaries, and secure in their identities, will automatically provide relationships through which the child can define itself, even without any conscious attempt to address this problem. Parents who are unclear in this matter tend to attribute feelings to the child which belong to themselves, and vice versa, making the infant's task of self-definition more difficult. Moreover, even the earliest stages of nurture of the infant, when some degree of fusion between mother and child is appropriate through the mother making her boundaries more permeable, empathizing with the infant's experiences (Winnicott's (1958) state of "Primary Maternal Preoccupation") may be rendered impossible if the mother's fragile sense of identity makes her fearful of entering into this kind of relationship, with all its vulnerability. Nevertheless, if all goes well, mother and infant are able at first to enter this symbiotic state, with father and perhaps other relatives protecting them.

As the child grows, the mother is able to re-establish her own boundaries once again, "failing" the child's expectations sufficiently to enable it progressively to define itself. In this she will usually be aided by the father, who not only protects the family boundary at this stage but "holds the life line" permitting the mother to enter safely into this degree of regressive interaction with the infant, and "hauling her back" by stages towards a primary investment in the marital relationship, rather than in the child. It is perhaps this crucial function of the father in assisting the mother and child to grow apart progressively, thereby facilitating self-definition and independence, which makes the presence and active involvement of the father so important in the next stage, comprising roughly the second and third years of life. He needs not only to restore close affectional and sexual bonds with the mother as the child needs her less, but by forming a close and trusting relationship with the child, by nature of the fact that he is inevitably a different person in some respects, he provides another dimension through which the child can find out who he is, as a ship, by taking two bearings on different landmarks, can establish its position. If the first year of the infant's life is concerned more with the taking-in of matter/energy and information, with the establishment of a *base*, then in this second period, the infant ventures out and explores the environment. Increasing maturation of the nervous system brings with it increasing control of movement, freedom of action, and the possibility of impinging actively on the surroundings. The child begins to walk, talk and gain control of its sphincters, and with these new powers comes the possibility of collaborating with, or resisting, the parents.

E.   Parenting and Social Information

It is during this phase therefore, that the foundations are laid for self-control and initiative, the achievement of some compromise between the demands for social conformity and the satisfaction of personal needs, and the development of a sense of identity, difference and separateness from others.

If the child is to accomplish this, the parents and other adult figures must achieve a satisfactory compromise between on the one hand providing freedom and space to try out these new powers, in order to test out the developing will and initiative, and to explore the world, while on the other hand also providing sufficient firmness, limits, controls and requirements that social demands be heeded, in order to enable the child to feel safe in his explorations, and to internalize those social values needed to make satisfactory relationships with others. The prominence of the issue of toilet training during this period led Freud to call it the "anal" phase, though it seems likely that the importance of this issue is due to the fact that it is the first battleground on which the conflict between the desires of the individual and the demands of the society are fought out.

In the second stage, problems may be caused if the parents are uncertain about their own identity or have unresolved conflicts over accepting authority or social demands, as well as where the father is absent or ineffective, or the parents are unable to collaborate over discipline and setting of limits.

F. Parenting and Sexuality in Childhood

A third phase, reaching its height around 4-5 years of age, is characterized by childhood precursors of adult sexual feeling, by interest in the genitals of the self and others, and in the origin of babies. Something like a love affair with the parent of the opposite sex becomes apparent, together with jealousy of the parent of the same sex.

If the parents are at ease with their own sexuality, have a satisfying sexual relationship themselves, and treat these manifestations with respect and natural-ness, the foundations are laid for sexual confidence in later life. The son discovers that mother finds his sexuality pleasurable, but that she belongs to father and is not available; the daughter likewise with her father. The child gets the message that its sexuality is good, but that it cannot marry its parents and must first grow to adulthood and find a partner of its own. Thus, the stage is set for entry into the wider world to learn, to socialize, to join the peer-group from which the eventual mate will have to be selected.

Once again, a balance is needed in the parental response between over-and-under reaction to the child's sexual initiatives. The combination of infantile sexuality, the oedipal conflict and the incest taboo provides, as it were, a powerful motive force towards differentiating from the family (since sex cannot be obtained there) and learning to cope with the wider society (where sex will ultimately be available). Parental prudishness, or complete denial of parental sexual response to the initiatives of the child, removes the carrot from the donkey, as it were. At the other extreme, incest allows the donkey to eat the carrot, but in either case a vital motivation towards differentiation and growth is removed.

As in other periods, several related developmental tasks are being addressed simultaneously, and the achievement of one automatically helps the others. During this third period, the child not only has to accept that the parents are more powerful, but that they have a special relationship with each other and some pleasurable and indeed profoundly exciting activity from which he or she is excluded. The child has to cope with *jealousy* and *exclusion* from relationship. Not only does omnipotence suffer a further necessary reduction; in addition, if this stage is successfully surmounted, the foundations of the capacity for *sharing*, and so for group membership, are soundly laid.

The child is now well prepared to join the peer-group, a capability which may have been enhanced by previous experience of coping with siblings, and the child goes to school. Interest and energy are transferred increasingly from the earlier biological tasks towards learning and socialization. The earlier, more open expression of sexuality appears to go underground, though interest remains active enough, even if confined to discussions or satisfactions of curiosity with peers. Males and females divide into separate groups, and even become antagonistic. Teachers and other adults provide new models, additional landmarks on which children can take their bearings to find their own preferred positions and directions. The parents become less important, though still providing a safe base and refuge.

For the parents, perhaps the main need is to let the children go. Mothers who themselves find it hard to separate and differentiate, and have gratified themselves vicariously during the earlier period, make separation difficult for the child. But in normal circumstances, separation is aided by the fact that the mother is glad to be freed of the burdens of the first five years, and is able to resume her separate interests and activities. Almost all studies of marital satisfaction have shown that during the period between the birth of children and the time they go to school, marital satisfaction reaches its lowest ebb, increasing in general thereafter just as it decreased before.

G. Parenting and Sexuality in Adolescence

The approach of puberty sees a return of the interest in sexual issues which burst into prominence with the hormonal changes at the beginning of adolescence. The child is under biological and social pressures to accept and gratify the emerging sexual needs, and to move away from the primary attachment to the parents and the family towards the loyalties of the peer-group. At the same time, the struggles towards independence alternate with a resurgence of childish dependence, while demands for sexual freedom are counter-balanced by equal fears and a desire that the parents will set limits within which experimentation can be safely attempted. All being well, the responsibilities of adult sexuality are gradually approached, first engaging with the opposite sex in the safety of the same-sex group; then pairing off, but in a crowd; then perhaps in small groups or foursomes; finally in couples.

The task of parents is particularly difficult at this stage, for whatever they do will by definition be "wrong". They will be seen as too restricting at one moment, uncaring at another; prudish kill-joys when they set limits, neglectful and indifferent when they do not.

Parents who are ill at ease with their own sexuality, or whose sexual relationship is unsatisfactory, will find the task more difficult. They may either become over-restrictive out of anxiety, provoking unnecessary rebellion, or avoid the provision of age-appropriate limits through their need to deny the problem. Such difficulties will be all the greater if the sexual relationship between the parents is unsatisfactory and precarious, since their inhibitions, which may not be unsuperable as long as sex is kept in the background as a low-key issue, may be magnified intolerably when they are confronted with the crude directness which can characterize adolescent sexuality.

What is required of the parents at this stage is that they themselves should have completed their own developmental tasks to an adequate degree. They need to be sufficiently at ease with their own sexuality to enable their adolescent child to be at ease too. The sexual relationship between the parents needs to be satisfying and enjoyable, so that it encounters no threat from the powerful sexuality developing in another member of the family. Instead, they can serve as a positive model to the adolescent that sex, within a loving and responsible relationship, can reach its greatest fulfilment. And the parents need to be sufficiently complete in themselves, as well as satisfied with each other, to contemplate the departure of their offspring from the home without being threatened with pain and loneliness, indeed, to anticipate with pleasure the prospect of freedom from child-rearing tasks.

H. Adulthood and the New Family

As the young person reaches "escape velocity" from the emotional "gravitational field" of the family, the tasks of gaining acceptance by, and finding a responsible place within, the wider society become paramount. The individual learns to work, becomes self-supporting, explores the social and physical environment more extensively, and after "playing the field" to gain more adequate experience of intimate and sexual relationships, is drawn increasingly towards a more permanent liaison, culminating in marriage. All these changes require an increasing ability to see oneself as part of a group, to see others as oneself, to accept a certain discipline and self-sacrifice to permit the performance of a common task, whether the production of goods in work, or collaboration in setting up a home.

The parents, during this time, will be enjoying their new-found freedom, if healthy; or experiencing loneliness and emptiness, behaving as the "interfering in-laws" of the stock music-hall jokes, and anxiously and impatiently awaiting the arrival of grandchildren, if not.

The arrival of the new-generation couple's first child brings profound changes and new stresses. The wife, who is likely to be working, is obliged to give this up, at least temporarily, and to undergo a total change of life-style. Overnight, she loses her former freedom, which may have been greater than she had ever possessed, and must devote most of her attention to serving another person who makes constant demands for attention by night as well as by day. The husband must at least continue to work and support his wife in this task, while much attention and care she formerly devoted to him is now suddenly transferred to the baby. If he shares more fully in the child-rearing activities, as is common nowadays, the change for him is greater still. Even the sexual relationship is disrupted for a period, and may be impaired for months or years through fatigue and distractions. The marriage comes under particular stress for all these reasons, and marital satisfaction reaches its lowest point over the next few years.

At this stage, and particularly around the time of the birth, the calm supportive presence of the original parents (now the grandparents) provides a crucial input. They have been through it all before, and can reassure by the way they take it in their stride. Through their affection and support, they can help to replace the mutual support which the couple formerly gave to each other, and now must give to the child-rearing task. Other relatives can play similarly supportive roles, and it is likely that the larger extended families of previous times sustained young parents through this stage more adequately than is commonly possible today.

I. The Life-cycle Completing

In our description, one cycle is now complete. The original parents, now grand-parents, will continue to play an important part in their children's and grand-children's lives, acting as supports and resources in times of stress and crisis, mediating between the parents and children at times, and providing alternative models. It remains to say something about the later phases of the life cycle, after the children have "left the nest".

The beginning of this later stage will tend to coincide with what is often called "the prime of life". The powers and achievements of the man will often be at their zenith. The woman, too, will still be vigorous and energetic. If she has maintained and developed her own separate life, identity and interests outside the child-ruling tasks, she can now enjoy a period of unprecedented freedom and achievement. Both partners will normally be still sexually vigorous, and if the relationship has been nourished, they may find the sexual relationship more enjoyable at this stage than at any previous time.

As they move beyond this phase towards the 60s physical strength and energy will diminish, and the most active pursuits will begin to be curtailed. If achieve-ment earlier has been adequate, success and recognition will seem increasingly unimportant. Interest and enjoyment turn increasingly inwards, and the satisfaction of these final years will depend on the extent to which an inner life has been preserved and built up through the earlier years. Simple activities and pleasures become increasingly valued, and life becomes easier as unnecessary complications, and meaningless ambitions, drop away. To the extent that this change is possible, and negotiated successfully, retirement becomes something to look forward to, and brings a new and different phase of enjoyment.

The death of the partner is part of this final phase, followed eventually by the death of the one remaining. To the extent that earlier phases have been success-fully surmounted and enjoyed, death will be experienced as a part of life, accepted like the rest.

During this last phase, the caring roles reverse, the parents taking on a caring and managerial role towards the grandparents as the powers of the later fail, even the grandchildren enjoying helping to look after them. By the time the grandparents die, the parents have already been prepared, therefore, for the new responsibility they undertake as they now become of grandparental age them-selves.

This last part of the cycle has been described here in terms of those who manage it well. They will usually be those who have managed earlier phases in the same satisfactory way, so that they have developed satisfactory resources within themselves, and are therefore able to give more willingly, and to demand less. For those who earlier have been deprived and unhappy, looking to each other or to their children to remedy their own deficiencies, the later years are likely to extenuate the feelings of loneliness and misery, so that far from being a support to their children and grandchildren that they become increasingly demanding and burdensome.

J. What makes for Success in the Family

For the process to proceed in a satisfactory, optimum fashion, there should be throughout life a steady decrease in the egocentricity and narcissism of the early infantile stages, counterbalanced by a progressive increase in real skills, interests and internal resources. The meaning and purpose of life must come increasingly to lie in something beyond the individual, ephemeral self, even beyond any one other person, and even ultimately beyond the family. For this to occur, not only must interest extend beyond the self to the family, and beyond the family to the wider community, but as we shall see from the Timberlawn Research, some sense of a transcendent value system is needed which can enable the individual to survive even the death of loved ones without destruction of meaning.

It should be clearly emphasized again, perhaps, that this chapter deals throughout with health in the sense of optimal function, in contrast to dysfunction of varying degree which receives adequate coverage in other chapters. Individuals and families conforming to these criteria are of course rare, as olympic athletes are rare, but we have enough evidence (outlined later in this chapter) to be confident that these high levels of effective function are approached in a small minority of the population. We will not expect to encounter them in our professional work with dysfunctional families, and we will not expect to raise the level of function of families we treat to this optimal level, not least because, as Beavers (1977) has pointed out, mental health professionals are most unlikely to be functioning at that level themselves (and might not be very good at the job, or might not be motivated to take it up, if they were). (See Chapter 2 for further discussion of what makes for a 'healthy' family.)

C. THE INNER-EXPERIENTIAL LIFE
OF THE FAMILY

I. INTRODUCTION

In the two preceding sections, we have looked at the functioning of the family and its individual members. First, we considered the family as an interacting system in the present, where we studied its cyclic operations without much reference to its past history. Secondly, we considered the family as a system developing over time, where newer members are being assisted by older ones to transcend a series of developmental stages (in psychoanalytic terms), or (in behavioural language) at age-appropriate times to acquire a series of behaviour patterns, transmitted by learning processes of one kind or another. In both cases, we were viewing the family and its members from outside, from an objective standpoint where the actual behaviour observed would suffice to describe the situation (as those with a behavioural orientation in fact strive to do). If we were confining our studies to central heating systems, steam engines or electronic calculators these approaches would suffice.

II. EXPERIENCING

A. A Human Function

But humans not only go through the motions of interacting and developing. Humans also achieve something called *experiencing* their lives. They can be "conscious" (whatever that means) of some aspects of their surroundings and even of themselves and their relation to others. How much this function is shared with other animals we do not know, and humans appear to have additional abilities, almost certainly not shared by animals, of being *aware of their experience*, of being able to be *aware that they are conscious*, to be critical and analytic towards it, and to communicate and share that second-order (or as in the case of the present communication between writer and reader, *third*-order) consciousness with other members of the species.

These functions *can* be described in behavioural terms and a visitor from space, studying the human race, might have no alternative. But therapists are themselves human, sharing the fact of consciousness and other characteristics of human functioning, so that we are able to *put ourselves in the place of* the different family members to some extent, approaching the problem from inside rather than outside.

It is customary to take these capacities we share for granted, to talk *as if* we do not need to examine or explain them and can safely use them without questioning their nature. This is adequate, when they are functioning effectively, and reflections upon the nature of consciousness can be left to philosophers. But family therapists (and indeed psychotherapists generally) have found their attention drawn particularly to this question because it appears to be precisely in this area of consciousness, communication and control that confusions arise which lead to family systems becoming dysfunctional.

Little or nothing is known, even at the present time, about the *purpose* of consciousness or self-awareness, if by "purpose" we mean the difference it makes to our functioning, the way we would be likely to operate if it did not exist. In his most recent book Bateson (1979) for example states that:

> . . . . the fact of image formation remains almost totally mysterious. How it is done, we know not — nor, indeed, for what purpose. . . . . there is no clear primary reason for using images at all or, indeed, for being *aware* of any part of our mental processes.

Bateson remarks only that

> . . . . speculation suggests that image formation is perhaps a convenient or economical method of passing information across some sort of interface. Notably, where a person must act in a context between two machines, it is convenient to have the machines feed their information to him or her in image form. [p.37] . . . . it will be reasonable to guess that mammals form images because the mental processes of mammals must deal with many interfaces. [p.38]

Bateson does not elaborate this, nor is there at present much help to be found, as far as the present writer is aware, from psychological or philosophical writings so far available. We must resort therefore to "common sense": that is, the writers of this monograph must speak from what they assume to be common among their own experience, and that of their readers. This, as we shall see, is fraught with difficulty, but it is at present the only way to proceed.

B. Consciousness, Insight and Change

For fifty years or more, it was "received wisdom" among most of those engaged in psychotherapy that "insight", that is, consciousness of certain connections between "symptoms" (limited aspects of present behaviour) and present behaviour in a more general sense (e.g. as shown through "transference") or with past experiences or memories, was necessary for change in such undesired behaviour patterns to be possible. *Why* consciousness of these connections should produce this effect was never explained very satisfactorily. The rise of behaviourism, and of behaviour modification techniques of treatment, bypassed the whole issue of consciousness and demonstrated that certain types of symptomatic behaviour, at least, could be altered by submitting the patient to new experiences, according to principles elaborated in learning theories. Later still, adherents of communication theory models, particularly those interested in the pathological and therapeutic effects of "double-binds", claimed that insight *followed* change, rather than the reverse. Yet others have discovered that "prescribing the symptom" (instructing people to try to stay the same, or to get worse) can also paradoxically result in relief of symptoms. And if we go beyond orthodox techniques of psychotherapy, we find that encounter groups emphasize the importance of insight and change, while *est* (Erhardt Seminars Training) claims similar improvements by getting people to accept that there is no need to change at all. Religious conversion experiences under powerful emotional pressures, or the emptying of the mind of its habitual activities in meditation, or concentration on some impossible question such as a Zen Koan, all appear capable of bringing about changes in habitual functioning which are more or less enduring.

It seems as though heightened consciousness or "insight" is *in some way* associated with the kind of changes psychotherapists are interested in bringing about, though the connection is clearly less simple than was at first thought.

C. Pathological Functioning and the Fragmentation of Experiencing

What does seem common to the problems that present to a psychotherapist is a kind of fragmentation of the individual's capacity for experience, whereby he cannot from time to time survey his life as a whole, and is therefore prevented from noting discrepancies which may have arisen between the functioning of different subsystems, upsetting the efficiency of the whole organism. Most human behaviour is carried out automatically or semi-automatically, by learned mechanisms which are outside awareness, even if conscious application is necessary to acquire the skills in the first place. Learning to drive a car, for example, we have for some time to give our full attention to the task to the exclusion of everything else, but it would be a disadvantage if driving continued to need the full range of our conscious attention. It is greatly to our advantage that "lower" centres of the nervous system take over this routine task, leaving our conscious attention free for other purposes (perhaps planning the rest of our day) except when unexpected emergencies alert the higher centres to the need for the maximum available attention.

We may reasonably surmise that many sub-systems develop integrated, efficient performances of this kind, which will not usually enter conscious awareness *unless something goes wrong* and threatens the organism's well-being or integrity. But if we survey the kinds of situation in which individuals or families complain of symptoms or relationship dysfunctions and seek psychological help, we soon discover that *one common feature of all such situations is a discrepancy or discordance between different parts of the total system concerned.* Some piece of behaviour or experience is labelled a "symptom" precisely because it does not appear to have meaning and purpose within the functioning of that individual as a whole; indeed, at first sight it appears *dys*functional, interfering with other functions. Similarly, when a family presents complaining of an individual member, the behaviour of that individual at first appears to be disruptive of the functioning of the whole family, and meaningless in terms of the way they are operating as a unit.

Whatever form of therapy is employed, it usually seems to require the therapist to bridge the fragmentation between the deviant individual and the group, or the deviant sub-system within the individual and the individual as a whole, from a birds-eye-view which not only makes a deeper sense of the discrepancy (even of the fragmentation) but which also discovers a more comprehensive organization in which the deviant sub-system can find a constructive place (once the fragmentation is overcome). Consciousness can then be regarded as something like a "working party" set up to view the functioning of some large organization, the various parts of which may be working effectively, but each of which has grown and changed in such a way as to be out of balance, and so impairs the functioning of the whole. Once the organization is brought into balance and is working effectively again, the working party has served its purpose and its energy can be turned to other tasks.

D. Consciousness as a Central Function

It is suggested, therefore, that consciousness (in the sense of that self-consciousness to which psychotherapists refer when they use the term "insight") plays some part in bringing subsystems into more harmonious relationship when some form of imbalance or fragmentation has occurred. As Bateson suggests, such consciousness is not an end in itself, but more a sign that the organism is undergoing some temporary period of self-examination and adjustment. When we are functioning most harmoniously, and are most in tune with our surroundings, we may be intensely aware (in the sense of alive and responding) but such "self-consciousness" is at a minimum.

In terms of our present concern, this would imply that healthy families are not, in general, particularly preoccupied with insight, with self-understanding, with self-consciousness in the sense of a self-absorbed, self-improving stance in relation to themselves and each other. We may expect that they will be open, responsive, spontaneous, alive, and that they will show evidence of a vivid and enjoyable inner world, but this is another matter altogether. We may nevertheless expect that they will have this faculty of self-examination readily available, and that they will not be inhibited in using it should some interruption to their fruitful interaction indicate that something is going wrong. They will be insightful in the sense that they will not hesitate to examine themselves and their relationships openly and objectively, as well as in the sense of having much information already available, but once the problem is resolved, we may expect that they will put this capacity for self examination aside until it is needed again, and get on with their lives. Watching the interaction of "optimal" healthy families in the Timberlawn Research Study videotapes one is struck by the openness, spontaneity and relaxed, alive, enjoyable exchange between the members. One is also struck both by their absence of self-preoccupation or morbid unnecessary introspection, as well as by their willingness to look frankly at themselves when this is made necessary to fulfil a task or because some problem has arisen.

E. Fragmentation as the Root of Conflict

Watching the operation of such healthy families, one is also impressed by the relative absence of persistent, irresolvable conflict, despite the remarkable individuality and difference among the members. Yet conflict and strife seem, much of the time and in most families and social situations, almost as if they are inevitable conditions of human functioning. Freud, among others, certainly took this view of human nature, believing that a constant struggle between the demands of society and the urges of man's animal nature was the price of civilisation.

There have nevertheless been exceptions to this pessimistic view, stemming from both secular and religious sources. It is interesting how Bateson (1972) links the two so naturally in the following quotation from one of his essays:

Aldous Huxley used to say that the central problem for humanity is the quest for *grace*. This word he used in what he thought was the sense in which it is used in the New Testament. He explained the word, however, in his own terms. He argued— like Walt Whitman—that the communication and behaviour of animals has a naïveté, a simplicity, which man has lost. Man's behaviour is corrupted by deceit— even self-deceit—by purpose, and by self-consciousness. As Aldous saw the matter, man has lost the 'grace' which animals still have. I shall argue that the problem of grace is fundamentally a problem of integration and that what is to be integrated is the diverse parts of the mind—especially those multiple levels of which one extreme is called 'consciousness' and the other the 'unconscious'. For the attainment of grace, the reasons of the heart must be integrated with the reasons of the reason (p.128-129)

In his thirteen-part BBC television series, exploring the world's religions, Ronald Eyre (1979) found, despite the diversity of theological views, that the ideas of being *whole*, of being *healthy*, and of being *holy* all had similar meanings, in the sense that Bateson has used above.

Our real dilemma appears to be this: That all man's achievements: the capacity to symbolize, the transmission and storage of knowledge through language, the development of science, technology and all that has stemmed from these, depend in fact on man's capacity to fragment, to isolate, to pursue in his thought and imagination ideas and structures which are *not* bound by his senses, which are not just a reflection of the world he experiences before him at a given moment. He can *abstract* from his experience (Korzybski, 1933) selecting those features of events which interest or attract him, and ignoring others. Having done so, he can play with these as a child plays with bricks, manipulating them and testing out different possible relationships as in logic, mathematics or physics. Then, these experiments with images or abstractions can be tested out and verified or refuted by actual experiment in the real world.

This is the process underlying all scientific discoveries, whereby experiments with inner experience which led to the formula $e = mc^2$ enables us to harness atomic energy. But the same principle underlies all human behaviour, beyond that described by the simplest principles of learning theory. Why is the process sometimes helpful and constructive, and what makes it often harmful and productive of inner and outer conflict? The answer has been expressed in many fashions, but is essentially simple. It seems we are so constructed that our capacity to abstract and isolate parts of our experience readily proceeds past the point where it ceases to be helpful and becomes harmful, this point being the stage at which *we focus our attention and interest on the isolated part to an extent where we forget its origin in the larger whole*. We are then no longer aware of the experience we are focussing on as part of a *system*. We cling to the isolated part, which becomes the "truth", and cease to return to the more profound and complicated source in our total living experience from which this "truth" derived. Moreover, experience is a flux, the world is in motion, we and others are changing constantly; yet, to employ this process of abstraction, to be able to "think", and above all in order to communicate in symbols, we must take static cross-sections of our experience of constant change.

All "truth" arrived at by this process must, for both these reasons, be partial, temporary. As long as we remember this, our abstractions help us to deal with, and adapt to, the real world. But as soon as we forget that ideas, abstractions are isolated, frozen elements of an interacting system, we lose touch with the real world (which is the same for all of us and about which we can hope to agree) and begin to live in different incompatible worlds in our heads (over which we can only argue and struggle).

F.   Fragmentation Perpetuated or Heated

The process can be seen at all levels of human interaction. In the individual, such clinging to a past reality explains the fact of "transference", where patterns of response appropriate within the family are carried into later social relationships, including marital interaction and the bringing-up of children. Even within the family, children may retain inappropriate dependent attitudes towards their parents, and their parents may retain infantilising attitudes towards them, though both are physically mature. Families as a whole can similarly fail to learn from experience, but perpetuate unrealistic images of the family, and of the outside world, over generations. Furthermore, whole societies may become arrested in their development through valuing isolated abstractions above the flux of experience from which they were originally derived, as in the Dark Ages when medicine stopped for 1500 years after the work of Galen.

Is there some crucial factor, open to the possibility of our control, influencing the use of our vital capacity for abstraction towards that constructive and creative use which remembers the whole system and does not confuse the part with the whole, rather than towards increasing identification with abstractions, uncontrolled imagination, and finally madness? No question is more important for the survival of mankind, and there is already some suggestive evidence from studies of child development and the functioning of healthy families, which may help us towards at least a partial answer. Studies such as those Bowlby (1969, 1973, 1980) and Winnicott (1958) with human infants, and similar experiments on infant monkeys by Harlow (1966) and others, demonstrate clearly that a certain basic stability, regularity, reliability and consistent support is needed from the mothering figure if the infant is to feel sufficiently secure to venture out into the environment, away from her, to explore and begin to cope with change, unfamiliarity, newness. The "attachment behaviour" described by Bowlby seems essential if the child is to leave the mother and venture increasingly into the strangeness of the surrounding world; the safety of Winnicott's "holding" situation is vital if the child is similarly to engage in the experimental, spontaneous activity of "play".

If this safe situation is not provided, the individual deprived of its security clings to the original mothering figure, or to some substitute for the order and regularity she should have provided, whether in the form of possessions, obsessional activities and routines, recurrent fantasies, or rigid forms of "thought" or belief that must be protected from correction by external reality for fear they may be changed and lost. The individual's development inevitably becomes arrested.

Once this situation exists, it is understandable that the individual concerned seeks contact with others who will not disturb it, or who will at least disturb it as little as possible. People with different views, and above all those who are open to experience, who are constantly learning, growing and revising their ideas, will represent threats to be avoided, and will be seen as aliens if not enemies. It will be safest to keep contact only with family members who share the same rigid beliefs. To the extent that social needs must be met outside the family, friends and acquaintances will be chosen because they hold similar views, rather than for the challenge and stimulation of difference. For the intimacy of marriage (if the individual is able to contemplate this step at all) a partner will be chosen at a similar level of developmental arrest, or in Bowen's (1978) term "degree of differentiation", who will reinforce rather than undermine the frozen belief system. And children, when they arrive, will be indoctrinated into the pattern and prevented from growing, or at least not helped to grow, beyond it. Thus the pattern can perpetuate itself over generations, as Bowen has pointed out and Fisher and Mendel (1956) have demonstrated experimentally.

III. COMMUNICATION AND FRAGMENTATION

A. The Influence of the Different Modes of Communication

In addition to Bateson, others influenced by his work at the Mental Research Institute at Palo Alto in California (Watzlawick *et al.*, 1967; Watzlawick *et al.*, 1972) as well as the Milan Group (Palazzoli-Selvini *et al.*, 1978) have emphasized the vital importance of the different modes of communication in relation to these processes. In the fragment of Bateson's writings quoted earlier, the most crucial phrase is his suggestion, following Aldous Huxley, ". . . that the communication and behaviour of animals has a naïveté, a simplicity, which man has lost. Man's behaviour is corrupted by deceit—even self-deceit . . ." The behaviour of animals, including their simplicity, their completeness, their "grace", has much to do with their limited capacity for communication, as compared with "civilised" human-kind. Though some higher animals show rudimentary capacities for symbolic communication, animals communicate almost entirely through non-verbal, analogic means. They express their relationships to one another, their feelings and intentions, through actual, though partial and incomplete, expression of them. A threat to attack another member of the species, as in competition between males for available females, is communicated by all the bodily preparations for such an attack (posture, gesture, facial expression, growling etc.) which is demonstrated to be a communication and not an actual attack only by the fact that it is inhibited in its development at a certain stage, and stops short of completion. And if the communication is successful (that is, if it intimidates the competitor without the need for an actual fight) the rival will respond with some bodily signs of submission, sufficient to reduce the threatening behaviour of the opponent. The weaker dog presents the jugular vein to its more powerful rival, whose attacking behaviour then ceases.

Such non-symbolic, analogic communication is *similar in form to what it represents;* it is communicative in that *certain relationships present in the event represented are actually reproduced.* The difference between the real thing and the communication about it, is that *a part of the whole is representing the whole.* Even the dance of the honey-bee, indicating to others in which direction nectar may be found, *reproduces* in the pattern of its dance the angle between the direction of the goal and the direction of the sun, and it similarly indicates the distance to be travelled by the speed of its dance, which bears a certain relation to it. The matter does not quite stop here, and Bateson (1979) has clearly demonstrated how the capacity of some higher mammals to engage in *play* is a vital step towards the kind of experimentation that humans can engage in through use of symbols.

In humans, non-verbal, analogic communication continues to play a vital part. It is the only form of communication possible in the earliest years of the infant's life, and probably remains the most important mode of communication mediating social control in small groups, including families. For example, children may ignore the verbal appeals or expressed threats of punishment by parents over a long period, but their behaviour immediately changes the moment they recognize that the parents "really mean it", through information conveyed by the non-verbal channel. The parents' glaring eyes, tight lips, flushed faces, harsh voices and tensed bodies are recognized as "for real" in a way that words may not be, for they *are* real, a part of the developing reality.

The closer humans remain to this non-verbal, analogic mode of communication, then the simpler, more natural, and more "graceful" their social behaviour is likely to be. "Primitive" tribes, or children and relatively uneducated country people in "civilized" societies are likely to retain more of the simplicity and grace of animals, since the nature of this form of communication makes self-deceit difficult. But both man's greatest achievements and his greatest vices are consequences, as we have already suggested, of his capacity for the symbolic, digital mode of communication: the capacity to let one thing *stand for* another in a way which is completely arbitrary (though of course *agreed*), where the symbol bears no relationship whatever to what it symbolizes. This ability to use *symbols* (together, of course, with the abstractions or concepts for which we agree they shall stand) enables us to create an infinite variety of inner worlds, differing in any way we wish from the actual one we inhabit. Among other logical expressions underlying this possibility is the word "not", indicating whether a communication is true or untrue, a communication impossible to make in the non-verbal, analogic mode except by beginning an action and stopping short of completing it (e.g. a threatening fist which does not actually strike) (Watzlawick *et al.*, 1967). "To be or not to be" is now a question which can be asked, of others or oneself.

B.   The Dangers of Symbolic Communication

However this development, which makes possible our greatest power, our knowledge, brings with it also the capacity for self-deceit; the ability to create, believe in, live in, a world at variance with the evidence of the senses. Expressed in mythical terms, man has "eaten of the tree of knowledge of good and evil": he has the possibility, which he did not possess before, of choosing between what is and what is not, of inhabiting an inner world at variance with the facts actually encountered. This new-found power brought with it, inevitably, a loss of that innocence, simplicity and "grace" that bound us tightly to the evidence of our senses. Now humans could arrest their development at any point they wished, choosing to maintain an inner world which fitted the facts at one stage of development, but which became increasingly inconsistent with later reality. If one wished, one could remain omnipotent, God, co-existent with the whole universe; where no other individual capable of independent action existed. Alternatively, one could remain a helpless baby to be perpetually looked after, a defiant toddler, or an endlessly competitive child in an Oedipal triangle, and so on. However, this is possible only if the individual restricts communication with others to a degree which prevents the discrepancy between the inner and outer worlds from being exposed. Where the discrepancy is at its most extreme, communication may have to be so completely restricted with others that the individual withdraws from all social contact, and is considered "mad". Where the discrepancy is less extreme, the individual may ally himself or herself only with those members of the family who support the fantasy, rejecting others; may choose friends, or a mate, who do not challenge it; and if there are children, may train them to behave in ways which reinforce rather than challenge the lack of congruence between the inner and outer world. Thus, families as a whole tend to develop shared systems of fantasy, or levels of developmental arrest, with which they collude to preserve from correction. The collusion may extend to communities, even nations, as exemplified in the fairy-tale about "The Emperor's New Clothes".

The real world cannot be got rid of, nevertheless, and maintaining the fiction must inevitably be a constant struggle. Unless a solution of complete social isolation is chosen, someone, sooner or later, may give the game away. The most complete family collusion will be threatened by the fact that children have to go to school, that parents need to meet others in the course of their work, or that members are forced into social contacts through other external pressures. Even within the family, some may find themselves paying a higher price than others to maintain the fantasy, and be more inclined to rebel or escape. In addition, the threat to the fantasy system does not come only from outside. The actual achievements of each individual, in work, in relationships, in sexual attractiveness, etc., somehow have to be reconciled with the fantasy system.

C. Communication, the Maintenance of Dysfunction and its Cure

As a natural result of these constraints, communication becomes extremely complex. Everything an individual says about himself will tend to be influenced by three criteria; or, to put it another way, three simultaneous messages will tend to be contained in every communication:

(1) What is said must somehow not contradict too obviously the inner fantasy-world.

(2) At the same time, it must somehow not be so inconsistent with social expectations that it will actually be challenged by others.

(3) A third message will also be sent (usually non-verbal) exerting emotional pressure on the recipient not to notice any discrepancy between messages 1 and 2, and also not to comment on the inevitable confusion that will have resulted from trying to express two incompatible messages at once.

Needless to say, persons are selected as mates or friends who will obey the non-verbal command and not challenge the contradictions. Those who do challenge them, including children in the family, will be rejected.

The above complexities in communication, which arise quite naturally from the possibility of clinging to a static inner world at variance with the changing outer world, have been much described under the general term "double-bind". However, the explanation given here for this disordered form of communication seems altogether simpler and more understandable than those offered previously. For example, the terrible power struggles, at once immensely destructive though totally denied, seen to characterize the families of schizophrenics by the Milan group (Palazzoli *et al.*, 1978), which they attribute to pride or "hubris", become explicable if each member of the family is in fact seeking to preserve a fantasy that he or she is omnipotent, has no boundaries or limits, is an unchallenged "Lord of Creation". The word "hubris", which indicates a pride which seeks to rival the Gods, is absolutely appropriate. If all family members cling to fantasies of God-like omnipotence, the very *presence* of others, independent beings challenges this fundamental assumption. And since to compete with them openly is to admit that they exist, even competition with such non-existent beings must be denied.

Some of this material will of course be dealt with more fully in later sections dealing with pathology, but it is necessary to mention such matters briefly here for clarity. We can also mention briefly at this point that where nature produces a poison, she usually also provides an antidote. And so it is with the fragmentation described above which forms the source of so many human ills. Though it is made possible by the unique human capacity for symbolic representation of abstractions from sense experience, by the human capacity for digital as well as analogic communication, our ability to use symbols also enables us to overcome some of these difficulties which symbols themselves make possible. For we can use language to speak *about* language, and to study *disorders of language,* if language enables us to step away from reality sufficiently to make independent conceptual thought possible, and so to create science. If it thereby also enables us to lose touch with reality and go mad, by taking a second step we can step outside the problem, stand back from the disorder of language itself, study it and correct it. Should something go wrong with this second order (meta-level) process, the detachment made possible by conceptual thought enables us to stand back from that in turn, and so to observe and correct our errors, indefinitely.

IV. RESEARCH INTO DIFFERENCES BETWEEN HEALTHY AND DYSFUNCTIONAL FAMILIES

In the preceding pages, we have tried to look at the family from various perspectives as a *system*, and by returning to the simplest first principles we have tried to understand what the concept of *healthy function* would mean in such a system. Let us now turn to a survey of some of the actual research findings available at the time of writing, derived from observation of actual family interaction. Needless to say, in the brief compass possible here, only an outline of the main findings can be given, leaving out many important details which restrict the validity of the results. References are given, however, whereby the reader can explore the subject further.

A. How much Health and Dysfunction is There?

We might ask first whether healthy function is common or rare. No adequate answer exists to this question as regards the family as a system, but we may judge that truly healthy families are few and far between from existing knowledge regarding the mental health of whole populations. The Midtown Mahattan Study (Srole *et al.*, 1962) for example found 23.4% of a representative sample of the population demonstrating clear psychological dysfunction, and discovered only 18.5% who were definitely well. The results for the Sterling County Study (Leighton *et al.*, 1963), though including a more rural area, found closely similar figures, with 20% clearly dysfunctional and 17% indisputably well. It is important to begin with this kind of information since many existing studies are faulted in that they compare the obviously ill not with the most well, the "optimal" extreme which forms the main focus of this chapter, but with a measure of "normality" based more on the statistical average (that is, the *mid-range* group), comprising about 60% of the population in the studies just mentioned, whose mental health was uncertain.

B. Unusual Degrees of Health: Research Studies

(1) Westley and Epstein
Westley and Epstein (1970) examined in detail the families of a group of college students who showed unusual emotional health, and compared these with families of others who were particularly disturbed. The differences observed were checked against a study of a sample of the college population. The main findings were as follows:
1. Regarding the degree of *role differentiation between the parents,* the parents of the healthiest children showed a *balance between separateness and overlap* whereby many of the parental functions were shared, but not to a point where there could be confusion between the male and female identities or paternal and maternal roles and responsibilities. Families where there was greater overlap in the roles and responsibilities of husband and wife, and less differentiation in the sexual roles, produced fewer healthy children, often suffering themselves from role confusion. The "traditional", role-segregated, male-

dominated family, was even worse in its effects, and the degree of ill health in the children was exceeded only in families where the traditional roles were reversed, with the father performing more than half of the "traditionally female" household and child-care tasks.

2. Regarding the issue of *power*, the healthiest families were found to be *father-led*. Next most healthy were those which were *father-dominant*, next *egalitarian* and worst *mother-dominant*.

3. In general, it was found that a *high frequency of sexual intercourse*, together with *increasing sexual satisfaction during the course of the marriage*, appeared related with mental health in the children. But this was not always so, and the existence of a *warm, loving and supportive relationship between the couple* appeared even more vital, compensating considerably for emotional ill health in either husband or wife. Where this was the case parental pathology appeared to be contained and coped with within the marriage, rather than passed on to the children.

Westley and Epstein were studying individual family members rather than family interaction, but in a comparison of matched pairs of families with or without a schizophrenic child, Mischler and Waxler (1968) found similar features. More healthy families showed a strong parental coalition, but with authority exerted through negotiation rather than in a rigid, authoritarian way. Communication was clearer and more direct in the more healthy families, and was either rigid and fearfully-controlled, or confusing and disruptive, in the patient-containing families.

(2) Stabenau, Tupin, Werner and Pollin
A third research study (Stabenau *et al.*, 1965) has already been summarized in some detail in a previous book by the present writer (Skynner, 1976 p.244-246). A comparison of families producing children who are either schizophrenic, delinquent or showing neither of these disorders, showed many features consistent with other studies mentioned here, and

> . . . in the families with a normal control, affect tended to be appropriate, modulated, positive and warm. Interaction featured considerable autonomy, a coping rather than manipulative or controlling pattern in dealing with the family members, and a goal of mutual understanding and satisfaction. Family organisation was flexible with clear role differentiation and expectancy. Empathic awareness with each other's role was evidenced, and the father and mother tended to interact in a complementary manner (p.50).

(3) MacGregor et al.
A fourth study, less scientifically rigorous than the others but reporting the treatment of families containing adolescent members who displayed various degrees of disturbance, (MacGregor *et al.*, 1964) has also been summarized in tabular form in the present writer's previous book (Skynner, 1976). It shows many differences between more healthy and less healthy families, corresponding to those of the other studies. In moving from the description of families of the most disturbed children to families of the least disturbed children, one is struck again

Table I.

Level of function of children	Severe dysfunction	Mid-range function	Healthy function
Types of disorder	"Process' (chronic) schizophrenia Psychopathy (Sociopathy)	Reactive psychosis/Behaviour Disorders/ Neurosis	No evidence of psychiatric disorder; effective functioning
Power-structure	*chaotic* Parent-child coalition (usually between mother and index patient, father ineffective and excluded)	*structured/rigid* Rigid control, little negotiation. Parents either competing for dominance (behaviour disorders) or dominant-submissive relationship (neuroses)	*structured/flexible* Strong, equal-powered parental coalition, but children consulted and decisions through negotiation. Clear hierarchy with mutual respect.
Differentiation	*fusion* Blurred boundaries, unclear identities, shifting roles. Blaming, scapegoating, evasion of responsibility. Invasiveness.	*separateness through distancing* Identities more defined but at cost of emotional distancing, restriction of potential and of spontaneity. Role stereotyping, including male/female.	*clear identity + intimacy* Identities highly defined and secure, permitting also high levels of closeness and intimacy. High individual responsibility.
Communication	Vague, confused, evasive, contradictory. Double-binds. Mystification.	Clearer than in severely dysfunctional, but in rigid, stereotyped way (so often superficially clearer than in healthy).	Open, clear, direct, frank. Lively and spontaneous.
	Imperviousness.	Impervious to new ideas; non-mutual.	Receptive and responsive to new ideas.

	oppositional	*oppositional*	*affiliative*
Relationship	Distrust, expectation of evil (betrayal, desertion). Ambivalent feelings unintegrated, swings between extremes; inconsistancy dealt with by denial. Marriage highly unsatisfactory; split by parent/child coalition.	Relative *distrust*; human nature seen as basically evil, needing rigid control of self and others. Repression, suppression. Ambivalence not accepted, dealt with by repression and reaction formation against "bad" impulses. Lack of marital satisfaction; competing or dominant/submissive roles.	*Trust*; basic expectation of positive response to positive approach. Warm, caring, mutual regard and responsibility. Ambivalent feelings accepted as normal. Both sides included and integrated. Mutually satisfying, complementary marital roles; sexuality mutually satisfying also.
Reality-sense	Reality denied; escape into fantasy satisfactions.	Adequate reality sense to function effectively, but with some distortion and incongruent family "myths".	Image of self and family congruent with reality.
Affect	Cynicism; hostility; sadism; hopeless and despair.	Hostility (behaviour disorders) but without the degree of sadism in severely dysfunctional. Subdued, joyless, restricted (neurotic disturbance).	Warmth, enjoyment; humour, wit. Tenderness, empathy.
Attitude to change, loss	Unable to cope with change and loss. Timeless, repetitive quality, with denial of separation and death, escape into fantasy.	Change and loss faced, but with great pain and difficulty. Separation and death not really worked through; substitutes for lost persons and feelings transferred, instead of internalization of lost person.	Change, growth, separation and death all accepted realistically and losses worked through, due to 1. Strong parental coalition (in relation to older and younger generations). 2. Strong, varied relationships outside family. 3. Transcendent value system.

by: the importance, for health, of parental co-operation and collaboration in the matter of authority; a clear inter-generational boundary whereby the children cannot disturb this coalition by forming stronger parent–child coalitions themselves; mutual acceptance and understanding; and an ability of the family as a whole to relate to, and accept help from, the larger community. Once again, moving from the families of the most- to the least-disturbed children, one is impressed by the dominant position of the mother, and exclusion of the father in the former; and the position of increasing leadership taken by the father as the degree or level of disturbance decreases.

(4) Timberlawn Studies

However, even though these studies show much agreement, none of them examined the actual behaviour and interaction of families which ranged from the most dysfunctional to the extreme of health. A first step in this direction has been taken by the group at the Timberlawn Psychiatric Research Foundation (Lewis *et al.*, 1976). Their research, which reports the first successful attempt to find and examine in depth the personalities, relationships and typical interaction found in families at the extremes of health (rather than the mid-range or "average") is of such crucial theoretical and practical importance that the reader is strongly urged to read the published material of the researchers themselves, either in the book just quoted or in the more popular presentation, omitting much of the detail of the research design (Lewis, 1979). In a previous publication (Skynner, 1981), the present writer has attempted to summarize the results in three tables, which have been seen and approved by Lewis, and which should help the reader to grasp their main findings rapidly. (see Table I)

In this first table, the spectrum of level of psychological function is divided into three main categories, for the sake of simplicity. It will be seen at once that in moving our attention from the characteristics of the most severely dysfunctional families, through the mid-range group, to the most healthy families, the change is not simply one of degree, nor is it simply a steady increase or lessening of certain features. Instead, in certain respects, progress towards health appears to take place in a step-wise fashion, by stages.

For example, the chaotic situation in the most severely dysfunctional families, where there is characteristically a parent/child coalition with the father most often ineffective and excluded, gives way at mid-range function to a rigid structure not only with rigid control of the children by the parents, but also a rigid hierarchy with one spouse dominant to the other. But when we come to the most healthy families, this situation is not simply exaggerated, but radically changed. Structure is present, but is sufficiently secure for the children to be consulted and decisions reached through negotiation, and the parental coalition has become equal powered.

Similarly, the fusion of the severely dysfunctional family gives way to individuality and separateness in mid-range function but only at the cost of emotional distancing and role stereotyping, including rigid differences in sexual role. In healthy families this is not taken further, but radically changed. The sense of identity and difference has become so secure that individuals can alternate between intense intimacy, and separateness. A similar transition is seen in regard to communication, where in the mid-range clarity is achieved at the cost of rigidity, while the latter is no longer necessary for healthy families.

As regards relationships, reality sense, and affect, the transition is more continuous. The same is true of the attitude to change, loss, separation and death. The Timberlawn Group found that the capacity to deal with these different aspects of change was an especially crucial and reliable feature in differentiating healthy from less healthy families, affecting physical as well as mental health. This one might expect, of course, in the light of our previous discussion, if "health" is connected with an ability to adapt to the ever changing flux of experience and the challenges posed by the developmental process, by constant change of inner "models" or "knowledge" to fit the new information.

Table I presents the findings in broadest outline. But the Timberlawn Researchers also examined in more detail the families producing healthy children, comparing the six families whose function approximated most closely to mid-range function, to those which showed the functioning of the "healthy" group at its greatest extreme. The former they called "adequate", the latter "optimal", and an outline of the findings regarding this comparison is given in Tables II and III.

Table II needs little explanation and shows that the "optimal" families could be differentiated from the "adequate" on 7 out of 8 criteria, while Table III

Table II.   Main characteristics of "optimal" families,
in order of apparent importance

"Optimal families could be differentiated from "adequate" families on all these characteristics except No. 7 (Initiative) to level of statistical significance. Both produced healthy children, but "adequates showed many "Mid-range" features.

---

(1) *Affiliative attitude* to human encounter — open, reaching-out, basically trusting (as contrasted with *oppositional* — distrust, withdrawal etc.)

(2) *High respect for separateness, individuality,* autonomy, privacy (as contrasted with expectation of agreement, conformity, "speaking for others").

(3) *Open, clear, frank communication* (as contrasted with confusion, evasion, restriction etc.).

(4) *Firm parental coalition,* egalitarian with shared power between parents (as contrasted with parental splits and parent/child coalitions).

(5) *Control flexible, by negotiation,* within basic parent/child hierarchy (as contrasted with rigid, inflexible control and unchangeable rules).

(6) *Highly spontaneous interaction,* with considerable humour and wit — "three-ring circus, but all under control" (as contrasted with rigid, stereotyped interaction).

(7) *High levels of initiative* (as contrasted to passivity).

(8) *Uniqueness and difference encouraged* and appreciated — liveliness, strong "characters" (as contrasted with bland, stereotyped, conformist types).

Reproduced by permission from "The Handbook of Family Therapy", 1981, (A. Gurman and D. Kniskern, eds), Brunner/Mazel, New York.

Table III.   Differences in marital and sexual function between "adequate"
             and "optimal" families, all producing healthy children

	Adequate	Optimal
ROLES	Generally traditional gender roles but in rigid, stereotyped, highly role-segregated way.	Generally traditional gender roles but seemingly from choice, with rewarding, mutually pleasurable complementarity and reciprocity.
RELATION-SHIP	*Husbands* successful, agressively work-oriented. More satisfied with lives than wives — distant and providing material but not emotional support.	*Both husbands and wives* express mutual pleasure and enjoyment with relationship and life generally. Husbands involved in work but responsive to wife's needs, supportive and emotionally aware.
	Wives generally unhappy, needy, lonely, feeling isolated from husbands and overwhelmed by children. Tending to obesity, depression and fatigue. Interests outside home limited.	Wives feel appreciated, cherished. Many, active interests outside home, though role of mother and wife central and satisfying.
SEXUALITY	Regular, generally similar frequency (about twice-weekly). Mostly satisfying to husbands. Wives generally dissatisfied (too much, too little, unpleasurable etc.)	More variable in frequency between couples (several times weekly to twice a month) but highly, mutually pleasurable and satisfying to both partners. Pattern of long-term marital fidelity.
LEISURE	Limited involvement of couple with community.	More involvement of couple outside the home and family alone.

Both "adequate" and "optimal" families shared very high belief and involvement in the idea of the family, and their children's activities.

Reproduced by permission from "The Handbook of Family Therapy", 1981, (A Gurman and D. Kniskern, eds), Brunner/Mazel, New York.

shows that there were striking differences between the "optimal" and "adequate" families as regards the marital relationships. It is reassuring to see that many couples showing evidence of considerable degrees of mid-range function can nevertheless produce healthy children by dint of hard work, effort and struggle, even at considerable cost. But it is even more reassuring to see that the greatest health and well-being in family function, like the highest development of all other human skills, appears after the basic knowledge and skills are so well established that they no longer require anxious effort, giving space and time to allow spontaneity, playfulness and enjoyment, reminding one of Bateson's use of the word "grace".

REFERENCES

Bateson, G. (1972). "Steps Towards an Ecology of Mind". Chandler, New York.

Bateson, G. (1979). "Mind and Nature", Wildwood House, London.

Beavers, R. (1977). "Psychotherapy and Growth: A Family Systems Perspective", Brunner/Mazel, New York.

Bertalanffy, L. V. (1968). "General System Theory", Brazillier, New York.

Bowen, M. (1978). "Family Therapy in Clinical Practice", Jason Aronson, New York.

Bowlby, J. (1967). "Attachment and Loss. Vol I: Attachment", Hogarth Press, London.

Bowlby, J. (1973). "Attachment and Loss. Vol II. Separation: Anxiety and Anger", Hogarth Press, London.

Bowlby, J. (1980). "Attachment and Loss. Vol III. Sadness and Depression", Hogarth Press, London.

Eyre, R. (1979). "Ronald Eyre on The Long Search", Collins, London.

Fisher, S. and Mendell, D. (1956). The Communication of Neurotic Patterns over Two and Three Generations. _Psychiatry_ 19, 41-46.

Harlow, H. F., Harlow, M. K., Dodsworth, R. O. and Arling, G. L. (1966). Maternal Behaviour of Rhesus Monkeys Deprived of Mothering and Peer Associations in Infancy. _Proceedings of the American Philosophical Society_ 110, 58-66.

Klein, M. (1932). "The Psychoanalysis of Children", Hogarth, London.

Korzybski, A. (1933). "General Semantics", Science Press, Lancaster, Pennsylvania.

Leighton, D., Harding, J. S., Macklin, D. B., Hughes, C. C. and Leighton, A. H. (1963). Psychiatric Findings of the Stirling County Study. _American Journal of Psychiatry_. 119, 1021-1026.

Lewis, J. M., Beavers, W. R., Gossett, J. T. and Phillips, V. A. (1976). "No Single Thread: Psychological Health in Family Systems", Brunner/Mazel, New York.

Lewis, J. M. (1979). "How's Your Family?" Brunner/Mazel, New York.

MacGregor, R., Ritchie, A. M., Serrano, A. C., Schuster, F. P., McDonald, E. C. and Goolishian, H. A. (1964). "Multiple Impact Therapy with families", McGraw-Hill, New York.

Miller, J. G. (1965). Living Systems, Basic Concepts. _Behavioural Science,_ 10, 193-245.

Mischler, E. and Waxler, N. (1968). "Interaction in Families", Wiley, New York.

Palazzoli-Selvini, M., Boscolo, L., Cecchin, G. and Prata, G. (1978). "Paradox and Counterparadox", Jason Aronson, New York.

Skynner, A. C. R. (1976). "One Flesh: Separate Persons", Constable, London. (US edition entitled "Systems of Family and Marital Psychotherapy", Brunner/Mazel, New York, 1976).

Skynner, A. C. R. (1981). An Open-Systems, Group-Analytic Approach to Family Therapy. _In_ "The Handbook of Family Therapy", (A. Gurman and D. Kniskern, eds). Brunner/Mazel, New York.

Srole, L., Langer, T. S., Michael, S. T., Opler, M. K. and Rennie, T. A. C. (1962). "Mental Health in the Metropolis", McGraw-Hill, New York.

Stabenau, J. R., Tupin, J., Werner, M. and Pollin, W. A. (1965). A Comparative Study of Families of Schizophrenics, Delinquents and Normals. _Psychiatry_ 28, 45-59.

Watzlawick, P., Beavin, J. H. and Jackson, D. D. (1967). "Pragmatics of Human Communication", Norton, New York.

Watzlawick, P., Weakland, J. and Fisch, R. (1972). "Change", Norton, New York.

Westley, W. A. and Epstein, N. B. (1969). "The Silent Majority", Jossey-Bass, San Francisco.

Winnicott, D. W. (1958). "Collected Papers; Through Paediatrics to Psychoanalysis", Tavistock, London.

┌─────────────────── Chapter 2 ───────────────────┐
│   │
│   Different Views of a   │
│   Healthy Family   │
│   │
│   A. Bentovim, J. Byng-Hall, G. Gorell Barnes,│
│   A. Cooklin, R. Skynner   │
└───┘

I. INTRODUCTION

To illustrate some of the themes concerning healthy families explored in the earlier chapter by Skynner: he and the authors of later chapters were invited to view and participate in a discussion of a healthy family's interaction while occupied in carrying out a task as a family. A number of writers have commented on the use of "tasks" given to healthy families to stimulate interaction, which can then be recorded, viewed and re-viewed (Riskin, 1976). As part of the basic research of the Family Studies Group of the Hospital for Sick Children, Great Ormond Street, a series of tasks have been administered to a variety of families who were "healthy" and "unhealthy" (Kinston, 1980).

The research aim was to define a way of *describing* family interaction and *rating* it. A "family description format" has been produced (Loader *et al.*, 1981) and family health scales are being developed and evaluated (Kinston, 1979). There are many similarities with the research of the Timberlawn Group described in Chapter (1) by Skynner (Lewis *et al.*, 1976) which appeared while the research was in train. It seemed a good way of exploring the issues of what makes for a healthy family interaction by viewing one of the tapes produced for the Great Ormond Street research. Although the validity of the way families tackle tasks in "laboratory" conditions has not been generalized to the families own life at home, Hansen's (1981) description of "living-in" with normal families shows how families repeat patterns seen in the clinic endlessly.

Two tasks were chosen from a series of six tasks, from tapes of families without a "defined" psychiatrically disturbed member. They were recruited from successive attenders at a coeliac disease clinic (Kinston, 1980) on the basis that children with coeliac disease have no *known* psychiatric or psychosomatic symptoms once treated satisfactorily. They are seen every year in the gastro-enterology clinic to check on the dietary treatment and to ensure growth is satisfactory. They are not handicapped by their disorder apart from needing a special diet free of gluten which is not too restrictive. Among the group of 17 families, a family rated by the experimenters as being among the healthiest and least dysfunctional was chosen to show the group of experienced family therapists: Robin Skynner, Alan Cooklin, Gill Gorell Barnes, John Byng-Hall and Arnon Bentovim.

The tasks chosen were a 5-minute "build a tower with blocks" which shows the family in action, and a task which asks the family to express feelings and fantasies about an accident between a car and a motor bike which they have seen. This shows the way they tackle an affectively laden topic. The group saw tapes through completely once, and then had a discussion following a second viewing which was taped and this account has been edited.

II. THE FIRST TASK

A. The Family

The "M" family is an intact family of two parents and three children. Father is a consultant advisor on computers to a large multi-national firm and mother is a housewife. There are three children, all girls: Valerie aged 12 years, Jaqui, aged 9 years, and Naomi aged 6 years at the time of the interview. Naomi, the youngest has coeliac disease and is very well. The parents were asked to bring all the children to take part in the research interviews and Kinston (1980) has described the very considerable efforts needed to recruit and hold families for such research efforts. They knew their participation would not benefit themselves directly, but they were willing to participate and gave permission for video recordings. The tasks which were part of the general procedure were administered by "tape-recorder" and the whole interview which took approximately one hour, was video-taped.

B. "Build A Tower Task"

This task is introduced by the experimenter on tape and audio, and they are told previously that the tasks are to enable them to show how they do things as a family and there are no right or wrong answers.

Experimenter: "Take the box next to the recorder and use them to build a tower — I'll be back in about 5 minutes."

C. Description of Response

Father advances to the box and takes it back to a low table which is placed among a circle of chairs where the family have been sitting, and as he does so, says "come on", and they rise at his signal to surround him kneeling around the table.

The family themselves are good looking and dressed attractively, father in shirt sleeves, mother smartly but simply dressed in trousers and shirt, the oldest girl in trousers and the two younger girls in pretty dresses.

As the father spills the blocks out on to the table, the girls giggle and push forward. Father says "Hey steady on", and the giggling and obvious pleasure of the family continues. The mother hangs back slightly, Valerie and Jaqui kneeling down facing each other, Naomi and father making the sides of the square with mother behind father. Although Valerie starts to pick up the blocks, father takes over two large blocks and makes them into the base while Valerie adds a third.

Father: We'll have to make a solid base.

Mother: Yes make it solid.	Jaqui puts a block on top of her father's and mother leans across to add another one.
Mother: See if you can make it solid and build it right up.	Then sits back as if to leave it to them. Father neatens up the blocks to make them all square and the girls continue to put blocks on top of the base.
Father: Put this one on top.	
Valerie: Put it on the top. We've got lots of small ones.	Echoing father. Rifling through the blocks left on the table.
Mother: Is that a big one over there.	Reaches across to two bricks on the side. Naomi is "helping" by leaning across to put bricks on top rather clumsily and on the second occasion Valerie takes it off her and puts it on herself.
Mother: We've got these enormous ones, we should use them at some stage.	Fingering them.
Father: Where are they then; big ones here.	Mother passes them to him, as he goes on building, very much in the centre, controlling the building, the girls taking turns to add bricks themselves.
Mother and Father [in unison]: That's not very good.	When completed. [laughing]
Mother: You could have an architecturally wonderful tower, high at the sides, hollow inside.	Children laugh.
Father: We've got to have it symmetrical, otherwise it will never stand up.	Adjusts the bricks.
Mother: Here's one which is a different size.	Leaning across.

Naomi pushes one on top and makes the whole structure sway.

Mother: You have to be careful—do be careful Naomi.

The children laugh, especially father, with much enjoyment.

Father: It's still lopsided.
What about your bit Naomi.
Steady.

Valerie laughs.
She puts it on top.

Father: It's very warm.

An aside to mother.

Mother: Very warm.

Valerie takes off her coat!

Father: What does that look like.

Naomi throws her arms up in the air with exultation and pleasure.

Mother: As long as no one breathes it'll be all right.

Father: mmm.

Valerie then fiddles with the blocks on top and Jaqui follows.

Mother: That's rather good actually.

Naomi claps.

Father: Yes.

Valerie closes the box.

Mother: Do you think we have to put them back in the box.

Father: Leave them there.

All go back to seats.

Mother: I wonder how high we could have made it.

Father: We could have gone higher than that.

Jaqui: It could have been very [inaudible].

Father: It's very conservative.

Mother: Very—there's a green teacup perhaps we could hang it on there.

Father and Mother [together]: Put it on the top.

Jaqui puts the cup on the top.

Mother: See if it will balance—no, the other way up darling.

and changes it around.

Father: No, the other way—right in the middle.

All laugh—Naomi clapping her hands again with delight.

Mother: That's it—there.

Father: Have to see if we could put the box on top.

Children [in unison]: No, no, then the lot will fall down, it wouldn't balance.

More laughter.

Father: It might—it's not that important —five minutes is up.

All sit back quietly, murmurming and smiling.

Experimenter [on tape]: That's fine.

D. Therapists' Discussion

Bentovim: Who would like to start?

Byng-Hall: The thing that struck me was how much this family was able to use the situation to enjoy itself. Immediately they picked up that potential in the task and the kids joked and laughed. The parents were able to manage the level of excitement in this family very well. If you listened carefully, you could hear both mother and father saying "Steady, steady", or "Don't knock it over", and the kids responded to this quite readily. The whole task could have been wrecked if the kids' behaviour had been allowed to escalate. I was impressed too by the imagination in the family, in particular mother in the background was quietly drawing up a plan for the building; she was suggesting the form it might take and the process by which the whole task might be managed while the rest of the family were picking up these ideas and putting them into practice. But it wasn't just a mechanical task: they added some flowery ideas to the whole business and mother, for instance, suggested they might make an architectural masterpiece, or words to that effect.

Skynner: I had a similar response to the fun and enjoyment, it was a lovely family to watch. I was thinking in terms of the Timberlawn classification and having seen some of their tapes, I thought this showed most of the characteristics of their optimal families. There was a very affiliative attitude to human encounter: very open, reaching out, basically trusting. I thought there was very high respect for separateness and individuality throughout the whole family, great enjoyment of difference; they were very lively, strong characters, everyone seemed to like that and encourage it. There was great spontaneity and liveliness but, at the same time, there was a quite remarkable sort of control and calm which didn't seem to be coming from anywhere in particular; the parents were putting in some help or guidance a little bit, as John mentioned, but somehow that seemed to be a part, a characteristic, of the whole system; the children were excited, and yet there was this calm quietness at the same time, whereby they could concentrate on the tasks. There was also very open, clear, frank communication; they all seemed to express their feelings and to feel they would be accepted, with one exceptionally emotional minute, and I didn't get a feeling of inhibition. The parents showed a coalition; power seemed to be shared between them and control seemed to be flexible, by negotiation between the parents and children. The father took the lead in this, the mother as well, but the father more in that he picked up the box and generally helped them and led them, but he didn't take over nor did he prevent them from using their ideas as well, but he helped them to express themselves; so the control was not *rigid*. They showed very high levels of initiative, they seemed to be very quick to have the ideas and to put them into practice, and what they built was a very constructive, integrated kind of activity.

The only negative comment I could make about them was that the mother seemed to me a bit inhibited, a little bit anxious, not markedly so, but a little; it was striking in contrast with the father who was very relaxed and involved and quietly cheerful. The mother seemed a bit self-conscious and nervous and anxious, a bit in the background, the last to get up, rushing in a little bit at times as if she was doing so from her own anxiety, rather than as part of the whole group. Otherwise I would say this struck me as a very healthy and very, very nice family.

Cooklin: I was thinking of two things really from a slightly different perspective. Firstly, the form of the interaction over time from the beginning of the task to the end and secondly, if we had been told they were a treatment what might we have reframed differently. For example, I saw the main axis of interaction between the father and Naomi, and in the early part of the task, it looked as though it was a relatively fixed, stable state of affairs. The relationship between the father and the mother was complementary, with father the activator, the one who was going to engage the children and act like their teacher or Scout Master, and mother the advisor commentator who did not engage actively.

If those roles were fixed, one might have jumped onto it and said that there may not be sufficient sharing and so on. Looking at the whole interaction over time, however, I felt that this family tackled this task as an issue of presenting the families' self-esteem. What seemed healthy to me about the family was that there was relatively little doubt at any point, except just at the first giggle when they started the task, as to whether they had reasonable esteem about themselves as a family and about each other. The way they maintained the task was impressive, they wanted to do it as quickly as possible, as efficiently as possible, and as soon as they'd done it they sat back. There was a little bit of concern as to whether they were going to be rewarded, or what was going to happen and they waited and then gave their own comment that it was "conservative".

The response could certainly have been called competitive. If the family had been in some kind of competitive escalation with some other agency, or some other family, or somebody else, then one might have said that this was a potentially non-creative and pathological response, but the fact was that the task united the family rather than the family were united in their difficulties with the task.

Gorell Barnes: I just wanted to say something about the family organization as I observed it. It seemed to me that the family performed this task well because they all gave the father authority to be the leader, but in fact apart from the middle child who actually tried to do something different on a couple of occasions, the children otherwise fitted in with the ideas that father was putting to them the way the tower should be built. I felt that the father was producing a tower, that he said "You've got to have symmetry," and "It's got to be balanced at the bottom to work at the top", and was producing very practical concrete kinds of ideas about how to build towers, whereas the mother was pushing the imaginative possibilities of towers. She talked about building a "wonderful" tower and this seemed to me to be a very good balance. I thought that they managed the children extremely well; the youngest knocked something down when the task was almost completed and they did not get too cross—they all laughed a bit and then rebuilt it. But I felt that the children really weren't given much imaginative scope at all to develop this tower.

In the end, it seemed to me that the family were a little bit dissatisfied with their tower and looked at this quite chirpily: "We could have gone higher than that", they said; but Dad said "That's not bad in five minutes", and on the whole, they were quite pleased with themselves at having achieved the task. Then I noticed an interesting bit which perhaps showed how Dad can join with Mum in this, in which he said "Let's put the box on top", and the children said "No, it would fall down", and so he had a naughty impulse to spoil the tower, then he was stopped by the family, so it seemed to me they were good at balancing one another's impulses.

Bentovim: The only thing I'd add is father's role in actually acting as the negotiator with the people setting the task, his response to this, his watching the time. He seemed very much involved with the boundary between outside and inside, and the family were safe in his care of the situation. He made it clear he would deal with whoever had set the situation up.

Byng-Hall: It was interesting to listen to the discussion and to realize that perhaps different members of the group had identified with different people. Certainly I think I must have been. I found myself listening to mother's imaginative and planning comments, and as a man I was taking the executive role, before I was in his shoes as it were, listening to the others. I was much more aware of mother's role in the whole process, which seemed to be guiding; not controlling, but suggesting and highly imaginative. I didn't pick up the anxiety as much as Robin did, although I could get some sense of what you were talking about.

Skynner: That difference in the power of the two: the dominance of the father, is the one thing I would question about them as an optimal family. I was also struck by the thought (joking) that when you have much more active mothers, perhaps you get Eriksonian enclosures being jointly built, rather than magnificent Eriksonian towers! [Erikson, 1963]

Cooklin: I would like to return to what would be the cut-off if this wasn't a healthy family. For example, one thing which was positive was that there was no conflict about the father's position, and relatively little conflict about the mother's position and relatively little conflict, despite some jockeying for positions, between the children. Now one could say that was very healthy because they knew their place and could function within it, or you could say that these were rigid roles that they had to stick to and were linked with myths and so on and so forth. My feeling was that there was something which identified this family as healthy, which was the kind of degree of Brownian movement within those roles; that they weren't absolutely rigid, even over that short space of time. It is still true that the relationships were nearly all complementary rather than oscillating between complementary and symmetrical. As such they were somewhat fixed. But there was no kind of battling that could have been said to be symmetrical, except for the little bits of laughter, but even this limited amount and some good humoured jockeying for position would identify them as being a healthy family.

Byng-Hall: Just one comment: the father being able to take the "little boy" role right at the end seemed to me to be an important indicator that the roles were not too rigid.

III. THE SECOND TASK AND DISCUSSION

A. The Expression of Feelings and Fantasies Task

Experimenter: Discuss your reactions to the following. The family has just seen an accident between a car and a motor bike and the ambulance has been and gone.

Father: What's your reaction; the ambulance has gone. [speaking quietly]

Valerie: Blood. [quietly]

Naomi: Glass broken.

Father: Glass?

Naomi: Because the windows might be broken. The windows might be broken of the car.

Father: We ought to sweep the glass up, should we mother? We haven't got a brush though.

Naomi: No, but can we get one.

Father: We can use an old bit of something to sweep it up.

Naomi: If we bought one we could sweep it up.

Jaqui: Well, how do we buy a brush, Naomi?

Father: Did we actually see the accident?

Valerie: Yes, she said we'd just seen an accident.

Mother: Assuming we did, wouldn't we all be rather shattered?

Valerie: Oh, I feel sorry for that poor man.

Jaqui: Which one?

Father: Which one — the one on the motor cycle or the one in the car? [Seriously] We don't know how many were hurt or anything like that do we?

Jaqui: No.

Father: Have you ever seen an accident?

Valerie: No.

Jaqui: No.

Mother: We saw one on the way home — on the way from school, didn't we?

Father: Did you have a lump in your tummy?

B. First Discussion

Bentovim: I think we should discuss this first section as it seems to be the end of a sequence. It seemed to me that the parents were protective of the children over this emotionally laden task, e.g. Father: "Did we actually see the accident", with a general atmosphere of irritation with the topic. However, encouraged by mother saying "Wouldn't we all be shattered?", Valerie enacted the role by saying she "felt sorry for the poor man". Then the father immediately responded by changing the content and asked if anyone had seen an accident which introduced a discussion about the task itself.

Cooklin: It seemed to me that, whether this is healthy or not, this family had clear boundaries about how far one could go in that kind of direction.

Byng-Hall: The thing that interests me was the way in which the family as a whole, I think guided by the parents and directed by them, managed to change the level at which the family was engaging. The immediate response was blood, and then they switched off that frightening topic back to glass and sweeping up the glass and so on; but the family didn't then keep avoiding the painful issues: they kept on dipping back into more painful areas and then coming out again which seemed to be a reasonable way of handling something which really carried enormously emotive aspects.

Gorell Barnes: Yes, I think that's true, but it seems to me at this point that the father is still the one that is consistently doing that, because he shifts uneasily and says "marvellous" in a slightly sarcastic tone of voice. It's father who suggests that the glass be swept up. When Naomi's imagination gets going, it's father who keeps it in bounds. Then the older sib joins in and says "We haven't got a brush, Naomi", and it seems to me that whenever some enjoyment about the accident comes in, the father keeps it in bounds whether for good or bad; that's what's happening at this point. And then we get onto "Have you ever seen an accident?" and I quite agree I think the level changes.

Cooklin: Mother verbally cues in the eldest girl and it appears that she also looks towards the girl at the same time. It's very difficult in the sequence to see which comes first, whether it is a non-verbal cue as well as a verbal one, but I thought they *were* congruent. Maybe in this family there is a tendency to keep things light, but it is not a conducted session that people in the family can express what they are feeling, although there is some sense in which especially Valerie is constantly looking at her parents for permission to say things, so the cue may come in there, in giving permission rather than directing.

Skynner: I saw the mother's intervention as anxious, as wanting to talk about something rather morbid because of her own needs, and the father as being more relaxed about it and behaving as if there was no point in getting worked up about something which wasn't actually happening and just a bit of imagination. How one would view that would depend upon what one thinks "normal" is. The children presumably, would respond to the parents anyway and would be watching for cues; I don't know how one could describe that as being either "normal" or "abnormal". However, I am interested that we are already into the problem of what's normal and abnormal, and we are using our own personal criteria.

Gorell Barnes: Maybe one thinks about the two different things, the two different tasks we've seen, and it seems to me that mother is again pushing in the same direction as in the first task, i.e. towards imagination, encouraging them to use their feeling component "I assume we'd all be shattered", and father, as you say Robin, is really saying "Well, you know, is it necessary to get into that". I don't know whether this is healthy or not. He says things like "We don't know how many were hurt, do we?": he is not wanting to engage at the level she is pushing them towards at that moment; in the same way, when they were building a tower, she wanted to build something wonderful and he wanted to build something practical that would stand up. So I think it is quite interesting to see how they have been complementary in a different way in relation to this task, which is a very emotional task.

Skynner: Can I respond to what Gill said there? I think that's a good explanation of that incident, in that you're putting it in terms of two dimensions: one is to do with the complementarity of the father and the mother as regards "instrumentality" and "expression" of emotion which I would see as normal or possibly normal; but the other thing is the *content* of the emotion, and the content of the emotion the mother was putting in seemed to me to be rather morbid and father was playing that down. So I would see those as two different dimensions, both equally relevant.

Byng-Hall: The word she uses was "shattered" wasn't it, which could refer to either the emotion or to the visual imagery of the shattered windowscreen.

Gorell Barnes: I think it interesting that she is making a push to get them into a different feeling level and father is resisting that as I see it. She is acting for her own needs, at this point rather than on behalf of the family task and that's the point he was making I think.

Bentovim: I also wonder whether he was protecting the family from the intrusion as in the first one; one felt again that he was interposing and saying "Why in hell's name do we have to go into this sort of thing?", and possibly, knowing that his wife was quite anxious about it, so he would be protective of her.

Cooklin: The other issue which is raised when trying to watch a piece of normal behaviour, as when trying to discuss a piece of therapeutic behaviour, is do we have a common language? Robin said earlier that he did not listen too much to the content; maybe we ought to discuss what you mean by "content". Are you talking about attending to the process of the language, rather than to the content of the language.

Byng-Hall: I thought I was simply looking at how the sequences formed in the first part and at what point the sequence changed.

Skynner: What you are saying is very informative and educational to me.

I suppose it would be better if I got rid of the word "content" as far as my response is concerned and talked more about "verbal" and "non-verbal". I'm responding more to the *non-verbal*, the feeling of fun and laughter and spontaneous movement, the way the little girl raises her hands when they have done something they like, and how they move around, and what they look like, rather than the actual words they are saying.

Byng-Hall: The discussion has made me realize that I was trying to follow a theme in both its form and content. The verbal and non-verbal communications were giving me information about this. The theme I was trying to follow was how much this family could get in touch with painful imagery and feelings and frightening imagery. Both the verbal and the non-verbal behaviour showed an ebb and flow which was interesting and as it developed through the session, the ebb and flow was able to increase in amplitude, so that we know from our first general overview of the session that father was able to describe a very, very unpleasant experience indeed. This made me feel this was a healthy family.

Gorell Barnes: I think that one of the things I'm always following is what sort of different cues are the parents giving the children and what are the implications of this for the way the children are going to relate to certain situations, so it's a combination of the behaviour but also the actual words used, rather than themes; I think it's the actual words and what the messages mean. It's interesting that the themes we are talking about are marginally different.

Cooklin: There is just one other thing that occurred to me as differentiators for me of healthy *vs* non-healthy. One was that they found a metaphor which was given to them by the parents for painful feelings which was not a kind of grossly exaggerated or very disturbing metaphor; it was the "lump" that was passed around for the metaphor for feeling upset and I thought that was, in a sense, the parents giving the children a healthy way of communicating about being upset or feeling something.

C. Continuing the Sequence:

Valerie: It was an accident between a motor-scooter and a car.
Father: It was just like that one then.
Valerie: No, I didn't actually see it happen, but the ambulances were there. We went past it on the way home.
Mother: We saw one the other day.
Jaqui: A lady used to look after me when you were at school somewhere round by the butchers, you know. We were walking home and we saw it. We came out at 3 o'clock and you [to Valerie] came out at half past or something.
Mother: When I first went back to school?
Jaqui: Yes.
Father: And, anyway what did you feel like. [picks up the task]
Jaqui: Horrible. Your tummy sort of goes whoo.
Mother: It does, doesn't it.

Father: Mmm.
Jaqui: You feel glad that you weren't . . .
Mother: Exactly.
Jaqui: In it.
Mother: It could have been you.
Valerie: And wish people were more careful.
Father: Does it make you become more careful yourself?
Valerie: Yes. [nodding and Naomi nods with her]
Jaqui: We don't drive.
Father: You have bikes.
Valerie: We don't ride in the road.
Father: It's a good thing.
Jacqui: When we came home from granny there was a boy riding a bicycle very
    dangerously.
Mother: [noticing Naomi fiddling] If you pull that, the buttons will come off so
    could you just leave them please, darling.

D.   Second Discussion

Gorell Barnes: I was interested in Robin's comments that he saw the mother as
morbid and it seemed to me that she was relating to the children as though they
were her own age, rather than as children, and she was very much saying to them
"It's horrible isn't it" and she said. "You're glad it wasn't you", and I agree she
seems to be very much egging them on into feeling it at a different sort of level. I
was very impressed at the way the parents tolerated the child trying to remember
the event and encouraged her. I think that was handled very nicely.

Byng-Hall: I saw it very differently; I saw what mother was doing was giving
permission for these children to be in touch with real past experiences and not to
have to shy away from them and I could see that she was saying it as if she was at
their level, but that seemed to me to be a way of encouraging them. By being
empathic and putting herself inside them she really enabled them to explore the
experience and remember it.

Skynner: I would like to respond to that. I did see the mother as continuing from
the previous section to show further evidence of an insistent need to talk about
something disturbing to herself, and to put that kind of emotion into the system
when it wasn't asked for: that was her contribution to it. I felt she was quiet to
start with and then she comes forward with quite a harsh, insistent voice with a
compulsive quality to it; the father is quiet, relaxed, tends to tone her down,
rather switches away from her and again, the one thing I am concerned about in
the family is the mother and the relationship between her and the father. They
are alright with each other, but somehow it disturbs me that he performs so well
and she can only get in by shoving some of this sort of stuff in.

Cooklin: I think, overall, that it is a fairly healthy piece of interaction, just
comparing it with a family I've seen with the same number of children. The first

thing is that the children actually respond to what each other have said; I mean, they respond to a similar rhythm, they don't cut across or jump to another level or change metaphor halfway through in discussing this little sequence. Secondly, although there was something a bit clumsy about the way the mother said "You're glad it wasn't you", I thought that it was a rather clumsy attempt to find something to say at the children's level, and that she was a little uneasy in that role, but nevertheless it was an attempt to do that for the children rather than just an expression of her own feeling. The father then balances it. That's the thing I feel slightly worried about. Each time the mother does express something of her own, you could see this as healthy or unhealthy, he re-establishes the boundaries; he did it on this occasion by saying "Do you learn to be more careful yourself?" He moved it to a moral: Is there a moral in this for all of your children, in response to the mother being more personal.

Byng-Hall: I was watching and listening to the sequence between the mother and the girls as they expressed their horror and she usually followed them as a matter of fact with some comment; it may be that she followed them a little bit quickly, which indicated that she was very much alive inside trying to empathize with the children, and to that extent I think I'm beginning to tune into Robin's feelings that this mother is a bit anxious, but I didn't get the sense that she was going to stuff her distress into the kids.

Skynner: Well, I agree with John. I don't feel that either she or the father are intrusive, or trying to lay down these feelings, or project them, into the children, even though the children may take cues from them, but I did see the mother as wanting to express what I am calling the morbid feelings, and the father as looking after her and cooling that off. However as I commented, it does seem important that we are developing a kind of polarization among ourselves, which may be something of interest to look at later, about how normal it is to express what I'm calling "morbid" feelings here. I think that, as we are professionals in the business of *studying* morbid feelings, and maybe we enjoy morbid feelings and patients have to express them for us to do our work, healthy families don't function like that, because they don't want to do that and they can't be bothered to waste their energy on negative things like that.

Cooklin: The thing that struck me when Robin and John were talking, is that Robin seemed to be referring to what the mother actually did, and John was talking about the mother/husband system. Individually it might be unhealthy for the mother to say what she did, but the family system is so structured that the husband is cued in to rescue her at an appropriate time. The resulting family structure might be healthy whilst the specific intervention of the mother's might have been a bit clumsy and a bit over-anxious. The family structure is organized in such a way that the father rescues her without a great deal of anxiety or difficulty and without her really looking put down.

Gorell Barnes: Thinking of the healthy aspects of this family puts me in mind of the sequence when Naomi fiddles with the buttons on her dress. It is just that that little girl is demonstrating a 6-year-old rhyme which goes "Chinese, Japanese, spidernese, look at these", and they point to their bosoms with great enthusiasm!

Cooklin: The trouble is that this is a kind of piece of interaction which is extremely difficult to look at because it's so enjoyable. It's so lovely, it's what you call "family life". On the other hand, it seemed to me that in the same vein you could look at it as a significant response on the little girl's part to what is taking place. In the content of the whole family, you could look on it as a punctuator; a manoeuvre which in fact leads them to change gear. It establishes the mother as an authority and it distances her from the role she was in saying "This is the way one might feel and you might feel glad it wasn't you", and getting too close to the children. In that sense it may well be a healthy function, a process which really reinstates the mother's parental function.

Skynner: I'd like to agree with what Alan said there. I felt much happier about the mother, having seen that sequence, because she came in as someone with responsibility and authority in her own right and spoke in a way which seemed to have an appropriate degree of firmness, but not too much, and one could see that she had her power too, and that it was respected.

Gorell Barnes: I would like to comment on the question of whether this 6-year-old is reacting to something that is going on in the family, or is the 6-year-old reacting to simply the normal instincts of being a 6-year-old by fiddling with her buttons, and the way this gets used I think is interesting, as Alan says, as a punctuator. I'd just like to comment that I don't think the child is particularly respectful of her mother; she observes her but then she makes this mocking bosoms motion which is really about "Shut up you silly old lady", often observed in 6-year-olds. I mean I think she is quite healthy in the way she responds.

Skynner: Well, I agree with Gill; that's a healthy disrespect for one's mother which I was very pleased to see. Also I thought the mother's authority comes in there in an area which is very much, certainly traditionally, her domain, which is "buttons which she may have to sew on if they are pulled off". But also I wondered whether she was also coming in at that point because mothers have to teach daughters that they mustn't be too free with their breasts and bodies, and she may be, as it were, stopping the girl from being too exhibitionistic, which again would be a perfectly legitimate function.

E. Tape (continuing)

Father: Does it make you not want to ride a motor cycle.
Jaqui: No.
Father: You don't want to ride a motor cycle?
Valerie: I do.
Naomi: I do. [makes a face]
Mother: All I can say is, if you are going to ride a motor-bike, for goodness sake get the right gear, wear skid boots.

Valerie: It's illegal not to, isn't it?

Father: Yes, that's true.

Jaqui: Do the proficiency tests cover motor bikes too?

Father: No—you have to have a licence for a motor cycle—you don't have to for a bicycle.

Pause

Father: It's difficult to discuss your reaction.

Mother: It *is* difficult—but for the Grace of God there go I.

   (at this point Naomi comes to her father for a kiss and he says under his breath something like "mad . . . completely".)

F. Third Discussion

Cooklin: This is quite different from all the other bits in one way and I still think it's a healthy family function but one which is very difficult for us to categorize. It seemed to me that the family suddenly moved in with the metaphor of a motor bicycle into the area of metaphorical fantasying, and when Valerie asks "do the proficiency tests cover motor bikes?", it seemed to me that there was a metaphorical statement about the issue in the family: that if you move into danger, is there some kind of protective operation available. If the family was in therapy, some kind of meta-statement about the family would have been possible. The fact that the father then quickly takes it back to a factual level in this context is healthy. I would suspect that if he did this in a situation where such a statement needed to be made, it would be healthy, and I think if you saw it as a treatment situation you would see it as unhealthy and blocking movement.

Skynner: I thought they showed a very healthy enjoyment at the idea of riding a dangerous motor cycle, except for mother who could be seen I suppose as exercising a traditional maternal function of looking after the family's safety and welfare, and making sure they *do* wear crash helmets. But the *way* she came in with that seemed unnecessarily anxious and emphatic, and I thought that was the main expression, or the most obvious way, in which she was expressing a pervasive anxiety within herself which was not appropriate to the situation, and which bothered me a bit throughout the whole session.

Byng-Hall: I'm now preoccupied with the idea as to whether father is in touch with something pretty painful inside himself and is defending against it or not and for clues which will tell us one way or the other, and since we know from our first viewing that he is going to tell the family about a painful sequence when a man died in his arms; e.g. I wondered what brought Naomi across the room to kiss him.

Bentovim: Yes, I think one of the things you missed was that immediately after she does that motor bike signalling, he says "completely" and I think we missed out a bit when she said something and he said "mad", in a very nice way and having seen this three or four times, I think that she comes across to kiss him because he had said these two really quite affectionately nasty things to her, following the reprimand from her mother about the buttons.

Skynner: I didn't catch that on the tape, but I have the idea that healthy families *are* mad in the sense that they can be "mad" without worrying about it, and can tease each other and call each other mad and all that kind of thing, so if that's what was going on there I would be reassured about their health by that inter-action.

G.   Tape (continuing)

Mother: You can have feelings in your stomach.

Jaqui: It feels as if there is a lump in your throat.

Valerie: And your throat goes all dry—when you're scared of something your throat goes all dry.

Father: [turns to mother] This seems rather morbid—does it do any good discussing one's reactions to this sort of thing—I mean does it make you any more careful or . . .

Mother: I don't know, because I think when it comes to the crunch everybody behaves in a different fashion. If you were involved in an accident, would one be calm or would one panic?

Valerie: Panic I suppose.

Naomi: Panic.

Mother: Not necessarily panic. I mean very often the most unexpected people are calm in an emergency.

Father: Yes.

Mother: Other people who you think would be splendid, panic.

Father: You have never had an accident?

Mother: Yes I have actually; I've been involved in two—Daddy drove into some-body.

[Family laugh]

Mother: He's always driving into somebody. Granny was in the front and I don't know, we had chickens, or eggs or something . . .

Jaqui: It was eggs. I remember Uncle Peter told us once. We were sitting in the car and we had just come back from Granny's . . .

Mother: This was outside a place called Bude in Cornwall, and another time I had an accident myself.

Father: It's changing the subject you know.

Mother: Yes.

Father: I'm sure everybody would be very interested.

Mother: I'm sure they would be fascinated.

Valerie: You've actually knocked over a rhubarb lady? [laughs]

Father: Oh, you have actually knocked over a rhubarb lady.

Mother: That was taking my driving test.

Valerie: Did you pass?

Father: [laughing] Of course not.

Mother: No — no consideration shown towards cyclists.

Father: It is a bit thick crushing the rhubarb lady.

Mother: I didn't crush her, she wobbled.

Valerie: She wobbled because of your dangerous driving.

Jaqui: And the rhubarb fell all over the road.

Mother: No, the rhubarb was tied on the back; she fell off the bike and the rhubarb went in the road and I ran over it — the rhubarb.

Father: You crushed the rhubarb?

Valerie: Did you have to pay?

Mother: No.

Father: No, she just failed her test. How many times did you fail?

Mother: Only once; I took it twice. So did Jenny, so did Ken. Jenny took hers three times.

Father: Ken failed did he?

Mother: Yes, we all did, it was quite fair. Jenny did a three-point turn straight into the dustbin . . .

Father: She still does.

Mother: So she failed on that and Ken, . . . oh, I don't know, he went through traffic lights or something. We were both delighted that Ken failed as well because he was very confident.

Jaqui: What car did you take your test in?

Mother: I took it in a Morris 1000, dual controls. When you turned your wheel his went the same way.

Pause

Father: Well, we have successfully murdered that subject.

Mother: Yes. My mind travels on to the body in the ambulance again.

Father: Twig-hopping again.

Mother: I know, but I do; I mean I always think "I wonder what's going to happen when we get to the hospital, the next of kin and relations".

Father: Well, that's what they want to know.

Mother: All right. Well, that's what I was thinking about.

Father: Well I don't see how that fits with you and the rhubarb.

Naomi: Mummy, my friend was telling me that she saw an actual accident happen between a lorry and a van.

Mother: [interrupting Naomi and addressing father] Well you got somebody out didn't you. You got those people out of the upturned car the other day.

Father: And then the poor bloke died when he hit a wall.

Mother: When?

Father: I had to haul him out of his car several years ago . . .

Mother: Oh, yes that's right, he died on you.

Father: He died in my arms yes — he had a stroke. [puts hand to head]

Mother: What happened then?

Father: I had to haul him out of the car and put him in the ambulance.

Mother: Yes I know, were you on your own?

Experimenter: Let's stop there.

H. Final Discussion

Cooklin: It seemed to me that this sequence was in parts. First of all there was a symmetrical interchange with the two girls then Naomi joins the mother and she gains a kind of strength which allows the father to describe the man who dies in his arms. Now you could see that getting somebody to talk about their feelings means putting them down, or you could see it as the mother giving the father space to talk about an experience that he needed to talk about. In fact, both seem to me to be true, in one sense it was a way of her re-achieving a symmetrical relationship with him by getting him to do the thing that she had done. On the other hand, it was also a way in which he could healthily talk about it and share a bit more.

Gorell Barnes: It was interesting that everybody did have a chance to say something and that one person at a time seemed to be expressing, or drawing, the family back to a more serious purpose and that this gets handed around. I was interested in the bit where Naomi gave somebody a chance to get back to the serious topic, and so it does seem as though within the family there is a lot of room for the exchange of feeling which I thought was very good. But it's monitored very carefully, and nobody lets too much out at a time. That may be fine, but it seemed to me that the children, apart from the eldest daughter who was rather too compliant, were quite free in being able to pick up themes and then pass them back to their parents.

Skynner: Well I had the same response to this whole task as I did to the first one—viewing it in terms of the Timberlawn classification. I still feel a bit unhappy about the relationship between the father and the mother, and the problem seems more obvious in the mother. One could see this complementarity that Gill mentioned as functional and healthy; the father says "Does it do good to discuss reactions?", talking about intellectual functions, and the mother then goes on to talking about feelings of panic and calmness, so she is getting to the feeling level. Then the child, I think the youngest one, gets mother in touch with deeper feelings and mother then cues father in to talk about this very deeply moving event, which I thought he handled very naturally, with feeling, but also as if the whole family could handle it very well. But I was still a bit worried about the parental relationship which seemed to have a *slightly* distant, abrasive quality in it which made me a bit uncomfortable but, otherwise, I thought the family functioned well and there was a lot of spontaneity and pleasure and fun, and I would still say this was a healthy family.

Byng-Hall: Yes, it does seem to be a healthy way of handling something which was very painful. It was curious to see how the family almost proclaimed that they had forgotten about this awful accident and it was as if they were giving father permission to withdraw from having to talk about it if he did not wish to You could look at it that way, or you could say that this father had not talked about it in front of the kids. Is that healthy or is it unhealthy? I had a feeling that the family was aware of his discomfort as he sat there leaning forward talking about the dead man having a stroke, and putting his hand to one side of his face, which seemed to me to indicate that he was identifying with the dead man who had the stroke. To me it is still a bit of a puzzle—I don't think we see enough healthy families as clinicians to know whether this was the right level to handle a highly painful memory, or whether there is evidence here that in fact it had been screened out and that the family would act together to deny it if necessary.

Bentovim: To draw matters to a close, I felt again the theme I've been reiterating, which is the context of how the father seems to be expressing some irritation again at the impingement on his family by this very painful thing ("Is it helpful to talk about this thing"), which I felt was a sort of statement to the researchers . . . I wondered whether his screening himself was, again, an attempt to protect the children and say that the world is a place where a certain amount of screening or a boundary formation around what actually happens to children is necessary, if they are to grow up with sufficient experiencing—but not too much.

REFERENCES

Erickson, E. H. (1963). "Childhood and Society", Norton, New York; Penguin, London.

Hansen, C. (1981). Living in with Normal Families. *Family Process*, **20**, 53–75.

Kinston, W. (1979). "A reliable standardised clinical interview with the whole family", Family Studies Group, London. (Unpublished).

Kinston, W. (1980). The Healthy and Unhealthy Family: Research in Family Interaction. Proc. VII. Int. Cong. Group Psychotherapy.

Lewis, J. M., Beavers, W. R., Gossett, J. T. and Phillips, V. A. (1976). "*No Single Thread: Psychological Health in Family Systems*", Brunner/Mazel, New York.

Loader, P., Burck, C., Kinston, W. and Bentovim, A. (1981). A Method of Organising the Clinical Description of Family Interaction. The Family Interaction Format. *Aust. J. Fam. Ther.* 2:3, 131–141.

Riskin, J. (1976). Non-labelled Family Interaction: Preliminary Report on a Prospective Study. *Fam. Proc.* **15**, 433–439.

Part II

The Family and Therapy

Chapter 3

Dialogues on a Family in Treatment

G. Gorell Barnes, A. Bentovim, J. Byng-Hall,
A. Cooklin, R. Skynner

I. INTRODUCTION

In this chapter we examine the shift from a functional to a dysfunctional family system. We will follow a similar procedure to the section on the healthy family by presenting extracts of tape from an interview with a family in treatment.

II. FORMAT OF DISCUSSION

Brief extracts of tape were shown to a group consisting of Arnon Bentovim, John Byng-Hall, Alan Cooklin and Robin Skynner to gather their ideas on how dysfunction in the family was identifiable, how to track the sequences involved, how the therapist had been drawn into the dysfunction in the system, and as a stimulus to gather different ideas on frameworks for therapy. The session had taken place a year earlier, so there was no intention of receiving consultation from the group. This is not offered therefore as a model of a supervisory or consultative group, but to show different therapists' thinking in relation to material the reader himself can relate to directly, working out himself the question "How might I proceed?" The therapist was Gill Gorell Barnes.

III. DESCRIPTION OF FAMILY

The Horovitz family were referred by their general practitioner for family therapy following many years of unsuccessful treatment for physical symptoms in the two children, Claire and Joseph. Unusual identifying symptoms will not be described, but others included facial ticks, acute stomach cramps, obsessional hair pulling and ritualistic hand washing. The family treatment consisted of twelve sessions over five months with four follow-up sessions in the autumn. The children were rapidly symptom-free following engagement in regular family work, although a brief symptom substitution, stealing, had to be dealt with following the fifth session. The family considered the work they did together as extremely valuable, subsequently referring other families for therapy. They chose to return to review work once a term for a second year to make sure the commnication channels within the family were remaining open.

IV. META STATEMENTS

Each therapist was given a copy of the transcribed tape and asked to make a brief comment on the theoretical position from which they had made their comments. These follow below.

A. Meta Statements: Arnon Bentovim

My frame here is to attempt to clarify the "surface" action of the family: the "compulsive" interactional patterns, which takes over the family's attempt to achieve anything, and which to the outsider renders what is said as "meaning-less". Surface action by this definition would include the generational crossing of boundaries and triangling in of children to parental arguments. It has to be seen in the context of depth structure of dysfunctional shared family beliefs, myths, or meanings, many of which were expressed by others: e.g. the notions about children in this family, having to be happy at any cost, having insoluble problems, comfort can be given across generational lines between sons and mothers, but not within generations.

I am interested to see how the therapist gets pulled into these surface action and depth structure phenomena and how they relate to the way in which the family "interprets" or deals with their shared history.

B. John Byng-Hall

I have a hypothesis about the function of symptoms with which I always start. If it does not fit then I discard it. Symptoms often arise out of a conflict over regulation of distance, which occurs when a relationship is simultaneously experienced as potentially too close or intimate but also potentially too distant, with the threat of a break-up hovering in the background. In that situation, either coming closer or moving away creates anxiety. A symptom solves both problems. Looking after the "patient" provides safe non-intimate closeness, and it provides a reason for staying together. The greatest threat to a family unit is a distance conflict between the executive couple, usually parents, sometimes others, e.g. mother and grandmother. In this case other people, usually children, but sometimes in-laws, are triangled in to regulate the distance, stepping in between when the couple gets too close, or bringing them together when they get too separated. A symptom or problem in the children again performs both functions, bringing them together as parents to cope, but frequently provided a source of disagreement thus also preventing intimacy.

Therapy is designed to move distance boundaries so that there is no longer an approach/avoidance conflict. Anxieties about loss and intimacy are reduced in two ways: first by giving new safe experiences of both closeness and distance in the session, either by using structural techniques or experientially through exercises such as family sculpting; secondly by use of understanding, either of what happens in the session or of the historical roots of the anxiety. I like to use metaphors to illustrate the family dilemmas, e.g. a "push-me-pull-you".

I think of the entrenched family perceptions built up around the dysfunctional family patterns as myths. I try to re-edit or modify, not explode, the family mythology so that it provides healthier guidelines for action.

C. Alan Cooklin

My goal in considering these excerpts was to try and find routes of entry for therapeutic change. I was not therefore concerned with making an extensive formulation of the meaning of all that I observed. Rather I was looking for workable realities which could be expanded, and in which a therapeutic process would be facilitated. The tools which I was using were derived from the principles of structural family therapy. Thus I was looking for where in the system it was easiest to join at any particular time, where an enactment of a typical family pattern could be created, and how more functional boundaries could be established. Finally, I was looking for moves which could potentially lead to an unbalancing of any fixed dysfunctional patterns.

I was therefore not in conflict with the other discussants over formulations, but was looking for entries through which to create therapeutic events.

D. Robin Skynner

My comments following the clips derive from two principles already enunciated about the functions of healthy families. First, I believe that subject to a certain amount of negotiation and two-way communication between parents and children, a fairly clear hierarchy and generational boundary is of importance for health, with the main sexual relationship between the parents, relatively unaffected by the children's desire to disrupt it. I have always believed that; since the female parental figure is likely to bear, suckle and take the main responsibility for nurture in the earliest years, it will therefore more often fall to the father to assist them in the process of separation/individuation when the time is ripe. This provides a natural division or function between male and female parents, although I acknowledge that there may be exceptions. These views have been supported by almost all available research, and are now adopted by most family therapists. Any intervention I would make would therefore be directed, as the discussion indicates, towards establishing this clear boundary and restoring the primary involvement to that between the parents: "getting the marriage back where it belongs".

The other principle my comments derive from is that normal, healthy parents bring up normal, healthy children without worrying too much about it, more or less automatically. Unhappy, unhealthy, abnormal parents are concerned, implicitly or explicitly, that they will not be satisfactory parents and are either too indifferent to the needs of their children, or too concerned about them. The latter group are seeking to remedy the deficiencies of their own childhood by giving their children what they did not receive themselves, or trying to correct the mistakes of their own parents by being better parents themselves. This is obviously doomed to failure and can do nothing but harm, because the parents are *using* their children to relive their own lives, living *through* their children, occupying their children's territory, as it were, instead of letting the children differentiate and become separate persons. I refer to this point explicitly in the discussion, although I do not propose any specific intervention.

EXTRACTS

The extracts that follow were taken from the fourth session where the focus of parental concern had moved from symptoms to the patterns of relationship. Within the family, the children were now overtly symptom-free but the parents, who expressed "helplessness", had moved on from physical symptom issues to handling emotions within the family.

V.   EXTRACT 1

Father (Ben), Mother (Sarah), Daughter (Claire), son (Joseph).

Dad: Most of the time Sarah and Claire fight, I understand what it's about and honestly the majority of my time I agree with Sarah, anyway over these sorts of things, we're talking about and — er — Sarah knows it and I suppose . . . if either of us know how to solve it we wouldn't be here, in part anyway.

Mum: [to T] I suppose if I could turn around and say "Look she's been told she's not getting a new skirt, the zip is broken, it's got to go to the menders, and get the zip repaired, she'll have to wear the old one, if I could just — if that was it — but because she walks around being miserable it goes on affecting me.

T: So that's a tactic — a very good tactic.

Mum: Yes.

Dad: It's terrific.

Mo: [looking at T all the time] So how do I deal with it? I'd very much like to be told how to deal with it.

Dad: And the answer is "ignore it" and be told later, "I don't like being ignored", or "Don't ignore it", and be told, "Leave me alone", which comes back to what I was saying um — we want the children to be happy.

Mum: It's not just Claire, Joseph flares up and does the same thing, but he flares up very quickly — if he can't get something he wants when he wants it.

Dad: He flares up — but in 10 minutes it's over and forgotten [to Joseph] Am I right?

Mo: [to Joseph] If you don't like it, you do get in quite a temper but it's over very quickly; there's no cold war going on afterwards.

Dad: Joseph's tempers last for ten minutes.

Joseph: No, not all of them.

Dad: *Five* minutes some of them.

Joseph: Twenty minutes some of them.

Dad: OK Claire's will go on for ever and a day.

T: [indicating Mother] And her mother's used to go on for about a fortnight.

Mum: Mine used to as well.

Dad: Oh yes, I can see it happening and I can see a repeating performance and I knew Sarah when she went through this with her mum, but it doesn't help.

T: It probably makes it worse.

Dad: I find it terribly frustrating I really do because I can't find an answer to it.

T: I don't think there's an answer in the sense you're trying to find it.

Dad: I can't find a way of dealing with it and you're asking how do you deal with it. It may be totally natural and happen to every family in the land: but I can't find a way of dealing with it whether it happens to be, "I want to be alone," or "Give me total attention".

A. Discussion

Cooklin: The Father's statement "We want the children to be happy", would be a good road in. The way I had heard it so far was that the father says he understands what is going on, and says he agreed with his wife. But in some curious way, by agreeing with her he actually disqualifies her. He, in a sense agrees with *her being incompetent,* and then the mother makes what sounded like quite a hostile demand: "I want to be told how to deal with it". Even if the therapist was going to answer, he doesn't actually let her, and says that what he wants is for the children to be happy. I think I would have wanted to have responded to that statement in some way, maybe to say that, "He was too ambitious", or that "He shouldn't be trying to make the children happy yet . . .", something like that; I would have wanted to intervene in some way at that point.

Byng-Hall: I would like to have somehow linked with the processes that were going on at the beginning of the clip. I'm not quite sure how I would have done it, but father, in the very first statement, is edging towards the idea of, "If either of us knew how to solve it we wouldn't be here". This could have led on to a discussion about how the two of them together, as husband and wife, might have solved this particular problem. However, mother, with quite a lot of pressure, zooms straight off towards her daughter and focusses on the very symptom which can always catch her; being miserable. I would like to have somehow drawn attention to the process of *Claire drawing to herself parental energies at the point when the parents might have been doing something together.* I think probably after Mum had finished her talk I might have said something to Claire like, "Claire, you only have to be miserable and you know you have Mum's full attention, like just now in the session Mum was able to think about your feeling depressed and talk about that rather than talk with your Dad about how they might solve their problem together." Probably from then on I would have kept to the strategy of demonstrating how the kids constantly come in between the parents whenever they might actually resolve something and then I would actively block that process, supporting the parents in getting something worked out, via content introduced by a member of the family or via the process in the room.

Bentovim: It seems to me too that the issue is what sort of alliances are being split up and when, and that a big question is how to triangle the therapist in. There is this very strong appeal from mother to the therapist: "Well how do I deal with it?" —

and father's comment, "Well if we knew what to do we wouldn't be here", which is something to do with the same process of making a demand of the therapist for something which, because it comes two different ways, she really can't respond to.

Byng-Hall: Yes, you become dislocated if you respond to it?

Bentovim: Yes, you become dislocated and there is something here about Claire perhaps being described as having some sort of loyalty both ways on; both to her mother in terms of fighting and to her father in terms of failing.

Skynner: I don't think I would disagree with any of that. I would like to focus on it slightly differently. If one is taking the core of what they are saying here, then the father begins by saying that he and his wife agree about all these things, but he says "Umm" and "Ah" and "I suppose", and it's clear that they don't really agree because if they did agree they wouldn't be having these problems anyway, and they wouldn't be there. Now the other two points which would identify this as a family likely to be dysfunctional straight away to me, would be the excessive effect of the children's emotions on the parents; that is, the parents are too dependent on the children's reactions and happiness. This would imply to me that they are in fact trying to make up for some deprivation of their own through giving to their children what they haven't received, and thereby there is not a clear parent–child hierarchy.

Mum says, "because she looks rather miserable, it goes on affecting me". Well, obviously if it affects her I thought the therapist's intervention there was a very good one. She identified this as a tactic, in other words it's a little game to which she should not be responding, and Dad says, "terrific" as he rewards that intervention. Then Dad says, "The answer is to ignore it", but then he goes on to say that in fact he can't ignore it. Again he wouldn't be having the problem if he could. He comes back in the end to a very clear diagnosis of why they are having these problems; he says, "We want the children to be happy". If this was a healthy family that would not be said.

Cooklin: I agree with what Robin said about the state of the family. What I was looking for was some way of getting a hook on to this. The thing that occurred to me was that there was a useful metaphor running through this which was to do with *wastefulness*, a "redundancy" in both senses of the word, in the sense of something repetitive and something wasteful. I was thinking that one could create a construction such as "It's extremely wasteful for the father to be saying that he understands what it is all about. Mother can hear that. Why not make use of this information? She should ask *him*". So I would either try and get her to ask him and make sure she is absolutely certain that she is not wasting any of his knowledge or information, or alternatively, it occurred to me to say that it is really quite wasteful for the two parents to say the same thing. It would be better if they said something different to each other which, in a sense, is prescribing what is really happening.

Skynner: I would like to differentiate between my thinking and what I might have said. I would obviously not *say* any of those comments that I made, in fact I think the comment made by the therapist, in a sense the "tactic", is very nice. I would have liked to have *said* that, but generally speaking I would probably not *say* anything for quite a long time except "How dreadful", "It must be awful for you", and that sort of thing.

Cooklin: I was thinking about the dysfunctional element. It seemed to me, this was the way in which Joseph is pushed away and Claire is kept as the link between the parents. In some curious way it seemed to me that by saying "Joseph's all right, he's free, we are not held by him, his rows only last ten minutes . . .", and by defining *him* as "good": this is part of a move to maintain Claire in the *same* position. Joseph tries to resist being put in this position. He said, "It isn't always just 20 minutes, sometimes it can be more". And when the therapist tried to change the kind of epistemology or the whole way this thing was being seen, the whole framework of this, then the father responded with a massive disqualification. Then it seemed to me the therapist tried to go along with this so that he couldn't fight, and he disqualifies again, saying, "I find it terribly frustrating". The question is what you would have done in the end . . .

Bentovim: The game in this bit struck me very much: "His tempers last for 10 minutes." "No, not all of them." "5 minutes?" "No, 20 minutes some of them." This sort of game-playing, knocking backwards and forwards, really disqualifying the feeling and putting his father down. And there is that strange way of talking which I found quite disturbing. I mean as if there was an exaggerated way in which father was actually talking to Gill and getting her going . . . . very dramatic and false, really activating and capturing her and really enjoying it I thought. I thought the father was enjoying sending Gill up. There was something about the quality of it which was very forced, and the dys-functional element in my view, was that it was just going on without any meaning. I didn't believe what father was actually talking about for a minute, because father and son had already established a principle whereby whatever he says is wrong—5 minutes, 10, and it goes on in that way. So you get a sense of unreality.

Gorell Barnes: I'm going to abstain from commenting. I'm going to leave it all to you.

Byng-Hall: I would like, somehow, to get a simple phrase or metaphor for what is going on and the one that comes to mind is "the power of being an insoluble problem". That is maybe something that the whole family could respond to and I might have pointed out to Claire what part she had by being an insoluble problem, having both parents extremely concerned about her for a long time. Even her younger brother wanted to get a bit of that power, he wanted to have it for longer than just a measly 5 minutes. Maybe I would have left it at that, because it would follow on the strategy in the first invention that I suggested, which was to try and illuminate for the family some of the family game, which is how the children take away the depression and the fight and the potential disruption from the marital interaction.

Bentovim: Just to add a bit to what I was saying: it's father talking with the royal "I" — "I can't find a way of dealing with it" — "Poor me, it's all on me and you can't help and nobody can help. I can't do it". This is very much avoiding affect that is a *"we"*, that these are *two* parents, and he is really crying about "I"— I have the whole burden; look at her just like her mother—all on "I".

Byng-Hall: So then you can use the metaphor, the insoluble problem, each parent thinking they have to solve it on their own, which is made impossible by someone else.

Cooklin: The only bit I disagree with you about, Arnon, is that I didn't see the child as putting his father down in that situation so much as defending against being used to show up his sister. That I know is just another alternative punctuation, but that's the one *I* saw most clearly. I agree with John about wanting to find a simple metaphor and I'm still toying around with something about "waste" which I got from the thing about the new skirt. I don't think I would have spoken to the girl at this stage because I think somehow I would have needed to give the children a message that I was going to intervene in what the parents were doing, and so I think I would have followed what Gill did later. I was wondering where one could start doing it. There were two places that occurred to me: one was when the mother had said at the beginning, "So how do I deal with it, I'd very much like to be told how to deal with it", and the husband then says, "The answer is ignore it". I think I might have said, "That's an extremely inefficient way of letting your husband help you. Is that the way you try and get an answer from him or alternatively is that the way he answers you? Because that is not going to help." Perhaps I would have taken up again at the end—that the husband uses two alternatives and this would be the second way. He says, "I can't deal with either, whether it's leave me alone or give me total attention". I think I would have tried perhaps to frame these two as one and say that it's impossible for them to try and do so much at once, perhaps they should tolerate either, "Leave me alone" or, "Give me total attention", and work with one of those bits. Then I would make the parents do it and discuss how to do it together in the session.

Skynner: I found that I'm still mainly impressed by what I suppose has already been said in other ways, the lack of a parental coalition; by the lack of a parent/ child generational boundary. I would assume they are like four kids. I disagree a bit with Arnon as it seemed as if father is at least attempting outwardly to take a more responsible attitude towards doing something about this, whereas the mother is behaving more like an older child. I would take different sides there, but then that may be just different slants on it. Another thing that strikes me is I suppose the same thing; which is just as though this boundary also shows itself by the way in which the parents are so affected by the children and whether they are happy or not, and whether they are agreeing or not and whether they are having tempers or not. It seems to me that that's bound to lead to difficulties if they are almost anticipating trouble and thinking they ought not to have any, ought not to stop it because they feel like it.

Bentovim: Yes, that really fits in with the way in which presumably the father tries to take control through the therapist. He does it by an appeal to the therapist: "What can I do about it?"

Skynner: At least he's asking which the mother isn't. She's just sort of battling on and so fast one can't even hear. I feel that at least you can address something to him. But I can see that the danger would be to go through him; I see the point there. I think that's a very important view.

Cooklin: I think if I hadn't yet said any of the other things, I would have liked to have said at that point to the mother, "My goodness, is that how you ask your husband for help, because if you do, you aren't going to get very far". I think there is one point at which you can challenge the way in which both parents have serially disqualified any attempt by the therapist to put some pressure on the marital coalition.

Byng-Hall: I just feel fairly comfortable with the metaphor of "the insoluble problem" because it seems the power of that has become more and more evident. The mother really says, "It's my problem and I have to solve it", but on a meta-level she is saying, "*You* must somehow solve it if anything is going to change", and so on, and it's this theme going on and on and round and round. This is also addressed to the therapist at some level: "You must solve it, but you won't; it's insoluble".

VI. EXTRACT 2

Dad: But Sarah feels these rows so deeply that whatever I say or do she'll come back to it and it might be 5 minutes, 20 minutes, two hours or a day later. She'll come back to it.

T: Joseph, do you think there's anything your Dad can do to make your Mum feel better when she's feeling like that?

Joseph: No.

T: Nothing she can do?

Joseph: No nothing. I can't think of anything.

T: Why, because she's so out of reach?

Joseph: Yes, that's the feeling sometimes.

T: How does she show it, how does she behave?

Joseph: Sometimes she ignores you, she's done that to me before and just gets in a temper.

T: And you can see it on her face.

Joseph: Yes it sort of goes (pulls a face).

Dad: That's true actually I think, I mean you can look at Sarah and know um . . . but it affects everybody else but it spills . . . I mean it certainly affects Joseph and it certainly affects me . . . it spills over.

Mo: Joseph has a very effective way of tackling me; a very good way of tackling me.

Dad: It spills over.

T: What does he do?

Mo: He hasn't mentioned it. I'm surprised, [to Joseph] you have a very good way of coping with me if I'm irritable or miserable; a lot of the time you do something that's very nice to me if I'm tired or irritable or miserable: don't you know what it is?

Joseph: No.

Mo: I'm very aware of it.

Joseph: I might just *do* it, but I don't *know* what it is.

T: [to Mum] Why don't you tell him?

Dad: Why don't you tell *me*?

Mo: He comes and cuddles me.

Joseph: [thoughtfully] Oh yeah.

Mo: Yes, you haven't mentioned that.

Joseph: I always cuddle you.

Mo: Particularly if he senses if I'm down he always shows me a lot of affection Joseph . . . [in an apologetic voice she adds] . . . So does Ben.

Joseph: [high squeaky voice] Not as much.

Mum: Pardon.

Joseph: Not as much.

Mum: Yes, he does.

Joseph: Ooooh.

T: Does that reach you?

Mo: Yes. I'm very aware of that.

Dad: [pointing to Claire] But it also has the effect of making that gap much wider because Claire by nature is not particularly demonstrative. I've seen her do it. She sits and glowers while it's going on: I've seen her do it.

END OF EXTRACT

A. Discussion

Gorell Barnes: I liked that clip particularly because it represents for me the issue of what level of intervention is required in order to work on something overtly extremely simple. This appears a very simple interaction, but there are a number of ways you could approach it.

Bentovim: Well, what is so beautiful about it is that mother is really saying how marvellous Joseph is at doing it.

Gorell Barnes: She's setting him up.

Bentovim: Then she suddenly remembers that Ben is quite good at it too; at which point Joseph says, "Not as good as Daddy of course".

Gorell Barnes: No, on the contrary, he says Dad *isn't* as good as he is. That's the point of that.

Cooklin: But with a false voice.

Bentovim: I must say that I actually read it in the sense that he was actually putting himself down, but you are right.

Gorell Barnes: He's putting Dad down there; it's straight rivalry.

Byng-Hall: But he is putting himself down at the same time with this little jokey voice.

Cooklin: I'm still with Joseph and it's possible that he isn't putting his father down and it simply is true.

Gorell Barnes: But he still doesn't still speak the truth in a straightforward voice.

Cooklin: That's right. But he has been put in the position of having to speak the "truth". That voice I think interests me a lot. It struck me that two people in a sense initiated this child into a "bean-spilling" position. First of all you, asking him whether it was true that his father couldn't help his mother and then the mother saying, "Well he has this technique for helping me," and Joseph tried not to answer about this. They said they are surprised he hasn't mentioned it. One way of looking at it is that he is really trying to get into that position.

Gorell Barnes: I see this dichotomy quite differently. I think it's a question of how aspects of family patterns have got split up in the current system. Father is working at a head level and Joseph is working at an instinct level. He says, "I may just *do* it, but I don't *know* what it is". I think that's exactly the issue confronting these two parents, how to bring their thinking and feeling together in a complementary manner to act. The way the father is arguing the whole time is to do with logic and finding the right way of going about something through talk. His messages are at a different level to his wife's or his son's.

Bentovim: And yet she comes back every time.

Gorell Barnes: I'm going to stop talking, as the idea is for all of you to use the material as a vehicle for *your* ideas.

Skynner: It's interesting this, because I've watched this and read it three or four times and it has only just dawned on me that it's the *child* who is saying this. I mean if I'd been watching the tape three or four times I might have noticed it, but it's unbelievable a child saying this.

Cooklin: The child is saying what, Robin?

Skynner: Well he is saying he is cuddling the mother. I thought this was what the father was saying and I thought well, you're home and dry.

Cooklin: The mother says the child does it.

Skynner: Yes, that's right but somehow Joseph is saying all these things with mother; this dialogue is going on between the boy and the mother in which he is in fact speaking for the father's role, as you said. It has only just dawned on me that the child could possibly be saying this and not the father. And I suppose, as you say, it is all there, the same old parent/child coalition in a very extreme form. I suppose I would just stop them at that point and just keep them at that for the rest of the time however long it was.

Byng-Hall: I think I would be pursuing the metaphor of the insoluble problem because it still has some potential, in that at this point you might actually start to tease out what *was* the insoluble problem. It seemed to be to do with what happens if you either get too close to someone or if you get angry; they disappear forever, and yet if you don't make any approach, then they may still disappear. There is some problem like that, which I am not clear about yet. The insoluble problem seems to be between the parents. You already know that mother has the longest temper, so what is she like when you get close: can she be very angry, it somehow is safer for the son to get really close and cuddly with her, not the father. There is something about father and mother getting close which is a problem. I would be using that and thinking about ways of saying something simple, which I can't at this moment!

Bentovim: I just wonder whether the insoluble problem which has been reiterated is this. You see Dad is saying somewhere Mum "spills over" too, and it goes on and on and on. The daughter is the same and what can you do about it. This is saying something about the ineffectiveness of logic *vs* emotional feelings. It seems to me that the insoluble problem is a couple who will communicate on different levels. When Gill, really stirring it quite a bit I thought, says, "Well what could Daddy do to help Mummy?" (which of course he couldn't possibly know) . . .

Gorell Barnes: Why not?

Bentovim: Father follows by saying, "Well it spills everywhere". Mother then brings Joseph in and says, "Well look, it's quite simple really; when somebody is emotionally close to me then it's all right", but that *can* only be someone across a generation boundary; it's not allowed between people of the same age.

Byng-Hall: It seems that is one of the insoluble problems; that at one level depression and feeling sad absolutely draws the other person into being close, and then when you are close you are pushed away. It is something to do with that conflict which is much more insoluble at parental level.

Bentovim: Because it's closeness across a generational boundary, not on the same level.

Byng-Hall: I don't know. I don't know enough about this family. I would want to know a great deal more about them to be able to say something which I would feel to be accurate for the parental relationship.

Cooklin: I think I would be happy to work for the moment with simply that clip, the last-one minute clip, because I think that Joseph—my view of it which I know was different from yours, Gill—showed immense discomfort when he was placed in this position. I thought about his voice in the frame of Watzlawick's statement that this was an attempt "not to communicate". It wasn't actually Joseph communicating any more, it was "somebody else". I would have taken that, I think, as a marker that I needed to pull the children out more in some way and to put more pressure on the parental subsystem. I think I would push the mother to get more help from the father. If the father is saying he can't give it, I would push the mother to try and get it from him. For her to say he can't help would in fact have to create a conflict anyway. She has to try and get it from him; if she says she can't before she even starts, then you could push her to work with what's wrong with him that she can't get some help from him.

Byng-Hall: I would, having used the idea of them presenting this as an insoluble problem, really challenge them on it: "Maybe it's more comfortable to feel that you can't solve this problem". I would define the "insolubility" as a myth used to protect them from doing something.

Skynner: I want to find some simple way, and I would like to have said, "Where's the marriage?" and then find some positive way of expressing the things people are doing. Mother needs help but can't ask, and the father wants to give it but somehow can't bend forwards to give it as he's frightened of the children . . . In the end, we see the same things happening between the father and the daughter. It's very unhappy for all of them, and we have to get the marriage to where it belongs!

END NOTE

Although this discussion will be at least two years old before it is read, the reader will see interesting choices of therapeutic procedure in the debate which continue very much as choices today. These are around achieving change through doing things differently in the session, stressing the system and enacting change or observing things with a different frame and a different choice of emphasis from which change will be anticipated. Clear agreement exists between all four discussants (and the therapist) on the need to get the parental alliance working more clearly and effectively both for each other and for the children, but the means by which the aim would be achieved are varied.

Chapter 4

Change in "Here-and-Now" Systems
vs
Systems over Time

— A. Cooklin —

I.   INTRODUCTION

Family Therapy may have an in-built predilection to develop controversies about its models of change, if only because its task—to develop a holistic view of the ecological system we call the family—is essentially impossible. Each theory of change can only reflect segments of reality. It may be necessary to stress the boundaries around these theories of change, or segments, in order that each should be sufficiently clear, and readily applicable. However, the relationship between apparently opposing theories needs to be identified if we are to continue the search for a holistic view of what we are about in Family Therapy.

Consider the analogy of the holograph, that surprising phenomenon which has been an off-shoot of laser technology. The laser is a fine, intense beam of "coherent" light. If the beam is split so that part of it falls on a photographic plate, and part of it on to an object from which it rebounds on to the same plate, a recording of light interference patterns is produced. An observer of the developed plate will see a three dimensional image of the object. This image will vary depending on the position from which it is viewed. Furthermore, if the observer smashes the plate into fragments, each fragment will contain an image of the whole object, although from a restricted "telescoped" view-point. The images contained by these fragments can even be of almost opposite views of an object. The fragments of the whole can contain "opposite view-points". The hologram is the most sophisticated image of reality we have so far been able to record photographically, but to understand its process of formation we may have to look at microscopic segments. The purpose of this chapter is to examine the relationship between two now fairly well differentiated segments of family theory: that which considers change in "here-and-now" systems (that is, short segments of time) on the one hand, and that which considers change in "systems over time" (that is, long segments of time) on the other.

I find the analogy of the holograph a useful one, so I shall refer to it from time to time. I shall also make fairly liberal use of other analogies drawn from the natural sciences. This is not intended to present a mechanistic view of human relationships, but to assist in gaining a meta-perspective of the processes of these relationships. The models developed within the natural sciences are somewhat clearer precisely because they can more closely approximate a bird's eye view of the total environment. We are much more a part of any human relationship we observe, and therefore the *generalizations* (not necessarily the observations themselves) we can make from our observations are more restricted. However, it must be stressed that these analogies are only used to convey the kind of model, rather than the particular process within the model itself. To do the latter would indeed imply that humans behave like chemical reactions.

A.   Practices, Ideas and Belief Systems

In the field of human relations therapy, it is inevitable that there will be a continuous pull towards describing practices (that is, organized sets of events in which a therapist plays a particular part) rather than ideas. This is partly because it is so difficult to establish sets of ideas which are other than temporary constructs about human relations. We cannot make fixed three dimensional models of these as we can with the holograph. Also, the pain and turmoil of some family interactions make such urgent demands on a therapist that he must have *methods* rather than just *theories*. (Haley, 1977; Sluzki, 1978; Treacher and Street, 1980; Street and Treacher, 1980)

Family therapists will sometimes make such statements as:
— The therapist does or does not try to display his or her emotional reactions;
— The therapist makes people stand-up, do this or that task, or does not;
— The therapist asks certain people to talk to each other or relates all questions himself;
— The therapist remains neutral, asks "circular" questions, and "positively connotes" the interactions.

These are sets of behaviour prescribed for therapists which, when clustered in a particular way make up a practice. These sets of therapists' behaviours are a necessary armamentarium not only for survival as an effective therapist in the turmoil of family interactions, but also because it would be quite impracticable to try and base each move on rethinking one's theory from first principles. The therapist would be unable to act. There is, however, a bridge between the ideas and the actions which I shall call "belief systems". They can be found in all therapies. Examples of psychoanalytic beliefs might be that "Change occurs in relation to the reintrojection of object relationships that have become modified in the therapeutic process", or "Change occurs through the medium of the transference relationships from the family members to the therapist".

Other beliefs might include "Change occurs when 'here-and-now' events are influenced actively as they happen", or "Change occurs as the context or significance of events in time is changed". These are the segments of reality which I shall now examine.

II.   THE PATTERN OF EVENTS IN HUMAN SYSTEMS

Changes in here-and-now family systems, such as might be sought in Structural Family Therapy, (Minuchin, 1972) and certain forms of Strategic Family

Therapy (Haley, 1977) are in fact changes in *short* sequences of time, and therefore segments of time with a relatively short "wave-length". The changes in family systems over time, such as might be sought by therapists using a psycho-analytic or transgenerational model of family therapy, are changes in relatively long sequences of time which have a long "wave-length". The difference in *quantity* of the two wave-lengths means a difference in the *quality* in the nature of the processes which can be influenced by different methods. Changes in short segments of behaviour may be effected *in vitro* by enacting the actual sequence within the time available for a therapy session. The changes *may* ultimately be *transferred* to the relevant *in vivo* setting. Changes in long sequences (where the length of the sequence may be that of a generation, or even two or more generations) may only be effected by attending to the control processes (sometimes referred to as governing concepts) which maintain the pattern of the sequence (Gorell Barnes, 1981). The nature of these control processes may be found macroscopically by examining the function of family myths (Ferriera, 1963; Byng-Hall, 1973) the Family Group Preoccupation (Cooklin, 1974, 1979) or the Patterning of Intersubjective Meanings (Kinston and Bentovim, 1981). Various techniques may be used either to change these control processes, or "interfere" with their effectiveness.

Some therapies are directed almost entirely to short sequences (particularly structural therapy, and certain kinds of behavioural approaches to family therapy), although in the course of achieving changes in short sequences, they may also effect some changes in the processes which control longer sequences. Some therapies are directed almost exclusively to influencing the longer sequences, such as transgenerational therapy (Lieberman, 1979; Bowen, 1975, 1976) psychoanalytic approaches to therapy (Zinner and Shapiro, 1972, 1974; Box, 1979) and the use of "mourning" techniques (Paul, 1967), while the Milan group (Palazzoli *et al.*, 1980) have attempted to devise interventions which relate current behaviour (short sequences) to the wider system (spatially and in terms of longer sequences). As family therapists have been preoccupied with the relationship between homeostasis and transformation in family systems, it is the thesis of this chapter that it is necessary to develop an understanding of both models of change, and of the relationship between them.

A. Models of Change and their Mythology

Within family therapy there has long been a concern to distinguish what adherents of a particular method do from what they say they do (Beels and Ferber, 1969). This has been possible as therapeutic secrecy has been dissolved by the use of one-way mirrors and video. Most therapists have been anxious to dissociate themselves from the nosological labelling of the identified patient, but in its extreme form, this concern has sometimes been expressed by an avoidance of all nosology. When this has happened, the description of theories and of their therapeutic practices has often been neglected. In addition, the practices are themselves very hard to define, despite a number of attempts some of which have been quite rigorous (Beels and Ferber, 1969; Cooklin, 1978; Dowling, 1979;

Kinston *et al.*, 1979). Even Epstein's group of experienced researchers in the field have loosely described the techniques employed in one of their studies as "systems-orientated family therapy" (Santa-Barbara *et al.*, 1980). In fact the field is now so complex that for the practitioner beginning work in family therapy, misconceptions and misquotations are almost inevitable. The confusion surrounding such misconceptions has sometimes led to emotional attacks by the representatives of one school on the spectres of another (Treacher and Street, 1980).

The naming of theoretical models has sometimes compounded the problem. For example, in Britain General Systems Theory has been used on the one hand by family therapists to devise Structural and Strategic Interventions in family systems, and on the other hand by workers such as Rice and Miller (1967) to develop a "psychoanalytic" model of organizations which they have applied to industries and other social systems. Psychoanalysts have been seen as being concerned with the past. Yet many British analysts would claim that they were dealing predominantly with what happens here and now, in the present, within the intensified strictures of the analytic situation. Some would even claim that they make little or no reference to the past even in reconstructions.

Within family therapy, controversy has flourished between therapists who observe "behaviour" and those who observe "feelings". Adherents to the communications school have stressed the "black box" approach. They do not need to know what goes on inside the box, but are satisfied to study it's connections. A consequence of this view is that they will only look at the behavioural expressions of feeling, rather than assuming knowledge of the feelings themselves. Thus instead of "Ann is feeling despondent today", they will say "Ann is behaving despondent today". It is interesting that many philosophers of mind would support the latter view, not so much because it is more "true", but because it does not create a false dichotomy between feelings and perceptions on the one hand, and behaviour on the other.

Describing feelings and behaviour separately propagates the "two worlds view"; often represented as the mind on the one hand, and the body on the other (Ryle, 1949). That this is a false dichotomy in neuro-physiological terms has been stressed by Pribam (1971). With this diversity of approaches, there has been an understandable and probably necessary tendency to focus on one or other segment or model. As a result, the particular segment may be coherently illuminated to return to the analogy of the holograph. While this is an essential process in the development of therapeutic methods, it is also important to be reminded that one is only responding to a segment of reality. On the other hand, attempts to achieve some coherence in one's position by attacking the image of another have been unhelpful to the development of coherence in the field, as they have often replaced a satisfactory analysis of the position from which the views are expounded (Treacher and Street, 1980; Wrate, 1980). The real struggle in family therapy is to maintain the observer/therapist's freedom from a perception of "linear causality" (Watzlawick *et al.*, 1969). That is, to replace the perception of events as between victim and aggressor, or from "these events caused what is now happening" with a picture of events and the context or structure within which they occur fitting snugly together and underwriting each other.

Many approaches have been used to try and help the therapist to experience the processes of family interaction in terms other than victim and aggressor. Live supervision techniques, or interviewing methods where the therapist stays "distant" from the family, or even some of the approaches to "working with" the therapist's own family, may all be geared to helping the therapist maintain a circular view of causality. The "schizophrenogenic mother" gave way first to the schizophrenogenic family, and later the "victimized" and "victimizer" gave way to the realization that the "victimizer" is as much a victim of the relationship as is the "victimized". In fact, the move has been from "What causes what?" to "In what way do particular symptoms or symptomatic individuals co-exist more or less comfortably with particular kinds of family structure, and how does each maintain the other?" Conceptually, the models used by the natural sciences may again be of some help. In physics and biology, a different view of the inter-relatedness of events, and the processes which control them, has long replaced the linear view. Not only are energy and matter one, but at the most pragmatic level, the biologist and physicist have been aware of the interrelatedness of electrical, physical, chemical and social influences on any phenomenon, and particularly the feed-back loops which effect a response to change in any one of these. Such an example can be seen in the increasingly complex and circular view which has been developed of glucose metabolism in the body as represented by Kreb's cycle, and the feed-back loops which control this.

So far I have been discussing models of change principally in relation to ideas and belief systems. I have touched on the macroscopic counterpoint of psycho-analysis *vs* systems theory, and the more operational microscopic counterpoint of "feelings" *vs* "behaviour". My purpose in reviewing these ideas is to set a background for the consideration of patterns over short and long sequences of time. When considering questions of causality, natural scientists have also given importance to the time relationship between different events. In a symposium on the philosophy of science, Northrop (1958) points out:

> Two factors in any deductively formulated theory of modern physics must command the focus of one's attention. These two factors are 1) the definition of the state of the system at any given moment of time and 2) the definition of the time relation between states of the system at different times . . .
>
> There is a second possibility with respect to the nature of the time relation between states of an isolated system. The relation may be one of necessary connection characterised by a repetition of constant time relations that hold true not merely for past and present but also for future cases; but it is a relation such that in any first observed instance, given the initial state of the system, one cannot predict the future state until one has observed the present state passing into the future or final state in at least one instance. The physical system in which the initial state is that of the acorn and the final state that of the oak constitutes an example. (p.204)

If this is a valid analogy for events in families, we can not only look at the micro-scopic time relationships between events, but also at the time relationships between events on the level of the life-cycle and beyond.

B. Communication of Meaning through the Ordering of Time

The arrangement of time sequence is what gives meaning to events. If one cleans one's teeth before eating, the event of cleaning one's teeth becomes meaningless in terms of dental hygiene, even though the configuration might have meaning in some other context such as defying parental authority. Also in all language, it is the time relationship which punctuates the meaning of an interaction: "If you do that, then I *will* smack you", rephrased: "I *am* (now) telling you that your action, if in the future you can carry it out (or repeat it), will subsequently be *followed* by my doing to you what I am (now) telling you that I will do". Or to a greater degree of complexity: "If you go on like that you will land up as your father did", reads as "I am *now* defining your behaviour as having consequences in the *future* which *will* need you to be defined by me as I *now* define your father as having been in the *past*". This is only illustrating the obvious, namely, the frequency and potential complexity of the time component in all communication.

The controlling power of time, the fact that in common parlance we usually see it as unidirectional, is a constant preoccupation in family life as in other contexts. We talk of "recapturing the past" (to control it) or of being "haunted by the past" (controlled by it). The fascination of the Dr Who myth, the power to break the rules of the tyranny of the unidirectional nature of time, has always been "present". The prophets and oracles had a limited franchise to read the future as though it were the past. These were only minor infringements in that they only *read* the future. On the other hand, "putting the clock back" as Orpheus tried to do by bringing Euridyce back to life, is breaking rules of a higher order, and risks turning to stone (or timelessness). Again, these examples only point to the obvious human preoccupation with time, in that it punctuates birth, generation and death.

Many have used analogies drawn from relativity theory to give shape to this preoccupation and the way its manifestations are structured. This has either been explicit (Calcroft, 1980) or in terms such as "the curvature of emotional space" (Friedman, 1980). Friedman has illustrated how ceremonies as "Rites of Passage", can give meaning and structure to the periodic wave-like fluctuations over time. As a result, such fluctuations cease to be rigid repetitious two-dimensional oscillations; e.g. son challenges father, father entrenches, son replaces father, grandson challenges son, son entrenches etc.; and are replaced by more three dimensional spirals which lead to new possibilities (Hoffman, 1981). It may be that family therapists' attempts to dissociate from time relationships by talking of "here-and-now" behaviour were partly influenced by the concern to move away from a linear model of causality. Because time is generally seen as going in one direction, prior events are always liable to be "blamed" for "causing" subsequent events. Carter and McGoldrick (1980) have proposed a two dimensional solution to this dilemma by breaking up the in-put to a family into horizontal stressors; life-cycle developmental transitions, and external events on the one hand, and vertical stressors; family patterns, myths, etc. on the other.

C.   The Question of Transmission

The question of the transmission of one pattern of events through the family life-cycle and beyond from one generation to another has long preoccupied family therapists. To some extent, it has also been studiously avoided by the "structural" group as it implies some kind of causality. In a paper designed to develop a systemic model from a psychoanalytic framework (Cooklin, 1979), I proposed a model whereby one could see certain patterns of behaviour "leap-frogging" through the generations. On the simplest level, stern parents frequently seem to produce children who in their turn grow up to become more lenient parents, whose children may well return to a model of parenting closer to that used by their grandparents. This was a causal model and it implied some kind of chain reaction going on throughout generations. However it would not explain the way in which certain patterns of behaviours, and familiar attitudes to these, may be passed down through the generations even for hundreds of years as described by Byng-Hall (1982). He gave illustrations of how the court martial and execution of his ancestor Admiral Byng for "cowardice" had laid a pattern on the interpretation of certain sets of events in later generations including that of his own family. He was able to give an elegant demonstration of how recent events in his own family were coded in terms of "cowardice or courage", "innocence or guilt", in a pattern whose form seemed to be isomorphic to the events of 200 years ago.

Bentovim and Kinston (1980) have proposed that a family may process such patterns in three possible ways: (a) by denial, which could be manifested by a kind of superinsensitivity to events which resonate closely with the pattern, e.g. the parents of an immigrant family manifesting unusual insensitivity to a child's difficulties in joining new groups; (b) by repetition without resolution; (c) by reversal, as in Hardy's novel "Tess of the D'Urbervilles", wealth and poverty oscillate with each other in a pattern which codes how the heroine resolves the dilemma of "being owned" vs personal autonomy.

I shall return later to the question of the transmission of sequences of different lengths, and the different processes involved in transmitting a sequence of a few minutes, as opposed to one of a generation or more. But first I want to consider an important building block of transmission: the communication process.

D.   The Communication Process

Consider the relationship between digital and analogic communication (Watzlawick et al., 1969). Digital communication refers to verbal, or symbolic communication and includes in it certain formal agreements between the transmitter and the receiver of the communication. For example there is little about the word car which describes the experience of seeing, being in, or being in any other relationship to a car. However the communicator, and receiver of the word car by accepting the formal syntax of language, will have accepted that the sound of the word car, will represent the object car. Because of this communication by labelled symbols, it is possible to distinguish between a digital statement and its opposite. The concept of opposites cannot be communicated analogically. One can say that the word light is the opposite of the word dark. However if one was to communicate about the word light by shining a torch at night, one could only communicate that there was either light or no light. Analogic, or imitative communication requires that the communication in some way directly represents the event about which it communicates. Humans are capable (Watzlawick, 1969) of both analogic and digital communication. With the possible exception of the whale and related mammals, they are the only creatures in the animal kingdom who can use both modalities. Analogic communication is phylogenetically more primitive than digital communication, but different phylogenetic levels of communication can also be distinguished within it. Digital communication is restricted by the formal syntax of language. Therefore although one can use badly written English, or badly spoken English, the actual meaning of the phrases still has to be based on an agreement between the transmitter and receiver of the words about their meaning. Within analogic communication there are more gradations. For example at a sophisticated level, an individual may signify that he wishes to withdraw from some aspect of a relationship by only slightly averting his eyes. At the other extreme, a child may signify a much more total withdrawal by curling into a ball, sucking its thumb, rocking, and being unresponsive to either spoken word or touch.

One important component of analogic or imitative behaviour is that like will respond with like. Some people who talk at length with somebody with a lisp may find themselves using a lisp. Yawns are notoriously infectious. To respond to a smile with a smile is often quite involuntary. Reaching for the natural sciences again, Bateson (1979) has produced a very elegant theory for the self-reproduction of patterns throughout nature. However one only has to look at the phenomena of resonance in physics. One pendulum will initiate oscillation in another close by. Although we can impute transmission of pressure changes through the air for this example, we cannot when looking at the transmission of electro-magnetic waves through space and the way in which they set up analogous waves in instruments which are attuned to them. This is an example of one method of pattern reproduction; i.e. the pattern has implicated in it a different order of pattern for its own reproduction. This is a phenomenon which is being increasingly recognized throughout nature. It is not the DNA in a cell which reproduces the cell, but the DNA/cytoplasm system. This is a different way of conceptualizing transmission from the idea of internal objects being projected and introjected, and it does not slip so easily into our common picture of the universe. Physicists after all were for years searching for the "ether" to explain the transmission of electromagnetic waves. At this stage, one may not need to say more in explanatory terms than that patterns have a tendency to reproduce similar patterns. This phenomenon is given acknowledgement by Minuchin (1972) in the process he calls mimesis. This refers to a communication which a therapist may make, often unconsciously, which is in some way an analogue of a style of communication by some member of the family. It could be that the therapist leans back and stretches his legs soon after the father in the family has done the same, or finds himself adopting a similar tone of voice, or accent, or removing his coat at a similar time. When I had asked one father to tell me about the problem in the family he became very vague and whispered "It is about the one on the left". I asked him to be blunt, to which he responded by leaning forward and telling me earnestly "You know I have not had very much preparation for this interview, you know". When later I saw the video tape, I discovered that I had leant forward in my chair, looked at him earnestly, and said "You know I have not either". Although there was a verbal component to this, I found I was using his tone and accent in a way which was not consciously mocking or ironic. Another example can be found in the powerful pressure people often feel to adopt the local accent or voice pattern when moving to a new locality.

The notion that relationship patterns are transmitted as though like sound waves is represented in current English metaphor;

"We are not on the same wave length"

"We are in step with each other"

"I get strange vibrations from him"

These are metaphors for communicational patterns, and the content suggests a perception of some kind of periodicity. There are other metaphors which portray the periodic nature of much communication and interaction. When we talk of "going round in circles", "vicious circles", "ups and downs", or "coming and going", there is always an implied movement to and from a certain state of affairs. Returning to natural science models, in Fourier's theorem, any pattern can be represented in terms of sine waves. Thus we can see in any apparently continuous event, such as a waterfall, that it is made up of periodic elements, while at the same time the whole event goes through regular changes: the waterfall for example ebbs and flows with the seasons.

Is there any advantage in using the wave motion analogy for human communication? It certainly seems to fit snugly enough for much imitative behaviour, but its importance is that a medium of transmission is unnecessary. That is to say one does not have to ask the question "Who or what caused these events to happen?" It allows one to take a step back and perceive the pattern, rather as one hears the sound instead of each individual wave. While it is interesting to consider individual behaviour in these terms it becomes essential in making sense of the reproduction of patterns in families.

A model of transmission I had previously proposed (Cooklin, 1979) was based on the Object Relations Theory of the personality developed by Fairbairn (1952). In this model, relationship patterns which have been perceived as threatening to the survival of the individual are internalized. Thereafter the individual seeks to be reunited with the aspects of him or herself which have been internalized and seeks others who will play the part of the original "other" in the relationship. In this model, it appeared as though relationship patterns were passed on like quantum packages from one generation to another, in contrast to a "wave" model. It now seems clear to me that this model is too limited. It treats events as though they were sequential, while in reality, any event contains components from all parts of the system simultaneously. A more coherent model for the reproduction of patterns of events would need to include three components;

(1)   The sequence of events
(2)   The arrangement of the parts at any one time
(3)   The wave form of the periodic or episodic nature of the sequence

Let us consider these in terms of a hypothetical short sequence. Such a sequence might be: Mother is upset, Father responds angrily, Susan responds to Father's anger by sulking, Johnny responds to these events by placating, Mother joins with Johnny, Susan joins with Father, the children then fight, the parents unite to control them. Thus the intensity of interaction in the sequence can be represented as in Fig. 1.

Six stages are represented here. The pattern must include the configuration of the relationships in each, the sequential order, and the wave form. Thus it could be

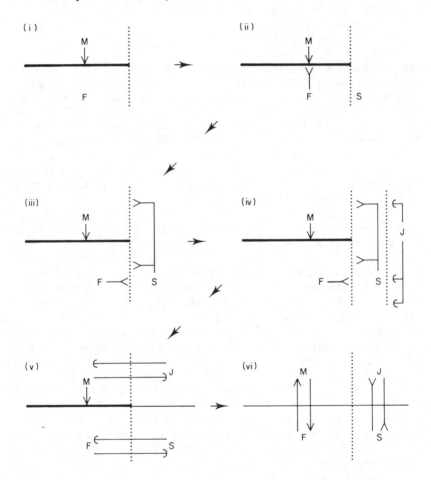

Fig. 1

that the interaction intensifies slowly through stages (i) to (iii), then escalates and is rapidly controlled: Fig. 2. Any other shape would be possible. The intensity could rise slowly and fall slowly (Fig. 3). Also, as shown in Fig. 4, the sequences may occur in rapid succession (a) or with long intervals between them (b). If one asks families to describe a common sequence of this kind, they can nearly always provide more than one. Furthermore each family member can usually predict more or less accurately how a particular sequence will "end", and will often be surprised to find they can do this.

In the view of the communications school, these sequences will in a sense be their own reproducers. In their view it is not necessary to impute either a causal or a transmission link between one sequence and another. Although each sequence may be different in content (the row may not be about mother being upset but perhaps about Susan bullying Johnny), they will nevertheless display the same formal relationships. That is, the overall patterns of interactions will remain the same. A group at the Department of Children and Parents in the Tavistock Clinic led by David Campbell are currently trying to verify the formal pattern in a common sequence observed with certain families (Byng-Hall,

Structure — Interaction — Sex

- Weak affiliation or disengagement
- Strong affiliation
- Overinvolvement
- Diffuse boundary
- Clear boundary
- Rigid boundary

- Overture, request or demand
- Positive response
- Negative response

- Male
- Female
- Died

"Key to Fig. 1 and Figs 7-15 (modified after Minuchin, 1974)."

1981). These are families where the identified patient (usually a child) interacts with the parents in such a way that the physical and metaphorical distance between the parents is kept within certain fixed limits (neither too near nor too far).

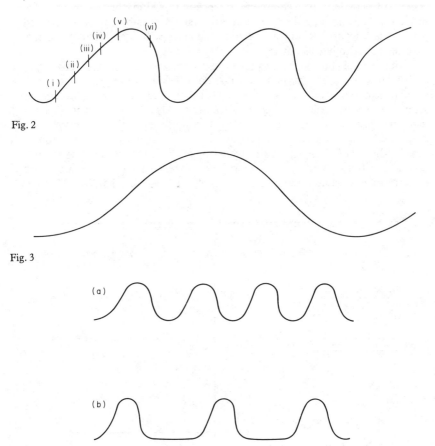

Fig. 2

Fig. 3

Fig. 4

III.   EFFECTING CHANGE

A.   Change in Short Sequence

A change in such a pattern would require that the sequence goes beyond its usual level of intensity of interaction. For example if in a family a sequence commonly ends with a mother rushing out of the house, saying "I am leaving for good", and returning an hour later, that event will not mean that mother is leaving to anyone in the system, but rather that that is the end of the sequence. If on the other hand, against this background the mother stays out for a week, and does not telephone, the event changes its context and meaning, and will probably have to be resolved in a new way. It is a central goal of Structural Family Therapy that a pattern of events is pushed beyond the usual limiting factor, so that new limiting factors have to be found, and thus new sequences. There is often a two-fold goal:

(a) to change immediate sequences by the therapist directly intervening in these sequences.

(b) through the medium of changing sequences to differentiate relevant subsystems, particularly executive subsystems (Minuchin, 1974; Camp, 1973).

In the service of these two goals the therapist will try to maintain and enhance the intensity of the interactions in the family's common sequences, and as a result put the members of the family through an experience of stress. The therapist will try to enact a sequence in the course of the therapy session, or even to enact the same sequence several times and in various ways try to influence its outcome.

A classical example of this approach is demonstrated when Minuchin "pushes the parents of an anorectic girl to make her eat". That is, he provides a backcloth and frame—"she must eat or she will die" . . . "you must make her eat"—and the shape of the communicational pattern then unfolds in front of him. For example, commonly the parents will each use gentle coaxing, pleading, cajoling, blaming and denouncement in rhythmic rotation, and each will disqualify the attempts of the other as the interactions approach a certain pitch of intensity (ironically just that pitch at which the pattern could be broken). In a variety of ways, one of which is to repeat at intervals his instruction to the parents, Minuchin will intensify this pattern beyond the usual level of tolerance allowed by the family. In one well-known case he stops the interaction just as the father is trying to force a sausage down his daughter's throat. He tells the daughter that she has humiliated her parents in front of him, because this is so far the only way she can fight them. She will need to learn more competent ways of fighting them, but in the meantime she must eat. The fact that she then eats is accompanied by two other changes:

(1) She allows her development to continue, achieves some greater autonomy, and increases the emotional distance from her parents.

(2) Her parents can no longer avoid conflict by their "helplessness" in relation to her "illness", partly because they have been shamed into finding some new solution and partly because her continuing development makes her less available to be engaged in their relationship. They thus have to organize themselves into an executive, parental pair.

The rationale for trying to separate out a more defined executive pair or sub-system in a family can be seen from two points of view. First, in terms of general systems theory, this has the effect of increasing the state of order or "negentropy" (the ordering of randomness) in the system. This is a necessary precursor to developmental change, because the individual's development requires a transformation in the shape of the family: a reorganization of the pattern of alliances and coalitions. Any system requires a degree of order in its internal state before it can effectively and safely (without a threat to its survival) undergo such a transition.

Secondly, the definition of an executive subsystem in a family can have a powerful impact on the communicational patterns. One thesis of communications theory is that when a child presents as symptomatic, the parents may make digital statements geared towards control. However analogic communications from either or both parents will frequently invalidate these messages, so that the symptomatic child can either oscillate between responding to one or the other message, or is unable to respond to either. This is close in analogy to an electromagnetic sine wave. If an alternating current is to be "rectified" for direct current use, half of the sine wave has to be "cut off", otherwise the two waves cancel each other out. A strategy analogous to this "rectification" has been used by therapists from the Strategic school of family therapy (Haley, 1977) an example of which has recently been described by Madanes (1980). She advocates that the therapist should respond to only one of these apparently conflicting communications. By enhancing and supporting one of the communications (in this case the one which supports the hierarchical nature of the parents' authority) the other communication becomes relatively less powerful, the control of the reverberating sequence is lost, and a new sequence has to develop.

B.   Change in Short vs Long Sequences

Using a Structural approach to family therapy, it is possible to enact a relevant sequence within a session. However if one is considering sequences whose "wavelengths" might be over many years, then clearly this is not possible. Also, increasing the time-span of the sequence beyond a certain limit not only means a quantitative difference, but also the nature of the sequences becomes qualitatively different. Using again the analogy of electromagnetic wave forms, infra-red light is a very different phenomenon from ultra-violet light, which has a much shorter wave-length and ultra-violet light is a quite different phenomenon from radio waves or X-rays or gamma rays. They all have quite different transmission properties, and the effects of their impact on matter and particularly on biological tissue differ entirely.

One example of a short sequence in a family has been given. In another let us say that the mother complains of tiredness and asks her husband to help prepare a meal. He asks Susan to "do more for your mother". Susan complains that Johnny is "let off". Johnny offers to help the mother. The father stands up for Susan. Susan calls Johnny a sneak "you wouldn't do it if I weren't in trouble". The father then provokes Johnny to do something for which he can punish him. This sequence ends slightly differently from the earlier one but the formal relationships are almost the same; that is, the interrelationship of the parts is similar. For example, in relation to Johnny and Mother, Susan and Father are in alliance; in relation to Susan or Father, Johnny and Mother are in alliance.

.

Within particular families the content may change but the form may remain remarkably constant.

However the *longer* the sequence is, the more difficult it is to describe accurately, or even to identify clearly. If one does examine a family history and sees that for example every second generation for three generations there is a "favourite child" who is in some way done down by a "black sheep" sibling, then one may be observing the manifestations at least of a long sequence. This may only be the visible manifestations on which hang a whole series of complex relationship patterns. In one family it could be clearly seen that there was a pattern through three generations of a "brother not speaking to a sister" for long periods. Other relationships between their parents and respective spouses could be seen to be organized around the periodic nature of these disaffections, and the latter could be seen to occur in relation to patterns in the former. Other such sequences of varying lengths are illustrated in the examples described later.

Structural family therapy, using interventions designed to influence relatively short sequences, nevertheless assumes that these relatively short focussed sequences of behaviour will represent some part of the whole functioning of the family system. This coincides nicely with the holograph analogy: each segment contains an image of the whole. Thus a structural family therapist may take one segment of the whole picture, usually that which contains the presenting symptom brought by the parents, and he will assume that this represents a restricted view of the whole system, not in terms of content, but in terms of its formal relationships. For example he will assume that if Johnny has a problem about bedtime which interferes with the parents' sleep, and perhaps their sex life, that a change in this sequence will potentially represent changes in the whole pattern of relationships between the boy and his mother, the boy and his father, the parents with each other, and perhaps all of them with siblings. Such an approach is fully congruent with much general systems and cybernetic thinking. For example the idea that each element in a system or in each subsystem will contain patterns which are analogous to those in the larger system, is implicit in the concept of isomorphism (Ashby, 1956). Recently this concept has gained neurophysiological validation in the description of "enfoldment" or the "implicate order" of the sensory/motor cortex (Pribram, 1971). It has been shown that while on the one hand, different cells in the cortex respond to different frequencies in the environment, a pattern of the whole is recorded and stored by each cell.

It is after all implicit in the concept of a system rather than a "heap" (to use the systems jargon), that a change in one segment will reverberate throughout the whole system. This phenomenon is illustrated by Ashby's Homeostat* (1956). The use of this model also demonstrates how events with a different "time space" manifest different properties. For example the time that this machine takes to go through all its gyrations and eventually achieve a "steady state", can vary depending on the kind of change initiated in any element of the machine

---

*A mechanical model whose parts are interconnected in such a way that a change in one leads ultimately to a change in all the others until a new equilibrium is established.

and on the relative position of this element within the machine. It could take anything from a few milliseconds to several hours for the machine to re-establish equilibrium. The change which takes fractions of a second leads to a change of state which is of different order to that which takes hours. In the former case the machine is "stable" much of the time. In the latter case, the machine is in a state of *establishing* stability for much of the time.

C.   The "Event Shape in Time Space"

I have so far drawn heavily on analogies from other events in working towards a framework for the shape of events in human systems. My purpose in this liberal use of analogy has been to try and disengage temporarily from our innate subjectiveness in order to isolate some generalizations. Before moving to the more vexed question of "How does it all happen?—"What controls it all?", I shall summarize the points I am making and some of the analogies used.

(1)   Patterns all have a shape, and patterns of human interaction all are events in time, and thus have a shape in time.

(2)   Such patterns have a tendency to reproduce themselves. Thus each event will tend to repeat itself at regular intervals, if other variables remain constant. I have drawn on sound and electromagnetic wave analogies to illustrate this point.

(3)   Each part of an event, while being a mini-whole event itself, also contains the pattern of the main whole event. As well as illustrating the practical application of this point in structural family therapy, I have also used analogies from the holograph and from the connections to the sensory/motor cortex.

(4)   The properties of an event are principally governed by the time space within which it occurs, as well as by the event shape.

(5)   Thus the interventions required to change the shape of an event in a short time space will differ from those in a long time space.

In the case of short sequences, occupying a relatively short time space of a few minutes, hours or days, these principles could form the basis of guidelines for interventions of the kind used in structural family therapy. The answer to the question "What keeps the pattern going?" can be assumed to be "the pattern itself". On the other hand, there is a relationship between sequences of different lengths. Short sequences can be components of medium sequences, which in turn can be components of longer sequences (see Fig. 5). Theoretically, a change in the pattern of short sequences could ultimately lead to a change in the pattern of long sequences. The husband/wife pair who successfully break a family tradition of a pattern of "alcoholic husband/long-suffering wife" characterized by sequences of drinking—violence—recriminations—and contrite guilt, could possibly have influenced a long-term family pattern for the future. This assumes that there is not some specific governor or control process, which remains relatively unaffected by such short-term changes, and which will tend to maintain the traditional pattern. Carter and McGoldrick (1980) have used the term *vertical stressors* to describe relatively stable family patterns or myths which seem to have a life of their own. If this happens, and I believe there is evidence that it does, then it is necessary to try and identify the nature of this governor or control process. I prefer the term "control process" to "governor" because I think there is evidence that it is itself an event rather than a fixed entity, such as a "thing" or a particular person. The Ps of systems terminology denotes a point in the interactional process; "the nodal point", rather than a particular element or person.

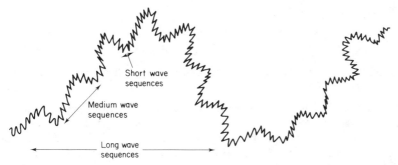

Fig. 5

D. The Nature of Control Processes

Both object relations theory, and attachment theory (Fairbairn, 1952; Cooklin, 1979; Bowlby, 1969) have provided models for control processes over longer-term sequences. Object relations theory suggests that the individual carries an internal model of an unresolved relationship which he continues to try and resolve in new relationships which are out of context. They are out of context because he is trying to solve the original relationship rather than the new one. Attachment theory suggests that in dysfunctional relationships, the individual is "anxiously attached" to a familiar albeit unsatisfactory relationship. More satisfying opportunities raise anxiety about giving up the known relationship on which one's own internal model is based. One aim of structural family therapy is that an individual will experience a new set of relationships, and thus members will participate in a new set of sequences. However sometimes the internal working models are so powerful in families that they act as a kind of "giro" or to use an electronic analogy as "reverberating circuits" which provide their own overwhelming positive feedback. It is in these situations that some different order of intervention is required.

From a different standpoint, Madanes (1980) makes a similar point about the individual adolescent:

> It may be that the disruptive behaviour *had* a protective function, but when the incongruous hierarchy stabilises and the system of interaction becomes chronic, the disturbed behaviour persists as a function of the system and independently of what set it off. It may be that at a certain point in time, there is no longer a hierarchical incongruity but simply a hierarchical reversal with the youth in a

superior position of power over the parents and with few or no situations in which the reverse is true.

This sees the "giro" as throughout the system, but the youth may be continuing to behave in a manner which has its own momentum although the behaviour may have lost any protective function. I believe for a similar reason Rosenberg and Lindblad (1978) from the Philadelphia Child Guidance Clinic recommend the use of behaviour therapy (specifically counter-conditioning) in addition to family therapy for the treatment of elective mutism.

> The individual work with the child is crucial since it affords the child an opportunity to work at changing in a context different from the one that allowed for the development of the symptom. Together these approaches offer a complimentarity that both speeds the change in the child and allows for this change to hold after a "return" to the family.

At this point however, a truly "systems" view of the control processes has not been satisfactorily described here. In fact the traditional psychiatric view of the "illness" or "condition" causing behaviour would almost fulfil the criteria that I have so far used for a control process. It could be argued that in Rosenberg and Lindblad's model, the child is seen as "embodying" the control process, but this would be an over-simplified anthropomorphic attempt to understand a complex phenomenon. Ferreira (1963) and Byng-Hall (1973) have explored the place of family myths as the "governors" controlling the course of long-term sequences. Watzlawick and others (1969) used the function of myths in regulating short and medium-term sequences. I have previously described the role of the Family Group Preoccupation (1974, 1979) around which potentially conflictual relationships are bound, as a governor of long-term sequences in certain families. The Family Group preoccupation is closely allied to the role of ghosts in family life: both those that are "as if" as well as those that are "believed in".

But all these ideas beg the question "What really is the control process?" Myths, the Family Group Preoccupation, and ghosts are after all only visual, representative, projections of patterns. Ghosts maintain an image which is often embodied in an event; a person's death in a particular way for example. Myths are patterns of relationships; the parts which the members play. It follows therefore that the control processors are themselves patterns, or at least patterns of patterns, rather as the patterns of amino acids in a protein are reproduced by the patterns of DNA in the chromosomes. It is really the configuration itself which is in charge of the sequences.

An intervention in a family can allow an apparently "impossible" father, mother, or child to leave that role. So what was impossible? It must have been the pattern itself. It is true that a pattern may be continued by an individual in a country far from his family of origin. The object relations model does provide a framework for the transmission of a pattern through such an individual. On the other hand, it is relatively rare for an individual to be totally cut off from his or her family with absolutely no communication, and if that state is approximated, the cultural context will play an even greater part in what pattern is continued. In addition, the strategic and paradoxical interventions of Haley, Madanes,

Pallazolli and others could not be effective if one followed through the logical conclusion of object relations theory as originally described. This is because all the object relations models of change rely heavily on the concept of "working through". Although made up of many repeated events in the therapeutic relationship, "working through" appears as a relatively smooth continuous process. Changes following strategic and paradoxical interventions, on the other hand, are often sudden. The shape of the event of change is more that of a step function (Hoffman, 1980) and occurs in jumps. The pattern of such change has been most clearly illustrated by Zeeman (1978) from the point of view of catastrophe theory. Because these interventions frequently do not involve the therapist in active persuasive "change encouraging" moves, in contrast with structural family therapy, they must act at the level of the patterns which control the patterns (Gorell Barnes, 1981). They achieve this by making the control processes irrelevant and therefore powerless. They do not make the actual relationship irrelevant or meaningless, a point often mistaken by therapists "trying out" paradoxical techniques. They may in fact lead to the same relationships being experienced with increased authenticity. I believe this is close to what Watzlawick *et al.* (1974) have described as second-order change. I believe this can be represented by returning to the wave form analogy (Fig. 5).

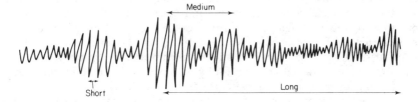

Fig. 6

This is of course a gross oversimplification, and the patterns could be represented by changes in different dimensions (Fig. 6). Second order change would have to be accompanied by some change in reality, and therefore one would expect by some change in the medium and long-term sequences.

E. Change in Short-Term Sequences Effecting Medium-Term Sequences

It has been stressed that in some situations patterns can apparently reproduce themselves. It has also been argued that when this is the predominant process, a relatively minor change in a short-term sequence could ultimately lead to change in longer-term sequences, rather as a small change in a river's banks can divert the whole course of that river. Thus small changes enacted during a family session might ultimately lead not only to change in those sequences enacted, but also to change in the family's structure and patterns of interaction. An example follows from the Anton family.

Paul was aged 13, and came with his sister Angie aged 10 and their grandmother,

Ann. The problem presented was that Paul suffered from regular, recurrent and severe vomiting, what would usually be described as Periodic Syndrome. The vomiting was said by his grandmother to occur in bouts at approximately weekly intervals, and about once a month it reached sufficient severity for him to require admission to hospital and treatment for dehydration. These events severely interfered with his life, and with those of this current family. The precipitant to the family's referral was a failed holiday in the Channel Islands. Paul had soon been admitted to hospital and the holiday was ruined. He was said to have suffered from this disorder since about the age of three, and he had been seen by at least two previous psychiatrists. In the folklore of the family, it had been talked of as having "developed from jealousy after the birth of his younger sister". The family had moved to the United States, and four years before I saw them the children's two parents had been killed in a car crash. Within the family there had been some relatively public heart searchings about whether the parents had been drinking at a party that evening, or whether any family row could have contributed to the event. At the time, the children's maternal grandmother had been on a short visit to the family. Two years before the accident, she had been divorced by her own husband just after her sixtieth birthday. Having now lost her only child as well, the opportunity to take over the children seemed to offer her a welcome new purpose to her life. In fact before the accident, Paul's symptoms had abated somewhat, at least in frequency, but within a year of the formation of this new family of three back in England, the symptoms had reappeared with all their previous ferocity. Paul also had been assessed by a local psychiatrist for learning difficulties, and had been placed in a special school. His sister Angie rarely missed an opportunity to rub in his relative incompetence with reading, by parading her own eloquence, results of tests etc.

When the three (grandmother and children) came for a family session, it was also clear that Angie was in as much of a battle with her grandmother for domination as she was with Paul. Paul presented himself as rather passive, and all his behaviour seemed directed to the goal of "keeping things calm". The family were seen for eight sessions in all. Within three sessions Paul's symptoms had subsided, and after another two, they had disappeared, apart from one relapse during Christmas which he was able to handle himself without recourse to hospital. The grandmother became less involved and preoccupied with Paul's symptoms, more able to control Angie and with less "sisterly" battles. She was also more able to enjoy activities of her own in a way which seemed in keeping with her own time of life.

Now let us consider this case in terms of stable short-term sequences, without seeking relevant long-term sequences. Paul's symptoms had disappeared relatively quickly. Although the therapist had spent some effort in encouraging and pushing the grandmother and children to re-experience more fully the mourning of the loss of the parents, at first sight this did not appear to be crucial. Recounting the details of the loss did not seem to be followed by any major change, particularly in Paul's symptom, and this symptom had been present almost continuously long before his parents' death.

The relationship Paul had with Angie and the grandmother appeared to have similarities to certain patterns in his relationship to his parents (Fig. 7). For example it appeared that by Paul staying closely involved with his mother, he had in some way acted as a safety valve in what was at times a stormy relationship between his parents. A similar kind of stormy relationship now existed between

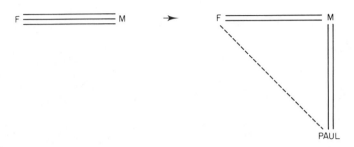

Fig. 7

Angie and his grandmother. The grandmother was often unable to control Angie, would threaten to have her "put away", while Angie would usually "win and get her own way". As the tension rose, Paul would begin to vomit. Paul's mother had responded to mounting tension in the marriage by threatening to return to her mother. Paul's father seemed unable to back down, so that an escalating series of threats would be exchanged until Paul began to vomit. Thus the relationship pattern between Paul and his grandmother and Angie, was isomorphic to that which had previously existed between him and his parents. Although the content was quite different, the pattern was the same (Fig. 8).

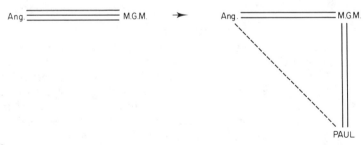

Fig. 8

The therapist directed his attention towards trying to establish a controlled hierarchy between the grandmother and children. He aimed to intensify the grandmother's attempts to control Angie, so that Paul could eventually be allowed a place as an elder brother to Angie. The effect of this was to place Angie and Paul on a similar level together, and relatively speaking more distant from the grandmother (Fig. 9). Angie, as a result, fought her grandmother less and Paul was less involved in their struggle.

It would appear that the historical significance of these encounters was less relevant to the changes in the short-term sequences. Nevertheless it could also be argued that the shared experience of mourning effected the outcome of medium-term sequences in the family. An example of such a sequence would be the pattern of over-engagement, oscillating with threats of abandonment, which

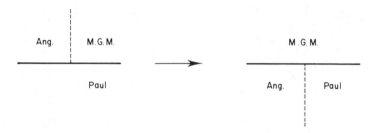

Fig. 9

occurred between Angie and grandmother, and which in turn was regulated by Paul's symptoms. If such a sequence changed, then the shifts in the more short-term sequences could be accommodated. The mourning process in which they were engaged during therapy could have led to a differentiation of the present pattern of interactions from the previous set which it emulated. The present pattern could therefore be governed more by the immediate needs of the family and less by a requirement to continue an old pattern. However, one could not predict at all how these medium-term changes might effect the longer-term pattern of relationships in Paul's or Angie's families of procreation.

F. Change in Short Sequences Leading to Interventions in the Control Process of Long Sequences

John and Sue Losey were a young couple with a 2-year-old son. John was a moderately successful businessman, and Sue had been competent in her own work as well as being a capable housewife. They had been referred by a paediatrician because their child George was described as "hyperactive". He would not sleep at night, got up early in the morning, often damaged things around the house, had tantrums if he could not get his own way, and was always on the move. Apart from slightly retarded speech, he was an otherwise normal and healthily developed boy. At different times the paediatrician had previously prescribed both tranquillisers and amphetamine-related stimulants, without effect.

John was smiling and affable, Sue worried looking, tense and rather bitter. George oscillated between them in an excitable manner until I engaged the two parents on the question of how they could co-operate in his management. As, with my encouragement, the two parents began to negotiate with each other about their approach to George, George seemed to forget them and eventually went to sleep, remaining so for the following hour. As this was some 15 minutes into a session and was dramatically different from anything which the parents had seen happen before, I was somewhat thrown from my goal of intensifying current sequences and trying to achieve shifts in their outcome. I could have encouraged them to waken George, but something about the unusual experience of peace with him asleep triggered the two of them to reminisce about how they had come to form this family. Sue's father had committed suicide shortly before George's birth. She had experienced this as extremely traumatic, feeling that she was responsible as she "should have known that things were not right", and experiencing the loss intensely as she had viewed her father as her only close support. His death had intensified what had been a previous pattern in her relationships. She would respond to potentially close relationships by hardening and distancing herself. With John this had been easy because his "happy-go-lucky" approach to life made little intrusion on her privacy. However, George's robust demands led her to retreat even further into herself, to which George naturally responded by making increasingly excited demands. Sue had been pregnant by John before the marriage but had insisted on having this aborted "because I didn't want to have to get married for that reason and then be told by my mother 'I told you so' ". John claimed to have been very distressed about this abortion, and thought that it had coloured his protective attitude to George. In the same breath he talked about a younger sibling in his own family who died as a "cot death". John had made efforts to make up to his own parents for their loss, and had developed a very protective and "soft" attitude to little children. This had been intensified by his hurt about Sue's abortion. Therefore in response to George he would be "kind and explain things", rather than assert relevant controls. This of course undermined Sue, and intensified her "hardness".

This family was seen for only three sessions, during which time the parents gained control of George, who had calmed down considerably, and Sue had ceased to distance herself so much from John, thus allowing John to be more assertive and direct with her. In this case, one could argue that Susan was able to change the way in which she distanced her husband once she was able to allow him to help her with the suffering and self-blame with which she continued to burden herself about her father's suicide. Similarly, John's need to "nurture and protect little children" could be seen both in the context of this immediate family, and as part of a longer-term sequence relating to his role in the family of origin. Although it was in fact the use of "Structural Moves" to enact and intensify the interactions related to the problems the family brought which was followed by this dramatic change of mood, it was the change in the control processes which allowed the new sequences to continue. In this case, the control processes were at the first level the nature of the triad between John, Sue and George, but at the second level, the processes were related to the roles which John and Sue were both asking each other to fulfil. The reason that these roles fulfilled the function of control processes was because they were non-explicit. Thus each had to fit more or less comfortably into the other's demands in order to remain within the system. Making these roles both explicit, and providing a context for their development was I believe an important part of the recalibration of the control processes in this case.

G. Integrating Change in Short and Long Sequences

So far it has been stressed that change in short-term sequences can be affected by the techniques of structural family therapy: enactment, intensification, boundary-making, unbalancing. When used in conjunction with techniques for changing realities, and "changing epistemology", such changes will sometimes lead to a shift in the balance of interactions throughout the system in such a way that the control processes themselves will be recalibrated. In this case, a change in the pattern of the longer-term sequences may also result. However when the control processes and the longer-term sequences which they control carry a powerful momentum, then efforts to intervene with these directly will be complementary to changes effected in short-term sequences. The control processes may be effected by a number of strategic techniques (Gorell Barnes, 1982a, b) or by exploring their original context which has now become potentially irrelevant. I say potentially because, in fact, the context has not become irrelevant if the processes are continuing in the present. The typing or coding of events as belonging to the past is only useful if it relegates these events to the past. This can be achieved by changing their current context so that they no longer have a place in the present. This last point is illustrated by the following example:

The Arkwright family consisted of the mother June who was a pottery teacher, the father Stan who was a landscape gardener, and their two children, Shelley aged 10 and Neil aged 8. Shelley was in trouble at school, her work was deteriorating, and teachers had complained about her. She was involved in escalating battles with her mother, ostensibly about homework, and her mother was alarmed by the degree of violence in which the two of them were engaging. Viewing the family from the point of view of its formal relationships, Shelley and her mother were over-engaged with each other, and Stan was relatively distant. There was no hierarchical differentiation between Shelley's and her mother's roles, and Stan treated his wife in a patronizing way, as though she and Shelley were sisters. At the same time, if Stan began to address either Shelley or her mother directly, he was usually interrupted. Neil behaved "as good as gold", which engaged him actively with Shelley by irritating her, and relatively distancing himself from his parents (Fig. 10).

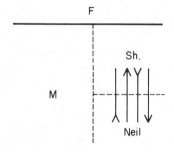

Fig. 10

In the first two sessions, I asked June to show me what happened when she tried to talk to Shelley the "way she wanted to". She asked Shelley "what is it about me that annoys you?" At first Shelley would not answer. Eventually Shelley responded "Why do I annoy you?" The analogic components of this question conveyed that she was asking her mother if that was what the mother's question meant. At another level, it also conveyed her confusion manifested from the lack of hierarchical clarity. In intensifying the sequence I had moved the father's chair so that he could not directly intervene with Shelley, but could only see his wife. I had asked Neil not to interrupt but to listen "for the time being". I had asked Stan to find out from his wife what she wanted to do when Shelley kept leaving her chair. After several attempts to ask June in which he made such statements as "What you want to do is . . ." or "I mean you want to make her sit down, don't you . . ." or "shall I make her sit down . . . ", he finally asked his wife "what do you want Shelley to do?" June responded that she wanted Shelley to sit down. He was then helped to support his wife in achieving this. As Shelley continued to have tantrums in the room, the therapist was able to intensify the interaction between the parents in the task of successfully managing these tantrums (Fig. 11). By the third session, the mother had established control over

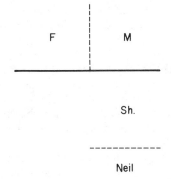

Fig. 11

Shelley, and Shelley was scowling less and looking more relaxed. However in relation to her father, she was even more mocking and dismissive (Fig. 12).

Fig. 12

The father was asked to enact what the mother had been able to achieve, and the mother was asked to sit out and watch. After several episodes, when the mother could not restrain herself from "rescuing" her husband each time as she saw it he "did it wrong", the father was in fact able to have a quite reasonable and age-appropriate conversation with his daughter. Meanwhile Neil had said to his sister "Shelley do hurry up otherwise Dr Cooklin will only be talking about you and I will never get dealt with".

I asked the mother how she thought her husband was managing to which she replied rather reluctantly and a little sourly "I think he is doing rather well". I then left the room and went behind the one-way screen having asked the father to "continue". A sequence similar to the ones I have described developed again. At a certain point, the mother leant forward to "help" her husband by talking to Shelley. This was the point of "repeat" which I had been waiting for. I entered the room and said to the mother "really, I don't understand why you must keep rescuing him. Why is it? Why must you keep rescuing him? He is really doing very well". At first she smiled nodding, and then burst into tears apparently communicating a degree of distress which seemed quite out of keeping with this setting. I had asked her "why must you keep rescuing him?"

I stopped this part of the session and asked about the origins of the family. The mother showed the same distress as she began to tell me about the death of her father when she was aged 15. She and her younger sister (at that time aged 10, the same age as Shelley now was) had been playing with an old gramophone trying to make it work. Her younger sister Sarah had been nagging her father to make the gramophone work. "Make it work Daddy, make it work for me". The father had checked the connections on the electric motor and plugged it in. He was electrocuted and killed instantly. June had told her sister that her father was not really dead, just unconscious. There was nobody else around and she had had to get help, but none of the adults would believe her story. She and her sister had never discussed the event.

What I had responded to analogically was that she was treating her husband in an inappropriately fragile way. Following this session, Shelley's relationship with her mother changed markedly, and she became increasingly engaged in school. June met her sister and discussed the incident for the first time, both acknowledging how afraid they had been about facing each other. June and Stan were seen for a number of marital sessions before June was able to treat Stan as potent enough to be of use to her. The complimentary side of this shift was that he had to acknowledge his wife as a potential adversary rather than the "best child he had got". Once the couple had separated themselves out as a marital pair, Shelley and Neil began to be more actively competitive. The therapy had lasted for 12 sessions in all, but two months later the parents returned on their own to ask for advice about Neil. I did little other than to ask them to enact discussing it together. They went home and found an easy solution to a minor control problem with the little boy (Fig. 13).

There are other frameworks within which these events could be considered. Shelley's behaviour certainly played an important part in distance regulation between the parents (Byng-Hall, 1980). They maintained some engagement through her, but did not become so intently engaged with each other that the confusions of hierarchy in their marriage would be confronted, thus avoiding the dangers of violence or abandonment between them.

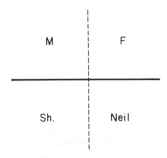

Fig. 13

There was a shift in balance between the different parts of the system through the initial work of intensification, boundary-making, and unbalancing. However, there was an overall pattern of interactions of the husband/wife pair which seemed to override these short-term changes. The intensely emotional event of the wife seeing the link between the way she treated her husband (which only could have been seen in the context of her as *mother* in the presence of *her children and* her husband), recalibrated the control process. Without this second-order change, the scene could have been set for the propagation of a longer-term sequence from generation to generation or in alternate generations. However the pattern was not carried alone by June (or of course her husband's component by him) but by the configuration, which involved her mother, her sister, and others.

H. Medium Sequence Change

In the final example three wavelengths of sequences can be distinguished; short repetitive cycles occurring regularly throughout a session, medium sequences repeated over a cycle of a few months or years, and longer-term sequences spanning a generation or more.

The family consisted of Annie, Jack her husband, and Sheila their daughter of 24. The problem presented was that Annie was "having a nervous breakdown". The timing of this coincided with Sheila's latest bid to leave home, and to separate from the intense triangular relationship between the three of them. The short-term sequence refers to the regular pattern of interaction between the family members. This is characterized by the following moves: as Jack withdraws from Annie, so Annie becomes increasingly extreme in her demands. Jack then withdraws further. As the pitch of interaction rises, Sheila makes moves to leave the triangle. The pitch of interaction between Jack and Annie then further increases in intensity until Sheila becomes engaged in taking one side or the other. This is an example of the short-term sequence, which could occur several times in a session. The pattern will show a remarkable constancy of form although, as can be seen from the example below, the roles assigned may be swopped from time to time. The starting point of the sequence I have used is quite arbitrary as the pattern is both cyclical and continuous. The medium-term sequence is similar in form but different in its time space or wave length. The peaks of intensity are when Sheila prepares to leave home, and are ultimately followed by Annie "having a nervous breakdown", or at least Jack's complaint that she is. The wavelength varies between a few months and a year or more.

The long-term sequence refers to the pattern of relatively stable triangles giving way to relatively unstable dyadic relationships, which would in turn be replaced by stable, and therefore "clung to", triangular relationships throughout the family's available history.

Annie had come from a family where triangular relationships, those in which three people were "reliably" involved, were the stable unit. She had remained closely involved with her parents while her elder and younger siblings had responded to the freedom which this arrangement afforded them by "leaving us to it". Her own separation from her parents had not occurred until her mother died. Without her mother, the relationship with her father was unstable, and she soon began to try to distance herself. She married Jack in 1937. They had met "in service" (they were both servants in a country house), but he was soon drafted into the Army. By the time of his return from the war, she was living with another man. After an initial refusal she returned to Jack and almost immediately became pregnant. She gave birth to a boy with spina bifida who died ten days later.

Jack was the middle child in his family. His father was engrossed in his elder brother and his mother heavily involved with his young sister. The latter two were still living together. Although he often felt lonely and depressed, he was most comfortable when being relatively ignored. He had to "force" his attentions on Annie who for a time had responded to him and then withdrawn again, after the death of their child. Jack's attempts to woo Annie were infrequent, and he would usually seem relieved when he settled back into a more or less comfortable isolation. It appeared that this cycle of events lasted about ten years. They had married in 1937, the first child was conceived ten years later, and Sheila was conceived after another ten years in 1957. Annie, however, had remained closely involved with the child that died. This ghost seemed to maintain the stability of her relationship with Jack, as it completed the triangle. This "child" required Jack to stay in the marriage for the myth to maintain its authenticity. It kept Jack at a distance so that the question of whether or not the child was really alive would not be confronted. For Jack's part, the child myth had not only kept the marriage safe, not too intimate but to be preserved at all costs, for fear the myth be exploded; it also became reminiscent of the elder brother he could not displace. In fact he felt most comfortable and "knew his place" in such a context. This arrangement continued to operate throughout a cycle of about ten years. Annie maintained that the child had not really died. Jack responded to this contention as a reason why he must treat her carefully, and the myth was never truly challenged; not, that is, until the birth of Sheila.

Thus Jack had moved from being the relative outsider in a series of triangular relationships in his family of origin, to being the relative outsider in this new triangle. Annie had moved from being closely involved with her mother in such a way that her father was kept "in the picture" but comfortably at bay from both of them, to being closely involved with the dead child in such a way that Jack was kept involved but kept at a distance comfortable for both (Fig. 14).

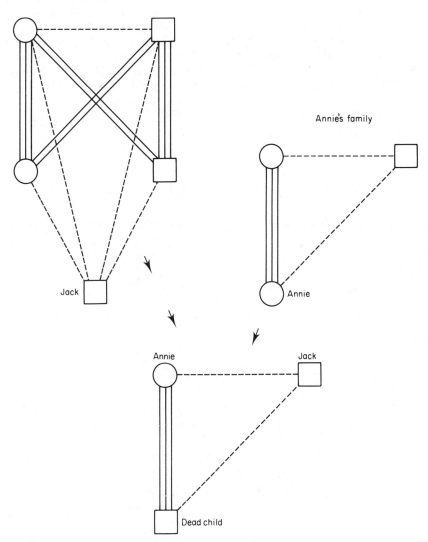

Fig. 14

This whole system was therefore initially destabilized by Sheila's birth. For her to be accepted, the myth had to be exploded, and the raison d'être of the marriage brought into question. Neither partner could contemplate this. Jack became Sheila's "protector" from Annie. Annie's position became more untenable, and she is said to have tried to smother or strangle Sheila. This then became a new myth: "Annie had tried to get rid of Sheila". As the system restabilized, Sheila became the pivot of the new triangle. The myths of Annie's attack on her, and of the son "who had not died" served only to cement this arrangement. That is the "guilt" of "having tried to kill" Sheila meant that Annie kept closely involved with her, and Jack ministered over the relationship but was outside it. The dead baby was therefore replaced by Sheila, but hovered in the background threatening to return if Sheila should leave. The implication of the return of the dead child myth was that Annie would have a "nervous breakdown", and the system would destabilize (Fig. 15).

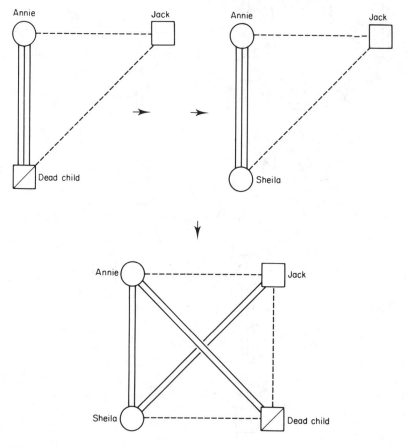

Fig. 15

Thus both myths prevented a challenge to Annie's role: "she was disturbed, could not be challenged, and needed Jack and Sheila", and her role protected the relationship between Jack and Sheila, as supportive but distant. Only the developmental process in the form of independent strivings from Sheila could really challenge this arrangement. Until recently, Sheila had shown little evidence of any such strivings. She had often stayed home from school to look after Annie, and Annie had often kept her off school to "protect her daughter". Annie would have "paranoid breakdowns", and Jack remained "long-suffering" and continued to minister to Annie and Sheila.

The family had been the subject of many therapeutic endeavours, including hospitalization and medication for Annie, medication and later psychotherapy for Sheila, "investigations" for weight loss in Jack, and recently "supportive psychotherapy" for Annie combined with family therapy for all three. When I first saw them, a medium-term sequence was in the process of being repeated. After many years of school refusal, Sheila had had similar difficulties with work, but was now settled in a reasonable clerical job. However she was isolated, without friends and did everything with her parents. The previous year she had made enquiries about training as a nurse, about thirty miles from home. She applied and was accepted. Her father began to reassure her that she'd be all right. Her mother began to complain about "spiritualists plotting against me", and Sheila wrote turning down the place on the course. However, although she stayed at home and isolated, she began fighting her mother about what she called "you trying to control me" and her father about his handling of her mother. A few months before I saw them, Sheila had again stated her intention to leave home and train as a nurse. Jack then admitted to Annie that he'd been having an affair with another woman. The nature of this affair was very unclear, and it appeared anyway that it had been going on for some years. Thus it seemed clear that it was less important whether or not this affair had happened than that it was presented as a challenge to the system. That is a different kind of triangle, in which Jack *was* involved with a third person, suddenly appeared like an omen to warn of the possible consequences of Sheila leaving, and breaking the stable pattern. The system produced an effective error-correcting negative feedback loop.

The initial response to this apparent piece of new information was an escalation in the standard pattern of medium-term sequences. Annie insisted the spiritualists were controlling her thoughts and once or twice "let out her feelings" on some members of a bus queue. Jack was demanding in-patient treatment for Annie. An increasing number of professionals became involved with the family in various ways.

The longer-term consequences were the way the families of both partners had transmitted a requirement for stable relationships, and the patterns which surrounded these. The medium-term sequences were those which maintained this pattern; the way Jack and Annie came together, separated and came together, in the company of another man, another woman, a dead child, and Sheila. Part of these medium-term sequences was enacted by the way Jack and Annie responded to Sheila's attempts to separate, each responding to Sheila and each other in a way which disqualified Sheila's bid for independence. Sheila also showed evidence of patent relief as these sequences completed their cycle and leaving became irrelevant. The interactions which I'll summarize occurred over the course of some ten sessions:

(1) "Paying off" the other therapists (no reflection on their skill but rather on their place in these sequences), and were in three phases.

(2) Dislodging Annie's role as the "one who is crazy and must be treated with kid gloves".

(3) Marshalling Annie and Jack to "parent" Sheila.

(4) Using a paradoxical challenge to Sheila to divert her from "completing the sequence" and returning home.

In the first session, Jack was insisting that Annie was "having a nervous breakdown". I asked Jack to explain what he meant in detail.

Jack: Well, you know she's imagining things.

Dr C: Please be more specific, exactly what do you mean?

Jack: If you've been a psychiatrist all these years you should know what a nervous breakdown is like.

Dr C: Not this one . . . look, let me help . . . get Annie to show me the behaviour you're worried about—try and make her show me.

Jack: [to Annie] Well you tell the Doctor what you told me—about these things you're imagining.

Annie: I'm not mad.

Jack: I never said you was.

Annie: I just said I was being victimized—the people in the office they were spiritualists and they were going to victimize me out of my job and they were right.

Jack: [to Dr C] There you are, you see . . .

Annie: [shouting] I was being victimized out of my job I tell you . . . [now screaming and standing over Jack threatening him with her fist]. You bastard . . . you won't believe me . . . why won't you listen?

Jack: [to Dr C] Now you see why I don't like coming up here . . .

Dr C: Go on—continue . . .

Jack: No, I'm not going on because this is . . .

Dr C: You know Jack I am amazed at the amount of extremism you tolerate in your wife . . . why do you allow it?

[Jack appears somewhat taken aback]

Dr C. continuing: I mean it can't allow for any pleasure, peace, *or* tranquillity . . . why do you allow it? . . . I wouldn't allow it with my wife . . . why do you?

Jack: Because . . . someone's got to keep on an even keel . . .

Annie: [taunting] Why don't you leave me?

Jack: . . . because if I didn't . . . I can see I could land up like these wife bashers.

Annie: But it's good to let go of your feelings . . . a row is good . . . why are you so passive?

Dr C: So is it, Annie, that the more passive and calm Jack gets, the more emotional and emphatic you become, the more passive and unsure Jack becomes, which makes you more determined?

Annie: Yes, he won't fight me.

Jack: Well I will sometimes . . . at least I'll argue . . .

This short sequence had occurred many times between this couple. The intervention pushed it beyond its normal limits, reframed it as a relationship pattern, and at the same time reframed Annie's behaviour in "behavioural" rather than "illness" terms. Later in the same session, much of the above history was also related by the couple. Some interventions were also made around the question of the myth of the dead baby. For example Annie claimed Jack had never shown her the death certificate, but added that she wouldn't have believed it anyway. It was therefore agreed that Jack would obtain a copy of the death certificate but keep it hidden from Annie. They might visit the grave together, but not observe the name on the headstone. Such interventions which by *reductio ad absurdum* gradually dislodged the "live-dead baby myth", also intensified the triangular relationship between Annie, Jack and Sheila. Thus within 2-3 sessions, the first phase of therapy had been completed, but with Sheila now *more* engaged in her parents' relationship. Although attention had been paid to the long-term sequences as manifested in the "live-dead baby myth", I do not believe these were effective in influencing the course of these sequences. They were, however, relevant to the short-term goal of dislodging Annie from the role of "mad woman".

I have acknowledged that the first phase left Sheila more rather than less engaged with her parents. In fact by the fourth session, Sheila had moved back into her mother's bed, while her father moved into the living room. It was reported that this was because Sheila was said to have been hearing noises in her room "like a cat scratching". I had initially responded to this information as though it were a perfectly common place state of affairs, and asked the father to join me at the blackboard to help me construct a detailed diagram of the house and where it connected with the neighbours so that we could "ascertain the nature of this sound". Eventually this was interrupted by Annie in a triumphant voice "well it was the vase coming off the mantle piece that really frightened her . . . she thought it was a ghost . . . *so* she's coming in with *me*".

Dr C: Ah, because you've got the edge on these supernatural things?

Annie: [a bit deflated]: Oh well I don't know about that.

Sheila: Yes, well I did think it might be a poltergeist.

Dr C: Now wait a minute, do you mean a poltergeist or do you mean a ghost? Let's be clear.

Sheila: Well I'm not sure . . . I think a poltergeist . . .

Annie: She thought it might be a ghost, that's why she's coming . . .

Dr C: Wait Annie, I want to hear from Sheila . . . was it a poltergeist or a ghost?

Sheila: I'm not sure . . . may be it was a ghost but . . .

Annie: It must have been a ghost because . . .

Dr C: Now wait Annie, was it you or Sheila who had this experience . . .

Annie: I expect it wasn't anything at all really.

Dr C: Sheila, what was it? A ghost or a poltergeist?

Sheila: Well . . . I think . . . yes, I'm sure it was a poltergeist.

Dr C: Good . . .

This was an example of a common short-term sequence which ended with Sheila defining her own reality. Although one might feel the content was crazy or at least bizarre, the formal relationships were isomorphic with other sequences in which the content was quite different. In future similar sessions, similar in form but not in content, Sheila gradually increased her distance from her parents to the point where she insisted she would "do the training whatever happens to them". She had moved out from her mother's bed. The parents were keeping their own conflict in check by engaging in supporting Sheila's bids for greater independence. So far, therapeutic interventions had only shifted the short-term sequence. There was no evidence that the medium-term sequence would not be completed as before, as she began to move out, so that she would not leave. A variety of strategic moves, aimed at interfering with the control process of this medium-term sequence, were used. For example Sheila was told that she certainly would not do the training, but it was a good myth to keep up as it would prevent her parents from feeling demoralized or worried that they had kept her too close. Later she was told that although she would not be able to leave, it was good training for when the time was ripe. Against this background of "training for maturity", the parents were asked to have a violent row in the next room to Sheila and see for how long she could keep the door closed and "stay out".

Sheila took up the challenge, left home five months before the training was due to start and spent this time on a kibbutz in Israel. She is now doing well in the nurse training, has had a boyfriend and has developed some other social relationships. It would appear that the medium-term sequence has been altered. It is impossible to say what will happen to the longer-term sequence, transmitted through Sheila. Annie and Jack have settled down. From time to time, Jack complains of various physical symptoms. Annie worries about him and then complains of being "victimized", but their modus vivendi is fairly stable.

IV. CONCLUSIONS

The following points have already been made (p.88):

(1) Patterns all have a shape, and patterns of human interaction are all events in time, and thus have a shape in time.

(2) Such patterns have a tendency to reproduce themselves. Thus each event will tend to repeat itself at regular intervals, if other variables remain constant.

(3) Each part of an event, while being a mini-whole event itself, also contains the pattern of the main whole event.

(4) The properties of an event are principally governed by the time space within which it occurs, as well as by the event shape.

(5) The interventions required to change the shape of an event in a short time space will differ from those in a long time space.

The following additional points have been made:

(6)   The notions of "here-and-now" change in systems as opposed to "systems over time" are artifacts. "Here-and-now" change occurs in the spatial and temporal form of short-term sequences. Interventions in systems over time can only happen "now" and *may* then influence the shape of future sequences.

(7)   The approach of structural family therapy is most powerful when the short-term patterns repeat themselves, when the parts of an event or pattern have a similar formal shape, or are isomorphic with, the larger pattern of which they are a part. When the latter is the case, the structural approach is most likely to be effective in sequences which are longer than the therapy itself.

(8)   Long-term sequences may imply a governor or control process which although itself a pattern of events, is a pattern of a different order from day to day interactions. Although this pattern will sometimes be influenced by changes in short-term sequences, sometimes it will not. In the latter case a different form of intervention is required.

(9)   While I have previously described an approach to these control processes based on object relations theory, in this chapter I have stressed the relevance of strategic and paradoxical interventions. These interventions change the pattern by removing the control process "from office", as it were, and thus making them inoperative by placing them in an untenable context. On the other hand, in my second and third examples (the Losey and Arkwright families), I contend that the control processes were manifested by the couples maintaining roles which were inappropriate to their present context. By establishing the context in which these roles *had* been appropriate in their families of origin, they were divested of their potency as control processes in the present context.

Thus when the control process is vested in crucial relationship patterns hinged to powerfully emotive events, it may be necessary to name these events in the process of shifting the locus of control. In the work of the Milan group, one can see both principles operating.

This leaves the question of "what to do when?" The nature of control processes can only be implied. Any attempt to search for the "real truth" carries with it dangers. One of these is of entering a "linear pursuit" for the "true culprit" or cause. Another is of entering into a cognitive search for this "truth" with the family, which keeps the intensity of interactions below a level at which change can occur. It follows that a structural approach to short-term sequences is a rational starting point, not only because it attends to the bread and butter of what the family has brought, but also because one cannot at the outset know where a small change will end.

REFERENCES

Ashby, W. R. (1956). "Introduction to cybernetics", John Wiley & Sons, New York and London.
Bateson, G. (1979). Mind and Nature, Wildwood House, London.

Beels, C. C. and Ferber, A. (1969). Family Therapy: a view. *Family Process,* **8,** 280-332.
Bentovim, A. (1979). Theories of Family Interaction and Techniques of Intervention. *Journal of Family Therapy* **1,** 321-345.
Bowen, M. (1975). Family Therapy After 20 Years. *In* "American Handbook of Psychiatry V", Basic Books, New York.
Bowen, M. (1976). Theory in the Practice of Psychotherapy. *In* "Family Therapy" (P. J. Guerin, ed.), Gardener Press, New York.
Bowlby, J. (1969). "Attachment and Loss, Vol. I, Attachment", Hogarth Press, London.
Box, S. J. (1979). The Elucidation of a Family Myth. *Journal of Family Therapy* **1,** 75-86.
Byng-Hall, J. (1973). Family Myths Used as a Defence in Conjoint Family Therapy. *British Journal of Medical Psychology,* **131,** 433-447.
Byng-Hall, J. (1979). Re-Editing Family Mythology During Family Therapy. *Journal of Family Therapy* **1,** 103-116.
Byng-Hall, J. (1980). Symptom Bearer as Marital Distance Regulator: Clinical Implications. *Family Process* **19,** 355-365.
Calcraft, L. (1980). *In* "Einstein: The First Hundred Years", (M. Goldsmith, A. Mackay and J. Woudhuysen, eds), Pergamon, London.
Camp, H. (1973). Structural Family Therapy: An Outsider's Perspective. *Family Process* **12,** 269-277.
Carter, E. and McGoldrick, M. (1980). The Family Life Cycle: An Overview. *In* "The Family Life Cycle", (E. Carter and M. McGoldrick, eds), Gardner, New York.
Cooklin, A. (1974). Family Preoccupation and Role in Conjoint Therapy. Paper to Royal College of Psychiatrists, June 1974.
Cooklin, A. (1978). Cultural reflections in British Family Therapy, *Group Analysis XI.* **3,** 212-222.
Cooklin, A. (1979). A Psychoanalytic Framework for a Systemic Approach to Family Therapy. *Journal of Family Therapy* **1,** 153-165.
Dowling, E. (1979). Cotherapy: A Clinical Researcher's View. *In* "Family and Marital Psychotherapy: A Critical Approach", (Walrond-Skinner, ed.), Routledge & Kegan Paul, London.
Fairbairn, W. R. D. (1952). "Psychoanalytic Studies of the Personality", Tavistock Publications, London.
Ferreira, A. J. (1963). Family Myths and Homeostasis. *Archives of General Psychiatry* **9,** 457-463.
Friedman, E. (1981). Systems and Ceremonies: A Family View of Rites of Passage. *In* "The Family Life Cycle", (E. Carter and M. McGoldrick, eds), Gardner, New York.
Gorell Barnes, G. (1982a). A difference that makes a difference. I. *Journal of Family Therapy* (in press).
Gorell Barnes, G., Jones, E., de Carteret, J. (1982b). A difference that makes a difference. II. *Journal of Family Therapy* (in press).
Hardy, T. (1891). "Tess of the D'Urbervilles", MacMillan, London.
Haley, J. (1977). "Problem Solving Therapy", Jossey-Bass, California.
Hoffman, L. (1980). The Family Life Cycle and Discontinuous Change. *In* "The Family Life Cycle" (E. Carter and M. McGoldrick, eds), Gardner, New York.
Kinston, W., Loader, P. and Stratford, J. (1979). Clinical Assessment of Family Interaction: a reliability study. *Journal of Family Therapy* **1,** 291-312.
Kinston, W. and Bentovim, A. (1981). Creating a Focus for Brief Marital or Family Therapy. *In* "Forms of Brief Therapy", (S. Budman, ed.), Guildford Press, New York.
Lieberman, S. (1979). Transgenerational Analysis: The Geneogram as a Technique in Family Therapy. *Journal of Family Therapy* **1,** 51-64.

Madanes, C. and Haley, J. (1977). Dimensions of Family Therapy. *Journal of Nervous and Mental Disease,* **165**, 88-98.

Madanes, C. (1980). The Prevention of Rehospitalization of Adolescents and Young Adults. *Family Process,* **19**, 179-191.

Miller, E. J. and Rice, A. K. (1967). "Systems of Organisation", Tavistock Publications, London.

Minuchin, S. (1972). Structural Family Therapy. *In* "American Handbook of Psychiatry Vol 3" (G. Caplan, ed.), Basic Books, New York.

Minuchin, S. (1974). "Families and Family Therapy", Tavistock Publications, London.

Northrop, F. (1958). Causation Determinism, and the 'Good'. *In* "Determinism and Freedom", (Hook, ed.), New York University Press, New York.

Palazzoli, M. S., Boscolo, L., Cecchin, G. and Prata, G. (1980). Hypothesising—Circularity—Neutrality: Three Guidelines for the Conductor of the Session. *Family Process* **19**, 3-11.

Paul, N. L. (1967). The Role of Mourning and Empathy in Conjoint Marital Therapy. *In* "Family Therapy and Disturbed Families". (G. Zuk and I. Boszormenyi-Nagy, eds), Science and Behaviour Books, Palo Alto, California.

Pribram (1971). "Languages of the Brain: Experimental Paradoxes and Principles in Neuropsychology", Prentice-Hall Inc., Englewood Cliffs, New Jersey.

Rosenberg, J. and Lindblad, M. (1978). Behaviour Therapy in a Family Context: Elective Mutism. *Family Process* **17**, 77-82.

Ryle, G. (1949). "The Concept of Mind", Hutchinson, London.

Santa-Barbara, J., Woodward, C. A., Levin, S., Goodman, J., Streiner, D. and Epstein, N. B. (1977). The McMaster Family Therapy Outcome Study: I. An Overview of Methods and Results (unpublished manuscript).

Sluzki, C. (1978). Marital Therapy from a Systems Theory Perspective. *In* "Marriage and Marital Therapy" (I. Paolino and S. McReady, eds), Brunner/Mazel, New York.

Street, E. and Treacher, A. (1980). Microtraining and Family Therapy Skills—Towards a Possible Synthesis. *Journal of Family Therapy* **2**, 243-257.

Treacher, A. and Street, E. (1980). Some Further Reflections on Family Therapists as Scapegoats—A Reply to Robin Skynner. *Journal of Family Therapy* **2**, 1-22.

Watzlawick, P., Bevin, J. H. and Jackson, D. D. (1969). "Pragmatics of Human Communication", Norton, New York.

Watzlawick, P., Weakland, J. and Fish, R. (1974). "Change", Norton, New York.

Wrate, R. (1980). The Development of Family Therapy in the U.K.: A Minority View? Newsletter for The Association of Family Therapy. Autumn: 14-18.

Zeeman, E. C. (1978). A Catastrophe Theory of Anorexia Nervosa in Hunger Models (Booth, ed.), Academic Press, London and New York.

Zinner, J. and Shapiro, R. (1972). Projective Indentification as a Mode of Perception and Behaviour in Families of Adolescents. *International Review of Psychoanalysis,* **43**, 523-530.

Zinner, J. and Shapiro, R. (1974). The Family Group as a Single Psychic Entity: Implications for Acting Out in Adolescence. *International Review of Psychoanalysis* **1**, 179-186.

Chapter 5

Dysfunction of Feeling: Experiential Life of the Family

J. Byng-Hall

I. INTRODUCTION

Emotion provides the thread and the colour in the tapestry of family life. The full range of every experience is felt most profoundly within family relationships: bliss, contentment, sexual ecstasy, loyalty, remorse, loneliness, frustration, boredom, fear, murderous rage and so on. Feelings provide the impetus for staying together and for leaving. They energize relationships. The experiential life of the family is generated by the interplay between feelings and interaction. This interplay is creative when each facilitates the other. A husband feeling affectionate reaches out to touch his wife on the arm. She feels warm and smiles back; seeing this exchange, the children settle to play together.

When an experience is, or has been intolerable, the family may defend itself by avoiding the situations in which either the affect or the action may arise. This may be called family defence. The parents in the family might have experienced intolerable rejections. The husband feeling affectionate but not sure how to express it, may tentatively put his hand out to touch his wife; she withdraws, perceiving the hesitancy in his approach as showing insincerity. The children, sensing the parents' vulnerability, start a fight which draws attention away from this marital interaction. The danger is past. The risk of putting intimacy to the test has been avoided. Every family needs some defence. However, dysfunction may follow when there is a serious disconnection between the feeling and the appropriate action; either the disconnected feelings such as depression, or the out of kilter action such as vandalism may then be experienced as the problem.

Experiential techniques in family therapy are aimed at helping family members experience feelings in their appropriate interpersonal context. Experiential family therapy can be described as a method or school of family therapy (Kemplar, 1973; Duhl et al., 1973), or it can be one set of techniques within a much wider repertoire, which is the author's practice. Madanes and Haley (1977) stated that a major characteristic of experiential techniques is the introduction of new experiences within the session. In order to choose an appropriate therapeutic strategy, it becomes imperative to understand the family system: to know what is dysfunctional and what is not. For this reason, the author will describe various experiential techniques in relation to his formulation of family conflict; he will not list techniques 'à la carte'. Readers who espouse a different conceptual framework must also undertake a similar linking exercise. Without this discipline a mish-mash can occur; indeed the therapist can find himself merely reinforcing the family defences by following their cues to avoid particular actions or feelings.

II. THE ROLE OF AFFECT IN HOMEOSTASIS

Homeostasis, the way the family system maintains itself and prevents any major changes, provides limits to excesses of experience by curbing certain interactions and feelings in the family. Hence it may be used in the service of defence.

A. Establishing Experiential Limits: Marking Boundaries

The limits are set down in the family script which each member of the family is taught. The homeostatic boundary is tested, often by adolescents and the consequences remembered and handed on by being recounted in family stories and legends (Byng-Hall, 1979). If a member of the family approaches the limit, warning will be given, if this does not check him sufficiently, threats of what will happen follow. Sometimes these threats are carried out. In this way, the imagination or phantasy life of the family and its memories play important roles in boundary-setting. The emotions of guilt, fear, anxiety and loyalty are all evoked.

A family drama may be enacted etching the family script on the family memory. In one particularly tragic example, the 14-year-old girl drowned following a rough and tumble with some boys on the jetty of a harbour. The parents labelled this as murder and their two sons were warned that the murderers were outside waiting for them as well. Needless to say the family became totally housebound; their boundary became the front door.

The drama can represent a replay of a scene from the family script. It emerged that the mother of the drowned girl had nearly been drowned herself by some boys when she was six. She warned her daughter never to go swimming, indeed she prevented her from learning to swim, and even identified the fatal jetty in her warnings. The drowned girl had acted a role in her mother's script. In the family sessions following this tragedy, it became clear that the murderousness within the family, especially between the father and mother was very intense. These dangerous impulses had been displaced and they were now united against the outside world. Murderers were now seen to lurk everywhere. In this instance, the replay of the script led to a fearful narrowing of the external boundary as the price for reinforcing limits within the family itself.

III. AFFECTIVE BALANCING

Most families, however, are able to adjust and extend their boundaries in the light of experience. One reason for a failure to adjust may be that an excessive preoccupation with one boundary is used to distract from or balance another diametrically opposite boundary. For instance, a fear of intimacy may be hidden by a preoccupation with loss. It is easy to imagine that someone who cannot bear to be left alone is automatically at ease in intimate situations. This is often not so. Conversely, someone who cannot tolerate being held down by anyone may appear to be free of anxiety about being alone. Again this is often not so. If a couple with these two styles get together, they may establish an interaction in which one is overtly clinging and the other overtly pulling away. The clinging spouse can then deny her fear of intimacy, and the independent spouse can deny his fear of loss. This results in what is known as a too close/too far system (Byng-Hall, 1980) in which the relationship is simultaneously too close for comfort and too distant to feel secure. This, however, is a potentially unstable bond. The more she clings, the more he tries to escape. This can escalate in what in cybernetics is known as mutual positive feedback. That is, each person's action produces a reaction which in turn encourages an increase in that action. The resulting escalation can break up the relationship.

The parents of the drowned girl had separated for a while, father demanding that his wife should stop holding him down. Byng-Hall (1980) goes on to describe how a third party, often a child who is ambivalent about the marriage may be given the role of distance-regulator or stabilizer to the marriage, holding them together if they become too far separated, and keeping them apart if too close. Parents, relieved that they do not have to take responsibility themselves for their tensions, unwittingly exploit their "go-between" child's role. The child's natural ambivalence, wanting to get each parent to herself, but also wanting them to stay together, becomes increasingly intolerable and he or she becomes a patient.

Before she drowned, the girl had been depressed. This brought father home again to help mother look after her. She was also sleeping with her father, with the collusion of her mother who on her part had one of the adolescent boys sleeping in her room. Thus the girl kept her father at home but also kept her mother out of his bed.

The drowning provided a classic, although tragic, example of how the symptom is frequently a compromise between opposing themes. She went dangerously far away from home, but in her physical contact with the boys on the jetty became too close, dramatically proving the danger of this contact through the final enactment. On examining the evidence, it was clear that she provoked the boys to throw her in. Her incestuous guilt was finally punished. Following the drowning her parents became united, in order to hunt down her killers. In her death she became an even more effective distance regulator.

This family is of course a highly dramatic and unusual one. They were used by the author because they vividly illustrate several aspects of his thesis. Byng-Hall and Whiffen (1981) describe how mood swings can be countered in the family. Depression in one member may for instance be balanced by elation in another. If the mood reaches certain thresholds, family anxiety may trigger a swing into the opposite mood. This anxiety might for instance be about suicide in depression or loss of control in manic episodes. It can be seen then that either excessive affect or extreme action provokes homeostatic controls.

IV. EXPERIENTIAL TECHNIQUES IN FAMILY THERAPY

A. Changing Boundaries: The Therapist as Boundary Marker

Who monitors boundaries? Often it appears to be one person concerned with limits. However, on careful examination the whole family is involved, and if the boundary keeper is away someone else takes over. Even the person who most frequently transgresses can take over this role, much to everyone's surprise. This can be vividly demonstrated when the therapist asks family members to change roles. One delinquent boy was asked to reverse roles with his father. He ticked his father off with such intense feeling that neither could doubt that his disapproval of delinquency was his own, not merely belonging to his father. The ultimate power to control the homeostasis, however, lies with the person who can change or reset the boundary: the boundary marker. If that person is in the family, then the potential for change and growth is present. If the boundary marker is in the extended family, or in the form of an internal unmourned dead family member, or disputed in the family, change can be more difficult.

The therapist can become a temporary boundary marker (Byng-Hall and Campbell, 1981). He can become an attachment figure (Bowlby, 1969) who can provide a safe base from which to explore. Winnicott (1971) discusses the role of *play* in which symbols are used to explore new dimensions to feelings and relationships. If exploring new forms of interaction in the presence of the family therapist shows them to be safe, these can then be added to the permitted family repertoire.

Winnicott (1971) contrasts play with playing *games* where rules are firmly established and then experienced within the intense action of the game. The authority of the therapist can be further enhanced by setting new rules for family interaction and then ensuring that the accompanying interaction occurs. He can then give blessing to new boundaries. This approach is found in structural family therapy described by Minuchin (1974), and discussed by Cooklin (Chapter 4). In this technique, family members are taken during the session beyond their normal homeostatic limits. The therapist has established a boundary beyond the family norm. The intensity required to break through the barrier may be provided either by the severity of the symptom, as in anorexia nervosa, or by the therapist's very active pushing of the family homeostasis. In both situations, the therapist's skill lies in keeping the family to the task and preventing them from defusing the tension or from using homeostatic mechanisms. Finally, sometimes quite suddenly, they are forced into quite a new way of relating.

In one family, the daughter had reached 6 stone, and her weight was dropping steadily. In an outpatient session, it emerged that father covertly undermined his wife's attempt to force their daughter to go to hospital if this was needed. The therapist discussed with the family the weight at which she might die. The tension rose. The girl shrieked at her mother that she would rather kill herself than go into hospital, adding that she would eat enough anyway. Mother countered this by pointing out that that was what she had said every time but nothing had changed. The therapist noticed father sitting back. He sided heavily with mother while making them decide when she should come into hospital. Both parents shouted at each other. Mother screamed "murderer" at father who suddenly switched into making a decision about how his daughter should come into hospital the next day both to stop her "suicide" and her self-starvation. The tension dropped, the daughter started to eat, and hospitalization was not needed. Here the rule forbidding any hostility between parents was changed, allowing them to set effective limits.

B.   Extending the Therapist's Own Emotional Thresholds

This work engages the therapist in emotional experiences which are often way beyond his own family norms. Empathy is the key to experiential change. The therapist cannot carry his clients beyond where he himself can journey, which through empathic process is only as far as his own emotional defensive cut-off point. When he retreats, they have to as well. To be helpful to a wide range of clients, the therapist's experiential journey has to be beyond not only his family but also the social norm. In analogy a surgeon who does not get over his normal revulsion to cutting flesh, will be of no help to his patients. The other side of the coin is that he has to be sensitive to his patients' pain, or he may indulge in surgical practices which increase rather than decrease suffering. Similarly, the therapist also needs to acknowledge and even value his own limits, but he should ponder their significance.

Family therapy training must provide the setting for trainee therapists to extend their emotional limits. This may be done through live supervision (Whiffen and Byng-Hall, 1981), in which the supervisor watches the therapist working and keeps him to the task, thus preventing him from using too many homeostatic manoeuvres of his own. Another approach is to work with the trainees' own families, either as it is represented internally, or by helping him (Bowen, 1972) to go beyond his normal lifelong routines within his family. McGoldrick (1981) describes very vividly how all three methods can be used together to reset trainee and family boundaries simultaneously. She selects what she calls trigger families, that is, those families which have similar difficulties to the trainee therapist (e.g. failure to mourn), and then works on that issue as it manifests in trainee and family. This can lead to a break through for both family and therapist. In these techniques, the trainer becomes the attachment figure, or potential boundary marker for the trainee therapist.

Personal therapy: either family, marital, group or individual can provide settings where experience is allowed to extend and blossom. Support groups consisting of colleagues can help to share the task of going beyond the norm. Sometimes personal reflection provides the means for change.

I was able to work with the grieving and despair in the drowned girl's family. I could stand the pain of standing by the dead girl's bed with the whole family weeping and wailing. I could even ask, "Where is she now?" to be told, "There sitting next to you on the bench"! When, however, the murderous rage started to emerge in full force, I and my co-worker became seen by the family as potential murderers. I was unable to tolerate the anxiety despite my co-worker's willingness to soldier on. I stopped the therapy. Instead I alerted the network to the danger; for instance, the housing department was warned that to carry out an eviction order might be very dangerous. There was plenty of evidence to support this thesis. For example, father threatened to use an axe on us if we came again, and he told us that he and his sons were going out to discover and hunt down the murderers.

I ponder whether my anxiety provided a link to reality and appropriate limit setting, or whether through my limits, this family missed a crucial opportunity to resolve their fundamental problem. My co-worker experienced the threats as having a histrionic quality. Probably she was right. My inability to contain the murderous fury that we were being asked to hold for the family was nevertheless making further work impossible, whatever the reality. I need to learn to defuse hostility before it reaches this level in the future. As I write this, I become aware of the need to examine whether my own fury coloured my view of the family. One hour later I have. It was helpful but uncomfortable. Reflection is one important method for re-experiencing and *preparing* to reset the point at which one has to cut out of experience: to "not know" or "not do". My boundary will not actually be changed until after the next encounter with an experience which resonates in type or intensity with the previous one. Reflection and action must complement each other; one must not be used to avoid the other.

Most experiential exercises can, and should if possible be entered into by the therapist himself beforehand. This usually involves working with a group of colleagues who will simulate or enact a family in therapy while the therapist tries out the technique. This gives the therapist the experience of doing it and also the participants an inside view of what it feels like. These groups are best led by an experienced teacher, or by someone who has used experiential techniques. Watching an experienced therapist treating a family with experiential techniques either on video-tape, through a one-way screen, or by sitting in the same room is also invaluable. If these opportunities are absolutely unavailable, it is possible to start afresh. I started using some techniques in this way.

Therapists and agencies have a duty to structure enough time for reflection and training. It is far easier to labour greatly, rushing from one task to another without experiencing the pain of growth. The cost of this defensive manoeuvre is diminishing efficiency, absenteeism, and a failure to confront society with the realities of employees' appropriate emotional boundaries. This perpetuates the syndrome of an overworked inefficient demoralized system, which is often merely a reflection of the client population. On the other hand, endless navel gazing can of course be equally task avoiding.

V. SPECIFIC EXPERIENTIAL TECHNIQUES

Some guidelines can now be given. But unlike a game with strict rules, the most alive experience for the therapist and the family is play, where their combined creativity will give a fresh and refreshing twist to each and every situation. Once a technique has become stereotyped and boring to the therapist, it is no longer experiential. The family only moves in an experiential event if the therapist is also on the move. Luckily like all play, there are an infinite number of possibilities allowing for something new to emerge each time. It is, however, probably best to weave the variations around some basic strategies. This provides more security for play. Occasionally a completely new approach can be tried, but devising some totally new game each time will be too confusing.

VI.   SPACE

A.   Altering the Balance Between Verbal and Non-Verbal Communication

The family system is often expressed in seating arrangements at home, or in the arrangement of the house. These become routine, and are frequently reflected in the way the family sits in the therapist's office. A therapist who wants to provoke minimal change in spatial experience (a quite legitimate strategy), will go to the family home and sit in the visitor's seat. There are a myriad ways of providing new spatial experiences.

The power of changing the usual spatial arrangement was discovered by Freud. He put his clients lying down with the therapist out of sight. Not surprisingly, he discovered that among other things, this evoked experiences related to childhood and to sleep: namely, dreams. It also removed much of the non-verbal interaction and placed what remains out of sight, thus freeing the patient's phantasy to roam. The family therapist, who wants to promote phantasy can ask family members to close their eyes, while he is asking them to imagine something. An example would be in asking for metaphorical images to represent each family member. Animal imagery can for instance reveal that a son perceives his father like a huge grizzly bear and himself as a mouse, something not easy to appreciate when visually that son is a hefty 27-year-old and the father an arthritic 60-year-old. Visual cues can also be removed by the therapist putting two members back to back and asking them to discuss something, thus forcing them to communicate accurately with words; a valuable communication exercise especially for families who are typically non-verbal.

The aim of the therapist may in contrast be to increase the use of all the modes of communication. In one family, whenever conflict emerged all members of the family would look away from each other, even shutting their eyes. When the next topic of disagreement emerged, he asked the parents to sort out the disagreement together, not to address everything to him. After several promptings they talked to each other, but looked at the therapist. He moved the patients' chairs to face each other, and looked away himself if they tried to catch his eye. Only then were they able to engage in discussion and to reach an agreement.

B.   Triangles: How to Discover a Dyad

In one family, everyone continuously monitored everyone else with their eyes. Whenever the therapist wanted the parents to work something out together, one of the children, often cued in by a parent, created a lively distraction. He put the children together to play on one side and placed his own chair so that it blocked the view between parents and children. This gave the whole family the experience of parents being able to resolve conflict without the children intervening. The alternative of seeing parents on their own does not provide this experience.

The one-way screen can also be used for this purpose. In one very enmeshed family, the 19-year-old girl monitored and dominated her parents' every action. They were "separated" but still living at home while father was awaiting new housing. The girl was sent to sit next door to watch the therapist and her parents through the screen. They discussed how to find father a flat. After a while, the therapist joined the daughter who was agitated about what would happen to each parent. He discussed her fears of her parents' possible suicides. The discrepancy between this nightmare vision and the middle aged couple sitting next door calmly discussing arrangements enabled the therapist to confront the daughter with what she was projecting onto them. After a while, the parents got bored, mother took out a book, curled up on the couch and started to read. The therapist and girl burst out laughing. On returning to the room, the parents exclaimed how much easier it had been without their daughter's "help". The issue of suicide was then discussed openly and realistically.

C.   Symbolic Use of Space

One couple asked to discuss their marriage. They talked endlessly about "mother-in-law" instead. After some time, the therapist said that he was going to play mother-in-law. He stood in between them, and insisted that they continue their discussion. He moved repeatedly to block their views. Getting exasperated, each in turn asked him to sit down but he merely responded by swivelling round to look at the other. When they consulted with each other and asked together he finally sat down. They laughed. They no longer brought the topic of mother-in-law up as a diversion, or if they did, the therapist merely made a move to get up and they stopped with a laugh. This family is described in detail in Byng-Hall (1980).

One couple, Sarah and George, presented with serious fights and wife-battering. They described an incident in which a row had escalated into violence after shouting at each other through a closed door. This had followed an earlier row in which George had threatened to leave, and then locked himself into the sitting room. When the door was finally opened, George punched Sarah, breaking her nose. The therapist tried to get the couple to discuss the episode. They were too agitated. The therapist decided to role play the door. He stood between them, told them that he would represent the door, and asked each to say exactly what was shouted.

Sarah (S): Let me in!

Therapist (T): [to George (G)] What did that make you feel?

G: I just wanted space to think.

T: What happened next?

S: I said, "Don't leave like this when you're upset".

T: How was it, George?

G: I felt hemmed in.

> [The therapist asked where the door was. It was the only exit from the sitting room and *en route* to the front door.]

T: You were hemmed in. Sarah, could you say it a different way?

S: I—er—I could have said, "Are you going to go away again?".

G: Yes, then I would have just explained.

T: You see, Sarah, "Are you going?" feels different to "Don't go", when you feel hemmed in.

T: [turns to G] How did you respond?

G: I said, "Leave me alone!"

T: But Sarah was afraid of being left, I expect she heard the "leaving" bit.

G: I could have given more detail.

T: Such as?

G: Leave me for a while.

T: Sarah, how would you have reacted?

S: It would have reassured me a bit.

T: But not enough?

G: Perhaps, "I need time to think".

S: It would have left me in doubt, I just needed reassurance that he wasn't leaving.

T: George, could you have given that promise at that time? Let's be realistic.

G: I just needed five minutes to think. I didn't know what to do, I locked the door because I knew she would be at me.

T: Does that give us a lead?

G: How do you mean?

For several minutes the therapist struggles to get George to think about what he might have said. Finally:

T: You remember the five minutes?

G: When? Oh yes, I suppose I could have said, "Just give me five minutes, I don't know what to do".

Sarah: [relaxing visibly] "I would have stopped pestering you then.

The therapist, still standing between them, says, "The problem is that you, George need space. But Sarah, you want to be close because you're afraid of desertion. Unfortunately the messages you each got through the door was (T advancing towards George, arms out in enclosing gesture) "I've trapped you"! So you respond by replying to Sarah, "Go away"! Therapist turns round and gives sudden dramatic pushing away gesture to Sarah. "The trouble is that makes you cling even tighter—and you George end up punching her to get her away—and so on." All three then sat down and discussed ways in which they could make simple clear factual statements to each other when a similar situation next occurred. They could then choose to de-escalate rather than escalate.

This example illustrates the problem of experiential work. It was unique to the situation, and will never be repeated in precisely the same form. It followed a failure to get the couple to confront each other. The therapist wanted to maintain the intensity of the situation. His involvement and proximity ensured this, but it also provided the safety each needed. The therapist took on the distance-regulation role in a very concrete way. One technique, that of asking the couple to re-enact what happened, suitable to some situations, was too frightening here. The way in which the exercise developed reflected his theoretical view of the too close/too far system found in this family (Byng-Hall, 1980) in which Sarah was too close for George and George too far away for Sarah. The therapist wanted to provide a way in which each could back off the impending escalation always incipient within that system.

It cannot be emphasized enough that experiential exercises are only as good as their aim. If the therapist has a hypothesis about what is wrong and what needs changing, he can improvise on the technique. The flourish in which the therapist enacted the reciprocal phantasy of envelopment/rejection only occurred to the therapist as the intervention unfolded; it was not foreseen. Indeed it would be dishonest to say that what he was going to do was planned. He only started with a rough idea. Another approach might have been to interpret George locking himself up as representing his wish to stay and to be controlled, and Sarah's combination of provocation and then staying to be punched after the door was unlocked as representing her wish to be punished. This would have clashed with the therapist's aim at that moment to interrupt the mutual positive feedback which was acting to escalate each other's behaviour. Later when the fighting had stopped, there were plenty of opportunities to make those inter-pretations.

VII. FAMILY SCULPTING, VIDEO-REPLAY AND MIME

A. Family Sculpting: Methods

Family sculpting in which family members are placed in spatial relation-ships symbolic of their relationships, has a specific methodology and can be learned and used in a more planned manner. The technique was developed at the Boston Family Institute (Duhl et al., 1973) and described by Simon (1972) and Walrond-Skinner (1976). Those interested should read further, and preferably explore the technique using colleagues before trying with a client family.

Dolls can be arranged in relationship to each other by a client to show his picture of his family. In family sculpting, the dolls are dispensed with and the actual family members used instead. Needless to say this provides a powerful and vivid picture of the family as well as a profound experience for each family member. For instance, one father who saw himself in the very bosom of his family, was profoundly shocked when placed by his son outside the door. He had to acknowledge how little time he spent at home and what this meant to his family.

Each member of the family is asked by the therapist to place family members, including himself in positions which represent the family as he sees them now. This is done with as little talking as possible, thus forcing the person to act in non-verbal mode. He should be asked to position limbs, body and head to represent each person's typical attitude, and to do this without thinking too much. It is not, however, a non-verbal technique. After the whole family tableau has been set up, each family member is then asked to share his or her experience of being placed in this position. This provides material for therapeutic work either at the time or later. After this procedure is finished, each person is asked to put the family in the positions that they would prefer, which is usually closer and more loving. This second stage provides some goals for therapy. It also provides an experience of how things could be improved, and of how good that might feel.

B. Sculpting: Facilitating the Process

This represents the bare bones of the technique, which like any art has to be practised. Some brief hints may be useful. First, how do you start? Standing up, the therapist may say,

> As a way of helping me to get to know your family, can you show me how you see yourselves? First can you stand up please? Joan (he walks over to her and holds her by the arm), can you put your family as you see them? Who is close to whom, put them in a position which shows their personality, what they are like [pause] each of you will have a turn to give me your picture of the family. Now Joan, whom do you want to start with?

Each therapist and each family has a different style. Many require further explanation, but the use of too many words at this point can block the exercise. The therapist has to model what he wants the family to do. Note how he stands up first and then goes to Joan to hold her arm just as she is going to be asked to mould or sculpt her family. The family usually looks perplexed and the therapist may say, "O.K. you've chosen Mum — now how do you see her, head up? angry? [miming this for the family] or down trodden? or sad?" [therapist drops his head in despair]. Humour obviously facilitates this process, and the family usually gets the point quickly, especially when the therapist is himself at ease with the process.

C. Sculpting: Indications for Use

When do you use it? Some therapists use sculpting routinely at some point to expose and explore relationships in the family. It can even be done within a few minutes of the beginning of the first session. The author prefers to use sculpting for specific reasons. When a family is very verbal, with many intellectual insights, a sculpt can cut right across this and reach the raw emotions underneath.

It may be done when the therapy has reached a standstill, or lost direction. In other families, where words are woefully inadequate, they can tell the therapist, and each other much more in a sculpt. It should be remembered that the technique is symbolic and aimed at generating understanding. This might interrupt problem-solving techniques. It should then be avoided or postponed if the therapist is struggling painfully to help the family solve a particular real-life problem. To sculpt at that time might be a defensive manoeuvre. Space should in that case be used to provide a better setting for resolving that problem, in which case structural family therapy techniques such as changing seating arrangements may be more appropriate.

D.   Sculpting: Case Example

In George and Sarah's family, a sculpt was used in the second session. George was being ultra-intellectual about his view of Sarah's problem. The therapist asked him to sculpt how he saw the family. He placed himself "out in front" leading the family with Sarah and their two children, Derek aged five and Florence aged three, five strides behind. He held his arm out sideways in front of Sarah. When asked how he would like it, he said that he wanted her more equal. The therapist explored how this change could happen. He could fall back. No!, he did not want that. For her to step forward meant that she had to drag the children with her or leave them behind. The therapist asked the family to rearrange itself. Two interesting things happened. Sarah struggled forward, the five-year-old son, Derek, tripped up and hurt himself as he was dragged forward, and simultaneously she banged her face into George's outstretched arm. She already had a black eye from a fight with George, and so the therapist worked on the idea that George's shield was also his punching arm which kept her down. George was able to share his fear that she might walk right past him and do better than him. As he was out of work, this fear was more vivid. Sarah was asked how she would like the family. She wanted to be level. How was this to be symbolized? She let go of Derek's hand, stepped forward and held George's shielding hand, thus lowering it. Derek lay on the floor crying. The therapist asked how they could manage this. Sarah let go three-year-old Florence's hand and picked up Derek. Now Florence was adrift. Eventually after much struggling with what to do, George picked Florence up and held her. In this exercise the rivalrous tensions between the parental subsystem, and mother/child subsystem were revealed. Sarah's need for George's help in parenting emerged as the problem and not Sarah's depression which George had initially been complaining about.

The difficulties in the dimension of closeness/distance can be revealed in sculpting. In one very tense family, the 8-year-old Timothy placed his mother in the middle of the room with his 5-year-old brother Jack hidden behind her and · his father in front of her. When asked what he felt about this, father said that this was probably to put his wife in between himself and Jack to stop him beating Jack.

This led to a discussion about how mother interfered with her husband's discipline. Jack's behaviour had for long been out of control and the therapist pointed out to mother how she needed the help of her husband's authority. In the meantime, Jack lay on the floor kicking and screaming. His mother tried to stop him, failed, and then picked him up and exasperated, carried him over to her husband. Jack continued playing up. The tension rose considerably and the therapist felt a very powerful pressure to intervene but managed to restrain himself. Finally father, who was furious, smacked Jack on the arm. Jack glanced at his mother who showed that she supported what his father had done, and he stopped misbehaving. For the next ten minutes Jack leaned up against his father in a relaxed manner. His disobedience started to decrease after this session.

This episode illustrates how the therapist should be able to allow the tension to rise until resolution occurs. If he had intervened, he would merely have become another part of the family homeostasis, proving that father was dangerous to Jack and reinforcing the need for mother to go on policing father's smacking, which incidentally also provided a distancing mechanism between the parents: they fought over his discipline.

E. Sculpting: Adding Video Play-Back

This theme required further work. Single therapeutic interventions rarely completely change a system, as so often implied in the literature. In a later session, Jack was disobedient again, rushing over to Timothy to grab his drawing. His parents failed to discipline him. The therapist stopped the action and suggested a replay or rerun of this episode. They returned to their original places, Jack again with gusto making to grab Timothy's drawings. Father held his arms. Jack continued to struggle. Mother looked on. Jack watched her to see her reactions. After his mother said, "Stop it," he quite suddenly relaxed and stopped misbehaviour. The therapist wanted them to have an experience of success and to see for themselves how they had achieved it. He replayed a videotape of this segment of the session four times to the family. Finally they were able to see for themselves how they had succeeded when acting as a team, which was when mother supported her husband. Video playback provides a particularly powerful experience. Members observe themselves in context. They see themselves contributing to something instead of merely responding to things being done to them.

F. Sculpting—Adding Intensity

Intensity can and should be an ingredient of experiential exercises. Sometimes, as with Jack, a child or another member of the family adds fuel to the situation. On occasions, however, it is the therapist who has to ensure this. In one family described in detail by Byng-Hall and Whiffen (1981), in a typical ending to the family sculpt, Zoe aged 9, the identified patient, when asked to put the family as she wanted them, placed them in a small entwined hugging circle. Everyone agreed that this was lovely and close. The therapists let this go on until the tension rose intolerably. Zoe then said, "We can't stay like this. Dad won't be able to go away to work and Mum—she couldn't go shopping". This led to laughter and disentangling of the group. The conflict between clinging and autonomy was experienced. Byng-Hall (1981) discusses other methods of adding intensity to sculpting.

G.   Sculpting with Miming Added

Mime can be added to sculpting. Instead of keeping their positions still, the participants can be asked to mime some daily event without words. This could for instance be father coming home from work and his family's response (or lack of it). The family can then be asked to repeat this many times until they are thoroughly fed up with it. The intensity and energy is now available for change. If they are asked to do it in a new way the next step can be taken. In the family discussed earlier in which the therapist role-played the mother-in-law (Byng-Hall, 1980), the couple was able to mime a symbolic interaction between themselves.

> Margaret stood still facing her husband. He came toward her, opened his arms when he got closer as if to hug her. Margaret then put her hands up to keep him at a slight distance. David dropped his hands to his side in a resigned way and walked away towards the door as if to leave, however, before reaching the door he turned back and walked towards Margaret once more. The whole cycle would then be repeated. After this cycle had been repeated about ten times, with an increasing sense of frustration, Dr B. asked the couple whether they would like to try the cycle in a way in which they would both prefer. After a series of tentative efforts, they finally managed to embrace each other. Dr B. stood by silently and allowed the tension to rise. Finally they had to pull away again from each other. The therapist asked what it was that they were afraid of in their intimate contact. They said that they did not know but that they would like some help with their sexual relationships which were unsatisfactory.

The last two families illustrate how important it is to allow tension to build up in the close apparently loving positions. In too close/too far families, intimacy is as problematical as loss. The family may recognize the need for work on it after this exercise.

VIII.   TIME: PAST AND FUTURE IN THE PRESENT

A.   Exploring Time Past

Changing the experience of time can alter current behaviour. Usually the therapist takes the family, or an individual in a family session, back in time to re-experience in the present what was avoided in the past. Time can be taken forward as well. In the Right family, each member presented with great vehemence, conviction and in detail how he or she had been badly done by by the rest. The therapist listened patiently to each story. He then said, with equal conviction because he felt it was true,

> You, Angela, are *absolutely* right—completely correct—you, Ben, are equally right . . . etc.

Saying this to each member of the family in turn.

> Isn't it marvellous! You have all worked out a beautiful system in which you can be so perfectly right — *every* one of you! It would be a shame to change that. Clearly in your family being right is more important than sorting out differences. I suggest you continue this for a number of years. In my experience with such a beautifully balanced dance, you could carry on without changing it except for minor interesting variations for the next ten, fifteen years — perhaps shorter — usually a great deal longer. Let's see, Gill, you would be thirty-one after 15 years at home proving that you are entirely RIGHT! Marvellous! You, Alex, would be 29, etc.

Techniques for looking backward in time have a number of aims:
(1) To mourn unmourned figures from the past, who because their image is kept alive usually haunt a current member of the family;
(2) To give an appropriate historical context for the current family problem. This can save the scapegoat from feeling that he has caused all the problems *de novo;*
(3) To join in a therapeutic alliance with the family;
(4) Cementing alliances between family members by increasing empathy;
(5) To understand the origin of their current predicament;
(6) To alter or re-edit family legends from the past, and in this way change the family rules which are carried from generation to generation through its mythology (Byng-Hall, 1979).

The central technique involved is to evoke memories of past experiences, but the mode of change is through altering the relationships in the session. In families the past is the present; the memories or stories are there now, in the session.

Family sculpting can be used for this purpose, members of the family, and/or the therapist can be asked to represent figures from the past. Parents can be represented as they were envisaged before children were born, and then each child in turn placed in relationship to the couple. This is a powerful way of evoking the experience of the change in the couple that children bring. Usually the couple are together, the first child placed between them or in front of mother. Father then has less attention. When more children arrive, there is often no space for them. The experience of the new child struggling for a place is balanced by the feeling of the first child being displaced. Deaths can be portrayed by asking the dead person to lie down, or to stand on a chair like a haunting ghost. The feelings evoked can be very strong.

This method of exploration of family history is often done with groups of professional colleagues, where one colleague with help of a consultant sculpts his own family of origin or a client family. As many as sixty or more people can be involved in sculpting the extended family. This technique is such an effective way of demonstrating family systems evolving over time that it is often used in teaching events, and it may be what is best remembered by the participant. Indeed some novice therapists then imagine sculpting to *be* family therapy.

The technique can be used with client families. One dead, unmourned child was represented by a cushion. In another family, an empty chair represented a dead grandfather. The therapists can be used to represent grandparents, which is like sculpting the family transference.

B. Family Trees: Genograms

The use of family trees or geneograms are described by Lieberman (1979). Some therapists do most of their family therapy around the family tree, in much the same way as the analyst uses the couch. Byng-Hall (1979) discusses when an exploration of history is necessary as opposed to when it is a tool that both therapist and family can choose to use because it suits them. Those families which misuse their history need help. Two misuses are common. First, those families that see the present merely replicating the past without any choice, and secondly those families that deny that the past has any relevance whatever. These misperceptions of the historical process appear to be opposites but are really similar. The families which deny the past usually unwittingly re-enact the past faithfully in the next generation, as do the families that know their family script and faithfully replicate it.

An appropriate historical context is one in which each family member has a sense that his background provides a tradition and impetus for what happens but that he is in charge of the form that his life takes. It is important for therapists to experience this sense of being supported by tradition while simultaneously holding one's own destiny in one's own hands. The best way of achieving this is for the trainee therapists to explore his own past family. This can be done unguided, although it is preferable to do this with the help of a supervisor, or of a colleague in which a co-counselling relationship can be established.

There are a number of ways in which the memory of past figures can be intensified in family therapy. When asking about figures in the family tree, it is valuable to ask for family legends or stories about them. These can then be written on the family tree. Sometimes children will draw faces in the squares or circles. These can be very informative. The therapist can ask for family photographs so that a visual image can be added. Getting out the old photos can also start the family reminiscing even before coming to the session.

C. Differentiating Images of the Past from Present Reality

Paul and Paul (1975 and personal communication) asks for a photograph of a client's parent of the same sex. He then enlarges it and videotapes the photograph. This makes the dead person seem alive. Furthermore he can, with his videotape mixer superimpose the living picture of the son on the photo of the father. This gives a quite extraordinary haunted look. The live picture can then be faded or the two images separated to either side of the screen. In this way he merges and then separates the two people in an attempt to disentangle the introject of the parent from the client's current self-image.

The equipment of course is not available to many therapists. Paul however uses audio cassettes of each session which the clients take home and play later. He also instructs them to play cassettes at the time of important anniversaries, to enable them not to unconsciously re-enact some unresolved drama. For instance, he may make a tape of a mourning experience that occurred in

October 1963 in October 1977. He will instruct the family or couple to listen to this tape every October, but especially October 1983.

There are many techniques for intensifying, and reliving a bereavement. Paul (1967) calls this operational mourning. The client, in the presence of the family, is asked to recount all the details of the death, of his or her reactions, of what happened and how were they told of the death. The therapist empathizes with the pain of the experience. In this way, the memory and the appropriate affect are both brought together, and re-experienced in a way in which proper mourning can be completed. The client can be asked to visit the grave. Williamson (1978) describes how he instructs the person to say the things which he would like to have said at the grave, in short to talk with the dead person. This can be recorded on a cassette recorder and brought back to the therapy session. This can provide a very powerful experience for the patient and therapist. Paul describes this when done by a man who visited Dachau where both his parents died. This tape provides an unforgettable experience for anyone who has heard it. Paul also uses material related to other families' mourning processes to play to new clients. This may be cassettes, videotapes or letters. They are chosen because they resonate with the client's problem. This stimulates the affect which has often been buried.

Past ceremonies which had disastrous effects can be rerun with a different outcome. In one family, the parents could be sexual together in private, but had to be stiff and formal in front of anyone else including their children. The children's developing sexual identity was threatened by this denial of adult sexuality. It emerged on exploration that neither parent had been properly given away at the wedding. Indeed both families had disapproved. The therapist asked whom on each side disapproved most: it was mother's father and father's grandfather. The therapist then conducted a marriage ritual in which he at first played the mother's father, in which he gave the bride away, and then as father's grandfather blessing the groom instead of disapproving. Following this the couple could be more demonstrative.

IX. SHARING THE THERAPIST'S EXPERIENCE WITH THE FAMILY

In all these techniques, the therapists obviously share the overall experience. This however can be taken further. Therapists can openly share their own pain, confusion or sense of madness with their clients. This can provide a profound linking experience. It is especially useful in rescuing the scapegoat. A girl was referred because she was crazy. Half way through the first session in which each parent bombarded the other, the client and the therapist with questions, demands and contradictory statements, the therapist felt he was going mad. He burst out: "If this goes on a moment longer I think I will go crazy, I feel smashed into a thousand pieces, if I can feel like this in half an hour I wonder what it is like at home twenty-four hours a day, seven days a week". For a while the family treated him as crazy, but his co-therapist rescued him and slowly over time, the focus shifted to what happened between people, not how crazy they were.

A direct interpretation of how the parents were driving their daughter crazy would have alienated the parents who would then have had to prove once and for all that she was crazy in her own right. Whitaker (1978) is a grand master in use of his own craziness and phantasy in entering the family system and then changing it. His approach is, "Hey! don't leave me out of this amazing world of yours, I want to enjoy it as well". He often uses a co-therapist to rescue him. The artistry with which he tunes into the family imagery is truly amazing. He uses the vitality of daily conflict but defuses the terrifying phantasies.

X. CONCLUSION

There are many more ways in which the therapists can introduce new experiences into the sessions, family drawings, tasks in the session such as "Arrange the furniture here to make a home," or "Draw your house as it is, then how you would like it," communication exercises, encounter techniques, Gestalt techniques etc. etc. Space in this chapter only allows a brief sketch of the techniques familiar to the author. The guiding principle is, *"Know what you are trying to achieve"*, then experiential techniques can add to the effectiveness of therapy. Doing exercises for their own sake confuses and defuses. The author uses experiential techniques at some time in most families varying from 5% to 15% of the treatment time, rarely more or less. Because they are fun to describe, they probably rate a higher percentage of his writing.

REFERENCES

Bowen, M. (1972). Towards the Differentiation of a Self in One's Own Family. *In* "Family Interaction", (J. L. Framo, ed.), Springer, New York.

Bowlby, J. (1969). "Attachment and Loss, Vol. I: Attachment", Hogarth, London.

Byng-Hall, J. (1979). Re-editing Family Mythology During Family Therapy. *Journal of Family Therapy* **1**, 103-116.

Byng-Hall, J. (1980). Symptom Bearer as Marital Distance Regulator: Clinical Implications. *Family Process* **19**, 355-365.

Byng-Hall, J. (1981). Therapeutic Confusion Produced by Too Close/Too Far Family Systems. *In* "Questions and Answers in the Practice of Family Therapy", (A. S. Gurman, ed.) Bruner/Mazel, New York.

Byng-Hall, J. and Campbell, D. (1981). Resolving Conflicts Arising Out Of Family Distance Regulation. *Journal of Family and Marital Therapy*.

Byng-Hall, J. and Whiffen, R. (1981). Family and Marital Therapy in Affective Disorders. *In* "Handbook of Affective Disorder", (E. S. Paykel, ed.), Churchill Livingston, Edinburgh.

Duhl, F., Kantor, D. and Duhl, B. (1973). Learning Space and Action in Family Therapy: A Primer of Sculpture. *in* "Techniques of Family Therapy: A Primer", (D. A. Bloch, ed.), Grune & Stratton, New York.

Kemplar, W. (1973). *Principles of Gestalt Family Therapy*. A. S. J. Nordahls Trykkeri, Oslo.

Lieberman, S. (1979). Transgenerational Analysis: The Geneogram as a Technique in Family Therapy. *Journal of Family Therapy*, **1**, 51-64.

Madanes, C. and Haley, J. Dimensions of Family Therapy. *Journal of Nervous and Mental Disease,* **165, 2,** 88-98, 1977.

McGoldrick, M. (1981). Through the Looking Glass: Supervision of a Trainees Trigger Family. *In* "Supervision in Family Therapy: Recent Advances", (R. Whiffen and J. Byng-Hall, eds), Academic Press, London and New York.

Minuchin, S. (1974). "Families and Family Therapy", Tavistock, London.

Paul, N. (1967). The Role of Mourning and Empathy in Conjoint Marital Therapy. *In* "Family Therapy and Disturbed Families". (G. Zuk and I. Boszormenyi-Nagy, eds), Science and Behaviour Books, Palo Alto, Calif.

Paul, N. L. and Paul, B. B. (1975). "A Marital Puzzle: Transgenerational Analysis in Marriage", Norton, New York.

Simon, R. M. (1972). Sculpting the Family. "Family Process", **11,** 49-58.

Walrond-Skinner, S. (1976). "Family Therapy: The Treatment of Natural Systems", Routledge & Kegan Paul, London and Boston.

Whiffen, R. and Byng-Hall, J. (1981). "Supervision of Family Therapy: Recent Advances", Academic Press, London and New York.

Whitaker, C. A. and Napier, A. Y. (1978). "The Family Crucible", Harper & Row, New York and London.

Williamson, D. S. (1978). New Life at the Graveyard: A Method of Therapy for Individuation from a Dead Former Parent. *Journal of Marriage and Family Counselling,* **1,** 93-101.

Winnicott, D. W. (1971). "Playing and Reality", Tavistock, London.

Chapter 6

Pattern and Intervention
Research Findings and the Development
of Family Therapy Theory

G. Gorell Barnes

I. RESEARCH AND CLINICAL WORK

A. Introduction

Researchers and clinicians in the field of human development and psychotherapy often find it hard to bridge the gap between their different kinds of enquiry. Researchers are concerned with the measurement of categories of things in a valid, reliable and replicable way while clinicians face each event as it comes to their clinical attention, responding to the unique qualities of the particular constellation that make up the person, family or problem before them. The two do not have to be mutually exclusive, but it is often difficult as a clinician to know where there are links with scientific thinking. How do the frameworks that people who class themselves as family therapists use, relate to other frameworks where change is studied. It seems important to me that the way in which people who work and teach in the family therapy field are seen to think, should not be characterized only by their difference from other more traditional psychotherapies, but by their areas of convergence with the approaches of different disciplines studying learning and change, and the research that has taken place within them.

According to the Oxford English Dictionary, a science consists of systematic and formulated knowledge. Hinde (1979) declares that,

> The study of interpersonal relationships and the treatment of these lacks as yet an overall and comprehensive measure for systematizing knowledge. Only when we can describe relationships, categorize their properties and classify them, can we transform our limited knowledge and experimental findings into generalizations with specific ranges of validity.

He covers many of the ways in which attempts are made to measure relationship, and charts some of the complexities of this process as it has been attempted within different disciplines.

131

B.   Relationship and Pattern

Following his approach, the variables involved are considered briefly here. Interpersonal relationships represent a coming together of individually specific constitutions and histories. There may be a shared social network and culture to provide common elements of history, or these also may be different and specific to each person involved. Many variables therefore affect the course of each relationship, and these are hard to differentiate within any given interaction. From the interactions developing between any two people over time, new and specific properties emerge, some of which can be observed, and others which are invisible and intangible. These can be classified as the behavioural and the emotional properties of relationship. While any pattern of interaction possesses subtle qualities that may be beyond the early reach of observational analysis, it is likely that most of the behavioural properties are accessible. What has preceded the interaction, as well as expectations of what will follow in the future, will inevitably influence its course.

C.   Measurement of Family Pattern

Measurement of such patterning is difficult.

> Given the possibilities for unidirectional, bidirectional, direct and indirect effects of
> individuals and for dyads, triads and quadrads, it is an understatement to say that a
> four element system is complex (Lewis and Feiring, 1978).

This is seen as a major obstacle to the transfer of scientific attention to units larger than the dyad and to the measurement of the notion of a system, a problem to which developmental psychologists have recently drawn attention.

In videotape recording of families, we have been greatly helped as clinicians in our observations of family pattern within sessions. For example, the child may produce a stomach pain or an obsessional symptom such as the need to wash his hands when tension in the room mounts. To measure this scientifically is possible but complex. Hartup (1978) has referred to "The tyranny of data"! In measuring family interaction, 30 minutes of observation yields 360 discrete, 5-second intervals on each participant in a dyadic situation. Scores may be generated on any number of different variables in each of these intervals. The reduction of such amounts of data is a task of staggering magnitude. Campbell (1981) recently described the Tavistock Clinic, Department for Children and Parents, Family Therapy Programme research team's 5-year struggle to do this, and the complexity of the task. Other British studies of family interaction related to measuring intervention include most notably the many studies from Great Ormond Street (Kinston *et al.*, 1979, Bentovim and Kinston, 1978 and Kinston *et al.*, 1981) in their developing work on Brief Focal intervention, have devised techniques for relating past and present patterns in a relatively economic way. In attempting to describe families more efficiently, they are looking at the reliability of clinical description and judgement of family atmosphere, based on the observation of behaviours and the inferred relationship of these to the underlying pattern of historical events.

D.   Variations in Traditional Family Pattern

Further variables would include the many family forms with which clinicians now meet. A "normal" model of family may still be a two-parent family with their own children, but it is equally likely to be two-parent families where one parent is not the original parent of the child, single parent families, multiparent families where divorce and remarriage has led to at least two sets of parents for the children, adoptive and foster families, and homosexual couples with children, who are seeking an outside viewpoint. It would not be possible to cover adequately in one model the variables these different family clusters add to the already rich complexity of a family life based on continuous development from birth.

E.   Intervention in Family Pattern

For clinicians, the relationship between interactions, relationships and the properties of these relationships; the overall family pattern and the symptoms of any one member may be said now to be the basis of family therapy. The debate about procedure in therapy, how to intervene in the organization of pattern over time, the family system, is related chiefly to whether intervention should be at the level of the interactions themselves as they occur in the room; or at the level of the pattern of their emergent properties, what the therapist understands about the meaning of the interactions he observes. Does he go for the more concrete or the less overtly definable aspects of relationship? Concern over what constitutes an effective therapeutic intervention and the proper role of the therapist, can be seen as centring here.

II.   FAMILY PATTERN AND INDIVIDUAL DEVELOPMENT

Pattern exists in the eye and mind of the observer, and the way he chooses to punctuate it will depend on his own context and vantage point. Nonetheless, to punctuate pattern at the boundary of the family can be said to be legitimate from the contextual viewpoint of professionals other than family therapists. While the boundary that focusses on the family, at the expense of school, of community or at a supra level, of region or cultural group, is an arbitrary boundary; research has shown that it can be an appropriate one for clinical rather than political attention. The family is a unit where leverage for change can be effectively applied both on behalf of individuals within the family, and in order to develop the family's capacity to act effectively on their environment. If the family can develop belief in their capacity for problem solving, they and the individuals they nurture, can develop the capacity for autonomous action, and can apply what has been learnt outside the family as well. Haley (1976) has pointed out that whatever radical position the therapist takes as citizen, his obligation as professional is to define the social unit that needs to change to solve the presenting problem of the client, and to act effectively on that.

The influence of family patterns on individuals has been shown in diverse ways, three of which are particularly relevant to professionals who work with and hope to influence families: pattern as it affects social change, pattern as it affects mental illness and antisocial behaviour; and pattern as it affects stress.

A.   Family Pattern and Social Change

Although the way in which the family mediates between its members and the world outside is so diverse that it cannot properly be noted here, the findings of Rutter and Madge (1976) in Cycles of Disadvantage are worth noting. They have shown that while familial continuities do exist especially with respect to intelligence, educational attainment, occupational status, psychiatric disorder and multi-problem families, there are also striking discontinuities. At least half of the children born into disadvantaged homes do not repeat the pattern in the next generation. Over half of all forms of disadvantage arise anew in each generation. Even where continuity is strongest, many individuals break out of the cycle. There is also a marked reduction in continuity over three generations. While the impact of professional intervention is not part of their study, it provides evidence that it is not misplaced to attempt intervention in family pattern.

B.   Family Pattern and Mental Illness

We know that family pattern has an effect on forms of illness and social behaviour. Four recent quite different research studies may serve as examples to demonstrate the effect of family interaction upon one of its members. The replication by Brown et al. (1972) of an earlier study predicting the relapse of discharged schizophrenic patients, found that the measure of "expressed emotion" and in particular the number of critical comments made by a key relative about a patient, was the most important predictor of relapse and a suitable target for intervention. Other components of expressed emotion were emotional "overinvolvement" and "hostility". Above 35 hours a week of face to face contact with a highly emotional relative greatly increased the chances of relapse. This was equally true whether the relative was a parent or a spouse. Falloon and his colleagues (Falloon et al., 1981) have recently reported some success using this as a target for sustained professional intervention. Kreitman (1970), studying 60 male patients receiving outpatient treatment for neurosis or personality disorder, found that while the patients' wives did not differ from the control group in terms of mental health early in marriage (i.e. it was not a question of assortative mating), at time of study they had higher ratings both of impaired health and of psychiatric illness. It was found that (as in Brown's study) more time was spent in face to face interaction with each other with no one else present than in the control group. It was hypothesized that in such a case of modelling process takes place in which the husband was the dominant model. In a third study, this time of behaviour problems among children in their own families, Patterson (1975) assessed the frequency with which hostile behaviour

from a child was followed by a response from another family member likely to
induce another hostile response, and found that such sequences were five times
more common than in the control group.

A fourth interesting and relevant study by Bugental (1971) analysed video-
taped parent/child communication in families containing a disturbed child of
8–12 years, referred by the school for chronic behaviour problems, and found
messages nearly six times as likely to contain conflict between the verbal, vocal
and visual channels than in the control group, (for example, a critical or
disapproving statement spoke in a positive or cooing voice). Conflict was found
between verbal content and facial expression and between verbal content and
tone of voice, but not between face and voice. Such behaviour is similar to that
described by Bateson and his colleagues (1956) and hypothesized as the basis of
the Double-bind theory of schizophrenia. While much of this theory is now
taken as an elegant model of transactional confusion and the basis for other kinds
of analysis of discrepancy in family message giving, rather than as relating
specifically to schizophrenic illness, the existence of such conflicting messages in
families with disturbed members is common knowledge among those who work
with them.

C. Family Pattern as it Affects Stress

It is clear that aspects of family patterns are also important under special circumstances of stress. In Brown and Harris's study of depression among women in
south London (1978) the presence of young children in women with a stressor
increased the risk of depression from 17% to 93%. On the positive side, the
presence of a good relationship with one parent does a lot to ameliorate the
effects of parental discord for the children (Rutter, 1971, 1979). Of the children
in discordant homes with a good relationship, only a quarter showed a conduct
disorder, compared with three quarters of those lacking such a relationship. A
similar finding is discussed by Lewis (1976) whose study of seriously disturbed,
midrange and optimal families will be referred to again. It is also discussed by
Skynner (Chapter 1, p.32).

III. MUTUAL INFLUENCE IN FAMILIES

In turning to the effects of pattern in families we can find much more open
acknowledgement of mutual influence than would have been the case 10 years
ago. Most interaction studies before that time were concerned with mothers and
infants. Studies have now demonstrated the impact which each member can have
on another. Fathers as well as mothers respond to their newborn infants, infants
respond to their fathers by 7 months at least (Lamb, 1976) and interactions with
elder siblings, cousins and other kin or network also play a crucial role in social
development and may be seen to compensate for parental deficiencies or parental
absence. Babies and children affect parents, both structurally and emotionally. It
is not a one way process (Lewis and Rosenblum, 1974). As Dunn (1977) states:

We can only understand the growth of a child's relationship with his parents if we see them as interacting pairs from the earliest days, and we can only understand the origin of later individual differences between children if we take real account of differences from birth.

A. Healthy Family Patterns and Stress

The development of the structure of the healthy family itself contains stresses. Dunn's work has also shown how ordinary family events like the arrival of new babies create stress in family patterns. She and her colleagues found that more than half of the forty 2- to 3-year-old children in their sample became more tearful after the birth of a sibling, nearly one half showed new toiletting problems, and a quarter developed sleeping difficulties. Mothers tended to play less with the first child and spent more time in prohibiting, confronting, and in negative verbal interactions (Dunn, 1980).

Intact families will vary in their response to life stresses such as illness, hospitalization or bereavement. Such stresses can impinge powerfully on the pattern of relationships. On discussing how stress affects later development, Rutter (1981) pointed out that stressful early events may operate on later action by altering sensitivity to stress or in modifying styles of coping which then protect from or predispose towards disorder in later life only in the presence of later stress events. All children are likely to encounter stress events as they grow up, and it is very unlikely that the long-term outcome will be determined by the number of such stresses. It is more probable that it will be determined by how the stress is dealt with at the time; and perhaps particularly on whether the result was successful adaptation or humiliating failure. We might cautiously say that helping families solve problems successfully in the present is also preventive against future stress, since if we help them achieve adaptive and flexible solutions to stress that simultaneously help diminish sense of failure and humiliation, they will have a larger repertoire of problem-solving behaviour to draw on (Aponte, 1978) and they will keep open a flexible, curious and hopeful attitude to the outside world and the dilemmas it imposes which Lewis et al. (1976) have shown is one of the characteristics of healthy and functional families.

B. Stress, Intervention and Future Development

While one could argue that helping a family cope better with current life events is a worthwhile aim in itself, those who observe families without the intention of intervening, suggest caution in attempting to alter interaction as a preventive measure (Dunn, 1976; Kagan, 1978; Stern, 1979). The predictions between particular influences in early childhood at any one time and the child's subsequent behaviour are not clear.

As Kagan puts it,

> Maturational forces direct the basic growth functions for many psychological systems that emerge during the first two years—reaction to discrepancy,

amplification of memory, object permanence and stranger and separation fears. Experience determines the age at which these competencies appear or disappear and during the period of their emergence the intensity and frequency of display.

Dunn and Bateson (1976) argue for the idea of equifinality as an important notion in development to which we should all attend. As children arrive at similar end-states by very different developmental routes, we should intervene in what may appear to be "abnormal" with caution. They remain scientifically cautious, however, about which aspects and parameters of relationship can be safely ignored. "We do not know which aspects of a relationship are essential, which can be transferred and which are harmful." Hard data on what family interactions are optimal is rare. Some of the epidemiological work in this country (Richman, 1978) would suggest fixed qualities in family relationship which correlate with persistent disturbance in young children, and the many studies from Professor Rutter and his colleagues give further guidelines on behaviours in families that correlate with psychiatric disturbance in older children (Rutter, 1975, 1978).

While on the one hand, behaviour relationships (and therefore patterns) in families are observed as changing over time, Dunn also comments that although behaviours themselves change, the core characteristics of a set towards behaviour is often maintained (Dunn, 1981, personal communication). This is a helpful and relevant observation for family therapists who have learnt to consider "classes" of behaviour with different discrete performances by family members at different times. It is relevant to the discussion on levels of change within systems which ends this chapter in which change is considered not only as it relates to particular interactions but to the class of interactions of which that behaviour is a member. The way in which change may be pushed through whole family systems in a change in subsystemic sequences, or alternatively the way in which a change in a class of behaviours will affect a series of interactions, links to this independent observation of family behaviours from a different source.

Dunn and Bateson (1976) also discuss the existence of stabilizing tendencies (homeostasis) both in given interactions and within the developing organism, pointing out that while not every aspect of mother/infant interaction matters, the absence or exaggerated presence of aspects of relationship may lead to divergence or disruption. Where stabilizing mechanisms do operate successfully, they will do so only as long as the divergence lies within certain limits. For example, small divergences such as a temporary loss of temper or withdrawal of attention may be unnoticed, moderate ones like brief or regulated absence adequately compensated, while larger ones such as severe physical abuse or sustained marital tension are disruptive. The consequences of any given degree of disruption will always depend on the impact of other variables in the system. The Tizard's work on children in different contexts both in institutions and in families, highlights this crucial variable of context (Tizard, 1975, 1977). Hinde states:

> We cannot yet tell without empirical data what aspects of a relationship are essential to its nature. Indeed the answer to that is liable to depend on circumstances.

In intervention with families, we would normally have to use clinical judgement about whether our job was to promote stabilizing tendencies within the family as in times of family crisis, or to increase divergent tendencies within a family who appeared to be stuck within a frame too narrow to enable them to cope with the problems confronting them, which might be necessary prior to better and healthier stabilization being achieved. This is unfortunately an area where clinicians must work with their own judgement in the absence of clear knowledge about what constitutes crucial aspects of relationship and therefore satisfactory resolution of crisis. As clinicians then we are still very much in the dark about what behaviours and what patterns exemplify the Winnicottean notion of "good enough parenting". Recent work (Rutter, 1978, 1979) has recently outlined further research evidence in this area.

C. The Circular Nature of Developmental Interaction

Within developmental psychology, the circular nature of developmental interaction has recently been emphasized by Lerner and Spanier (1978) whose dynamic interactional model proposes the view that individual development may only be adequately understood in the context of the constant reciprocal interaction between a changing person and his or her changing environment, and suggest that such continuous circularity implies a need for new statistical models and new conceptualizations of the variables analysed within these models.

> If development is conceptualized in a circular manner, then the utility of linear statistical models seems limited. In time the variables involved in this circularity may not be appropriately seen as antecedent to or consequences of one another. The components of development—the components of this circle, constantly change; as such, since each component is a source of every other, as each constantly changes, so do all others. Accordingly rather than the social universe being seen as constant and permanent and change being the to be explained phenomenon—this model assumes that change is the rule.

Such views chime closely with current thinking in family therapy where we are being urged to lose the constraints of Aristotelian logic and linear thinking (Dell, 1982). It seems important to remember at the same time a distinction between mutual influence and an awareness of the imbalance of power inherent in family relationships in the different developmental capacity to choose how action is taken upon the impact of that influence. The properties of a relationship involving a child are in a part a consequence of the child's immaturity, and whatever influences the child brings to bear in his interactions with parents, he does not have the same developmental capacity to choose how he acts (Stern, 1979, Brazelton and Main, 1974) in response to the influence of the other. To recognize the circularity of mutual influence is not to accord equality of power of thought, choice and action in terms of maturation, and it may be important to keep this in mind when the relationship between professional intervention and family distress is considered.

IV. MUTUAL INFLUENCE, PATTERN AND SYSTEM

In moving from interaction, relationship and pattern to considering how the relationship pattern is organized in time, we move into the concept of system. It is important to remember that a system is a model, an abstract representation of how a series of repeated events within a limited frame or boundary are construed. As an operational model for thinking about family functioning, it is worth asking in what ways thinking of families as systems have been useful. Systemic models of aspects of family functioning have been used in different ways in the theory building of family systems, and this difference is confusing, since the relationship properties described are not necessarily of the same category.

A. Physiological Systems Model

For example, in thinking about physiological response, a systems model has been used in describing the origins of reciprocity by Brazelton (1974); introducing the physiological component linking relationship pattern to individual organisms

> Just as there is an oscillating regulatory mechanism that maintains homeostasis in physiological parameters such as temperature control, cardiovascular mechanisms, the curve of activation, discharge and recovery seems to be necessary for attention in an ongoing interaction. The autonomic system is dominated by this kind of homeostatic mechanism. This homeostatic model which underlies all the physiological reactions of the enonate might also represent the immature organism's capacity to attend to messages in a communication system.

The relationship of system pattern to physiological response in the individual organism has been excellently documented in this country by Lask (1981) in relation to psychosomatic illness; chapter 23. It has been perhaps most strikingly demonstrated by Minuchin and his colleagues (1978) in a series of trials in which they measured the increase in free fatty acid response in diabetic children witnessing parental conflict from behind a one-way screen. This provided physiological evidence that psychosomatic diabetic children were not only more seriously affected by the family conflict than the control group of diabetic children, but that they took much longer to recover following termination of the witnessed parental row.

B. Systems Theory and Attachment Theory

Following John Bowlby's original work on attachment in systems theory in terms of set goals, goal correction and function leading to the maintenance of caregiver/infant proximity, Bischof (1975) modified Bowlby's systemic approach to include the move to maintenance of distance from the familiar and towards exploration of the stranger. Sroufe and Waters (1977) described attachment as an organizational construct which links individual difference to the requirements of development in different environmental situations.

"A behavioural system operating in terms of set goals mediated by feeling and in interaction with other behavioural systems." They make a distinction important to family therapy thinking, about behaviours and classes of behaviour; in response to criticism that specific behaviours as instances of attachment behaviour did not show stability over time. Sroufe and Waters argue:

> Since multiple behaviours can have similar meanings — prediction becomes not that behaviour A will be correlated with behaviour across situations of time but rather that behaviour A as members of class X will predict the occurrence of behaviours in class X in that same context.

(This is similar to Dunn's comment that while particular types of mother/child interactions show little consistency over time, patterns of interactions assessed as wholes do show consistency.)

This distinction between a single behaviour as an instance of a predictable class of behaviour is important as it relates to patterning in families, to the learning that is made possible or that is constrained by such patterns that I shall refer to later and to the class and level of interactional behaviours that are selected by the therapist for intervention.

Ainsworth (1977) emphasizes a distinction between attachment and the behavioural terms that mediate it; and views attachment as

> An inner organization of behavioural systems which not only controls the 'stable propensity' to seek proximity to an attachment figure but also is responsible for the distinctive quality of the organization of the specific attachment behaviours through which a given individual promotes proximity with a specific attachment figure.

Heard (1978) further extends the model to clinical work with the family system and suggests how it may be used both for assessment and as a design for therapeutic intervention (a) to evoke exploratory behaviour, and (b) to promote reappraisal of internal images of self and others in such a way that inner needs for attachment are assuaged by subsequent interactions.

C. A Systems Base for Family Intervention

Systems thinking derives principally from the concept of organization and reflects the proposition that events can usefully be represented in terms of their participation within a network of interrelated events. A system is usually defined as an organized arrangement of elements which comprise a network of inter-dependent and co-ordinated parts which function together as a unit. Open systems require energy and information from outside to accomplish their operations and to perform their functions. What the system can and cannot do at any particular place and time relates to its organization, the input it is receiving, and its environment. Systems can be categorized on a continuum from chaos (entropy) through rigidity toward greater flexibility with further evolution of coherent structure (negentropy). Families can be placed along this continuum in terms of their capacity to develop adaptive and flexible structures in response to feedback from the environment or from its members (Lewis *et al.*, 1976).

"Feedback" is characterized as either negative or deviation countering which maintains homeostasis, or as positive deviation amplifying operations, through which growth or creativity may occur within a system. The therapeutic intervention with families who are stuck rather than in dangerous crisis would be characterized by deviation amplification, i.e. the introduction of complexity to the system. In order to survive; complex, adaptive systems must be capable of positive feedback (i.e. move away from homeostasis) which leads to change in structure, organization and values as family or development requires it.

(1)   Health and Dysfunction in Family Patterns
Speer (1970) characterized a maximally viable social system (such as a healthy family) in the following way:
(a) Complex structural relationships in communication and interactions.
(b) A highly flexible organization capable of change from within the system.
(c) Highly autonomous components with a minimum of constraints in inter-component relationships.
(d) Considerable intrasystem determinism and causality of system and component behaviour.
(e) The ability to tolerate basic change in the system.
(f) The necessity of a constant flow of a wide range of information experience and input into the system.

The notion of health on families has been further discussed in the Timberlawn research comparing healthy and disturbed families (Lewis *et al.*, 1976) and is discussed at greater length by Skynner (in chapter 1). Two studies influencing their work are worth mention. The first by Westley and Epstein (1969) looked at a normal population of 96 college students, their health ratings by psychological testing, psychiatric interview and parental interview. Family variables distinguishing healthy from "sick" students included problem-solving capacity and style of communication, and the balance of autonomy and independence as important groups of variables. The factor critical to emotional health in children was the nature of the relationship between the parents. The second study by Mishler and Waxler reported a long-range interactional study comparing three groups of families, two with a schizophrenic child, with good and poor premorbid adjustment, and a control group with no child having a history of psychiatric hospitalization. These families were studied in a session involving the parents and a well sibling. Areas of differences among the groups were (1) expressiveness, (2) and (3) power: the strategy of attention and personal control, (4) disruptions in communications, (5) responsiveness. In the control families, there was more expressiveness, more positive affect and more flexibility. There were clear generation boundaries with a complexity of power although this was not exercised in a rigid or authoritarian manner. The parental coalition was strong, communications were more responsive and more disruptive than in families containing schizophrenics.

For the purposes of discussion in this chapter the Timberlawn findings about rigidity in dysfunctional family systems and flexibility in optimal family systems are worth noting. Speer (1970) in reviewing several interaction studies postulates a healthy family system as flexible with an absence of rigid constraints in system structure and a high capacity for tolerating autonomous behaviour.

The Timberlawn research interviewed 56 intact families with the oldest child in mid-adolescence in all, 31 of whom maintained 6-month records of family events, health and professional care. All families had no member in psychological or legal difficulty for the previous year. Each family was videotaped for initial data gathering, life history, medical history and interactional pattern. Four psychiatrists independently rated their health at a global rating and subsequently six families at either end of the health spectrum were interviewed for three hours. The findings bore out Speer's earlier work in confirming that physically healthy families with no evidence of psychiatric disorder and effective functioning were more open systems, tolerating a much greater receptivity and responsiveness to new ideas and capable of sustaining contradictory feelings and viewpoints without distress. There was greater respect for difference both within and outside the system boundary and greater individual autonomy. Severely dysfunctional families in contrast were run on a basis of "mutual intimidation"; responses had to be within narrow limits and little attention was paid to individual perception and feeling, or to any view that did not fit the family's "group think". Such families were reluctant to accept loss or change, and were held together by incongruous myths maintained by denial of reality and careful family teaching.

(2)   The Maintenance of Equilibrium
In family problem-solving, we are always confronted by some fear of change and a corresponding wish for "homeostasis" or the maintenance of things as they are. At one end of a continuum, this shows the wish for a healthy and necessary stability, as Hinde, Dunn and others have indicated; representing the family's capacity to survive over time and make healthy developmental adaptations as a social group with some cognitive congruence (common sets of meanings, values and expectations). At the other end of a continuum, however, it can become the stagnation of structure and the denial of individuation and growth, as the Timberlawn research demonstrates. What is important for the therapist is to be able to identify where the wish for homeostasis will actively prevent the intake of new information which might lead to new solutions because the family fear change more than they experience discomfort. If he does not take this fear into account, he will fail to understand why all that he does is useless. The family "tends to maintain itself" around some ideal (or idealized) point of equilibrium which has been established as the system evolves. As a system containing young children is a growth system and therefore on the move and not static, there is a continuous process of new input into it and thus a tendency for it to be pushed away from equilibrium. Over time, the family may develop certain repetitive enduring techniques or patterns of interaction for maintaining its equilibrium when confronted by stress and this pattern may be activated appropriately and inappropriately whether stress is internal or external, acute or chronic, trivial or gross. It is always essential to keep in mind the positive function of these homeostatic mechanisms for maintaining the "togetherness" of a family as they see it.

(3) How Does Systems Theory Help Family Problem Solving?
Haley, one of the original contributors to systems thinking in families, attacked systems theory recently (1978) as unhelpful to therapy.

> The merit of systems theory is that it makes things predictable—the demerit is that it focuses on how a family remains the same—it is not a theory of change but a theory of stability. In that it is not functional for a therapy based on restructuring and reorganizing the family hierarchy and in that it takes away individual responsibility from participants it is not a theory of how to proceed in therapy.

In the long-term debate on family systems theory which Haley is referring to, there was much emphasis from groups studying families with schizophrenic members and a cybernetic model based on closed-system feedback prevailed. The focus was on how the family homeostasis which involved the regular rehospitalization of the patient, was maintained. Many psychotherapists reacted against the way in which individuals in the debate appeared to be considered only as if they were components of a system. Focus was on input–output aspects of the system as reflected in family transactional processes which were assumed to be governed by rules based on maintaining homeostatic principles which both constrain and regulate intrasystemic behaviour. Discussion was largely based on clinical observations and studies of disturbed behaviour, and arose in reaction to clinical despair at the ineffectiveness of individual psychoanalytic psychotherapy for this patient group. Don Jackson said:

> It is significant in the development of family theory that it was the observation of homeostatic mechanisms in the families of psychiatric patients that led to hypothesis of family as homeostatic and eventually specifically as a rule governed system.

Dell (1981) has recently attacked the model as limited and inaccurate, and Hoffman (1981), in reviewing the development of systems thinking in the USA, confirms that this debate largely ignored biological systems with their innate capacity for adaptation and change. This may have been because much of the initial theory was based on work with young adults who were not seen to be developing further; and interest was drawn rather to communication patterns within the family. While a more cautious attitude to the cybernetic model has always prevailed in this country largely because of the development of family therapy within a health service and social service framework with a strong commitment to families with young children, the awareness the cybernetic model has offered of the transmission of rules in families at both verbal and non-verbal levels, and the potential for disturbance, held by conflict in the class of response required by a message, has been invaluable. It has inexorably led to the question of how the therapist himself should class his own messages and give information to a family, who themselves always communicate at conflicting levels. It has therefore led to the development of strategy and paradox in the interventions of the therapist (Watzlawick *et al.*, 1967, 1976, 1978; Cade, 1979; Papp, 1980; Madanes, 1981).

In family work with dependent and developing beings, we always need to keep the push for growth and development in mind as a force for creating change and not take too much upon ourselves. Alongside Winnicott, it may be useful to ask, "How little need we do?" As Dunn *et al.* (1976) have indicated, there is evidence that despite difficulties along the way, the same end-point may be reached by many different routes. Our job is often to provide the information that is missing to help the biological family system find its own solution to the dilemma in hand rather than offer a premature or forced solution ourselves. Bateson has defined information as "a difference that makes a difference", and it is exactly this that the professional, an outsider to the system, can provide if he can develop a clear hypothesis and understanding of what "information" is required. Clearly what will make a difference is the million dollar question; and it is around this question of what will make an effective difference to the family's capacity to find solutions to their problems that the wide variety of techniques incorporated into family therapy can be seen to be arrayed.

V. LEARNING AND PATTERN

A. Learning, Storage and Habit

Before some aspects of work with "rules to change the rules within a system" are examined, some interrelated issues such as learning (coding and classification), habit, i.e. what happens to previous learning and past experience, and how it is stored; will be touched on briefly. How experience is stored must be the source of most controversies in therapeutic attempts to help people retrieve; re-work undo and find new solutions. What follows is an arbitrary *aide memoire* to thinking afresh about changing pattern, not an academic review of different therapeutic positions.

Foss (1973) in talking about human learning, reminds us of the mechanisms brought into play by interaction between the main thinking and the object thought about, coding, classification and the learning of patterns.

> When an object is categorized this normally carries with it a process of coding; one remembers seeing 'an angry boy-bad girl', there is much less load on memory as compared with having to remember the total original percept . . . but this advantage is gained at the expense of discarding much of the original information.

The object is remembered not for its unique qualities but as more like a "typical instance" of the category in which it has been placed. Accuracy of learning and remembering, will therefore depend on the number of categories and sub-categories available to the learner which will vary from person to person. The remembering of pattern will depend on two main processes: (1) autonomous processes including possible tendencies to simplicity, symmetry and fading, (2) categorizing, in which the pattern will be recalled as a typical instance of the category in which it has been put.

Bateson (1967), relating to this learning of pattern as it is reprojected in art, discusses habit formation also; as the sinking of knowledge down to less conscious and more archaic levels. The unconscious contains not only the painful matters which consciousness prefers not to inspect; but also many matters which are so familiar that we do not need to inspect them. Habit therefore is a major economy of conscious thought. (p.114)

Both Foss and Bateson from very different positions point to the price paid in the problem of information storage. The "sinking" process, though economical, may lead to over simplification in how we think.

B.   Habit and New Learning

This may affect our capacity to think afresh since new learning depends on prior learning. Everything that we learn depends on constraints and predispositions resulting from what we are, and what we learn must include the rules that we learn and most of the rules determining what we learn (Seligman and Hager, 1972; Hinde and Stevenson Hinde, 1973). How learning takes place and how it is constrained remains a matter of differing opinion, but the debate is highly relevant to professionals intervening in a pattern since it relates to what can be undone, reworked and thought about in a new way.

What a person experiences depends both on physiological arousal and on how he labels the situation (Singer and Schachter, 1962). In interpersonal relations, emotions will therefore be affected by how an individual has learnt to label his feelings in the light of the circumstances he knows to have produced them. What he believes about what has happened, the meaning he ascribes to events, will determine the map he makes of his own experience and the way he subsequently describes them. Experience is stored as symbols which can be manipulated. In spite of selectivity and distortion there will be for him a relationship between what happened and what he describes about past interactions with others. His behaviour and emotions will also be influenced by his anticipations about the future. As Hinde (1979) points out, in spite of debate about precisely how it happens, A's perceptions of people, situations and behaviour, his feelings about them, his thoughts about his feeling, and his thoughts about the behaviour and feelings of others are coded, and stored in symbolic form (Hebb, 1969; Ash, 1959) which results in dynamically organized and interrelated schemata of cognitive representations of individuals and events (Neisser, 1976).

C.   Pattern and Anticipation

Neisser (1976) argues for models of learning based on anticipatory schemata which operate at ranging levels of generality. Perceptions and cognition are transactions with the world that do not merely inform but transform the perceiver, in turn modifying the anticipatory schemata. This affects the capacity to receive certain information where there is no prior anticipatory set "information can be picked up only if there is a developing format ready to accept it" (p.55) and has implications for what the therapist does in problem solving. How he prepares the ground for his own intervention and uses the material of the session as governing information for his input into the system will be crucial for its effectiveness.

D. Variety in Learning

Bindra (1978) has proposed a model of learning which is particularly relevant to the relationship between the influence of pattern and the choice of action. The essence of his proposal on how individuals learn relates to the variety in the conditions of learning and the resulting train of appropriate responses that any individual therefore has at his command in response to subsequent eliciting stimuli (a view widely held by ethologists). Where there has been a narrow learning pattern in the first place ("a limited range of environmental spatio-temporal patterning"), subsequent eliciting stimuli will therefore call forth limited rather than various and flexible chains of "overlapping" or "nesting" of association. By stimuli he includes a full range of human experience sights, sounds, smells, temperatures, crying children, sexual attraction and fear of attack.

Bindra says that the mechanism by which these "pexgos" (presently excited genetic organizations with spatially and temporally ordered activation) are translated into a particular act is not known; and that the problem of a meaningful relation between perception and action is a fundamental one for psychology. He suggests however that since a response is a fresh construction in the brain every time it occurs, we must look to the lack of variation in relationship between space and time in learning pattern to account for stereotypes of response. Where these are altered, flexibility in response can occur within the same context (what Bateson has called Learning II). He proposes therefore that the analysis of behaviour should rest not on relating specified responses to specified stimuli but on the study of the total range of actions that occur in relation to the larger patterning of areas of behaviour in space and time. He suggests that the alternation of uniformity and stability in the patterning within which individuals happened to be confined may well relieve them of possible continuing stereotypy and persistence in their own responses. The implications of this for therapy and intervention in pattern will be apparent. Similar ideas arising from different sources will be found in this book in chapters by Cooklin and Byng-Hall. From a different perspective again P. P. G. Bateson and Hinde have both emphasized the importance of diversity in learning. P. P. G. Bateson's experimental chicks developed flexibility in attaining the goals they were seeking in response to the introduction of slight novelty to the usual pattern of experiment, learning rules to change their own rules. Although the problem of identifying where the starting rules are stored "which may be largely cellular and beyond analysis at the level of the whole", remains; Bateson and Hinde both argue that presented with diversity of interactions in learning, young animals can be equipped with "rules for changing the rules" and thus develop greater functional reciprocity with their environment (Bateson and Hinde, 1976). This complements Fentress (1976) who states that in the early stages of activation of learning, a wide variety of behaviours may be facilitated, but as the organization increases, the dynamic structure becomes more tightly constrained, requires less information (i.e. becomes habitual), is less easily interrupted by external factors, produces more linked sequences and blocks behaviour patterns associated with other systems.

E.   Links to Learning in Families

Thus from different fields, we see strands of argument and thinking developing which are similar and relevant to systemic thinking within the field of family therapy. Pattern constrains the capacity of the individual interactions, affects their process and also affects the capacity to receive new information. Information will only be effective if attention is paid to context and to the pressure of time and space that if uninterrupted will constrain an increase in flexibility of responses whether in thought, feeling or action.

F.   Therapy as Punctuation of Pattern

All therapy may be seen as offering a new punctuation, arbitrarily imposed by the therapeutic persuasion of the professional, to the experience of the patient. The provision of a different experience to that to which the patient is habituated, and which is causing pain is the beginning of providing a basis for new learning.

A note from Piaget links the role of active participation in learning to the kind of punctuation family therapists tend to offer to the experience of the family. He distinguishes objective knowledge, i.e. something someone else knows about; knowledge that is integrated, calling these states *vs* transformations. He describes how children learn better when they act on the thing to be learned, rather than when they simply watch and remember the relations between mental images and operations.

> The image is useful to the operation, to the extent that it symbolizes an exact knowledge of states, but it is by no means sufficient to furnish an understanding of transformations. To understand those it is necessary to act on the object and to co-ordinate the modifications into a coherent whole. (Piaget, 1977)

Piaget emphasizes that the process of learning is a process of dialectic. Something is learnt through the process of application to the issue in hand in which the properties of the object are freed from the subjective illusions of the person who is learning. Piaget has called this process "decentration". It links to the question of how a problem for a family can be distanced enough for them to do some work on it. Minuchin (1967) made this an important feature of his early work with families talking about the movement from interpersonal blame within the family to a joint focus on the third thing "the thing to be learned" which the family could work at together. The Milan group provide a similar experience using the different method of neutrality and circularity in the way they ask questions, punctuating the experience of the family in new objective ways (Palazzoli *et al.*, 1980).

VI.   PROBLEM-SOLVING APPROACH TO WORK WITH FAMILIES

A.   What Stops Them Doing the Work Themselves

Problem-solving therapy as a whole may be seen as focussed on the issue of what stops a family from learning or from decentring themselves enough from the problems they have in hand to do the work necessary to finding solutions to them. A number of reasons have been discussed, including the lack of prior information and experience on which to draw, a difficulty in assigning appropriate common meanings to the nature of the problem, and an inability to hold onto and store problem-solving solutions, so that they can be experienced and used again.

Another potential set of situations which the various examples of how we may be said to learn point to, is where the nature of the problem activates unpleasant stimuli or "anticipatory schemata" or associative chains that are maladaptive to problem solving because prior experience has led to learning of the wrong kind. Incorrect or oversimplified classification may be the least difficult area to remedy since other classifications may involve physiological responses of a complex order. There may be conflict between one set of responses which might be appropriate and another set at a different level which prohibit the employment of the first. McFarland (1973) has described one of the constraints on learning as "ambivalence in the environment". A family may not solve a problem when the solution may be seen as creating another problem at another possibly more threatening level. Inability to solve problems in family life is both very common and sometimes very complex since it may involve pattern development over generations as well as over time within one generation. Because families live together and interact in close physical proximity, they arouse one another very deeply often in the course of minor events. What appears to an outsider to be a small problem such as a baby crying, a child refusing to eat his potatoes, or a child's wish to go out with friends rather than joining a family outing, can become the ingredients of major problem development within families; invested with dramatic feeling which relates to the context in which these events were originally experienced, coded, categorized and stored (Gorell Barnes, 1978).

Families may also try to solve problems from their store of available ideas, not seeing how their persistent attempts to solve the problem have become the problem. The system they have arrived at for attempting solutions has itself become the problem. For example, we observed the family of a child with a hysterical dislocation of the shoulder which could be performed at will (but not backwards apparently) and which had involved eight years of attendance at different hospitals. The family was observed to be in disagreement and concerned over a number of other issues. The function of the symptom appeared to be to unite the family in concern over her as a distraction from their quarrelling and anxiety. It also brought the secondary gain of personal concern and attention. However, the problem solution, to attend hospitals, as a way of uniting the family in common concern, had become the problem, since the maintenance of the problem-solving pattern in one area of family life or at one level depended on the symptom continuing in another.

In thinking about families so far we have considered interactions, relationships, and the properties and pattern of relationship, defining a family system as being the organization of this pattern over time. Over time, pattern itself influences the properties of a relationship and therefore interaction and individual perception. Many social psychology experiments have shown the effect of group influence on individual perception (Asch, 1952).

In families, permission to perceive in a certain way, the coding and categorizing of information, are framed by relationship properties expressed through interactions, and by the pattern that governs these.

B.   How Family Therapists Work with Rules

Rules constrain the system and control the way information is allowed in and processed; therapists struggle with these rules in their work with families and the different ways in which they address rules is the subject matter of this book. Here I would like to highlight briefly three styles of intervention as they relate to rule change in family systems.

Therapists aim to change rules so that new perception and action are permitted at different levels within the dysfunctional system the family show. However, there are different levels of rule that a professional might address themselves to in problem solving: a ground-level rule or rules at higher levels. The choice for the therapist will be which of these he will choose for his point of intervention in trying to change a pattern that has become habitual and simplified, distorted or rigid in ways that are causing distress.

Strategies for change in family systems, defined loosely here as structural, strategic and systemic work, can be seen as linked to Bateson's definition of the levels of learning of which organisms or systems are capable (Bateson, 1972). Ground rule problem-solving work, which includes structural work and some strategic work, is linked to a second level of learning, "Learning II"; in which through therapy, members of a family are moved beyond the stimulus response patterns of the first level of learning "Learning I", and learn to act on, not simply respond to their environment, in a variety of ways (generalized learning). The therapy aims to repunctuate their sequences of experience and have them enact a variety of new responses within the same context. The members of the family learn to learn, and learn also how to transfer their learning to new situations.

The structural model developed by Minuchin (1967, 1974) and Haley (1976) has taken on a more strategic layout in the more recently published work of Papp (1980) and Madanes (1981) which include the use of different kinds of strategy. It continues to address itself to change through the minutiae of interaction in subsystem sequences. These sequences which are in operation from the moment a child is born into a family generate certain characteristics of the individual self which are in turn fed back into the system. Bateson calls these "the cybernetic circularities of the self and the external world" and Stern (1979), watching mother–infant play sequences, Minuchin talking about therapy with families call these "the dance". While the family context remains unchanged, certain behaviours, whether verbal or non-verbal will be read within the family as cues (or markers) for sets of perceptions and expectations to be brought into play, which stimulate further predictable patterns of behaviour. Such expectations as have been discussed are normally determined without conscious thought, having sunk to the level of habit, and the original reasons for categorizing them in a particular way being forgotten. They are not therefore available for discussion and repetition. The way that the truth as the family see it, is punctuated, can neither be true nor false in any absolute sense since there is no such thing as objective truth, but it represents the powerful view of reality within which the dysfunctional behaviour or "problem" is embedded (Bateson, 1964).

The therapist using a problem-solving approach working at ground rules, would aim to repunctuate sequences between family members so that experience in these sequences takes on different meanings. Ground rules carry the detail of family structure. Many transactions obeying the same meta rule will therefore be equivalent to one another (isomorphic) so that challenging one transaction is not an isolated event. Such work requires energy, focus, precision and intensity, through repeated repunctuation of sequences that have rigidified thereby decreasing options for problem solving. By encouraging family members to enact new ways of talking and behaviour with one another, the repeated challenge of isomorphic ground-rule transactions will amount to a challenge to a meta rule. Minuchin (1981) recently summarized this elegantly: "Intervention can focus on therapeutically relevant transactions and bring seemingly disconnected events into a single organic meaning increasing family members' experience of the single constraining rule".

Strategic work also requires the therapist to work with the behaviours of the family, at ground-rule level to achieve change, but always aimed more specifically at reframing the meaning of the behaviours. Watzlawick defines reframing as "an alteration in the conceptual or emotional setting or viewpoint in relation to which a situation is experienced" and the placing of the experience in "another frame which fits the facts of the same concrete situation equally well or even better thereby changing its entire meaning". Systemic work (Palazzoli *et al.*, 1980; Campbell, this book chapter 17) does not require the therapist to act upon the behaviours of the family to achieve a change in the system, but thinks more specifically about a change in the context of *meaning* ("reframing") within which the behaviours take place, a change at the meta level or second order rule level (or higher), "the highest possible rule". Notions of step by step learning through action are not part of the session, which is used for circular questioning to gather information about the way the family view the problem and the way they view each other's perceptions. The therapist addresses himself to change in the system as a whole, usually in relation to a wider system that frames the meaning of what he sees before him with a message or a task at the end of the session. The mechanism of change resides with the therapist's positive connotation of all the behaviours in the family. The family is thrown into a bind by being asked to accept the positive qualities of the symptom they ambivalently ask to be rid of. This is one way of distinguishing different styles of strategic work since the system is always seen in the context of the family system unlike the work of Watzlawick and his colleagues (1967, 1976) where the unit of behaviour treated may be taken right outside the context of family. This way of working, the systemic approach in which the whole system is addressed through the highest rule that the therapist can understand (Campbell, 1981) can be related to Bateson's "Learning III". In this third level of learning, a system may theoretically be freed from the bondage created through adherence to its own processes of second-level learning by perceiving the issue of choice in a new way. The paradoxical rules that have developed as a result of the conflicting attribution of meaning over time that govern current perceptions and therefore learning, are transformed by the introduction of new meaning and experience that affects each member of the family simultaneously. An overall change in pattern is aimed at, not just a change in part of the pattern.

C.   A Hierarchy in Rule Change?

Haley, originally a pioneer in the use of strategic therapy (1963) suggests more recently a simpler way of viewing an approach to rule change or problem solving in families. He suggests

> A way to view the approach is to give directives doing directly to the goals, such as getting the child to school. For those families in which a direct approach is not effective, the therapist falls back on an alternative plan that will motivate the family toward the goal. If that alternative is not effective, fall back on yet another alternative plan.

The more clear the problem and the goal of the therapy, the easier it is to design directives.

Papp (1980) distinguishes a hierarchy in approach to rule change in systems between interventions that are compliance based or direct, referring to the therapist's expectation that the family will comply with them, and those that take the resistance of the family to change into account. Compliance-based interventions: advice, explanations, and suggestions; include promoting open communication, coaching parents on how to control children, redistributing jobs and privileges among family members, establishing disciplinary rules, regulating privacy, and providing information that the family members lack. *Defiance-based or paradoxical directives* are those that depend for success on the family's defying the therapist's instructions or following them to the point of absurdity and recoiling. They rely on (1) defining the symptom as benignly motivated to preserve family stability; (2) prescribing the symptom-producing cycle of interaction; and (3) *restraining* the family whenever they show signs of changing. Another way of thinking about her work would be to suggest that its success lies not only in the wish of the family to defy the therapist, but in the way the tasks prescribed show them the logical absurdities within their own rule system.

Within family therapy and within this book, the issue of how to address the rules relating to the problem behaviour with the system, is obviously a key one. It has resulted in many innovations in therapeutic technique devised to invite or organize the family into reframing their dilemma in such a way that therapeutic work is done on a number of levels. The size of the system that is seen by the therapist and the time scale required for the change in the system to be worked through, are among elements contributing to diversity of approach and technique used. The flexibility or rigidity of the family system relating to their degree of dysfunction is likely to be another. The development of different ways of addressing changes in family rule structure will be the subject of further discussion (Gorell Barnes, 1981; Gorell Barnes *et al.*, submitted, 1981).

This chapter, reviewing some aspects of work in related disciplines that are of relevance to family therapists, places their ideas in a different context. It has been shown that family therapy has potential and exciting links with other areas of system thought about pattern and change. The links with ethology and with the constraints on learning imposed by context, seems particularly exciting and relevant; relating as they do to different ideas about rule change, the possibilities of flexibility and rigidity in learning within a system, and the introduction of new information into dysfunctional family systems. It is important that we continue to jump context and consider the relevance to our work of what colleagues in other fields are thinking and doing, so that as a group of clinical practitioners, we continue to be an informed open and flexible system ourselves.

REFERENCES

Aponte, H. (1978). The anatomy of a therapist. "Full Length Case Studies", (P. Papp, ed.), Gardner Press, London and New York.

Asch, S. E. (1952). "Social Psychology", Prentice Hall, New York.

Asch, S. E. (1959). A perspective on social psychology. *In* "Psychology, a Study of Science", (S. Koch, ed.), Vol. 3, McGraw Hill, New York.

Bateson, G. (1964). The logical level of learning and communication. *Reprinted in* "Steps to an Ecology of Mind", (1973). pp. 250-279, Paladin, St. Albans.

Bateson, G., Jackson, D., Haley, J. and Weakland, J. (1956). Towards a theory of schizophrenia/Behavioural Science. *Reprinted in* "Steps to an Ecology of Mind", (1973). pp. 173-198, Paladin, St. Albans.

Bateson, P. P. G. and Hinde, R. (eds) (1976). "Growing Points in Ethology", Cambridge University Press, Cambridge.

Bateson, P. P. G. and Klopper, P. H. (1978). "Perspectives in Ethology 3: Social Behaviour", Plenum, New York.

Bentovim, A. and Kinston, W. (1978). Brief focal therapy when the child is the referred patient. *Journal of Child Psychology and Psychiatry*, **19**, 1-12.

Bindra, D. (1978). How adaptive behaviour is produced: a perceptual-motivational alternative to response—reinforcement. *The Behavioural and Brain Sciences*, **1**, 41-91.

Bischof, M. (1975). A systems approach towards the functional connections of attachment and fear. *Child Development*, **46**, 801-817.

Bowlby, J. (1973). "Attachment and Loss. Vol. I. Attachment", Hogarth Press, London.

Brazelton, T., Koslowski, B. and Main, M. (1974). The origins of reciprocity. "The Effect of the Infant on its Caregiver", (M. Lewis and L. Rosenblum, eds), Wiley, New York.

Brown, G. W., Birley, J. L. T. and Wing, J. K. (1972). Influence of family life on the course of schizophrenic disorders: A replication. *British Journal of Psychiatry*, **121**, 241-258.

Brown, G. W., Bhrolcrain, M. and Harris, T. (1975). Social class and psychiatric disturbance among women in an urban population. *Sociology*, **9**, 225-254.

Bugental, L., Love, L. E., Kaswan, J. W. and April, L. (1971). Verbal and non-verbal conflict in parental messages to normal and disturbed children. *Journal of Abnormal Psychology*, **77**, 6-10.

Cade, B. (1979). The use of paradox in therapy. *In* "Family and Marital Psychology: A Critical Approach", (S. Walrond-Skinner, ed.), Routledge & Kegan Paul, London.

Dell, P. (1982). Beyond homeostasis: Towards a concept of coherence. *Family Process,* **21**, 21-41.

Dunn, J. (1976). How far do early differences in mother-child relations affect later development. "Growing Points in Ethology", (P. P. G. Bateson and R. Hinde, eds), Cambridge University Press, Cambridge.

Dunn, J. (1977). Patterns of early interactions: Continuities and consequences. "Studies in Mother Infant Interaction", (H. R. Schaffer, ed.), Academic Press, London and New York.

Dunn, J. F. and Kendrick, C. (1980). The arrival of a sibling: changes in patterns of interaction between mother and first born child. *Journal of Child Psychology and Psychiatry,* **22**, 1-19.

Falloon, I., Liberman, R., Lillie, F. and Vaughn, C. (1981). Family therapy of schizophrenics with high rate of relapse. *Family Process,* **20**, 2, 211-222.

Fentress, J. (1976). Dynamic Boundaries of Patterned Behaviour. *In* "Reaction and self organization" *In* "Growing Points in Ethology", (P. P. G. Bateson and R. A. Hinde, eds), Cambridge University Press.

Foss, B. M. (1973). Human and Animal Learning: A Caution. *In* "Constraints on Learning", (R. Hinde and J. Hinde-Stevenson, eds), Academic Press, London and New York.

Gorell Barnes, G. (1978). Infant needs and angry responses. A look at violence in the family. "Family and Marital Psychotherapy: A Critical Approach", (S. Walrond-Skinner, ed.), Routledge & Kegan Paul, London.

Gorell Barnes, G. (1981). Family bits and pieces: Framing a workable reality. "Developments in Family Therapy", (S. Walrond-Skinner, ed.), Routledge & Kegan Paul, London.

Gorell Barnes, G. (1981). A Difference that makes a difference (1). *Journal of Family Therapy* (in press).

Gorell Barnes, G., Jones, E. and de Carteret, J. (1981). A Difference that makes a difference (2). *Journal of Family Therapy* (in press).

Haley, J. (1973). "Strategies of Psychotherapy", Grune & Stratton, New York.

Haley, J. (1976). *Problem Solving Therapy.* Harper Colophon Books.

Hartup, W. W. (1978). Perspectives on child and family interaction. "Child Influences on Family and Marital Interaction. A Life Span Perspective", (R. Lerner and G. Spainer, eds), Academic Press, London and New York.

Heard, D. H. (1978). From object relations to attachment theory. A basis for family therapy. *British Journal of Medical Psychology,* **51**, 67-76.

Hinde, R. and Stevenson-Hinde, J. (eds). (1973). "Constraints on Learning", Academic Press, London and New York.

Hinde, R. (1978). *Towards Understanding Relationships.* Academic Press, London and New York.

Hinde, R. (1981). Family influences. "Scientific Foundations of Developmental Psychiatry", (M. Rutter, ed.), Heinemann, London.

Hoffman, L. (1981). "Foundations of Family Therapy", Basic Books, New York.

Kagan, J. (1978). Continuity and stage in human development. "Perspectives in Ethology, Vol. 3", (P. P. G. Bateson and P. H. Klopter, eds), Plenum Press, New York.

Kinston, W., Loader, P. and Stratford, J. (1979). Clinical assessment and family interaction: a reliability study. *Journal of Family Therapy,* **1**, 291-312.

Kreitman, M., Collins, M. J., Nelson, B. and Troop, J. (1970). Neurosis and marital interaction, I. Personality and symptoms, II. Time-sharing and social activity. *British Journal of Psychiatry,* **117**, 33-46.

Lamb, M. (ed.). (1976). "The Role of the Father in Child Development", John Wiley & Sons, New York.

Lewis, J. M., Beaven, R., Gossett, J. T. and Phillips, V. A. (1976). "No Single Thread: Psychological Health in Family Systems", Brunner/Mazel, New York.

Lewis, M. and Feiring, C. (1978). The child's social world. "Child Influences of Marital and Family Interaction: A Life Span", (R. Lesner and G. Spanier, eds), Academic Press, London and New York.

Loader, P., Kinston, W. and Stratford, J. (1980). Is there a psychosomatogenic family. *Journal of Family Therapy*, **2**, 311-326.

McAuley, R. and McAuley, P. (1977). *Child Behaviour Problems: An Empirical Approach to Management*. Macmillan, London.

McFarland, B. J. (1973). Stimulus relevance and homeostasis. *In* "Constraints on Learning", (R. A. Hinde and J. Stevenson-Hinde, eds), Academic Press, London and New York.

Madanes, C. (1981). "Strategic Family Therapy", Jossey Bass, San Francisco.

Minuchin, S. (1976). *Families and Family Therapy*. Tavistock, London.

Minuchin, S. and Fishman, C. (1981). *Family Therapy Techniques*. Harvard University Press, Cambridge, Mass.

Minuchin, S., Rosman, B. and Baker, L. (1978). "Psychosomatic Families", Harvard University Press, Cambridge, Mass.

Mishler, E. and Waxler, M. (1968). "Interaction in Families", Wiley, London.

Neisser, U. (1976). "Cognition and Reality: Principles and Implications of Cognitive Psychology", Freeman, San Francisco.

Palazzoli, M. S., Boscolo, L., Cecchin, G. and Prata, G. (1978). Paradox and Counter Paradox: A New Model in the Therapy of the Family in Schizophrenic Transaction. Jason Aronson, London and New York.

Palazzoli, M. S., Boscolo, L., Cecchin, G. and Prata, G. (1980). Hypothesizing-circularity-neutrality: Three guidelines for the Conduction of the Session. *Family Process*, **19**, 1.

Papp, P. (1980). The Greek chorus and other techniques of family therapy. *Family Process*, **19**, 1, 45-58.

Patterson, G. R. (1975). A three stage functional analysis for children's coercive behaviour. "New Developments in Behavioural Research Theory, Methods and Applications", (B. C. Etzel, J. M. Le Blanc and D. M. Baer, eds), Elbaum & Hilldale, New Jersey.

Piaget, J. (1977). The role of action in the development of thinking. "Knowledge & Development Vol. 1. Advances in Research and Theory", (W. F. Overton and J. M. Gallagher, eds), Plenum Press, New York.

Rutter, M. (1978). Early sources of security and competence. *Human Growth and Development"*, (J. S. Brunner and A. Gorton, eds), Oxford University Press, London.

Rutter, M. (1979). Protective factors in children's responses to stress and disadvantage. *Primary Prevention of Psychopathology, Vol. 3. Social Competence in Children.* (M. W. Kent and J. E. Rolf, eds), University Press of New England, Hanover, N.H.

Rutter, M. (1981). Stress, Coping and Development: Some Issues and Some Questions. Emmanuel Miller Lecture. Association of Child Psychology and Psychiatry. To be published in the Journal of Child Psychology and Psychiatry.

Rutter, M. and Madge, M. (1976). *Cycles of Disadvantage: A Review of Research.* Heinemann, London.

Schachter, S. and Singer, J. E. (1962). Cognitive, social and physiological determinants of emotional state. *Psychological Review*, **69**, 379-399.

Speer, D. C. (1970). Family systems: Morphostasis and morphogenesis or is homeostasis enough. "Family Process", **9**, 259-278.

Sroufe, L. A. and Waters, E. (1977). Attachment as an organizational construct. *Child Development*, **48**, 1184-1199.

Tizard, B. (1977). "The adoption of children from institutions after infancy", Association of British Adoption and Fostering Agencies, London.

Tizard, B. (1977). "Adoption: a Second Chance", Open Books, New York.

Tizard, J. (1975). "Varieties of Residential Experience", Routledge & Kegan Paul, London.

Urban, H. (1978). Development from a systems perspective. "Life Span Development and Behaviour, Vol. 1", (P. Baltes, ed.), Academic Press, London and New York.

Watzlawick, P. (1978). "The Language of Change: Elements of Therapeutic Communication", Basic Books, New York.

Watzlawick, P., Bevin, J. and Jackson, D. (1967). "Pragmatics of Human Communication: A Study of Interactional Patterns, Pathologies & Paradoxes", W. W. Norton & Co., New York.

Watzlawick, P., Weakland, J. and Fisch, R. (1974). "Change: Principles of Problem Formation and Problem Resolution", W. W. Norton & Co., New York.

—— Part III ——

Practical Issues

Chapter 7

Preparation of the Referral Network
The Professional and the Family

W. Roberts

I. INTRODUCTION

Whether or not a family attends an initial therapeutic session will depend, to a large extent, upon the preparation of all concerned: that is, the family, the therapist, the referring agent and any other relevant professional workers. "Good enough" preparation should aim at ensuring that the expectations of all those involved in the process are understood and clarified, for although family therapy is a treatment method increasingly available in a variety of settings, it is still common practice for one member of the family to be selected as the nominated patient at the time that the referral is made. It is therefore essential that the therapist is alert to the many factors which are present during the referral process, and is able to take appropriate steps to ensure that progress is as smooth as possible.

II. ROUTES TO THE FAMILY THERAPIST

A. Varieties of Agencies

The avenues through which a family finds its way to an agency are numerous, and although some families are sufficiently motivated to refer themselves, it is still true to say that the majority come into therapy because one or more of its members is showing signs of stress, the symptoms being as varied as the agencies or settings in which they may be presented. The majority of helping agencies, whether voluntary or part of the Welfare State, tend to focus on a particular age group, symptom or disability, and although many are increasingly aware of the implications of a stress signal being transmitted by a family member, may still make the referral for family therapy in such a way that the family themselves are unaware that they are expected to be involved in the assessment of diagnostic procedure.

With the growth of understanding that individual disturbance may represent family dysfunction, it is not only "helping agencies" who make referrals to family therapists. Schools are often alert to the difficulties of the children they are teaching: disruptive behaviour, academic underfunctioning and inability to make relationships are, among others, commonplace foci for referral. In some areas, the Police Juvenile Bureau have been known to make appropriate referrals, and in one instance, at least, the leader of a holiday play group, concerned about an aggressive boy, sought the help of a family therapy practitioner.

B. Historical Factors

If one considers not only the variations among helping agencies, but also the orientation and training of their workers, it is hardly surprising that difficulties occur, and it is relevant to look back in history if we are to understand this. During the era of the Welfare State, services have developed piecemeal, and were generally planned as a response to individual needs as they were recognized. Thus, Infant and Child Welfare Clinics were set up to cater for the under-fives age group, while on the other hand, services for the physically and mentally handicapped, span all age groups but tend to have symptom-orientated boundaries. Education Welfare Officers deal with problems affecting school children and their families, with the availability of the school psychologist, should need arise. The blind, the deaf, the spastics and others had voluntary organizations available to them to meet those needs not met by the State services, and because of the multiplicity and overlap of services, choice often depended upon the attitude of the sufferer or of the referrer. Despite the fact that in recent years, steps have been taken to change and improve this situation, (Seebohm, 1968) many families continue to be attached to more than one agency, and are seldom recognized as a "whole".

C. Multiple Agency Allegiances

Examples of this are numerous, and the following situation is not as uncommon as one would hope it might be:

The M family consisted of Father, Mother and two daughters, Betty and Mary. At the time that they came to the notice of a family therapist, Father was the nominated patient and was referred by his general practitioner for depression, leading to outbursts of violence. When the family were seen together, it came to light that Mother and daughters had another general practitioner who had referred Betty to a hospital child psychiatric department because of her mother's complaints about her difficult behaviour. This was the first time that Father learned of this situation, and he was understandably angry at being kept in the dark. Before the family were seen for the second session, it was learned that Betty had also been seen by the school psychologist to whom the teacher had turned for help when she became so disruptive as to be threatened with suspension. The school psychologist had spoken to Mother, but she said nothing about the steps she herself had taken and agreed to be referred to the educational authorities child guidance clinic, although when she failed two offered appointments there, the referral was not pursued. This clinic overlooked communicating with the General Practitioner. Meanwhile, the child psychiatric department had seen Mother and Betty and offered individual treatment to both. Soon afterwards, the Education Welfare Officer called to investigate Betty's prolonged absence from school, having been asked to do so by her colleague who was attached to the School. (The reason for two E.W.O.'s being involved was because, at that time, the Department was organized in such a way that officers worked on a "patch" system, and in some instances the family home and the school were not in the same "patch".)

Later it was learned that Mary, who was 3 years of age, was known to a health visitor who was keeping closely in touch because of her concern about Mary's slow development. This concern had recently led her to alert the Social Services Department for she suspected ill-treatment, and wondered whether Mary should be entered on the "non-accidental injury" register. A social worker from that department had just begun to visit the home. This is not an unusual situation, horrific though it may appear when actually faced in this way. We need to ask ourselves what it is that makes it difficult to change or avoid such situations; for once they have occurred, changed they must be if family work is to be successfully undertaken, and what needs to change is the failure of agencies to effectively communicate with each other.

III. BLOCKS IN REFERRAL TO AGENCIES PROVIDING FAMILY THERAPY

Let us instead try and understand what it is that creates such situations in order that, as family therapists, we may be sensitive to the roles of other workers, the policy and structure of their agencies, and so aim at improving collaboration between us.

A. Problems within the Referral Agency

Agency workers, and in this context I include school teachers, G.P.'s, health visitors and all who are likely to make referrals to a family therapist, have generally received a training which befits them for the kind of work they are expected to undertake within the confines of the orientation of their profession, and although many such workers are increasingly aware of the dynamics of family relationships, they may be restricted both by training and agency boundaries to working with an individual family member. Referral to a family therapist, even where this is relevant, depends upon a number of factors: (Menzies, 1970; Hornby, 1979).

(1) The level of trust which has developed between their agency and others,

(2) The degree of responsibility they feel they carry (an example of this being the local authority social worker who has statutory responsibility for a family member)

(3) The desire to practise family therapy themselves, even although this is not considered to be a function of the agency

(4) The fear of having undermined or undervalued the work they have so far done and

(5) The often unrecognized fear of losing a patient or client.

There are no doubt many more, not so easily recognizable but equally important factors. Perhaps we all need, from time to time, to stop and remind ourselves of the motivation which led us to choose our particular area of work and to realize that this, and our investment in training, may lead to serious ambivalence in referring on to others those with whom we have become involved.

B.   Problems within the Family Therapy Agency

At the other end of the spectrum, family therapists may need to guard against inappropriate referrals which come their way because of the despair (or anger) of a worker. In this respect, unless the situation is appropriately handled and the reasons for refusal to accept such a referral fully understood, the resultant unexpressed feelings of frustration between referrer and family therapist may lead to a failure of future referrals being made. I cannot emphasize too often, the importance of "good enough" communication between family therapists and referrers if treatment is to be effectively carried out. Ambivalence between workers is not limited to inter-agency relationships. In some instances the agency offering family therapy as only one method of treatment, may have failed to resolve differences of opinion between its own workers about when it is appropriate to see and assess the whole family. In this case, they run the risk of the ambivalence and/or disagreement being conveyed to referrers in such a way that the referrers are confused about what is being offered and failure results (Skynner, 1976).

C.   Recognizing Mixed Messages

The manner in which referrers convey ambivalence is varied. In one clinic in which I worked for many years, we became familiar with the referrer who informed us that although he was convinced that the problem was linked with relationships in the family, he was equally convinced that either one or other of the parents would not attend, or that the parents would not agree to any of the children other than the nominated patient being present. Experience taught us to enquire whether the referrer had actually *seen* both parents together to discuss the question of attendance, or to clarify the relevance of the siblings being included. It was not unusual to learn that this had not happened, and that information given by one parent about another had been accepted as valid: "my husband leaves all the matters about the children to me", being a commonplace statement. We were remiss in not recognizing that we had failed to ensure the referrer understood the relevance of the presence of both parents and all the children at a therapeutic session.

Many family therapists will no doubt recall their own past misgivings in this respect, for I well remember the long and difficult discussions that took place in the clinic where I first practised family therapy; the doubts and fears that we aired then are still being expressed by those to whom the treatment of a whole family is a new and unknown procedure.

D. Who Gets Referred and Why

I think it is appropriate to state that currently, the majority of families who find their way to a family therapist do so because one or other of their children is seen as the nominated patient; although it is also true to say that other agencies such as Marriage Guidance Counsellors, Probation Officers and others, are increasingly recognizing that difficulties presented by adult family members may be symptomatic of family disequilibrium.

Where a child is the presenting problem, it is frequently because of the concern of somebody outside of the family. It therefore becomes essential for that person (school teacher, playgroup leader, or whoever it is who is feeling concern) to inform the parents. In so doing, it is not unusual for tentative ideas to be floated as to the possible cause of the difficulties; the general public are being increasingly alerted to the symptoms of psychological stress by the media, and in addition, the training of all of those in the helping professions includes some aspects of this.

Unfortunately the ideas floated may not only be inaccurate, but may tend to apportion blame: "it's because his father is always out", "his mother makes a favourite of his sister", and so on. Alternatively, the cause may be attributed to a particular event: "he's been like it ever since we came to live in this neighbourhood". Such discussion between informer and parent, or between professionals as a result of a conversation with a parent, provides the opportunity for thoughts and ideas to be aired in such a way that the focus is on one family member who is seen as the patient or client; as the "victim" to be helped or rescued, or as the family member with a vulnerable personality unable to deal with stress. These perceptions, and there are innumerable variations, must affect the attitude and expectations of all concerned.

IV. PRINCIPLES TO ENSURE SUCCESSFUL REFERRAL

From the foregoing, it is evident that if family work is to be successfully undertaken, as much care and attention must be given to those who, although outside the family, are part of its system (the supra-system), as to the family itself when it is eventually seen. I hope it is also evident that "good enough" preparation needs to allow time and opportunity for misunderstandings and differences of opinion to be aired, and if possible, resolved.

A. Have the Whole Family been Prepared for Invitation?

With the foregoing in mind, what steps can a family therapist take to ensure that a referral is more likely to achieve a successful outcome? In the first instance, unless the referrer is well known (or the referral document makes clear), it will be necessary to enquire whether or not the whole family have been prepared for an invitation. It is not sufficient to be told that one parent was seen alone and promised to *try* and get the other to attend. I discovered how risky this can be when a head teacher volunteered this information and I later learned that a wife's message to her husband had been: "The Head says you will have to go to the clinic because she thinks you are too soft with Tom"! On other occasions there was no message to father. Referrers sometimes need convincing (preferably by personal contact, but at least by a telephone conversation) of the importance of the need for them to speak directly with important family members. Their reluctance to do so can not only be attributed to the demands on their time, for in discussing this topic with numerous referrers, they have aired their anxieties about meeting with parents who are known to disagree, their fear being that they will not be able to handle the disagreement.

In such a situation, it may be helpful to arrange to join in the discussion about a referral, thus not only providing a model of how such a meeting may be conducted, but also allowing the opportunity for the parents, or whichever family members are attending, to meet an agency member and have answered some of their questions. Some agencies provide a form which referrers are asked to complete and which requests relevant information. A referral form with which I am familiar asks the following questions in addition to name, address, occupation or school, name and profession of referrer:

(1) Other agencies involved (e.g. Social Services, school psychologist, health visitor, voluntary bodies) etc.
(2) Are these agencies aware of this referral?
(3) Reason for referral (the problems and their duration) as seen by the referrer.
(4) *The problems and their duration.*
    (a) As seen by the patient(s), adult or child
    (b) As seen by the family
(5) What is the attitude to referral of the patient(s) or the family?

The form then requests specific details of all family members, i.e. name, age, occupation or school, etc. plus details of other important family members or friends (if known). An additional paragraph states: "Before completing this form (which is provided as a framework for your comments), please discuss the reasons for referral with the patient(s) or family concerned to ensure their agreement".

Do not ignore uncompleted parts of the form however much you are tempted to do so. Their incompleteness is probably very relevant. For example, a referrer may be aware of the involvement of other agencies but not considered them relevant; like the G.P. who had seen both parents of a child in trouble and from them learned about a problem with a neighbour and of their request for rehousing made to a Social Services Department. The General Practitioner presumed that the Social Worker concerned was dealing with the housing situation, whereas the request had been seen as symptomatic of other difficulties and exploratory home visiting was arranged. Failure to inform about this very relevant agency led to confusion for this particular family.

B.   Sharing Understanding with Agencies

What other steps may be taken to encourage "good enough" communication between professionals in order that the preparation of a family for therapy is adequately carried out? In some areas, regular meetings are arranged which provide an opportunity for workers to get together. Such meetings can be task-orientated, i.e. to discuss particular problems, but they nevertheless offer the chance for sharing ideas; for discovering what one has in common and what is the particular speciality of each; for learning about the problems and difficulties inherent in the work of each agency; for sharing understanding about the various methods of working and for developing trust. Care is needed in the arrangement of such meetings: place, timing and purpose need to be discussed and agreed. Changes of workers may necessitate a recurring series of meetings at agreed intervals. In the initial planning stages, ambivalence is almost inevitable and will be expressed in numerous ways: late arrival at meetings, misunderstandings about date, time and place, and so on. But if this can be recognized and tolerated so that negative feelings about frustrations, disappointments and unmet expectations are aired, there is a good chance of the group working well together. The knowledge that families are often expert in playing off one agency worker against another may be an incentive for attendance!

A commonplace criticism of family therapists is that they are fortunate in only working with families who are motivated. While there may be some truth in this, the demands made upon referrers in the preparation process make it clear that the degree of motivation depends, to some extent, upon their own contribution. Nevertheless, the complaint may be linked with the awareness that referrers are left with many difficult problems, particularly those instances where a family is resistant to treatment. Staff in schools and childrens' homes are examples of this and often feel that they are not helped with some of the more problematic situations which are daily occurrences. Some family therapists have found ways of helping by meeting regularly with interested staff to discuss ways in which they may work more effectively. This has also offered the opportunity for supporting workers who are often left feeling helpless and despairing. Better and more appropriate referrals can result from such meetings, particularly when the improved understanding between agency workers is reflected in discussions with families. The following model which was successfully established is offered as a guide to those who are interested in improving communication with prospective referrers:

Three team members, representing three disciplines in a Child Guidance Clinic arranged, after initial exploratory meetings with senior staff, to meet fortnightly with a group of Educational Welfare Officers. The place for meeting alternated between the working premises of each group, and the agreed plan was for the Educational Welfare Officers to present a situation with which they were experiencing difficulty. It was expected that the presenting problem would be discussed in depth so that sufficient understanding could be reached for practical suggestions to be made about how the situation could be handled more effectively, an important part of these meetings, for endless discussion without decisions can be an abortive experience!

The clinic workers, in turn, discussed families known to the Educational Welfare Officer, demonstrating in discussion their understanding of family dynamics and thus the relevance of the need for the whole family to be seen and assessed. As trust developed, the Educational Welfare Officer expressed fears that family therapy could be "dangerous" and lead to violence between family members; that getting everyone together was like "building a bonfire" to which the therapist would "set alight" with the additional risk of them being sent away leaving others (i.e. the Educational Welfare Officer) to "quell the flames". The Educational Welfare Officer who made these comments was not alone in expressing such anxieties; indeed, I recently learned of a teacher who had said to a parent:

> You should ask your doctor to send J to "X" Child Guidance Clinic where they'll see her by herself. If I ask our psychologist, he'll refer you to "Y" department where they insist on seeing all the family together, and *in my opinion*, that's not necessary as J's the problem, and needs the help.

It is evident that we should not be complacent about the presence of such anxieties and their effects on the preparation of a family when a referral is being made.

C. Sorting out Territorial Rights

Before initiating any meetings it is important to ensure that the appropriate agency staff have been approached and are in agreement. In schools for example, you may need to meet with those who have "professional territorial rights": the educational psychologist, the educational welfare officer and of course, the Head teacher. If you are interested in meeting with the staff of a residential institution, you will need to communicate with the appropriate hierarchy of the Social Services Department. Unless care is taken to work through the correct channels, your offers of help may prove abortive. Care must also be taken to ensure that your offer is not misunderstood, for a "them and us" situation is not unknown in some areas, the "us" being seen as the experts who have all the skills, and the "them" those who have none.

There are of course, other ways of dealing with resistances in professional workers once one is aware of their existence and of the need to try and overcome this in the interest of effective therapeutic work with a family. Case conferences to which all known workers are invited can be arranged, care being taken in considering the advantages and disadvantages for meeting before or after one has met with the family. Some therapists are resistant to having more than the minimum information about a family prior to their being seen, while on the other hand, where it is known that a family is likely to be resistant, it may be more helpful to gain the support of all known agencies before attempting to contact the family itself.

It is no doubt clear by now that I consider the preparation of referrers to be of the utmost importance if the majority of families requiring therapeutic help are to find their way to an appropriate agency. "Good enough" preparation not only deals with resistances, but gives support and encouragement to the family; prevents conflicting and confusing communications; and avoids the possibility of the family being pushed and pulled between rival agencies.

V. INVITING THE FAMILY

A therapist who feels confident that this groundwork has been successfully undertaken can now address himself to the preparatory work that is still required to be done by him. The referral having been received and accepted, the next step is to invite the family for the initial session, the invitation making clear who is being asked to attend. This may appear to be stating the obvious but in my experience, letters of invitation are sometimes so vague that it is hardly surprising when either the nominated patient only (in the case of an adult) or a parent and child alone respond to the letter.

A. Letters of Invitation

The letter needs to state very clearly that all of the family are expected to attend . . . "If I am to be of help to you, it will be important for all of the family to attend at least for the first session".

It may be helpful, in view of prior information you have received, to suggest other relevant persons be included . . . "you may feel it could be useful to include others in your household in addition to members of the immediate family".

In this case, the letter is worded in such a way that the therapist is indicating a knowledge of other persons who could appropriately be included, but leaves the final decision about their inclusion to the family members.

It can also be helpful to recognize that some adults in a family may be required to take time off from work . . . "should you require a letter for your employer in order to be allowed to take time from work, I will be pleased to provide this".

Since attendance of a whole family may mean that some members are likely to be inconvenienced and a compromise about availability reached, the therapist can be helpful in indicating that alternative appointment times are possible . . . "can you please confirm that you are able to accept this appointment. If, on the other hand, the day and time are not convenient for you all and you would like me to arrange an alternative, I will be pleased to do so". Such a statement can also prevent the waste of therapeutic time since most families seem able to respond to a request for confirmation.

It may be helpful to send a copy of the initial letter to the referrer, particularly when resistance has been met and worked with, for this enables the referrer to continue to be encouraging. Or, where authority issues are at stake, as may be the case with a school truant, or a Court report, the referrer can take whatever steps they may feel appropriate to ensure that the appointment is kept.

B.   Inviting Family Members not "Living Together"

Where a referrer indicates that:
   (i)   parents of a family are either separated or divorced,
   (ii) there is a co-habitee currently involved,
   (iii) a grandparent, or other relative is either living in the household or
sufficiently close as to be considered an important member to include,
then a decision must be made about whether and how they should be invited.
Parents who are apart may yet continue to share parenting functions in such a
way that unless they are both included, therapy will create conflict and confusion
even where this may not be already in evidence (Skynner, 1971).

One family known to me were considerably helped through the steps taken by
the therapist to ensure that a reluctant father (separated but maintaining contact
with some of his children) was present at the initial session. In order that this
could be possible, the therapist first met with the father and his current co-
habitee and helped them to understand why the request was being made. In this
instance, the letter had to be carefully worded and the co-operation of the mother
and the referrer gained.

Initial communication can also be made by telephone: to get permission to
invite a separated or divorced parent and ensure that the reasons for suggesting
this are fully understood; to arrange the first appointment and discuss who of
importance in the family should attend; or to talk with a reluctant member where
this is known about from prior information.

C.   Case Examples

This method worked well with the "J" family who were referred by an E.W.O.
when their 14-year-old daughter was refusing to attend school. The E.W.O.
reported that Mr J was unlikely to attend (information given by Mrs J); he
believed that his daughter, Betty was the problem and should be seen. The
therapist telephoned the home and spoke with Mrs J to whom he offered an
appointment while at the same time explaining that he would want to see the
whole family. He asked who would be coming and whether they would find it
helpful to have an appointment card or letter in order to have time off from work
or school. This conversation, relaxed and friendly but also enquiring, allowed
the opportunity for Mrs J to talk about her husband's doubts about therapeutic
help, and his unwillingness to be involved in any way. The therapist expressed
his wish to speak with Mr J and enquired about a convenient time to ring him,
having first gained Mrs J's agreement. When Mr J was contacted, the importance of his contribution in the understanding of his daughter's difficulties was
stressed and when he continued to prevaricate, the therapist said firmly that he
expected Mr J would want to take his share of the responsibility in any decisions
concerning his daughter. The therapist's expectations of the importance of Mr J
being present were evident throughout the telephone conversation, and days and
times when he could arrange to take time from work were discussed.

With another family, some considerable work was done by the therapist on the telephone before they were seen. The G.P. for the "P" family telephoned the hospital family therapy department to request an urgent appointment for a 14-year-old patient whom he considered to be seriously disturbed and a possible suicide risk. The boy's mother had been to see him to tell of her concern and described some worrying behaviour. The therapist rang the boy's home to offer an early appointment to which all the family were asked to attend, and the mother with whom he spoke, accepted. Some hours later Mr P telephoned to cancel the appointment saying that he had spoken with his son and there was no need for further intervention. Thereafter followed several calls from each parent in turn, Mrs P asking for an appointment, and Mr P cancelling. The therapist then spoke to each parent in turn saying that they would need to talk together and agree whether or not there was a problem, and that if they agreed there was, she could arrange to see them. The G.P. was informed of the situation.

Some days later, the school asked the parents to a meeting to discuss their son's continuous truancy and difficult behaviour in school. During the course of the interview, referral to a Child Guidance Clinic was suggested, whereupon Mrs P revealed the situation concerning the hospital appointments, and the disagreement between she and her husband. This led to the school stressing the importance of Mr P's involvement, and urging both parents to telephone and speak with the therapist with whom they had already had some contact.

Some therapists have expressed doubts about using the telephone in this way, particularly before they have met with a family in person, but where there is sufficient information to indicate that a telephone conversation may be helpful, it has been found to be very effective (Coppersmith, 1980). When members of a family are required to take time from their employment, it may be helpful to give some indication of the length of time they are likely to be in a session. This can be particularly helpful when the family are attending a hospital for the expectation may well be that of having to spend a long time waiting to be seen.

D. Practical Preparations

Next, therapists must address themselves to the practical preparations necessary for the initial assessment session. This should include a room with the approp-riate number of chairs arranged in a circle so that communications can be seen and heard by all. In addition, a low table and play materials for young children should be placed in the centre of the circle of chairs to ensure that the children's play can be observed. Materials are important and should be appropriate to the ages of the children, yet not likely to be intrusive. Plasticine, crayons, coloured pencils and paper are perhaps the most popular and the least noisy! For younger children, a small box of miniature dolls, farm and zoo animals, etc. may be useful.

E. Therapist's Personal Preparation

Finally, the therapist's own preparation will need to include an adequate space of time for thinking about the task ahead. Depending upon style of working, a preliminary hypothesis may need to be thought out, or a decision about a technical approach in relationship to a particular symptom or age of family members. If a co-therapist is to be used, time will be needed for both therapists to talk together about the family they plan to meet, and the manner in which they aim to work. It may also be necessary to make arrangements for supervision, and if a one-way screen is to be used, it will be important to ensure that therapists, supervisor, rooms and equipment are all available at the time planned for the family session. This is stating the obvious, but in the experience of myself and numerous other colleagues, the minute details of preparation are not infrequently overlooked until a late stage so that the therapist arrives at the scene of action with tensions additional to those inherent in the prospect of meeting a family for an initial session.

F.   Introduction to Family Therapy Notions

With the arrival of the family, the therapist now faces the task of introducing them to the notion of family therapy (Franklin and Proesky, 1973; Haley, 1976; Stierlin et al., 1981). Again this depends on the way the therapist works, whether "close" to the family or taking a more "distant" position (Minuchin, 1981).

Despite "good enough" preparation, it is possible that the family will have failed to all come together. In this case, it may be worth enquiring about this before taking the family to the room in which they will be seen and waiting for latecomers to arrive. If on the other hand, it is evident that important family members are not intending to come, the therapist will have to decide how this should be handled, and whether the initial session should be focussed on why the member has not come, and how he or she can be encouraged to attend the next session, or whether to work with the subsystem present.

Once seated in the room where the session is to take place, the next step is for the therapist to introduce him or herself. Then, if each member of the family is encouraged to introduce themself, not only may this throw light on how the family functions, but it can give the therapist the opportunity of indicating that he is beginning to understand this . . . "does your mum always like to help you by telling people your name?". Taking trouble to find out how each member wants to be known can help to relieve tension, and again indicates the therapist's wish to be attentive to everyone . . . "do you like to be called Mrs Smith, or do you have another name you'd like me to use?" if the family all wish to be known by their christian names, the therapist must decide about his or her own name. If you are quite clear about how you wish to be addressed, there is no problem, but on the other hand, you may prefer to give the family the choice. Having introduced yourself as "Bill Jones" initially, you can, after learning the family's names, ask . . . "What would you like to call me: Bill or Mr Jones? What would help you to feel most comfortable?" However you undertake this, it is important that everyone is clear about how they wish to be addressed.

The therapist may quickly discover that the family have come with the idea of presenting one of their members as the patient or problem, and skill will be needed in dealing with this. "Engaging with the family", "joining", "accommodating": these are some of the current terms used to describe this process (Minuchin, 1974, 1981).

Some therapists like to address themselves to one member (it could be the nominated patient), and to ask them to "help me to understand about your family: Who is the boss?; Do you do things together or are you all very separate?; See if you can give me a picture of the kind of family you are", and so on. Alternatively, they may ask one member to introduce the rest: "I'd like to get to know you and your family: Can you tell me who everyone is". Whatever opening comments are made are an attempt to convey the therapists' interest in the family as a whole.

Some families will rush to point out that "we've come because of Johnny", and then it can be helpful to ask Johnny whether he knows what they mean, and then to invite him to check out by asking his family directly. Generalized terms ("He's always difficult") should not be acceptable, and in such a discussion detail must be insisted upon: "Johnny, can you find out what your mum means when she says you are a problem"; or "Mrs T, how can Johnny help you to understand what he means when he says you always go on at him. See if you can get him to explain more fully". It is not unusual for family members to wrongly assume that they are talking about the same thing, and this method can lead to the opening up of an area of disagreement between family members allowing the therapist to learn something about the process of communication in the family.

However the beginning of a session is undertaken, whatever technique or approach the therapist may choose, the task is clearly that initially, the therapist must join the family, and in so doing must also introduce the notion that it is the family as a whole who are the focus of the session.

REFERENCES

Coppersmith, E. (1980). Expanding the uses of the telephone in family therapy. *Family Process*, **19**, 411-417.

Franklin, P. and Prosky, P. (1973). A standardized initial interview. *In* "Techniques of Family Psychotherapy A Primer", (D. Bloch, ed.), Grune & Stratton, New York.

Haley, J. (1976). "Problem Solving Therapy", Jossey-Bass, San Francisco.

Hornby, S. (1979). Collaboration—a report of an interagency consultation. (to be published).

Menzies, I. E. P. (1970). "The functioning of social systems as a defence against anxiety", London, Tavistock Institute of Human Relations.

Minuchin, S. (1974). "Families and Family Therapy", Harvard University Press, Cambridge, Mass.

Minuchin, S. and Fishman, H. C. (1981). "Family Therapy Techniques", Harvard University Press, Cambridge, Mass.

Seebohm Report (1968). Report of the Committee on Local Authority and Allied Personal Social Services. H.M.S.O., London.

Skynner, A. C. R. (1971). The Minimum Sufficient Network. *Social Work Today*, **2**, 9.3.

Stierlin, H., Rucker-Embden, I., Wetzel, N. and Wirsching, M. (1980). "The First Interview with the Family", Brunner/Mazel, New York.

Chapter 8

Initial Work
with the Family

G. Gorell Barnes

I. INTRODUCTION

Beginning work with a new family is always accompanied by a small surge of anxiety. On each occasion there is uncertainty about whether a claim to professional understanding and skill as vested in the therapist by his setting, and the expectations of those referring to him, will be justified. Although he may have had something to offer a family yesterday, or earlier in the same day, this new group may present themselves in ways that leave him newly helpless and wondering how to proceed. Therapists have developed many devices, and familiar routines to help them through this difficult period of joining with the family, and some of these will be recorded in this chapter; but there is a necessary uncertainty in each therapeutic encounter which is an essential aspect of exploration. Without this professional alertness, he is not fully tuned to a difference in information between this family system and others with which he is already familiar.

A. Initial Approaches

For the majority of those working with families regularly, there is now some agreement that certain sorts of beginning are more productive than others. Within the treatment setting created by therapist sitting down with family, there are processes that facilitate the family's capacity to work on their own anxiety; that help them begin to define why they think they have come or sought outside intervention (or face the reality of why it has been imposed upon them by law), and that are more likely to help them begin to do some work on this between them, with the outside agency of the therapist. There are, however, distinct divergencies between theoretical approaches to subsequent therapy with families related to the level at which the therapist chooses to intervene in the family system. Some of these differences in approach and their implications for engagement are discussed below.

B. The Problem in Context

A therapist who invites a family to see him has, for the purpose of that interview, committed himself to an approach to problem solving in which the person expressing the problem is interviewed within his primary social group. The therapist is availing himself of the opportunity to observe the problem in the context of the social situation which will largely be contributing to maintaining it. He may not as yet have committed himself to continuing with the whole group, since he may feel that professional intervention to bring about change will not be best offered in this way. But recognize it or not, he is beginning on the process of acknowledging that change will involve everyone. In this country, a greater proportion of professionals see families for first interviews than continue to work with them as a group (Gorell Barnes, 1980a) since nearly all therapy takes place within contexts that believe in offering a variety of professional interventions to the families they see. These other interventions and forms of treatment are however increasingly considered within the context of the family as a whole (see Roberts, Chapter 7).

II.   INITIAL WORK: THE PLACE

A.   The Home Interview

A very high proportion of first interview family work takes place within the family's own home, and yet this is little discussed. Bloch (1973) discussed the clinical home visit in a detailed way that reads strangely to those English professionals accustomed to conducting much of their work in the home. Exactly because he uses visits so purposively, he highlights many of those potential aspects of making a visit to the home that can easily go unconsidered. These include a tour of all areas of the house, including those not normally on show; consideration of contrast between public and private areas of the house; the assessment of emotional exchange through the serving of food; a considered view of the style and management of family space. Lindsey (1979), Cade and Southgate (1979) and Clarke (1980) have each written about family work in the home setting in this country. Lindsey in particular has emphasized the importance of establishing a setting which makes clear to all the members of the family that the purpose of the visit is for therapeutic work to be done. She emphasizes the importance of the workers' belief in their own authority and right to be there as essential to making the family take proposed work seriously, and comments that she neither sits down, nor starts the interview until all who are expected to be there are present.

Other problems commonly found on home visits include television, acceptance of hospitality, and seating arrangements. Each worker must make their own decision about whether they will work with the TV or not; but a statement such as, "Please turn it off because I can't work when it's on", emphasizes that the interview has a purpose. Similarly, cups of tea can be deferred with a suggestion that work be done first, postponing rather than rejecting offered hospitality. It is important that the worker finds a chair from which they can see all members of the family and they may have to settle for a small hard back chair, rather than an offered corner on a low sofa between the dog and the wall.

The use of pets and toys can be important information during the interview, so it may be necessary to emphasize that everything is available for comment during the time the worker is there. Children or adolescents will therefore not be allowed to skip out unnoticed during the session. I make my personal boundary for behaviour the door of the room, since I have started interviews with mother ironing, father reading the paper, eldest daughter dressmaking, middle daughter drying her hair and youngest daughter playing in a corner with the cat. The work of the early part of the session then became the involvement of the family in listening to each other and to me (see also Byng-Hall, Chapter 19, Vol. 2).

B.   The Agency Interview

An interview will start better if the therapist feels he is providing a reasonably comfortable environment for the family to be in. However, he does not want to create envy by having it too comfortable, nor curiosity by having it too personal. Problems of luxurious furnishings are unlikely to be affecting many people in the health or social services in Britain today, but too personal a style in the room should also be avoided. It is unsatisfactory for family work to be attempted in rooms that are too small for the right number of chairs to be included, in addition to containing a small table to have some toys or drawing material for younger children who will get restless without things other than "words" to relate to. Most agencies are able to provide at least one room which can be seen as a family or group room, in which adequate furniture is available for both purposes. It helps to have a large cardboard box labelled with the family name into which any drawings, or other offerings can be put, along with small toys or plasticine models which are kept safe between sessions. Children of all ages, as well as adults seem to enjoy plasticine. Felt tip pens and sheets of paper are useful.

III.   INITIAL WORK: WHO COMES

A.   Who is the Family?

Who comes to the first interview and who does not come is always of interest. Why does mother turn up with her own mother and not her husband? Why does a younger sister decide that her imminent exam is more important than her sister's threatened attempt at suicide, when her parents feel the case is too serious for them to delay the appointment until the following week when she could also come? Why do two parents refuse to bring their teenage children until they have "sniffed out" the "family" therapist, although they have been taking them to different hospital paediatric departments for the last seven years? Why does a mother whose son has been taken into care and whose daughter has been expelled from five schools insist that she has to carry the problem alone and that father cannot be involved because his job is too responsible? Why does a wife refer her first husband and girlfriend, her second husband and son and herself for help, and be the only one not to turn up at the arranged time? These are all questions that will involve us in understanding each different system the problem is lodged within, and the meaning of the symptom to each person in the system as well as to the system as a whole. My personal approach is to see whoever turns up, rather than insisting on whole family arrival, since if the preparatory work has been properly done, this is itself information about the way this family operate in relation to the outside world. The meaning of the absences and the absent members of the system always needs to be borne in mind during the interview, since it is in itself a communication that may be important. In this following extract, the inexperienced therapist is trying to focus on the meaning of the father's absence and is floundering in the face of the united solidarity of the three generational system of the women of the family.

B. Case Example

Extract 1: Mother, maternal grandmother, Brenda (14, I.P.) Paul (3)

MGM: Well he's been bullying her and ignoring her because she's not conforming.

Therapist: Tell me about Bill, why isn't he here.

Mother: Well, his job is important.

Therapist: You obviously don't think that's why he's not here.

MGM: (Shakes head sadly) He's not mature enough love, look I'll tell you what, he's got thousands in the bank and he won't buy himself new clothes. They have their food and he makes sure they have their £40 every month, but we buy in between—*I* do. Doreen hasn't had new clothes—she's had that coat three years—You couldn't go to Bill for help, he needs help himself in my opinion. (3-year-old son of Bill and Doreen bashes radiator loudly during this.)

Therapist: Is that why you think he isn't here.

MGM: He's not here because you can't tell him and you can't tell him lots of things.

Mother: (simultaneously) Because he's at work.

Therapist: I know he's at work but I wrote to both of you offering to make a time when he could come. Did he read the letter?

Mother: No, well to tell you the truth I didn't show it to him.

MGM: No, nor would I. Not Bill.

Mother: He would have gone mad.

MGM: Well, we don't know if he would have gone mad.

Mother: When the headmistress told us we should take Brenda to the Clinic he said yes, he would come.

Therapist: Then why didn't you show him the letter. Does he act for Brenda as her father—I'm not clear what happened to her own father.

MGM: Oh well, Doreen divorced him, he was no good for her, she'd known him as a child and she said, "I'm going to marry him", and I said I'd never interfere with my kids and I didn't. And what he wanted was a mother—he loved me —he needed my help.

Therapist: You're telling me now your daughter has married two men who need help—(looks to Brenda who is now giggling) is that right—you've a strong nan there Brenda (patting MGM—all laugh—youngest son stops bashing radiator and joins group).

C. Comment

In this extract it is only when the therapist temporarily "joins" the system by acknowledging the strength of the grandmother that she begins to make headway. In this family it became clear that the two independently powerful systems, that of maternal grandmother, daughter and granddaughter, and that of husband-wife-children could not meet in the same room. In order to begin work with the family that took primary responsibility for the children, it was first necessary to work with and make a boundary between the family of primary responsibility and the family to which the children ran away when things got too hot: their "dear hardworking nan" and her co-habitee.

The question of who to define as the family and who to work with in the system is never fixed, and will relate to any one person's "style" of therapy and theory of change. Since I have always worked in a setting where the parents or their surrogates appointed by law are legally responsible for the welfare of dependent children, I find a minimal systems boundary definition helpful. I work with those legally responsible as well as those actually taking care of the child referred. This often means that social workers and residential workers will be present as part of the family system. Further criteria that I use, in deciding who to work with relate to the age and stage of the children, their current developmental needs, and who may need to be brought into the therapy to see that these are being attended to. I emphasize this since if the successful development of the children is the focus of the therapist's rational attention in irrational or unconventional family systems, it helps the therapist to focus on "who should be there" (Bentovim and Gilmour, 1981; Bentovim, Chapter 28). Are the parents able to treat their children in a manner that appears to recognize the age they are at and the stage they are at? Are the children being used to look after their parents' needs in ways that are grossly inappropriate, by caring for them physically; or in terms of need for emotional companionship, or sexual titillation? Are children being asked to perform tasks that are wholly unsuitable for their age and abilities? If the parents are confused, and confusing their children in this way, who is acting to give the parenting instead? (Rutter, 1974; Gorell Barnes, 1978). Outside agencies often need to be involved as part of the process of helping the family face these issues in cases of gross distortion.

IV. DEFINING THE FAMILY

A. What is a Family?

What the "family" system is will to some extent be defined, by what the functions of the agency, carrying out its meta-parental role on behalf of society through the welfare state require it to be. In general, a family is a unit of more than one generation, although sibling sub-groups have been the focus of therapeutic work. In some families, the system requiring attention will be a man, a woman and some children, but increasingly different varieties of family structure present for help. Many families will have only one parent, although an essential part of the family system will be the person or group to whom mother or father turn for support and confirmation of their own adult capabilities, as well as for sexual needs. These partners may be either male or female. We are relatively unknowledgeable as yet in this country in attending to the family structures of homosexual couples and the ensuing problems (Lowenstein, 1980) that may develop in the child. For example, in a family where the nominal parents are a white lesbian couple, the children are all West Indian boys, and there are additional issues of cross generation coupling and sexual attraction. Here, it seems particularly important to be linking intervention to the developmental needs of the children and things that any *parent*, regardless of their sex, has to be able to do on behalf of a *child* of a particular age and stage in order to help the family discover what they can do as a healthy parent-and-child unit; rather than the worker setting up unrealistic goals of achieving "normality" which fail. Hopefully whatever the nature of the sexual relationship, the single parent will be relating to other adults who confirm her sense of identity in an age-appropriate way for herself; since many of the problems arising from single parent families relate to the crossing of generation boundaries to the disadvantage of the children. Sometimes the parent herself is infantilized by her own parents who insist on keeping her in their own "parent-to-child" relationship when she needs her adult identity to be confirmed, in which case three generational work will be needed at some stage.

B.   Step Families: a Case Example

The question of who should attend is often particularly complex in step families. Many step families use the help of professionals to sort out the problems of being a "second" family. Clarifying which of those in the former families need to attend in relation to the presenting problems may be an essential part of the first interview. I have focussed on this in some detail in the extract below.

The family is composed of husband and wife and three children, two from previous different families. The children have been invited to come on behalf of Vivian, mother to two children and stepmother to the two others in the household they all lived in most of the week. She has been severely depressed for two months and has ceased to care for the house at all following an attempt to leave with Sam, her lover. The therapist is trying to establish who should be there to work on the problems the family are bringing. The eldest girl has refused to come, but the other three children, who are father's son, mother's daughter and Jo, son of this marriage, are present; one child representing each of three marriages. The therapist is discussing the absence of one member, Sue aged 18, father's daughter and the eldest child in the combined sibling group.

Extract 2

Therapist: So Sue didn't think it would "help" — what is it she didn't think it would help?

Father: The situation between Vivian and I.

Therapist: I invited all the children to come today because there were several things I thought as a family unit you might want to think about.

Father: (frames Sue's absence in terms of her moving away from the family appropriate at her age)

Vivien: (cross) That's got nothing to do with it, if she didn't want to come, she didn't want to come.

Therapist: (to father) but Sue is one of the people *you* saw as very concerned and important to the family.

Vivien: (cutting in) Yes, but I think she saw this as a very private thing.

Therapist: Well it may be that that is how all the children see it — do you know what we are talking about Jo?

Jo (7): (shakes head)

Therapist: Well I don't think we should talk about things you don't understand — why did you think you had come here today?

Jo: (squeaking): I didn't know.

Therapist: Ask one of the others to help you.

Father: Yes, you did know Jo.

David (13): I told you in the kitchen when doing washing up.

Jo: I know; I've forgotten.

Therapist: David can you help Jo out?

David: Well Vivien and Dad are coming here to try and solve their problems.

Therapist: You see it as problems between Viv and Dad as well, do you?

David: I'm not sure.

Therapist: Janet what do you think?

Janet (14): I don't know either.

Therapist: But you see things going on at home.

Janet: Arguments.

Vivien: You do know really, it's alright you *can* say.

Janet: I don't really know it's so muddling.

Therapist: I don't *really* know either, which is one reason why we are meeting together to try and sort out what it is that's not working in the family.

Jo: Well, there's a man called Sam who tries to take mummy away from daddy.

Therapist: I see — and did that make you feel unhappy?

Jo: Yes.

Therapist: I see — and now Mummy's come back.

Jo: Yes, but they are *still* arguing.

Therapist: What happens when they argue Jo?

Jo: I don't know — I go away — I go with David or Janet.

Therapist: That sounds good, so you children all go somewhere and keep out of it.

Jo: Yes, normally in the kitchen eating food.

Vivien: (tries to minimize) "not always eating".

Jo: (emphatically) Yes we were, last time we were eating CARROTS.

(Therapist finds out more about how different children respond to "rows" in the family)

Therapist: David, you've been through some upsets before you came to live with Dad.

Did you know about that Jo?

(Jo denies) (He recounts his knowledge of the process of David joining family)

First Sue came to live here and went to school with Janet and then David came.

Therapist: Why was that David?

David: I didn't like school.

Therapist: I see. I thought it was also related to something that happened at your other house.

David: Yes, I took an overdose.

Therapist: Uh huh, what does that mean exactly, do you know what an overdose is, Jo?

Jo: No.

Therapist: Could you ask David?

Jo: What's an overdose David?

David: I took too many pills.

Jo: (interested) Oh and did they take you to hospital?

David: (very brief nod)

Therapist: Did you know about that Janet?

Janet: Yes

Therapist: Do you think it's right to know something about why he did it or do you think that's his business?

Janet: His business. I'm not really involved in David's business. (David is not any blood relation to Janet being her stepfather's son by his first marriage.)

Therapist: I see are you saying you like to keep yourself separate and he also can do this.

Janet: I suppose so, but we get on very well when together.

Therapist: Of course you also lived in another family before too.

Jo: She used to live with her nanny.

Therapist: When did you join *this* family?

Janet: A long time ago—I've been here for years.

Therapist: That's one thing you all have to manage in this family—that is the three families that are part of your present family.

Jo: What's that.

David: It's not the same for you Jo 'cos you only live in one.

Therapist: Can you explain that David, because Jo is very good at understanding.

David: You actually live with your *real* Mum and your *real* Dad which Janet does not and I don't, but also we have got our real mums and real dads which is a separate family. As you know I go home to see mum every weekend, and sometimes Janet goes to see her father and her nan.

C. Comment

In this extract we can see the therapist tracking the content, getting to know the family issues, and finding out something about the complex family patterns and the way family members function under stress, both in this present family and the other families they visit regularly. In such a complex family, it is important to bear the larger system which is *four* families not *one* in mind, and to see how these other three families (the ecostructure for the presenting family) interconnect. However, the focus for the therapeutic work has to be clearly defined and maintained so that it is the family who are coming that are worked with, rather than the three that are absent, which could be an evasion from what *was presenting* in the focal parent child unit.

V. INITIAL MOVES

A. Opening the Session: Theoretical Viewpoints

For many family therapists, questions of where they will do the work and who they are going to work with in the family relates to the theory of systemic change that they believe in. My ideas about change in systems, usually defined in family therapy as structural or strategic work, are linked to Bateson's ideas about levels of learning in systems (Bateson, 1964).

(1) A structural approach to change through work with sub-systems in the family can be seen as Learning II: *"A change in how the sequence of experience is punctuated"*, whereas

(2) a whole system strategic approach can be as a change at Level III; *"A corrective change in the system of sets of alternatives from which choice is made"*, (Gorell Barnes and Campbell, 1982).

Working at either of these two levels of change would be related to different ideas about the therapist's use of himself and the setting he is in.

B. Structural and Strategic Approaches

These levels can be loosely related to styles of work known as structural and strategic. As there are many ways of defining structural and strategic work, the following brief definition must be taken as personal and arbitrary. Structural work in practice addresses itself to change in family systems through the minutiae of interactions manifested in sub-system sequences. These sequences, in operation from the moment a child is born into a family (Stern, 1977), generate certain characteristics of the self. In rigid systems, or at time of crisis when a normally more flexible system rigifies, homeostasis prevents the discovery of new pathways to problem solving. A change created within a sub-systemic loop in the system will, however, spread and if properly focussed and intensified will make an impact on the system as a whole. Working in this way the therapist gets close to the family, uses many of their words and movements, and while maintaining necessary distance works within the systemic style that presents. This kind of work fits well with home as well as professional environments.

Strategic work may equally address itself to sub-systems, since all intervention is a form of strategy and can be directed towards creating learning in a system at level II or level III, but as I am using the term here, I am considering work that is primarily aimed at creating a change in the rules that govern the system as a whole. Such work aims at a transformation of the overall contexts within which the family views their situations (that they can see the frog as a potential prince rather than as a better class of frog) (Gorell Barnes and Campbell, 1981 in press). The therapist addresses himself then to change at Bateson's level III, aiming to change the frame of the rules governing the second-level behaviours. Working in this style, the therapist maintains professional neutrality and distance from the family in a manner more akin to analytic practice and often works with colleagues behind a screen; who help him make interventions that address the system as a whole rather than the individual or sub-systems within it (Palazzoli *et al.*, 1978). Work of this kind would be difficult to transfer to a home setting. However, there is in addition a style of strategic work that combines elements of both these approaches and that cheerfully moves levels within and between sessions. This style has developed through the Palo Alto group in California (Watzlawick, 1967, 1974; Haley, 1963; Madanes, 1980), and has been extensively developed by the Family Institute, Cardiff, in this country in both clinical and home settings (Cade, 1979; Gorell Barnes, 1982a, b).

C. Opening the Session – Practical Issues

Whichever style of addressing the system the therapist chooses, there are certain areas of family behaviour and family functioning he will want to attend to. Most family therapists prefer to dispel the anxiety to do with the setting itself in order to concentrate on the purpose for which the family have come. Preliminary courtesies are part of therapeutic work. There should be enquiry as to whether everyone knows why they are here today, personal contact with each family member to find out about their anticipations in coming to a family interview; discussion of neutral topics such as schools and work, clarification of family names and ages, and forms of address (see Roberts, chapter 7).

In the course of this process which different schools of theory give different names, the therapist has the chance to begin to learn about the relationships between family members, as well as demonstrating by his manner his respect for the family. He begins to assess their mood and pace. Is it appropriate to the occasion?: too angry, sad or hilarious? How do the parents treat the children, and how do the children respond to the requests of the parents? Do the family present a united front . . . if not, who looks at whom before speaking and who disagrees? Who sits next to whom is used as information by all therapists and commented on by some. In all his noting of the process, the therapist has to maintain an open mind about the meaning of the information.

Although he begins clocking up detail from the beginning, he is not in a position to use that valuably on behalf of the family until he has a greater overall view. He may or may not wish to use his observation for the family to change the rules of behaviour in the session: "I notice that you always look at your mother when you speak . . . in this time we are together I want you to speak for yourself . . ." This decision to change family rules, to intervene during the session, will of course depend on the style and theoretical frame of the therapist. However in general, in the first half of the session, it is of greater value to understand and observe accurately the rules of the family system than to be intent on creating new ones for the therapy. In some families, however, the problem is stated from the moment the family sit down in the room, as when a mother tells her 17-year-old son to take off his coat because the room is warm. It will be the therapist's choice about whether he makes the material the focus of his professional attention, and uses that issue as part of the joining process ("Well, Sam, I can see you have a mother who takes good care of you, does she always worry about you as well as that?") or whether he prefers to distinguish between a "hello" stage and a problem-focussed stage.

D. Slowing Down

Some families would not allow such a distinction, and the therapist has to slow them down enough to begin to keep himself and what he can offer separate from the huge network of professionals and expected solutions the family have already come to rely on.

> Well we're here today because my probation officer said you could help with Mandy's appeal; and when I told my general practitioner he said why not go and see if they can help her and it might do my depression good too. The psychologist at the school was very helpful to Mark although I didn't like the type of child at the school he recommended, and so I thought I'd ask you while I was here if you could help on that one as well, as the headmaster said well if you can get the clinic to support you it might pull some weight at County Hall.

In these moments when the therapist is about to go under, some distancing tactics are necessary. Commending mother on the speed and detail with which she has opened the session, but placing oneself in the position of the slow-witted outsider who needs more time to understand what is going on, is one way of putting on brakes; another might be to admire the teenage daughter Mandy's shoes and ask her if she bought these for herself. This could be used to repunctuate the stream of experience so that the topic could be broached from a different stance. Alternatively, the therapist could use this opening statement of mother's as the focus for further information gathering; trying to elicit difference in the family's perception of the problem by taking one aspect of the problem and asking one member of the family who between two other members is most anxious about it. However he proceeds, he will want to keep the details of his information precise and put it together piece by piece so that the family follow him as he proceeds.

VI.   DEFINING THE PROBLEM

A.   Sharpening the Focus

The therapist may find there is difficulty in getting to a problem. He may see the family busy chatting away in the *manner* of those presenting a problem and find himself concerned at the apparent ease with which they quarrel, complain and present material for him to work with. In these circumstances, to express bewilderment or curiosity about his own experience of the interview can be a very valuable way of learning more about the family dysfunction. For example, in a recent session where father and son were arguing vigorously about whether the boy looked after his dog and took him out for walks often enough, the therapist said, "I find I am anxious that in showing us how well you can worry about your dog, you will leave without having really shared with us your worries about each other". In another session with a different family bringing problems of uncontrolled violence in a teenage daughter, the therapist congratulated the parents on their ability to allow the young members of the family equal say on every topic but wondered if this was allowing *them* proper space in the session to express their concern as *parents* on behalf of their children.

B.   A Problem-centred Approach

In the extract below, the referred child is approached in the general context of a family and an area of skill which is seen as problematic by the family. The therapist is finding a way of joining the family while retaining neutrality, in a way that leaves her sufficiently comfortable to start noticing the anxieties and reactions of the family; the point of the first few minutes is not for the family to admire the therapist's technique. The therapist begins with the youngest child who is not the referred patient, and moves on to meet other family members from there. From the beginning, the family's own commonsense and awareness in relation to different areas of the information they are bringing is emphasized and restated to them, often with a slight reframing of the context to increase the opportunities for perceiving the problem in a different way. Issues such as age and sex can be highlighted to underline children's sense of competence. To an older sibling anticipating being in the hot seat, it is reassuring to have his additional two-years' wisdom pointed out by the therapist as an asset in approaching the anxieties about school which a younger child is voicing, and to be asked his views on how these anxieties might be handled in the light of his own experience. Similarly, a same-sex sibling can be brought in on the grounds of "special understanding" of a parent or another child, or a younger child can be used to teach an older child or a parent about ways of "reaching" a parent. While the therapist will always need to be sensitive not to violate the accustomed hierarchy of the family too early, he can nonetheless make it clear that each person present has something of value to contribute about how the family operate in their daily lives, and therefore potentially about how a problem is to be solved.

In this beginning sequence, the therapist is focussing on the difficulties the children are having to the exclusion of other aspects of the family and its functioning, because the parents had presented in a crisis around the issue of reading and the violence it provoked between mother and son. Exploring more positive or resourceful aspects of the family are delayed until later in the interview. However, while impressing the parents with the fact that the problem is being taken seriously, it does not free the children to participate and the therapist has to be prepared to sit with that polarized discomfort.

C.   A Problem-focussed Beginning

Therapist: [non-specific] [to parents] I've heard a bit about the problem from Mrs Smith [E.W.O.] and I thought it would be useful to meet as a family; no one has ever met you two girls and when something like this has been going on in a family for some time everyone has usually got something to say about it.

[to girls] — I don't know your names. [to youngest] You're . . . ?

Catherine: Catherine

Therapist: Catherine, and you're how old? Let's see now.

Catherine: Seven

Therapist: Seven, and which school do you go to?

Catherine: St Veronica's

Therapist: Is that the same school as Patrick? [Here therapist assumes naïve role of one who knows less about school system than children, so that they can tell her all about it, confirming them as experts in their own field.]

Catherine: No he's moved onto the big school now.

Therapist: So where does he go to school then? [remembering to talk directly to him rather than about him] Where do you go to school Patrick?

Patrick: St Christopher's

Therapist: What sort of school is that: girls and boys or just boys?

Patrick: Just boys.

Therapist: And was it difficult moving on from St Veronica's? [Attempt to be sympathetic too early is poor move to get child at ease.]

Patrick: [squeaky] Not much.

Therapist: Did you have to do much more work in your secondary school?

Patrick: Yes

Therapist: And is it more difficult?

Patrick: Yes much more.

Therapist: Is the reading more difficult?

Patrick: Yeah

Therapist: Uh huh: That's tough. How's the reading for you, Catherine?

Catherine: All right, sort of.

Therapist: Are you just starting to read?

Catherine: [nods and kicks her feet.]

Therapist: Can you read a little bit?

Catherine: [shakes her head.]

Therapist: Are you finding it quite difficult as well as Patrick?

Catherine: [nods vigorously.]

Therapist: Yes it *can* be difficult, words look very funny sometimes I think . . .
How about you, what's your name?

Angela: Angela.

Therapist: And you're . . . how old?

Angela: Ten

Therapist: Ten—what's your name, Angela—and Patrick you're 14—and
Catherine you're seven. Which school do you go to, Angela?

Angela: St Catherine's

Therapist: And how's reading for you—are you a good reader?

Angela: [nods and looks pleased.]

Therapist: Ah, you're a good reader are you—[looks at parents] is she a good
reader for the family?

Father: Yes, she's the one, she's the one that can do the reading for us all.

Therapist: Uh huh, I see, you're a good reader—well that must be quite difficult
for Patrick and for Catherine. That must be tough, Patrick, having a
10-year-old sister who can read so well (a mistake as he can only disagree to
save his pride here).

Patrick: [squeaks] No, I just ignore it.

Therapist: [realizes mistake, laughs] Well *I* would find it tough, I bet it's
difficult to ignore it sometimes.

Patrick: [relaxes six inches.]

Therapist: Well who else worries about reading in the family?

Mother: Well we do—Mum and Dad—we get very het up.

Therapist: Mum and Dad—mmm. What sort of effect does it have on you all
when Mum and Dad are worrying about reading? It must have quite an
effect on you all when they get so bothered about it.

D. Family Members as Expert Witnesses

The use of family members as experts on the detail of their own problems, and
eliciting of this detail, is a way of breaking down the process of the interview into
manageable sequences which is particularly valuable with young children. In the
following extract of a family where the 13-year-old is creating havoc in the class
at school and on the point of exclusion the children have been led to discuss the
process of disagreement *in the family* and the therapist is helping them track
some of the detail that lies behind the presenting problem.

Therapist: I don't know much about the detail of this but I gather the school is
complaining. What are they complaining about, Pearl?

Pearl (13): I don't go to maths and I don't like French. I don't do my homework.

Therapist: [repeats] You don't go to maths, you don't like French and you don't
do your homework . . . uh huh, and is there anything else?

Pearl: Well I do work, but I sometimes make trouble.

Therapist: In what way do you sometimes make trouble?

Pearl: Well I sit and I don't do what the teacher tells me and I'm rude to the teachers.

Therapist: I see. Are you rude to your parents?

Pearl: Yeah

Therapist: Which one are you rudest to?

Pearl: My Dad.

Therapist: You're rudest to your Dad. Why are you rude to him?

Pearl: Because he shouts at me.

Therapist: Tell me something more about your dad; what is it that makes you want to be rude to him?

Pearl: Well when there's been trouble with my sister and mother, he always takes their side.

Therapist: He doesn't listen to *you* then?

Pearl: Well he will listen to my mum more than he'll listen to me but he listens to Babsie most of all.

VII.   MIDDLE STAGES

A.   Focussing and Clarifying

To illustrate the issues of the middle stages of the initial interview, I will continue with the same family. Later in the session, the therapist is trying to make the children sort out and agree on their reality in such a way that they can do some work on it in an age-appropriate manner.

Therapist: Well make sure that's what she's trying to say.

Pearl: I think that's what she's trying to say.

Therapist: Well make sure, ask her.

Pearl: Is that what you're trying to say?

Babsie (7): No

Therapist: Are you sure that you two understand each other—let's just get straight what really happens between you two. [focusses] Now Babsie what happens when Clive comes into your room.

Babsie: If I'm doing something he comes and you know he just says "Oh you're doing that because you want to take the cat away from me", and he puts on his silly voice and then I get so annoyed.

Clive (5): Well she started it coming into *my* room.

Babsie: I didn't, silly, I didn't. You just annoy me putting on that silly voice, calling me a cissy girl and all that.

Clive: Well she started it, hitting me and sticking out her tongue like this. [makes horrible face to show T]

Therapist: Well now let's slow this down a little.

B. Tracking the Problem

Therapist: So then the problem is you two, is that right, you have a quarrel, a fight and you run into Pearl to sort it out?
Pearl: Yeah
Therapist: Is there anything else?
Pearl: No, that's most of it.
Therapist: How does that lead you to be rude to your Dad?
Pearl: Because he says I shouldn't smack them, but I think I'm supposed to look after them when Mum is out, then they cry and they go and tell Mum when she gets back and she says I shouldn't smack them and tells Dad and he yells —and bawls me out.
Therapist: So you would like your Mum and Dad to listen more to you and less to your sister and brother. O.K. It looks as though the responsibility . . . who's in charge . . . needs sorting out here. Who would you like to discuss this with Pearl, your Mum or your Dad—which one would you like to talk to first?*

In this last example we are moving towards the middle stage of a first session. The question of what the therapist should have achieved by the end of the session and the links he should be making to further work, will now be in his mind. The lesson we have all learnt most powerfully in our work with families has been the importance of accepting and confirming the system the family bring, however dysfunctional it appears in the therapist's eyes, and of not letting the family go away without this sense of confirmation well established. Only if they have received this somewhere along the line are they likely to accept any initiated change, to continue working in between sessions, and want to come back. Where a family have felt that their reality has been understood, accepted and confirmed as having validity in terms of the options they had open to them, it becomes possible to challenge what is dysfunctional in the system in a variety of ways. Some of these ways are the subject matter of further chapters.

C. Contracts

Where a family is anxious or suspicious about continuing to work in an open ended way, it can be helpful for them to agree that there is as yet no way they can know whether the process of family work is of any use and to set a contract of a limited number of sessions after which a review will take place with them to see how useful they are finding it. Such a review date should be used for joint examination of what has been achieved and for the basis for a further contract if this is thought useful on both sides.

This limiting of sessions is especially helpful for families who cannot plan very far ahead in any aspect of their lives. The power of renegotiation is very important. Where "family therapy" has been recommended as part of a court

---

*With thanks to Harry Aponte whose patient way of working with child sub-systems in families I would like to acknowledge here.

order, it is essential to plan with the magistrate (usually in the juvenile court) that the case can be brought back for review if this approach is *not* found to be useful *on either side and other plans made.* Especially where planned as part of a possible or an actual Care Order, it is important to stick to the length of the contract made since it gives both adolescent and parents a breathing space to consider further separation in a less dramatic and crisis centred way. The fixed number of sessions act as a containment for the family during which time they know they will have a third part intermediary in sorting out habitual quarrels within a different context.

There are also families who will come for therapy with a readiness to make the clinic their home and the therapist one of their family. In such cases, the therapist may find it valuable to fix a number of sessions and then review the work in order to prevent himself making a lifelong contract. However the need for contracts to provide therapist protection are likely to diminish as the experience and confidence of the therapist grows.

For many strategic therapists, the notion of a contract of more than one additional session at a time would go against the principles on which they are working. These would include the capacity of the family to change without the further interest of the therapist or therapeutic team provided the principles on which the prescriptive intervention they had formulated for the family were systemically correct. The notion of contract might be decided session by session depending on the self report of the family and the assessment of the therapist as to whether further involvement would be therapeutically valuable in achieving systemic change.

D. Tasks

Tasks are ways of giving families concrete aspects of the therapy to take home and continue themselves. These may be given in a straightforward or in a more complicated manner. In that tasks require performance, they remind the family of the therapist and whatever containment he represents to the family that makes it safe for them to risk the improbable, which is to activate a change in their habitual system. It is thus important that tasks are set with assurance within the context of the family's confidence in the overall competence of the therapy. Two kinds of task need distinguishing.

(1) Straight Tasks
Straight tasks should be directed towards changing some piece of action either within one or more subsystems in the family. If it is overtly addressed to one subsystem only, the therapist will have to warn the family of the likely consequences for the others so that they are not taken by surprise.

> If Tom does manage to make his bed every day this week and tidy his own room you, mother, are going to find yourself with time on your hands and you, father, will have to find something else for her to worry about — or you could even find her something to enjoy.

This kind of comment which addresses itself to only one small aspect of a subsystem in a very enmeshed family can be offered both as an encouraging directive, "Let's see if you can do it", where there really appears to be some willingness to change, or perhaps as a challenge which still ascribes the best intentions to the family for resisting: "I doubt if the family will be able to allow Tom to do it on his own because they are so good at worrying for their children that they will hate to let him make his own mistakes".

(2) Strategic Tasks

Strategic tasks which address themselves to the unconscious wishes of the family as well as to their conscious and declared wishes and which aim to address themselves to the rules governing the overall patterning of the family are of a greater possible complexity than can be properly covered here. They may be directed to the system as a whole with required instructions for each person's behaviour during the coming interval; they may give reasons for the requirement or they may withhold these; they may be delivered with optimism or pessimism, with humour or with the utmost gravity.

> We believe that as a family you have a latent talent for healthy arguing which is not being properly exercised. We would like it therefore if every night you sit together round the kitchen table with an alarm clock and each take ten minutes to hold forth on the topic of your choice. The others are not to interrupt but are to wait for their turn (Gorell Barnes et al., 1982b).

Alternatively, there may be no general request for action, but simply a systemic message which observes the meaning of the behaviours of each member on behalf of the system as a whole, and delegates the action to one member, often the referred patient: "It will be up to Julia to find a way to lead you to success." Letters may also be sent to ensure that the task is clearly understood by the whole family with an instruction that it be "read aloud to the family at breakfast".

The sense of humour in the average English family has provided some interesting feedback on the use of these messages. What remains fascinating is the power they have if properly construed, to bring about change even in the face of open family resistance."We had one of your funny letters last week; we agreed about the first part but the rest of it's a load of codswallop and we've been discussing it ever since . . ."

An essential feature of paradoxical work is the therapist's proper appreciation of the function of disturbed behaviours for the family system as a whole. He is therefore *unwilling* to prescribe change, respecting the family's grasp of their own safety margins. He may indeed prescribe no change: "It is very important that you two do not get any closer at the moment because the family just aren't ready to handle that; stay just that distance apart." Alternatively, he might thank the presenting patient for "keeping the family just the way they are" and ask the family to help the patient maintain their symptom, while putitng it more consciously under the patient's control for the following week: "It is important that you practice your temper for at least 15 minutes every day and you, mother, must make sure she is really taking it seriously. Tom and Father are to remind you when it's time to practise" (Gorell Barnes, 1982, a, b).

VIII. ENDING THE INITIAL WORK

It is important to end the first session with everyone agreed about when the next one is taking place. Whether this is in a week's time or a month's time, the family need to know how long they have got to digest whatever has taken place in the session. The length of time between sessions will largely depend on therapist style, choice of theoretical model, and time he has available rather than any known index of family need. A guideline is to consider how long the family can hold onto the "representation" of the therapy, or the change resulting from the session, and at what point these representations will be lost, and the system readjust to its former state, perhaps requiring another input. As yet we know little about this.

In the engagement phase of therapy, it is usually important for the gap to be small while family and therapist achieve a working alliance, but those who work primarily with paradox feel that the time span is lengthier and that at least a fortnight is needed between sessions. The therapist working with whole-system prescriptive strategy who is aiming at transformation of the overall rules of the game, would argue that if the family's view of reality has indeed been transformed, i.e. become a new entity with formal characteristics different from its predecessor, a much longer time must be allowed for the implications of this radical change in view to be carried through to the behaviours of the family members. Links with any previous view or with the person of the therapist, would be irrelevant so that a number of weeks or months might be left between appointments. The length of time, however, would be determined and stated before the prescriptive message was given, so that a date was firmly fixed in the family's mind.

Successful therapy, as we all know, is not achieved by sticking to a rule book; but each therapist has to learn the basic rules of the theories of change he is following. He can then develop his clinical judgement about appropriate procedures between him and each new family with a greater degree of confidence.

REFERENCES

Bentovim, A. and Gilmour, L. (1981). A family therapy interactional approach to decision making in child care, access and custody cases. *Family Therapy*, **3**, 65-78.

Bloch, D. (1973). The clinical home visit. *In* "Techniques of Family Psychotherapy", (D. Bloch, ed.), Grune & Stratton, New York.

Cade, B. and Southgate, P. (1979). Honesty is the best policy. *Journal of Family Therapy*, **1**, 23-32.

Cade, B. (1979). The use of Paradox in Therapy. *In* "Family and Marital Psychotherapy: A Critical Approach", (S. Walrond-Skinner, ed.), Routledge & Kegan Paul, London.

Clarke, A. (1980). (Unpublished paper), Kettering Family Centre, Northants.

Gorell Barnes, G. (1978). *In* "Good Enough Parenting", C.C.E.R.S.W. Study 1. Report of a group on work with children and young people and the implications for social work education.

Gorell Barnes, G. (1980). Family therapy in social work settings: a survey by questionnaire 1976-1978. *Journal of Family Therapy*, **2**, 357-378.

Gorell Barnes, G. (1982a). A difference that makes a difference. I. *Journal of Family Therapy*, (in press).

Gorell Barnes, G. (1982b). (With Jones, E. and de Carteret, J.) A difference that makes a difference. II. *Journal of Family Therapy*, (in press).

Gorell Barnes, G. and Campbell, D. (1982). From frog to prince: the impact of structural and strategic approaches on the supervisory process. *In Family Therapy Supervision: Recent Developments in Practice* (R. Whiffen and J. Byng-Hall, eds), Academic Press, London and New York.

Haley, J. (1963). *Strategies of Psychotherapy.* Grune & Stratton, New York.

Lindsey, C. (1979). Working with rage and anger—the establishment of a therapeutic setting in the homes of multi-problem families. *Journal of Family Therapy*, **1**, 117-124.

Lowenstein, S. (1980). Understanding lesbian women. *Social Casework: The Journal of Contemporary Social Work.*

Madanes, C. (1980). Play, paradox and pretending. *Family Process*, **19**, 73-85.

Palazzoli, M. S., Boscolo, L., Cecchini, G. and Prata, G. (1978). Paradox and Counter-paradox, Aronson, New York.

Rutter, M. (1974). *Helping Troubled Children.* Penguin, Harmondsworth.

Stern, M. (1977). *The First Relationship: Infant and Mother.* Fontana Open Books, New York.

Watzlawick, P., Beavin, J. H. and Jackson, D. D. (1967). "Pragmatics of human communication", Norton, New York.

Watzlawick, P., Weakland, J. H. and Fish, R. (1974). "Change: Principles of Problem Formation and Problem Solution", Norton, New York.

Chapter 9

Maintaining Family Motivation During Treatment

A. Elton

I. INTRODUCTION

Maintaining a family in treatment presents one of the greatest therapeutic challenges. This may apply equally to a planned short-term contract as to an open-ended long-term treatment. Perhaps it would be truer to say that keeping the family involved in and working actively to change is the problem, since there are many families as well as individuals who may come compliantly to sessions, but may, once there, appear to use them to maintain the family status quo; indeed there may be families who oppose finishing treatment out of just such a need to keep things the same.

A. Some Basic Factors Motivating Families

Families who attend do have some wish to change, and many put considerable energy and much hard work into the process. Their enthusiasm and capacity to do so relates to the presence of various conditions. First, they *hope for relief* from their presenting symptom, whether that be identified by them as behaviour of an individual or as relationship problems. Many families may experience some relief of such symptoms from the outset of treatment, or even if there is no early symptoms change, they may be very reassured by having their worries and complaints listened to and taken seriously. Continued experience of relief, even if periodic, occurring through treatment keeps the family hope of change alive. Secondly, families may *be interested, even excited, in discovering new facets about their behaviour;* in doing this, possibilities of expansion in their family life may become evident. Finally, *they may actually enjoy treatment* despite the hard work they put into it (sometimes indeed because of the hard work and their own and the therapist's acknowledgement of this). Naturally such enjoyment has to be transferable and transferred to other situations if the family is to be able to stop treatment without undue anxiety.

The therapist has to bear these three needs in mind throughout treatment and meet at least one of them for much of the time. Indeed, if he cannot meet any of these needs for a prolonged period, his own motivation with that family is likely to weaken and he, too, may become hopeless. This can obviously be fatal to the treatment since its continuance and success depends on the therapist's interest and enthusiasm as much as on the family's.

193

B. Resistances

In previous chapters, a variety of therapeutic approaches have been described, all of which may be employed to help bring relief of painful symptoms, to widen the family experience, and to deepen their understanding and appreciation of each other. However, it is not enough for therapists to be skilled in techniques of change and sensitive to understanding very indirect messages about a hope for change. All therapists come up against the strong need of the family not to change: the positive resistance to any real alteration in the current situation, however painful it is. It is this resistance which makes the task of maintaining the therapeutic alliance so difficult. All families, however great and true their wish to change the painful situation which brought them into treatment, have a simultaneous and powerful wish not to experience certain changes; the very changes which may be essential to the achievement of their motivating goal.

II. RESISTANCE AND PREVENTION OF CHANGE

A. Psychodynamic Theories

(1) Individual
Resistance to change has been observed since the early development of psycho-analysis. Freud described it as a "vigorous and tenacious resistance" maintained throughout the whole course of treatment. He went on to discuss the very varied and subtle forms such resistance can take, and understood the phenomenon to arise from the same powerful forces which produced the symptomatology, namely from repression. He postulated that certain impulses are felt to be too dangerous to allow into an individual's consciousness and so are repressed: A defence system is necessarily erected to keep these impulses unconscious, but in doing this, the defences become an integral part of the personality. Indeed, they are the part of the personality which has to be changed in order to allow expression and understanding of the original repressed impulse and so relief of the symptoms. Naturally, defences are very strong, necessarily to do their work of repression, and so of course they are also very competent to resist any attempt to modify them themselves.

(2) Group
While in 1916 Freud expected his audiences to regard this phenomenon and the strength of it as improbable, his influence, and that of other analysts since has led to its existence being generally accepted, and to analytic and psychodynamic treatments focussing on many aspects of the resistance. Working with groups in the 1950s, Ezriel developed the theory of required and avoided solutions, which mirrored the idea of repression and the defence system, but described it in group terms (Ezriel, 1956). The required solution, including the symptomatology, is manifest and is produced in order to avoid some more painful situation. This

situation, if not avoided, it is feared would lead to some catastrophic occurrence. More recently, Malan (1976) has restated this concept further, and describes the *required* solution as the defence system, the *avoided* solution as the impulse or wish, and the *catastrophe* as the painful feelings which would be experienced if the avoided solution was allowed to occur.

(3) Family

The understanding that symptoms arise as a result of the attempt to avoid painful conflicts does, of course, make the existence of resistance to change understandable, indeed logical. Who would court the very disaster they have spent their lives, individual or group, trying to avoid? The Ezrelian concepts of required and avoided solutions can as well be applied to family dynamic life as to group process. Family therapists who work with family myths such as Byng-Hall (1973), Stierlin (1977) and Ferreira (1963) emphasize the way in which family myths have a homeostatic function since they act as strong defences, often stronger because they are passed on from one generation to another and so cannot easily be challenged. Equally, it may be very difficult to challenge what Stierlin describes as "loose myths", vaguely formulated assumptions held by family members. Such assumptions are powerful defences against examining the truth of family relationships since they obscure the real quality and variations in such involvements. Being over-determined, myths inevitably lead to labelling either of individuals or of relationships, and so distort reality. As with repression in individuals, myths serve both a defensive and a protective function; defensive against forces from within (the individual or family) and protective against forces from without (the therapist). Thus they constitute a strong resistant mechanism.

B.   Systems Theories

(1) Steady State Maintenance

Systems theorists also postulate a force analogous to resistance to change as central to the maintenance of the system. They see systems as requiring a state of equilibrium or "steady state" in order to continue functioning successfully; this is produced by feedback mechanisms which convey information to the system allowing it to correct either for its own malfunctioning or for any environmental change. In this way a steady state or homeostasis is maintained. As Katz and Kahn (1966) stress, in open systems the most important principle is "the preservation of the character of the system" rather than a rigidly precise homeostasis. Thus, if one part of the system changes, another part will alter in a compensatory direction; this capacity of systems to adjust allows them to continue functioning in different situations. This principle provides the basic axiom of systems theory as applied to family therapy. If one part of the system (individual) changes, then other parts have to change too in order to preserve the system as a functioning whole. The simplest type of change is an adjustment made to compensate for the initial change; this means that the steady state of the system is maintained. However, the aim of family therapy is to alter the system, and the ready activity of natural feedback mechanisms provide the resistant force.

(2) The family's Special Ability to Resist

The fact of a family's being a group does not make it less resistant to change than an individual, but more so. A family will have a greater variety of possible manoeuvres to employ by way of indicating pseudo-change than an individual has. If an individual learns to accept unacceptable feelings or practice new behaviours, they may become a meaningful part of himself and so lead to a real change. But if family member A in the family context does this, he may not be indicating real system change, but merely expressing something hitherto manifested by another family member, B, and so in a sense borrowed from him, so that B has now lost it.

The essential circularity of systems which arises from their need to maintain a steady state can ensure this. For example, it is not unusual to meet families where one person acts as spokesman for all; their words may be listened to with eagerness, fear, impatience, or boredom by other members. During treatment, this phenomenon may be noted and commented on; other members will be encouraged to speak, and may do so. An apparent improvement may occur, but the therapist may then become aware that A's overwhelming monologue has just been replaced by B's intrusive chattering. The system has not changed; that would require every member to speak for him or herself with a frequency appropriate to their age, and to be able to listen attentively to others. It is precisely this change which is so difficult to achieve. As Wynne (1965) has put it, "families have a staggering capacity to remain the same". Framo (1965) has described the massive resistance presented by families in treatment, a description which echoes Freud. Ferreira (1963), as discussed above, has pointed to the power family myths have in maintaining homeostasis and keeping the required solution alive. The strength of the barriers to change raised within a family is greatly increased just because each individual may not only be resisting change within himself, but is also resisting change in other family members either protectively or in self-defence.

(3) Case Example: The K Family

A striking example of such openly manifest resistance was shown in the K family. the Ks were a family consisting of parents and three teenage children, girls of 17 and 13, and a boy of 15. There were frequent violent arguments in this family, and members tended to take up very entrenched positions, with a great deal of mutual labelling. The mother talked in a particularly battering and intrusive manner in a loud and high voice, often in the plural and at great length. She herself became aware of how aggressive her style of talking was, and of how easily it could spiral off one of the frequent rows. Her distress at recognizing this was quite real, and she made determined and sincere attempts to alter her way of speech. Although her son supported her, and as a result she and he greatly decreased their arguments, the daughters vigorously and openly opposed her quieter approach, even mocking it. Her husband more subtly opposed it by failing to notice the change. After a short time, the mother (and son) gave up the attempt to change. The pressure of the family as a whole was such that it could not adapt to this change without some other member having to make a totally unpalatable change; for example, the two girls to have more open disagreements with each other. Still less could the family bear to consider at this point what pain the system of continuous rows over trivia avoided.

In such ways there can be active, albeit at times secret, coalitions between family members to maintain people in their assigned and familiar rôles. Fortunately, the converse is also true, and is what contributes to the effectiveness of treatment; that is, co-operation to achieve change. The therapist has to work to keep this active co-operation alive throughout the treatment process. This means treading a difficult balance between pushing the more optimistic members to changes which the others might resist, and letting the whole family fall into despair at the lack of change if they go at the pace of the slowest. It means keeping alive hope for the family at the times when they are struggling to change and failing to see results. It means being sensitive to the family's fears and defences even if they are not openly acknowledged and recognizing when it is helpful to change therapeutic emphasis from process to content and vice versa. All this is done in the context of recognizing the immense struggle between the wish to change and the fear of doing so.

III. TECHNIQUES AIMED AT MAINTAINING MOTIVATION IN THE FAMILY

In order to maintain the therapeutic alliance, it is obviously essential to have the family's co-operation. In the previous chapter, the work of engaging the family, formulating the problems and agreeing on a work contract have been described in detail. I will only refer to some of these tasks insofar as the therapist may need to refer back to them himself in helping the family deal with its resistance and carry on with the work.

A. Establishment of the Therapist's Authority

As Skynner (1976) has pointed out, "issues of authority, hierarchy and control occupy a central place in the concepts and techniques of almost all family therapists". The therapist establishes his control at the beginning by deciding which members he will agree to see together, when he will do it, and how he works. The aims of work are agreed upon. Having done this, the therapist is then much more likely to be able to deal successfully with drop-outs, absences and other such manoeuvres designed to undermine the treatment at a later stage. Although the therapist's control is generally speaking confined to the actual sessions, he is much more likely to succeed in getting the family to carry out tasks between sessions if the family acknowledges his direction, and of course perceives the task as relevant.

Once the therapist has succeeded in getting the appropriate members present at an agreed time, he then has to show that he expects the family to do quite a lot of the work themselves. He neither can, nor will, provide the answers, nor will he take over care and control of family members during sessions, although he may help. These functions belong properly to the family. Parental failure to comfort, control or attend to children can only be assessed and worked on if it is clear to all that the therapist does not intend to take over these functions. Parents have to be asked to carry them out. In this way, it is possible to see how successfully they can care and control, and how well the children respond. Similarly, most questions raised within family sessions are implicitly, if not explicitly, directed at another family member; families really wish to hear their own relations' views on important issues and not just the therapist's. The therapist has to be able to redirect questions from himself to an appropriate family member. Minuchin (1974, 1981) has described the need to avoid getting too strongly put into the "helper" rôle; if this does occur, it can prevent the family discovering its own independent strengths and capacities. It also means that the family when struggling with its own resistance to change, is much more likely to be able to recognize that this resistance arises from within itself, and not attribute it to a mean withholding spirit in the therapist.

B.   Creating a Focus and Changing it

An essential part of the engagement process is the agreeing of a focus of work. The therapist may wish to concentrate on the presenting symptom, or he can make his initial formulation to the family in terms of broader issues in the system. For example, if a child is presented as having temper tantrums, the focus may be simply helping the family manage the tantrums, or it may be stated as including a parental difficulty in expressing anger. Whichever is the case, the family and therapist have to agree on the difficulties they wish to change at the outset. A working alliance can only be maintained until those initial aims are achieved. A common experience in family, as in individual, work is that as the work proceeds, more problems may be highlighted. A change of aim or focus may then be indicated. If that is the case, a new agreed target must be negotiated. This shared target is important in maintaining the working alliance, since it provides necessary boundaries to the work in hand which could otherwise be felt to be endless. It also allows the family space to think about what they really want. A common expression of resistance is a belittling of their own needs. Families say things like "there must be people worse off than us, aren't we just wasting your time?" and "perhaps things are not really so bad". Such moves commonly occur near the beginning of treatment, although they may also be heard around significant anniversaries or holidays. If the basic problems are still manifest, the family is usually helped by being able to re-identify them.

It seems to me very helpful to be able to formulate the focus in such a way that the family cannot only accept it, which is essential, but also make sense of it, enlarge on it, and broaden the area of work themselves. This means that they do much of the work of overcoming their own resistance to moving into new therapeutic areas. If we consider the situation suggested above of a family referred because of a child with tantrums, an agreed formulation which refers to the parents' difficulty in expressing anger can allow that couple to move into looking at their own relationship or their relationships with extended family should that seem appropriate.

C. On-going Therapeutic Approaches and Techniques

I feel that there are two major elements to the work done with families in treatment. One is directed at the *"here and now"* process, the current feeling atmosphere and style of interaction between family members, and between family and therapist. The second is concentration on the *"content and meaning"*, discussion and understanding of the topics raised which can be seen as reflecting the thoughts and preoccupations of the family. Work on family myths comes into this category. My own personal view is that in order to maintain a satisfactory and helpful alliance, the therapist has to take due account of both elements. This does not necessarily mean that he has to work directly with both, nor that he has to select the one the family is overtly presenting. Therapists are well aware that families may produce content issues as a defence against working on control difficulties and structural problems as a defence against intolerable fears.

Those struggling to learn the theory and techniques of family therapy may often feel that there is a basic dichotomy between these two elements. This feeling may be exacerbated by reading such papers as Beels and Ferber (1969) on types of therapy and therapist, distinguishing *"active conductor"* and *"passive reactor."* In addition, the fact that family therapists have come from a wide range of theoretical backgrounds means that they have introduced techniques from such different orientations as psychoanalysis and behavioural theory. It also means that some workers are definitely inclined to be more symptom-orientated, others less so. Behavioural approaches tend to be labelled as active and directive (which may be true), and as taking no account of complicated feelings and past experience (which is not so). In distinction to this, the psychoanalytic method is seen not just as undirective (which it is), but also as passive and purely concentrating on past experiences (which it is not). Indeed, the whole concept of transference brings a technique of working with here-and-now processes, albeit in the context of content about past as well as present.

Family therapists may incline much more strongly either to a model concentrating on current behaviour (including relationship) change or to one struggling to understand the roots of the problems and thus achieving change. However, I feel that in order to maintain the family's motivation and so help bring about change, it may be most appropriate to be flexible: to be able to concentrate on here-and-now processes at certain times, and at other times be content to let past experience be the focus. Above all, it seems to me important to be able to distinguish when one must work with one element in order to be free to work with the other.

IV. "HERE AND NOW" INTERVENTIONS TO MAINTAIN MOTIVATION

"Here and Now" interventions comprise those techniques aimed at working directly with the structure of the family: techniques such as work on communications, work on control and boundary issues, on family alliances and task setting; and those aimed at working on the family/therapist relationship, such as transference interpretations (transference in the traditional analytic sense). Use of paradox, which is a direct and immediate challenge to the resistance, is also a here-and-now move.

A. Communications and Boundaries

I am linking communication and boundary issues, since dysfunction in one almost inevitably is associated with dysfunction in the other. In clinical practice, we frequently see families with striking problems of confused communication pattern and boundary keeping. Some families continually interrupt each other, or more than one person speaks at once. Others avoid talking directly in the first person, or else the individual addressed does not respond, but rather another does for him. In a similar way, if one family member is requested to do something, another may take over and act for him. While all families obviously do most of these things some of the time, families presenting for help may manifest such patterns to a very high intensity. Clearly if A or B speak for C, as often as he does for himself, there is likely to be little real sense of boundaries between individuals. If a family's pattern is for all to talk at once, or indeed never to talk freely at all, there may be a very impoverished awareness of each other's thoughts and feelings. There is also likely to be a general feeling of lack of control; that is, a lack of caring and an absence of parental authority. Naturally the parents share in this feeling, as they share in not being heard, and consequently their actual capacity to exert control when appropriate is likely to be diminished.

Such families can confuse and overwhelm the therapist with the amount and speed of information given and feeling projected, as well as by the actual noise level. It is often worthwhile for the therapist to make a statement about his own confusion or his inability to hear anything clearly. If the family responds to that spontaneously, it indicates that their pressure of talk arises from anxiety in the new therapeutic situation and that they themselves can modify it. However as is more often the case, such a comment has no effect, the therapist may have to work directly on the communication pattern shown before he and the family can do any other work.

B. Case Example: Robert's Family

(1) Introduction
Robert was an 8-year-old boy who was referred because of fairly severe behaviour problems both at home and in school; he had tempers, was distractable and

disobedient and had had to be contained in a special small class. He was a boy who was excessively short for his age, being considerably smaller than his two younger sisters, Ann aged 7, and Susan aged 6. Mother was the only remaining parent, the father having deserted when the youngest child was only months old. It was immediately clear to the therapist that Robert was never treated as the oldest child in the family, Ann being given that rôle. It was also evident on meeting the family that Susan was at least as disruptive as Robert and that all three children talked and interrupted continuously. Mother rarely spoke except to give weak or ineffectual negative injunctions. As well as talking for each other the children haphazardly used each other's toys and drawings in such a continuous way that the victim of such an abuse often did not notice its occurrence until later.

(2) Initial Therapeutic Moves
The therapy initially concentrated on three issues. First, mother was asked to treat Robert as the oldest child giving him some obvious privileges such as a later bedtime. Secondly, the therapist made a rule that there was to be no interruption, and the children were asked to put up their hands when they wanted to speak. Thirdly, mother was asked to monitor this and attend when a child wanted to speak and had been waiting. During sessions the family were encouraged to talk to each other. Although the first task was fairly readily carried out, the family had more difficulty with the others. The children responded easily to the notion of raising their hands, after all such behaviour is often expected at school, but they continued to speak for each other. The therapist then teasingly asked who they were: if Ann answered for Robert, she was called Robert, and so on. This amused the children, but also was effective in helping them identify themselves and each other. They began to use each other's names much more often and more appropriately. Interestingly, some time later on in the treatment when the chidlren wanted to show off their prowess in writing to the therapist, what Robert and Ann chose to write was: "We are learning to listen", and this indeed had been the explicit message of much of the treatment. Other techniques were also used. The family played a game in which members took it in turns to build up a story; this necessitated listening carefully. They were also shown video playback of parts of their sessions, Robert and mother particularly being shown bits where they had switched off and stopped listening and then introduced a red herring topic.

It was most difficult to help mother take over an appropriately active rôle and also a listening one. In playing a structured game early on, she had demonstrated that she could teach the children how to do this and hold their attention success-fully. In that kind of unemotive situation, she could be both active and responsive. It needed more work, not only on the here and now, but on the feared content of what she *might* hear if she listened attentively to the children in more spontaneous interaction, for her to be able to begin to respond more positively to the children's general needs.

(3) General Implications
Robert's family was a complicated one with many problems. Nonetheless it was obvious that the children appreciated being listened to and given space as individuals from the outset and that mother eventually did so too. Many families with confused and interruptive communications may respond more quickly to having their interruptiveness pointed out. They may be relieved to be allowed to stop such undermining behaviour, and will readily continue to check interruptions themselves. Some families will follow such changes by admitting to shared feelings of low self-esteem (a feeling which was confirmed by knowing that no one ever really heard). This in itself may be enough change; the family may be able to start to enjoy each other's company in a much more positive way. If the family can recognize the painfulness of the pattern and yet not be able to stop it with help from the therapist, then it may be necessary to consider with them what it is that is too frightening or painful to hear.

Very enmeshed families often show more severely disturbed communication patterns which are more resistant to change and may be more difficult to identify in the first place. The use of "we" instead of "I", the silent looking to another family member for approval or permission to speak, coalitions to silence certain members, all occur. Such systems show an insidious encroachment on to one another's psychological territory; often it is not clear who is encroaching and who is the victim. The moves may not be as equal and balanced as in Robert's family. This causes deeper enmeshment and confusion. Nonetheless, although much work on understanding feelings and history may need to be done in gaining understanding of why, here and now work must be done in identifying the pattern and pointing out actual occurrences.

(4) Therapist's Rôle
The therapist's rôle in this is an active one insofar as he must be able to observe the communication patterns accurately and then help the family see them. The family then has to take over the task of monitoring those. Games and rules may help as may video playback if it is available. Indeed, some families derive enormous help from the impact of seeing themselves as they are, and can use this to increase their own motivation to change.

C. Changing Alliances

All families have numbers of natural alliances within them; that between parents, between certain siblings, between parent and child. Such closenesses occur inevitably and only lead to dysfunction if any given alliance prevents one or both members of it being as close as they might be to other family members. Obviously negative alliances or coalitions exist with the implicit purpose of preventing closeness between members (Haley, 1967) and such coalitions are always pathological.

(1) De-triangulating Children
They probably always indicate that there are significant problems in the marital relationship and the therapist's first task must be to detriangulate the child

caught in the coalition and then work with the parents together, either with the rest of the family there or not depending on the case and on the therapist's preference. My own is for working with the couple alone in such situations. However, in order to reach that point, it is necessary to have overcome their resistance to having the problem labelled primarily as a marital one. If a couple are able to acknowledge some difficulties they are more likely to see that they are drawing a child, or children, in unhealthily and so may well accept the reformulation. However in some situations, the couple are determined not to look at their own relationship, and in such situations, it may be impossible to let the child out of the treatment. Such families are again likely to be highly enmeshed and may need a long time before changing at all, and perhaps the highest drop-out rate is among such families. If they are not so resistant, they are likely to highlight the marital conflict fairly early on, often over management of the children, and from then on may agree to work on it; indeed, are often relieved to do so.

(2)   Strengthening Sibling Alliances

There are, however, many other ways of helping families change and shift the balance of alliances. Siblings may be helped to learn to enjoy activities together (as in Robert's family). Another common shift is in helping an adolescent or near-adolescent child make a closer alliance with the parent of the same sex. Often a young adolescent may be presented as having a problem such as not working in school, general negativism or mild unhappiness. Sometimes when the family is seen, what is revealed is a considerable distance between the adolescent and parent of the same sex. While this may co-exist with an apparently over-close relationship with the parent of the opposite sex, this may occur not because of significant distance between the parental couple or overprotectiveness from the close parent, but more from unfamiliarity in how to approach each other. Helping the child and parent find ways of getting together can alter such distance and so change the existing alliances. The two may do this over talking together or having an activity together.

(3)   John's Family: Case Example

John, a 15-year-old with a sister of 20, was presented as being completely disinterested in any activity: home, school or leisure-based. He and his mother appeared to be very over-involved with each other. Father was asked to talk with John and share with him his own experiences of growing up especially at this age. Following this John became much more lively and active, and it also became clear to the therapist that the parents still had a great deal actively in common and did pursue their joint interests together, despite mother's apparent closeness with John.

(4)   Lindsay's Family: Case Example

Lindsay was an attractive 13-year-old whose parents complained of her temper tantrums and generally negative behaviour. She was also failing in school and had a long-standing speech defect. During the treatment the difficulty she and her mother had in achieving any positive closeness was highlighted; it was clear that both felt they were in some ways failing the other's expectations and so were continually unable to make friendly approaches. Both parents were rather concerned about some of Lindsay's normal adolescent interests in dress and appearance etc.; father definitely more so. The therapist picked up on mother's sneaking sympathy with her daughter and with mother's own rigid upbringing, and got them to talk together ("girl talk") without father and younger brother in the room. Mother was able to open up to Lindsay about some of her own adolescent "goings on", and to help her daughter express some wishes about make-up and so on. The two then were set the task of going shopping for make-up together, and also of playing around with it at home together on occasions. In this way they began to feel closer to each other, and consequently less dissatisfied; father was able to take a back seat on this issue and allow his wife to deal with it alone.

D. Control

Problems in control clearly relate to boundary dysfunction. Many families with children present with difficulties in this area. Sometimes they themselves are complaining of their children's disobedient behaviour; at other times they are not aware of a control problem, and are afraid that the child is very unhappy, anxious and so on. Of course a child who is allowed to have inappropriate control over his own and his family's life is likely to be unhappy, but that may often be secondary to the problem. Tantrums, behaviour problems and school phobia are common examples of dysfunction in control.

(1) General Principles
With many symptoms parents can be encouraged to find ways of establishing appropriate control both within the sessions and at home. Setting tasks and then supporting the parents in carrying them out can help. If parents succeed in stopping their infants' temper tantrum or in getting their children to listen attentively in a session, they gain an experience of success which often provides a basis on which to build at home. Families presenting with a school-phobic child may respond immediately to a new or heightened awareness that this symptom is, in part at least, expression of a control problem, and the child can then return to school at once. Such symptom improvement is of course unlikely to be maintained unless some further work is done on the family system, and part of the initial aim must be to identify such needs.

(2) Martin's Family: Case Example
Martin, aged 13, was brought by his parents having been out of school for 6 weeks. The boy had increasing anxieties about his performance, and felt that he could not cope with the work. Significantly, his much older sister had had a change of schools at about 13 because her school "was not right for her". During the interview, Martin was able to say quite clearly that he felt burdened by his mother's anxiety, worse since a recent illness. The mother's anxiety and ambivalence about her son's growing up were obvious, the father's equally

strong although not manifest until later. Father, who was nearing retirement, was confused and rather ineffective, torn between supporting his wife and his son. All three could agree, however, that they would like the mother to be less anxious and protective. With the hope of this being achieved, the parents were able to reassert their authority and help Martin return to school the following day. (As often seems to happen, this was done after father made a telephone call to the therapist during his struggle to get Martin out of the house, asking for confirmation that it was alright to be firm.)

Having achieved this success, the family was then well motivated to continue in treatment for a number of sessions during which they could continue to work on the separation problems underlying the original symptom. As in many families, task-setting as well as discussion of anxieties around independence could be helpful. Ideally, tasks should either involve all family members in the therapeutic group together (such as a shared activity) or else should give each member separately some task, which individually they might wish to achieve, but also which involves all members dealing with the same feeling difficulty. In Martin's family, he was asked to go out to a football match with a friend (he had only been with father before), and the parents were asked to have an outing together. This allowed each member to have some chosen pleasure but at the cost of having to separate from the other generation.

E.   Transference Interpretations

A very different "here and now" technique, that of transference interpretation, is much more rarely used in family therapy, although certain groups of workers such as Boszormenyi-Nagy and his colleagues (1965), Zinner and Shapiro (1972), Box *et al.* (1981) and Stierlin (1977) have worked on intra-familial transferences. However, interpretation of family/therapist transference may be helpful in response to resistance at certain points, especially in long-term treatments. Distress and acting out around holidays may be one such time, or therapist behaviour may quite accidentally seem to mirror actual experiences in the family, and so arouse similar feelings of anger or sadness.

An example of this occurred in Robert's family (see above). On one occasion, one of the co-therapists had to miss a session to deal with an emergency. The children began talking about the mother's co-habitee, who had recently left the family, in such a way as to indicate direct fears about the therapist's capacity to wish to continue "caring." A transference comment about this produced open acknowledgement of such anxiety, and the children were then able to continue to discuss their feelings about the co-habitee much more freely.

Transference interpretations may be made in relation to the whole family, as in the above situation, or may be directed at one member only, usually the one who is most vigorously expressing the resistance. In some ways, this latter approach is one form of the familiar technique of allying strongly with a particular family member.

F. Paradoxical Injunction

During the last decade, various family therapists have developed techniques of utilizing the resistance and the very symptom itself. Watzlawick *et al.* (1974), Haley (1977) and others (who in any case eschew attempts to help clients gain understanding of their problems), instead focus on changing behaviour, and counter resistance to change by paradoxically agreeing that the patient has found a better way of life than others can help him achieve. Palazzoli and her colleagues (Palazzoli *et al.*, 1978) who do work to understand relationships, will in very resistant situations provide carefully worked out prescriptions which appear paradoxical in that they reframe the pathological behaviour or system positively. In fact, they are providing a counter-paradox to the conflicted and bound situation in which the clients find themselves. In connoting this painful situation positively, they give the family a new feeling of self-esteem which may then help them find a new solution and to continue in the therapeutic alliance. This is a different approach from that of Haley and others, who may facilitate change by altering the focus of the resistance. Instead of the family struggling to prevent change, they may now fight to stop *not* changing, so that any change must be labelled as "too fast" or potentially dangerous, and to be resisted.

Many families seem to be helped sufficiently by interventions in the "here and now." They make improvements which can be maintained without any underlying pathology being revealed. Such dysfunctional patterns may arise as a result of severe stress such as illness or bereavement. The family might have coped well had it not been for great accidental problems. Or it may have coped well with such problems on the feeling level, but been unaware that in doing so, the children had had to "grow up too fast" in one way, and so took over control inappropriately in other ways. Dysfunction may also arise because the parents have a particular difficulty in taking responsibility for setting limits. If a family can enjoy its new freer opener communication and happily take responsibility for control appropriately, the work may be confined to this sphere. The "avoided solution", acceptance of boundaries, proves to be a paper tiger, not a real toothed beast.

V. INTERVENTIONS IN CONTENT, MEANING AND HISTORY TO MAINTAIN MOTIVATION

A. Introduction

Some families present without striking problems in control or communication, but express feelings of not understanding each other. Equally there are many families who do not respond much to interventions in the here and now, or who, having been helped achieve a more open and shared communication, find that they are unhappy with it. In such cases, one suspects that the manifest inter-actional difficulties have arisen as a defence against underlying fears. Indeed, sometimes this is obvious right from the outset, but it may also be clear that the taboo about open discussion of such fears is very strong and time is needed for the family to develop trust enough to do it. These families may be defending against a feared and all too likely catastrophe; illness and breakdown in one or more members, loss, either by death or total separation. Such events may actually have occurred already in the family's life or may have occurred in the past. The parents may themselves have been brought up in deprived or very disturbed situations. It is also possible that such fears were present in past generations and so have been transmitted as a part of family history or myth.

Therapists like Pincus and Dare (1978) and Byng-Hall (1973) give numerous examples of families who presented with problems which had their roots in a fear of repeating past history and so reexperiencing the miseries of painful relationships. As Stierlin (1977) and Boszormenyi-Nagy and Spark (1973) have pointed out so forcefully, family loyalty is immensely powerful and people feel unable to break the pattern of dysfunction, however painful, set by their parents. Herein lies another resistance to change; even when the family may have gained some understanding of itself and its relationships, the parental loyalty to their own families of origin can make it very hard for them to change and do "better" than their parents.

Even if families are responding well to treatment, concentrating predominantly on current interaction, many may be interested in how they came to operate in their dysfunctional way. Often some exploration of history is helpful, both in revealing ways and in maintaining a therapeutic alliance, since the family curiosity deserves to have some satisfaction having been aroused (Martin, 1977). The therapist, too, may be able to use such information to appreciate and convey understanding of the family pain and fears without necessarily dwelling on it at length. This may happen very naturally if labelling people with rôles and personality types is marked in the family.

B.   Myth and Labelling

Exploration of family history and myth can free families to concentrate on working on their current relationships and may be a necessary first step when history is continually brought to the forefront.

(1)   The "G" Family: Case Example

The G's were a couple who requested marital help following an earlier period of family work. The husband, a rather depressed and anxious man, described himself as coming from a "bad" rather harsh and uncaring family, whereas the ebullient wife came from a very warm, close-knit family and saw the husband as the ill partner. The husband tended to share this view, and moreover felt guilty that all the problems in their family must stem from his rather deprived past. The couple were asked to bring their family trees and describe their extended families. In doing this, they threw a completely different light on the matter; the husband's family emerged as fairly ordinary and likeable, albeit with certain personality difficulties. The wife's family, on the contrary, came out as depressed and enmeshed; the wife had had a real period of painful separation and two siblings were severely disturbed. The normality and likeableness of the husband's "bad" family was conveyed by both partners, who agreed in their descriptions but did not realize that they were describing "nice" as opposed to "dreadful" people. When the therapist commented on this, it came as a revelation to both of them and relieved the husband of an enormous burden of guilt about his "hard" family. Indeed, it allowed him to establish warmer relationships with his family of origin. In the marital treatment, it brought the wife in equally as a patient, and the couple then allowed work to concentrate on their current relationship.

C. Content of History and Work with the Past

(1) Introduction
Exploration of family history is not only very rewarding therapeutically at times, but has the added advantage of bringing in past (and absent) generations and so putting the growth of problems into a multigenerational context (see chapters 10 and 12). This can help relieve the family in therapy from feeling inappropriate guilt for all their problems. In doing this, it cannot only help maintain the therapeutic alliance which might otherwise feel too persecuting, but it can gradually help the family feel appropriate guilt and responsibility and so motivate them to change. Often such change will extend to the grandparental generation and so go to improving relationships there. As Boszormenyi-Nagy and Spark (1973) and Stierlin (1977) have described, such work may be of considerable importance for families with severely disturbed and deprived relationships, not only in the present but also in the past. In such families, the avoided solution is always likely to contain such strong and persisting fears that they cannot be adequately relieved by work concentrating on present inter-actions. For families with less disturbed backgrounds, there is still often a bonus of gaining increased appreciation of the grandparental struggle and of then being able to forge closer bonds. Often these moves may come when the adults in treatment are able to identify themselves as clearly separate from their parents, even at the cost of some argument, and can then enjoy warmer, less tied relationships with the older generation.

(2) The "Y" Family: Case Example
The Y's were a family with seriously disturbed backgrounds. They were referred with an obsessional difficult 13-year-old girl. Initially they presented as a confused and enmeshed mass; the two children, especially the younger girl (a 10-year-old), were positively invited to tell the tragic and disturbed family history which was then discounted by the parents. During the first contracted period of work, issues of boundary and control were quite successfully worked on; each member did overtly want some more privacy and some increased parental control. The "history" was deliberately ignored by the therapists. A better balance between parents and children was achieved, the children feeling some relief. The improvements, however, highlighted the marital dissatisfactions

and their shared depression. At the end of the first contract, the couple were able to accept continuing help for the marriage. Although it was obvious that the difficulties related to deep-seated shared experiences of loss and deprivation, the wife was still unable to dare acknowledge her fears openly. These were made easier to hide as the husband's background was more dramatically disturbed and he became seriously depressed.

This resistance to looking at the past meant that the early part of the marital work still focussed on helping the couple work on their own communication problems, their shared distance from each other. Facing the past was avoided because of a feared catastrophe of total loss and madness, the loss which had been experienced in the husband's family and the madness in the wife's. Instead of facing the past, the couple turned every minor current event into a potential disaster. Very gradually this was understood and improved and along with this the couple were helped to dare look at their fears about themselves, their deep disappointments and their anger. Again, the husband led in this, the wife maintaining a front of denial about her depressed and frightened feelings for about a year. The husband, who could not bear to meet any of his wife's extended family, knew that this was because his parents-in-law were looking after two orphaned grandchildren. He himself had been partially brought up by grandparents after being deserted, and on marrying had hoped to be parented by his in-laws. His jealous rage at the intruding grandchildren had led him to quarrel bitterly with his mother-in-law and to fear his own violent feelings to the children.

Later, the wife was able to reveal something of the roots of her obsessional behaviour, understanding it as a retreat and defence against the loneliness and fears of living in a family which was supporting at least one overtly psychotic member. Once the couple were able to look more openly at their own experiences, they were able to understand why they had made such demands on each other and failed to meet them; they were now able to give each other more mutual caring and to accept less violently some of each other's failures. They also began to re-establish some of the broken relationships with their extended families, taking a more realistic view of the likely disappointments but also writing, telephoning and talking to their families in less hostile and provocative ways.

While the therapists had been aware of some of the history and of the weight of incipient depression from the beginning, the work had to be taken very slowly and to vary its overt focus in order to maintain an alliance and avoid a resistance which frequently threatened to take the couple out of treatment. The open focus of feared depression and the work on the history took about a year to reach and a further six months to work on.

VI.   DROP-OUT FROM TREATMENT AND ITS PREVENTION

A.   Therapist Alliances with "Doubtful" Motivation

In family, as in individual treatment, resistance can be acted upon by certain members of the family dropping out before they have achieved their stated aims.

Often this wish to stop is voiced openly or hinted at in a session. In such situations, it is likely to be helpful if the therapist can ally strongly and empathically with the resistant member. In the Y family described above the wife came to the final session of the initial contract determined to stop; the female therapist allied strongly with her, empathizing with her feelings of doubt, and to the husband's amazement she changed her mind and agreed to continue with the proposed marital therapy. During the initial period of marital work while the couple were still see-sawing with doubts about continuing, the therapists deliberately allied rather more strongly with the partner of the same sex, aware that both had particularly deprived relationships with the parent of the same sex. Once the couple were well settled into treatment, such specific sex-linked alliance was not necessary.

B. Dealing with Collusive Exclusion

In other families, it might be more helpful to make such alliances on a hetero-sexual basis because of client need. If the therapist has some knowledge of the family history, he is perhaps more likely to be sensitive to such need. Often too, one is working as a single therapist and so the possibility of choice does not arise. The family therapist, therefore, has to be able to ally with any member positively; he also has to be able to do so with what Stierlin (1977) describes as "involved impartiality" which conveys to the family trust in his basic fairness. If this trust is established, it can help avoid the major problem caused by drop-out of a family member.

One important technique designed to demonstrate this is the therapist's refusal to continue the "work" when anyone is out of the room. Should a child or adolescent actually fail to attend, the therapist can encourage the parents to use their authority to bring him back, thus confirming that control is in their hands. If an adult drops out, the situation is rather more complicated, but nonetheless the responsibility often lies with other family members who collusively wish for that person to absent himself. Situations of this kind often arise when one parent and child, or children, are in open or covert alliance against the other parent and so wish to exclude them. They may do this because they want to complain about them: "he is always drinking", "she is ill and can't stand the hassle", "he isn't really interested in the family anyhow." If the criticisms are open, the therapist can point out that people cannot usefully be discussed in their absence, since such discussion is not only unlikely to help the absent person but might well add fuel to the fire of existing disagreements. In this way, a manoeuvre to label the absent member as the difficult one can be foiled. The attending group may well decide that in that case, they would prefer everyone to come so that they can at least voice the complaints. The family then accepts the responsibility for negotiating with itself. If the alliance against the absentee is covert, the situation is more difficult since the family may present a front of concern for him. Under-standing of the kind of perverse coalition described by Haley (1967) can help the therapist intervene in ways which drive a wedge into the coalition either by unmasking it or by continuing an open empathy with the absentee.

C. Dealing with Drop-Outs

If a member drops out, the therapist can sometimes help him back by a letter or a telephone call. If the family resistance is all being carried by that person the more positive co-operation in the work is being carried by the others, and that coupled with their own warm feelings towards the absentee may help him return.

In my experience, it is more common for the whole family to stop attending than for one member to drop out. The fear of change, the exposing of myth or revealing of secrets, is likely to affect all together. A family may be unable to give up its symptom or scapegoat, and in resisting any improvement will of course feel that the treatment is useless, as it is in such cases. More commonly a family may get some gains from alleviation of the presenting problem only to discover a new discomfort which threatens their security more. A common example is the uncovering of marital unhappiness. Sometimes an offer to see part of the system may help overcome such resistance and help the family decide to return all together, or the therapist may decide to work only with a subsystem. The capacity of the therapist to be flexible enough to work when he considers it appropriate with part of the whole system may be as important a therapeutic technique as being able to use a variety of approaches.

REFERENCES

Beels, C. C. and Ferber, A. (1969). Family Therapy: A View. *Family Process*, **8**, 280-318.

Boszormenyi-Nagy, I. and Framo, J. L. (1965). "Intensive Family Therapy", Harper & Row, New York.

Boszormenyi-Nagy, I. and Spark, G. M. (1973). "Invisible Loyalties", Harper & Row, New York.

Box, S. *et al.* (1981).

Byng-Hall, J. (1973). Family Myths used as Defence in Conjoint Family Therapy. *Brit. J. Med. Psychol.*, **46**, 239-250.

Ezriel, H. (1956). Experimentation within the psychoanalytic session. *Brit. J. Philos. Sci.*, **7**, 25-41.

Ferreira, A. J. (1963). Family Myth and Homeostasis. *Arch. Gen. Psych.*, **9**, 457-463.

Framo, J. L. (1965). Rationale and Techniques of Intensive Family Therapy. *In* "Intensive Family Therapy", (I. Boszormenyi-Nagy and J. L. Framo, eds), Harper & Row, New York.

Haley, J. (1967). Towards a Theory of Pathological Systems. *In* "Family Therapy and Disturbed Families", (G. Zuk and I. Boszormenyi-Nagy, eds), Science and Behaviour Books, Palo Alto.

Haley, J. (1977). "Problem Solving Therapy", Jossey-Bass California.

Katz, D. and Kahn, R. (1969). Common Characteristics of Open Systems. *In* "Systems Thinking", (F. Emery, ed.), Penguin, London.

Malan, D. H. (1976). "The Frontier of Brief Psychotherapy", Plenum Press, New York.

Martin, F. (1977). Some implications from the theory and practice of family therapy and individual therapy. *Brit. J. Med. Psychol.*, **50**, 53-64.

Minuchin, S. (1974). "Families and Family Therapy", Harvard Univ. Press, Cambridge, Mass.

Minuchin, S. and Fishman, H. C. (1981). "Family Therapy Techniques", Harvard Univ. Press, Cambridge, Mass.

Palazzoli, M. S., Boscolo, L., Cecchin, G. F. and Prata, G. (1978). "Paradox and Counter-Paradox", Jason Aronson, New York.

Pincus, L. and Dare, C. (1978). "Secrets in the family", Faber & Faber, London.

Skynner, A. C. R. (1976). "One Flesh: Separate Persons", Constable, London.

Stierlin, H. (1977). "Psychoanalysis and Family Therapy", Aaronson, New York.

Watzlawick, P., Weakland, J. and Fish, R. (1974). 'Change: Principles of Problem Formation and Problem Resolution", Norton, New York.

Wynne, L. C. (1965). Some Indications and Contra-Indications for Exploratory Family Therapy. In "Intensive Family Therapy", (I. Boszormenyi-Nagy and J. L. Framo, eds), Harper & Row, New York.

Zinner, J. and Shapiro, R. (1972). Projective identification as a mode of perception and behaviour in families of adolescents. *Int. J. Psycho-analysis,* **43,** 523-530.

Chapter 10

Family Legends

Their Significance
for the Family Therapist

J. Byng-Hall

I. INTRODUCTION

Family mythology (Byng-Hall, 1979) consists of a complex set of self-perceptions and stories which give the family its sense of identity. Mythology is an interesting blend of reality and fantasy. Only outsiders see the distortion involved and hence would call it mythology. To the family it is their reality. Among the stories of mythology are legends. These are coloured and often colourful stories which are told and retold down through the generations. All families allow many fascinating episodes to fade into the past unless someone takes the trouble to go and ask the ageing members of the family before it is too late. Why in contrast is great care taken to make sure that certain stories are told to the next generation? The main thesis of this chapter is that these stories are often moral tales which convey the rules and obligations of family life. Legends are moulded by the narrator and are "here and now" not "past" phenomena. Each telling produces a version which is edited to fit current distortions in family myths (Ferreira, 1963; Byng-Hall, 1973) and family rules. Thus while the family system remains unchanged, so too do the family stories, and legends can help to prevent change because they have a homeostatic function. Neither teller nor listener is usually aware, however, of when re-editing takes place in line with a shift in family structure. Each imagines that the past, as now depicted, led up to the present family predicaments: a far cry from the idea that the past has just been altered by the present. Thus legends can also consolidate and maintain change, reinforcing the new "reality".

Because legends are involved in changing and maintaining family rules, family therapists should be aware of them, both as phenomena and as potential tools for change. As most families have some legends, there are opportunities for family therapists to explore this dimension within their own families. This chapter includes a description of the author's exploration of one of his own legends. The use of legends in family therapy and in training will also be discussed.

II. THE INFLUENCE OF FAMILY LEGEND:
A CLINICAL EXAMPLE

Both family myths and cultural myths are descriptive and prescriptive, but family myth differs from cultural mythology in one important respect: ownership has to be acknowledged. As implied in the old adage "blood will out", stories about ancestors are more compelling for each family member than are more general stories. The moralizing in family legend usually leaves it clear that the "black sheep" is the odd one out in the family; but of course every member then has to struggle hard to avoid being the one to follow suit. It is after all "lurking in the blood". Scanning the present family cast in order to spot the next villain becomes a powerful mechanism in self-fulfilling prophecy.

A. Clinical Example: The "X" Family

In the X family, as will become clear, violence was considered to be the problem. Mrs X, a pretty petite physiotherapist, referred the family over the telephone because of her two teenage sons fighting, but added that she was worried about telling her epileptic husband about making the appointment. He would, she said, be absolutely furious.

In the first session, it became clear that one of the functions of the boys fighting was to reroute potentially disastrous marital or father/son violence. Mr X would rush in to stop their fighting, his wife would then storm up to stop him damaging her sons. They would then disagree with each other on how to stop the fighting. The fighting acted as a distance regulator (Byng-Hall, 1980). It brought the parents together, but not too close. In that context, there was no danger of the intimate marital contact of which they were both so scared.

Father, who was a Scottish architect, described how in his family of origin:

> My father threw his father out when he was only ten. My alcoholic grandfather was drunk one day when he came home and started beating up my grandmother who was blind. My father got hold of a piece of wood, hit him, and threw him out of the house.

The therapist asked whether the rest of the family knew this story. They all contributed additional snippets of information showing that this was a well-worn legend. "He never came back, leaving his blind wife to look after him and his five blind brothers and sisters!" (there was a form of congenital blindness in the family). "The only one who could see properly was grandpa who was the youngest." The imagery of legend is often vivid. In this case it was epic in quality. There was a hero, a heroine, a villain and victims. The villain not only assaulted a blind wife but deserted his pathetic almost totally blind family.

B. Legends as Condensed History

Legends are condensed history. What takes a minute or two to tell often depicts something which unfolds over several years. The legend encapsulates a scenario, and stands as a graphic analogy for the whole process. In the X family, it was of course not one but many episodes which led to grandfather's departure. The implied blame was the family's own current interpretation of what must have been a breakdown in the family and marital systems of the previous generation.

III. RE-EDITING FAMILY MYTHOLOGY

A. The Illusion of Alternatives

It seems that one of the reasons that certain legends are told and retold is that there is an unresolved theme in the family involving an illusion of alternatives (Watzlawick, 1978), implying that one of two particular choices has to be taken, e.g. either you fight your father and get rid of him, or you let your father beat up your mother. Either way the son is wrong. The theme also remains unresolved, because the way the problem is framed implies that it is only the son(s) who can provide the answer. The chooser *has* to choose one of the alternatives. This is the illusion. He can of course choose not to get involved in parental battles at all, leaving them to resolve their own difficulties. The real alternative is to be, or not be, involved. By posing the question as, "In what way are you going to be involved?" the real choice is obscured. Watzlawick (1978) illustrates the illusion of alternatives with the Nazi slogan "National Socialism or Bolshevik chaos?" The real choice is of course between dictatorship or democracy.

The story illustrating the illusion of alternatives is then told to maintain the family structure, e.g. keeping sons triangled in, reminiscent of the binding dimension of double bind. The function is to avoid an even more feared solution, e.g. one or other parent may be damaged, or they might separate. When this pseudo dilemma is resolved by discovering other options (e.g. marital rows can be survived and sons can leave home), the stories pertaining to it may die out, unless that is, they are so entertaining that they survive for "after dinner" purposes.

B. Editing the Past to Fit the Present

Editing the past to fit the present is of course a well-known phenomenon. Linnemann (1966) describes the editing of Christ's sayings by the gospel writers so that the parables carried significance for the young church at that time. He describes a parable as a "language event". At each telling the context is different. Christ preaching in his lifetime to his uninitiated followers was done in a very different context from that of the gospel writers who believed him to be the Messiah. Preaching is, in Linnemann's words, "Updating or providing new exposition to each generation". The moral to be drawn in each context, as with family legends, is somewhat different. In a secular context, history has also often changed to fit the present. Stalin and Hitler changed the official histories of their countries and then changed the course of history.

IV. "BYNG MYTHOLOGY": IN SEARCH OF ALTERNATIVES TO ILLUSIONS

After writing the article on family mythology (1979), I realized that if I was going to take my own ideas seriously, I would have to examine my own family mythology.

A. The Choice of Legends

I sat down and set myself a number of rules. I would select one of my family legends and proceed chronologically throughout my life tabulating all events which linked with the theme of the legend. I would also try to read the moral of the story. The first legend which came to my mind seemed safe enough. It was 222 years old.

I tried to remember the legend as it was first told to me.

> Admiral Byng was an uncle of yours. He was only an admiral because his father, your great-great etc. grandfather was a famous Admiral of the Fleet. He was sent to relieve Minorca which was being attacked by the French. He was sent under-equipped, and when he got there, the French fleet was much larger and so he did the most sensible thing which was to keep out of range, exchange a few shots and sail home again. Unfortunately he was then found guilty of cowardice and shot on his own quarterdeck.

The illusion of alternatives was you either attack or run away, either way you die.

B. First Association

At first glance, this seemed to have very little personal relevance. I was brought up in Africa a full 300 miles from the sea. I then recalled that despite the remoteness of the sea, I had as a boy wanted to join the Navy. The ownership issue was however quite clear. I was to identify with the Great Admiral of the Fleet, of whom I was a direct descendant, as opposed to this uncle of whom we were all somewhat ashamed. I could not remember being told the date of the battle, 1756. Anyway to a child, the story would have been timeless and vivid.

What other connection did I have with ships? When I was eighteen months old, in 1939, my family was sailing through the Mediterranean when war was declared. My parents told me that much of the time was spent looking over the side for submarines and torpedoes. I have no recollections of this, but the impression made on a toddler must have been powerful.

By the time I was 12-years-old, my wish to join the Navy was very strong and was taken seriously by my parents, so when an old family friend who was captian of a British Naval Cruiser wrote to say that his ship was visiting Mombasa, my parents arranged for me to spend some time aboard to see if I enjoyed it. The whole experience was frightening. Naval discipline was totally mystifying to someone brought up on a huge farm. The most vivid memory for me was standing to attention, upright and rigid, on the quarterdeck, looking very intently at the second in command, terrified lest he saw that I was scared stiff. This episode had puzzled me until I saw it in the context of the legend. Now it made startlingly good sense. I recalled that Admiral Byng was said to have been shot by his own men on his own quarterdeck: presumably at the order of his second in command.

C. Cowardice as a Theme

The theme of cowardice evoked powerful themes for me. I spent all my childhood frightened. I lived through some dangerous times. Kenya was dangerous both in its wild life and during the African Mau Mau rebellion against us white colonials, during which we lived in an isolated farmhouse in the forest. The family was fully armed against a Mau Mau attack which was a constant possibility. Indeed it was discovered later than a main Mau Mau trail ran a few hundred yards from our house. By the time I was conscripted to the Army the fighting had died down, and much to my relief, I never needed to shoot at anyone. Some of my best friends were Kikuyu.

I was much preoccupied with the question of whether I was a coward or not. Was fear evidence of that shameful (and dangerous) condition? Faced with a charging lion or an attack would I prove cowardly and run? My problem then was that never having "engaged" the enemy, I had not dispelled the fear of being a coward.

The next contact with boats had until then also puzzled me. After leaving the Army, I spent a holiday on the East African coast. In a fishing boat with some friends and an African fisherman, I noticed a shoal of six or seven sharks, not very large ones, but about 20 yards from the boat. I found myself diving in and swimming towards them. My friends told me to get back aboard but I watched the fisherman. As soon as he looked anxious and beckoned to me, I came back and climbed aboard. The Byng legend helped me to understand how I sought out a "real" seaman to help me know when I had got close enough to "real" danger to dispel the haunting label of cowardice.

Soon after this I sailed to Britain to go to University. I slept on board deck through the Red Sea and developed acute pain in the back and paralysis of the legs. This was polio. One fleeting fantasy was, however, that I had been shot in the back. Where are you shot if you are a coward and run away? The illusion of alternatives seemed to hold its spell. The option of leaving the danger zone (an alternative to fight or flight) seemed to have the same catastrophic result as flight.

D. The Double-ended Catastrophe

Before re-editing this legend, something I clearly needed to do, I tried to experience the power of the legend's moral injunction. My theory at that time (Byng-Hall, 1979) proposed that legends acted as a guide to which choice to make when there was a dilemma. The way this legend was remembered implied that attack when outpowered by an opponent was potentially disastrous, but retreat was just as catastrophic, constituting a double-ended catastrophe (Byng-Hall, 1980). Put into relationship terms, either separating or becoming over close could in phantasy and/or fact lead to catastrophic results, and thus articulation of the dilemma acted as a bimodal homeostat, preventing relationships becoming too close or too distant. Features of too far/too close family systems are discussed further by Byng-Hall (1980, 1981).

In this legend, the scenario was set in a wider social context. If you get too close you may be wiped out, but moving too far leads to execution. As Watzlawick (1978) points out, the act of presenting an illusion of alternatives represents an exercise of power. The listener thinks he has to choose one or the other, thus obscuring the fact that there may be many other options. The only apparent solution to this dilemma which did not invite disaster was to hover between the two alternatives, ultimately to stand absolutely still. Anyone who knows wild life knows the wisdom of that rule; either running off or attacking invites an attack. It might also be said to be a wise stance if one is outnumbered 150 to 1 in a civil war. What is obscured is the option to refuse to get into or remain in the danger zone. British pride disallowed that. Another family legend which reinforced this whole stance went as follows: my grandfather, who at the time was Governor of Northern Nigeria, was warned of an imminent attack at dawn for which he was totally unprepared because of a late night party. He placed his chair outside the house, which was on a hill, and sat in it, quite still. He was wearing a white dinner jacket. At dawn, the attackers fled when confronted by this ghostly still figure.

The Admiral Byng legend, as it was told, implied that attack plus posthumous glory was on balance better than public shame and execution. The British Empire in the 1950s could not lose face by conceding that Mau Mau had a good cause to want Africa for the Africans. They could only do this after first defeating them (or appearing to have done so). Similarly two centuries earlier, the English could not accept that the French might reasonably be expected to have more influence in Minorca than the British. To concede that would have meant harbouring the idea that the whole British Empire was an outrageous anomaly.

E. Family and Cultural Overlap of Legends

In legends, family and cultural values often overlap. The twin set of rules: don't either go too far off or get too entangled clearly had a family function especially in a very isolated situation. British society as a whole is also rather preoccupied with maintaining the correct distance between people. The Byng legend proved to be particularly valuable to study because it is both an international and family legend, hence it is well documented from many perspectives, English, French and from within the Byng family. Because it is old, it is also possible to trace some of the editing, re-editing processes.

As I had experienced the power of this legend, I felt I needed to find out whether I had imposed it on the rest of my family. I asked my three sons separately the question, "Who was Admiral Byng and what did he do?" Our 13-year-old replied: "Well a message was sent and Admiral Byng was sensible and did not get into a battle he knew he would lose; but he was shot for cowardice". He had picked up the gist of the legend. As an afterthought he said, "When I was younger I thought he was shot aged 12". This came from the title of a book about Admiral Byng entitled *At 12 Mr Byng was Shot* (Pope, 1962). Our 12-year-old said: "He was the bloke who was shot at midnight by his own men, he gave the order himself". He did not know why. He got this idea from the cover of the same book about Admiral Byng. In the picture on the cover, Byng is shown dropping his handkerchief to order his own execution. (Note that the second in command did not order the execution.) The sky was painted dark blue, and it could have been midnight, not midday. Our 8-year-old son promptly replied: "He was Admiral of the Fleet, like Nelson". This was entirely correct, we had recently been to the Maritime Museum where a painting of Admiral Sir George Byng (the admirable admiral who was father of the Byng of the legend). When asked about the nephew, he did not know anything except, "Didn't something happen to him, wasn't his throat slit?"

I was intrigued by what each of my sons had focussed upon. Editing occurs at the hearing stage as well as through the telling. Each version seemed to me to reflect something of their personalities as well as age. Perhaps bravery or cowardice in face of the enemy and naval battles were now less powerful themes in our family and culture. Other themes were more relevant, e.g. danger at night.

I felt that because of the lack of consistency in their accounts, I had probably not talked much about the episode, nevertheless they had all picked up something ominous. Much of the information seemed to come from cultural sources, not from family story telling. If I had not chosen to take an interest in the legend, would it have died out in the next generation?

I asked the same question of my 18-year-old nephew whose second given name was Byng. He knew the legend in much the same form as my original legend (page 216). Despite all evidence to the contrary, it emerged that he was preoccupied by the idea that he was a coward. Family legends can of course be kept alive in some branches of the family and die in others.

V.   RE-EDITING THE BYNG LEGEND

A.   Exonerating Byng

I thought it was important to give my sons a more accurate picture. I told them about what I had learned from the book (Pope, 1962) which I had read 15 years before. The book had aimed to exonerate Byng and show that he had been scape-goated. This is what I told them.

> Newcastle, who was Prime Minister at the time, was politically insecure. He had been warned many times that the French were planning an invasion of Minorca but he did nothing. Minorca was attacked and he had to act. He sent Byng at short notice which meant that his ships were ill equipped and his crews untrained. The

battle itself was inconclusive, but the French and English Admirals in time honoured manner, each sent home news of their own great victory. Unfortunately for Byng, the British Secret Service was most efficient and intercepted the French message of a French victory long before Byng could sail home with an account of his victory. Newcastle was panic-stricken because he knew that he would be held responsible for the loss of Minorca through his tardy action. He launched a political campaign to blacken Byng's name before he arrived home. This included hiring professional writers to write damning lyrics about Byng, which were sung by bands of singers roaming the streets of Westminster. Byng was arrested on arrival at Portsmouth and the trial was rigged to find him guilty.

How much this account was also an edit of the book can be assessed by those who want to read the book which is incidentally fascinating reading. While I was giving this account, my 8-year-old wrote this poem:

> Newcastle was a silly old thing,
>   He sent Admiral Byng to fight over Minorca without a thing.
> Finally Byng was shot,
>   Do I like Newcastle? Not a lot!

One re-editing had been completed.

B.   Exploring the Context Removes the Illusion of Alternatives

I decided that I wanted to know more about Byng as a person and the context in which all this happened. I told the story to Professor Howard Feinstein who is a psychohistorian and psychiatrist. He became intrigued, and we went to the British Museum to find the documents about the Battle. Some of those old documents had clearly not been touched for 223 years; others had been handled only once or twice. This was an incredible experience. The smell and texture of the paper itself was mesmerizing. As paper after paper revealed more and more unexpected information, the pull of history was almost tangible. Beware therapists! You can be lured here for a lifetime.

The pictures were most exciting. Here was visual proof that Byng engaged the enemy. There was a picture and commentary for each half hour of the battle, which could be followed in detail. In one picture both fleets were shown closely engaged with each other. There was a written description of Byng coolly discussing tactics with his captain. No sense of cowardice here. At one moment he had to veer away from the enemy to avoid ramming the dismasted ship in front of him. This could be seen in one of the pictures, and was later used as evidence that he withdrew from the enemy. Perhaps the most moving account was that given by an English sailor who described a rising tide of cheers from the English crews and marines as the French sailed away. Clearly they considered that they had won.

Evidence about Byng's dignity was plentiful. He wrote a long speech to be delivered before his execution. This speech was angry; indignantly proclaiming his innocence, but also forgiving. It conveyed a presence of mind which was in conflict with the picture I had built up of him which was of a haughty pompous, rather stupid man who did indeed have a streak of cowardice in him. It took, however, a long time before I allowed myself to be convinced by my new findings. Howard kept on remarking how I took every piece of evidence and twisted it to fit my preconceptions. Sometimes I did not even see some evidence in front of my eyes, at others I reversed the evidence. For instance, Byng never read this speech. I took this as evidence of fear (which may be true) rather than consider that he was not given the opportunity to make the speech, especially as it placed his executioners in such a poor light. This confirms my clinical impression that family mythology is extraordinarily difficult to shift.

Much of the search was interesting in itself. There were of course no daily newspapers. Instead political pamphlets were distributed. These were often written by well-known writers. Dr Samuel Johnson wrote pamphlets which were pro-Byng and carried some marvellous political invective. He wrote two, each in a different style: one in similar vein to the popular press for the less sophisticated, with simple arguments; and the other in which he used highly complex reasoning, more like the *Times*. Unfortunately he overdid it, and his highly convoluted arguments lost credibility.

To a family therapist, scapegoating is a highly understandable process. But why execution? Countless commanders had made far worse muddles. Was there something in the context to explain this extreme form of scapegoating, or did he like some victims invite persecution?

I discovered that Tunstall (1928), a naval historian who was keen to place the blame on the politicians as opposed to the Navy, has painted a most intriguing picture. All the leading politicians were involved: Newcastle, Fox and Pitt, each apparently either trying to save face or exploit the situation. The court martial failed to find him guilty of cowardice, indeed all the evidence given suggested that he was courageous. To emphasize this, he insisted on ordering his own execution by dropping his handkerchief. The Court only found him guilty of an error of judgement, not itself an offence at all. Quite erroneously from a legal point of view, this was then equated with negligence, for which the death penalty was mandatory. Probably the court martial assumed that the King (George II) would be bound to grant a pardon, and hence they did not have to face the full consequences of the decision. Byng himself did not want a pardon. He wanted the verdict reversed. He preferred to die rather than accept a pardon and hence admit his guilt.

The king was outraged by the request for clemency. George's own position in England was insecure. He was seen as more German than English, and he needed the support of the City who sponsored his expensive operations in Hanover. The City merchants were most annoyed by Byng's failure to regain Minorca from the French. It was an important Mediterranean base for British trade. The King felt that the politicians had whipped up public fury against Byng about the loss of Minorca. If he were to pardon him, where would their fury then be directed? Here I felt were sufficient ingredients for killing a scapegoat; money, power and the throne at stake. Later the nation itself felt the need to purge itself of this legacy to Byng. There was a vast list of publications which depicted him as a political victim.

C. Further Exploration of the Context

This may have sufficed to salve the national conscience about Byng, but family scapegoating is different. Did he invite it? Also how did our family react? This sent me on another quest. To decide for myself, I needed further sense of the battle itself. Here was where I dug deepest. Was he really a coward? I had to forget what the world made of it afterwards; that is always falsified anyway. Systems theory told me that he must have colluded in some way. First of all, what were the odds he faced? I already knew that his fleet was ill-equipped, ill-manned and far from home, and that he was facing a well-prepared fleet, roughly equal in numbers, fresh out of harbour. For someone brought up in the spirit of the British Empire, however, victory would be expected in those circumstances!

A complete shift in my view occurred when I read that 15 000 of the best French troops commanded by Marshall Duc de Richelieu were already on the island besieging the English garrison at Fort Mahon, which was commanded by Lieutenant-General William Blakeney aged 84, suffering from gout, and in bed most of the time! Byng had only 13 ships, and had been refused extra marines by the commander at Gibraltar, despite orders from Whitehall that he should be given them. It was as if a myth had been exploded for me. At last the incredible British self-deception was fully exposed. It seemed that it had been easier to focus on the deeds of one man than to ask the whole nation to open its eyes to its own stupidity. I think this resonated strongly with my Kenyan childhood experience, where the illusion of everlasting superiority was maintained despite being outnumbered 150 to 1. Bluff carried the British far, but this included self-deception as well, often based on the idea of intrinsically superior British qualities and inferior foreigners.

In the forest, my family had to maintain the same myth. I knew the truth. One of my closest friends was a Kikuyu teenager of my own age. We hunted together. I knew that not only were we outnumbered, but that the Africans could, quite naturally, run rings round us in their own environment. (This situation is not to be confused with South Africa where racial ratios are very different.) I had now been able to re-edit my view of my childhood experience after re-editing the Byng legend. I could now ask the question, who were the cowards? Those who refused to see real dangers, or those who dared to look and risk being appropriately scared? I was now able to ask my parents and my sister about their experience during the Mau Mau period. We had, it appeared, all been frightened but each carried the idea that the others were not. We imagined that sharing our fears would have undermined the other's courage.

D. Byng's Collusion

I then pursued the question of how Byng might have colluded. Horace Walpole described Byng as haughty and arrogant. He seemed by most accounts to have been more concerned with doing the correct thing than with the pragmatics of the situation. At every decision point he called a council of war, a sort of committee meeting, in which the majority made the decision. This hardly made for dynamic leadership. For instance, he did not insist on being given the marine reinforcement by the Gibraltar garrison despite orders from Whitehall; he allowed a Council of war to override this order. He also fought the battle exactly according to instructions devised 50 years before. It seems he found it difficult to take an initiative, allowing the rules to decide the action rather than risk opting for one of the alternatives. He could have engaged the French for a second time and presumably risked victory or defeat. He could also have refused to engage the enemy in formal battle. Tunstall (1928) argues (with modern tactical hindsight available to him) that a better tactic would have been to ensure that no French ships landed on Minorca; a much easier objective, and one which could have led to a successful siege of the besiegers, because the island could not support 15 000 troops, whereas Fort Mahon had ample supplies. Yet Byng had other options. He could have fought in an unexpected way, instead of predictably following the rules. It is interesting that the slavish following of battle procedures used very successfully by his father possibly served him ill. Perhaps that was his real error of judgement. It would have been interesting to know what legends he was told about his father's famous victories. It seems that he was chosen to command this expedition partly because he was expected to somehow emulate his father's domination of the Mediterranean.

By exploring Byng's context, I had shattered the power of the illusion of alternatives. Catastrophe did not automatically follow either alternative. The illusion of alternatives itself now also dissolved as I sensed that there were instead multiple options open to him. I could sense, however, the power of his historical context to encourage him to behave in certain ways.

VI. PASSAGE OF THE LEGEND OVER TIME

A. The Enemy's Views

Scapegoating can always be seen more clearly from outside. The French saw it immediately. The Duc de Richelieu was indignant about what was happening to Byng. He wrote a letter to Voltaire which included

> Whatever I have seen or heard of him does him honour . . . all Admiral Byng's manoeuvres were excellent . . . had the English persisted in the engagement they would have lost their entire fleet [possibly a French myth?]. There has never been such an act of injustice as that now directed against Admiral Byng, and every officer and man of honour ought to take note of it.

Voltaire sent this letter straight to Byng for him to use in his defence. It was discounted as having been solicited by Byng. In *Candide*, which was published shortly afterwards, Voltaire describes how, to paraphrase the passage, Candide while in Portsmouth sees an admiral being shot and asks why. He is told that he was not close enough to the French admiral, to which Candide asks a good systems question: was the French admiral also not close enough to him?!

"Cela est incontestable", lui repliqua-t-on; "mais dans ce pays-ci il est bon de tuer en temps en temps un admiral pour encourager les autres".

This particular famous quotation has done more than anything else to ensure that Admiral Byng is remembered. It assured the story legendary status. This piece of history is, however, now taught less and less frequently in British schools. As the British Empire has gone, perhaps this is less interesting or relevant.

B. Some Conclusions

To explore details of the changes in the legend over time, requires further articles. Suffice it to say that there are quotes by historians which, interestingly enough, support my original version of the legend. For instance Macaulay, writing in 1834: "But he did not think fit to engage the French squadron and sailed". Guedalla, in 1913, wrote: "Was militarily wise as it was politically foolish". The message that it is more praiseworthy to lose one's life bravely than to survive with shame is important to convey especially when, as is so frequently the case, the battle at the front is so clearly a complete, horrifying, bungled mess. The knowledge that retreat might lead to being publicly shamed and punished is a universal phenomenon of war. The Byng execution provided a vivid scenario not only for his, but for all ages. Legends have to resonate with universal themes, otherwise why would they pass from tongue to tongue.

The family was apparently solidly and unreservedly behind Admiral Byng in his direst hour; in one case surprisingly so. The fifth Viscount Torrington was his nephew and had been looked after by Byng after his own father died when he was 8 years old. He wrote extensive diaries which were later published as the Torrington Diaries (1934). He had clearly hated his uncle. In one poem he wrote:

> But I, soon sent abroad, to range at large,
>   By death divested of a parent's charge.
> That parent so beloved so truly dear;
>   An uncle lived, like Hamlet's uncle he
> Meet that I set it down, such this to me!

(It sounds as if there is a good family secret to pursue!) Despite his hatred, when the time came, he sent a petition on behalf of his uncle. Byng's younger brother Edward hurried to Portsmouth to meet him despite extreme ill health; indeed he was so ill that he died the day after arrival. The most vigorous of his supporters was his youngest sister Sarah, married to Admiral Osborne. She petitioned and pleaded at each level and opportunity. Members of the family were depicted crying in handkerchiefs in one picture of the execution. I visited the family mausoleum. His plaque was just underneath his father's, Sir George Byng's; a place of honour. On it were the following words:

> To the Perpetual Disgrace
>   of Public Justice.

The Honourable John Byng, Esq.,
    Admiral of the Blue,
Fell a Martyr to Political Persecution,
    March 14th, in the year MDCCLVII;
When Bravery and Loyalty
    Were Insufficient Securities
For the Life and Honour
    Of a Naval Officer.

On the front page of Tunstall's (1928) book given to my father by one of his aunts who was the matriarch of the family, I found written:

> An ancestor of ours who became the scapegoat for the blunders of the Government of his day to "their everlasting shame".

In public anyway, the family refused to join in the scapegoating. By the time the legend reached me, however, he had clearly been disowned.

On reviewing my original legend, very little remained as "true", not even the detail of being shot on his own quarter deck. The Monaque was not his flag ship. Did that edit relate more to my childhood experience of danger on our "own" farm? The Byng legend is clearly unusual in its age and documentation. More recent legends can, however, be explored along similar lines except that information about the event has to be collected from people rather than books. This, of course, gives the exploration a greater significance as a family event.

VII. IMPLICATIONS FOR FAMILY THERAPY

A. Family Legends in Other Families

Is my family unique in the power of its legends? To investigate this, I have been exploring legends with client families, colleagues and trainees. I have used the following experiential exercise in family therapy workshops. I ask the participants to close their eyes and

> imagine some current unresolved issue: we all have them; it might be trivial such as whether to buy a new washing machine, or perhaps involves some more important issue. Try to build up a picture of yourself and other people grappling with this decision.

This is to elicit the unresolved theme for which the legend might provide rules.

> Now think of the first family story that comes into your mind which was told to you about a period before you can remember. Again it does not matter if it is trivial. Stick to the first story. Try to get a vivid picture of the person telling you and how it felt.

I give about 2 minutes for them to do this and then say, "Now turn to your neighbour and share this experience with each other". This part takes about 12-15 minutes. Then

Explore whether there was any connection between the unresolved dilemma and the story. There may or may not be. If there is a link, are there any clues from the story about how you should resolve your dilemma?

Not surprisingly, there is usually a significant connection reported; occasionally none. This proves nothing of course, but the reporting back is usually fascinating. Often a story pops into the participant's mind immediately without much internal scanning, and its relevance only emerges in discussion. Indeed some participants drop the story as irrelevant, hence the importance of the instructions to keep to the first story however apparently trivial. Legends have much in common with dreams. The connection between conflict and legend is frequently clearer to the listener than the narrator. If the workshop meets over a period of time, the way in which the story changes can be explored. Many participants have told me how important the story turned out to be, and that they have explored it further. The richness of the stories shows that they come in many forms. Those including an illusion of alternatives account for a number.

In some families story telling is less important, or the family is totally cut off from its past. In these families, exploring the stories "made up" or phantasies about past figures can be fascinating.

B.   Legends in Family Therapy

In family therapy, change may precede or follow re-editing of legends. In my practice (Byng-Hall and Campbell, 1981), at the beginning of therapy I usually work structurally to help change the current relationships, and work with history at a later stage. I work mostly with family interaction, and with history only for a small proportion of the time. Drawing a genogram reduces the intensity and speed of work produced by structural techniques. For this reason I have techniques for eliciting the relevant rules from the past as quickly as possible.

I may ask the family to think of the first story that came into their heads. This usually provides a rich source of material related to the current therapeutic theme. In the family with the epileptic father mentioned earlier, immediately following an exploration of their profound fears about epilepsy, I asked for their stories. Father's story was

> It is curious but this keeps popping into my mind . . . My father telling me about how he used to stand on the bank of a river and dive right under the barges and come up again on the other side.

The family produced a rich network of interlocking stories about danger at sea, near drownings, and saving others who were drowning. It was then possible to link these with the many aspects of the epilepsy experience. Like all fantasy material, it is so rich that the therapist has to focus and select the relevant stories. Like metaphor, the story which resonates best with the therapist provides the communication. It becomes important for the therapist to be aware of the colour he adds to the mix. The Byng legend resonated with this.

In longer-term therapy, the genogram (Leibermann, 1979) provides a useful format for exploring legends. The main modification of the technique is not to ask what an ancestor was like, but to ask for a story about him, or better a story to show how "those two" got along. The story is then written down (the paper needs to be large enough) and any subsequent editing can be noted. The other advantage of constructing a genogram this way is that the stories are interactional which is congruent with working with the family system.

Re-editing my legend had involved exploring the context of the legend, exploding some of its myths and seeing that other options were open.

C. Clinical Example: The "X" Family Legend

In the X family, as the family system stabilized, the legend of the drunken great-grandfather thrown out by his 10-year-old son was revisited several times. They decided that he could have chosen to come home, or perhaps his wife did not want him. It emerged that the blindness was of late onset and so only the great-grandmother would have been affected, not brothers and sisters. Mr X came to one session complaining bitterly about his son's rudeness to him. I asked the family to recall the legend. I suggested that perhaps it was ringing bells for them now which could be frightening. I asked them to put themselves in imagination into that legend, as if it were now. They could hardly bear to think about it, but keeping them to the task, they eventually accepted the roles while acknowledging them to be fantasy. Mr X discussed with Brian whether he felt he had to intervene to stop him beating up his wife. The reality of the present family interaction was compared and contrasted with the legend. I point out how they had corrected the legend so that father emerged as the strong one who could beat up his sons if necessary. The fighting which was valued was largely restricted to that between the brothers, a much more appropriate place. I also suggested that they had to exaggerate this correction perhaps unnecessarily, because they were haunted by the legend. Father's epilepsy made potential violence feel more real than it might have been otherwise. Fact and fantasy, past and present, were disentangled.

VII. EPILOGUE

One more important personal change came from quite an unexpected source. I was telling the Byng story at a party when someone, who possibly had the influence to put it into effect, suggested that Parliament should ask the Queen for a public pardon for Byng. A curious sense of release followed, perhaps because justice could finally be acknowledged, where it needed to be: with the monarch. Despite the fact that this was 224 years later the legacy had still weighed on me. Boszormenyi-Nagy and Spark (1973) discuss the concept of a family legacy. Although the nation had not repaid its debt to the family, in some symbolic way, it was now showing its willingness to do so. I could now feel free of the obligation to collect that debt, although it could be argued that I am doing so through this chapter.

REFERENCES

Boszormenyi-Nagy, I. and Spark, G. M. (1973). "Invisible Loyalties", Harper & Row, London.

Byng, J. (1934). Extract from a poem on his youth. *In* "The Torrington Diaries", (C. Andrew, ed.), Vol. 1. p. 345, Methuen, London.

Byng-Hall, J. (1973). Family myths used as defence in conjoint family therapy. *British Journal of Medical Psychology*, **46**, 239-249.

Byng-Hall, J. (1979). Re-editing family mythology during family therapy. *Journal of Family Therapy*, **1**, 103-116.

Byng-Hall, J. (1980). Symptom bearer as marital distance regulator: Clinical implications. *Family Process*, **19**, 355-367.

Byng-Hall, J. (1981). Therapeutic confusion produced by too close/too far family systems. *In* "Questions and Answers in the Practice of Family Therapy", (A. S. Gurman, ed.), 143-146, Brunner/Mazel, New York.

Byng-Hall, J. and Campbell, D. (1981). Resolving conflicts arising out of distance regulation. *Journal of Marital and Family Therapy*, **7**, 321-330.

Ferreira, A. J. (1963). Family Myths: The covert rules of the relationship. *Archives of General Psychiatry*, **9**, 457-463.

Lieberman, S. (1979). Transgenerational analysis: the geneogram as a technique in family therapy. *Journal of Family Therapy*, **1**, 51-64.

Linnemann, E. (1966). "Parables of Jesus: Introduction and Exposition", S.P.C.K., London.

Pope, D. (1962). "At 12 Mr. Byng was Shot", Weidenfeld & Nicholson, London.

Tunstall, B. (1928). "Admiral Byng and the Loss of Minorca", Philip Allan, London.

Watzlawick, P. (1978). "The Language of Change: Elements of Therapeutic Communication", Basic Books, New York.

Chapter 11

The Strengths and Weaknesses in Co-therapy

W. Roberts

I. INTRODUCTION

It would be true to say that when family therapy was first practised in England, it was commonplace for practitioners to work in pairs, and although initially it often appeared to take place because of the level of anxiety about the ability of one person to manage to work alone with the complexities of family interaction, it was also recognized that working as a therapeutic pair offered a number of additional advantages.

Currently the situation appears to be changing, and an increasing number of family therapists are choosing to work alone, or, if they have co-workers, to use them in a more supervisory role; whether or not this can be considered co-therapy is debatable (Hannum, 1980). How has this change come about? In part it can be attributed to the interchange of ideas and cross-cultural learning which arose from the visits of various American practitioners during the 1970s when new and relatively unfamiliar methods of working with families were introduced (methods which required more activity on the part of the therapist), reinforced by the contributions made by some of our own family therapists when they in turn visited the United States. It may also be due in part to the disenchantment experienced by therapists who had difficulties in establishing a satisfactory co-therapy relationship. My own view was personally influenced by the combination of these factors, and led to me choosing to see families alone rather than with a co-worker.

II. EARLY CO-THERAPY EXPERIENCES

A. Basis in Multi-disciplinary Clinic Settings

If we re-trace the development of the family therapy movement in this country, we find that initially it was most commonly practised in child-centred settings, i.e. Child Guidance Clinics or hospital departments of Child Psychiatry. This may be one of the reasons why co-therapy was so immediately popular, for these settings were generally staffed by inter-disciplinary teams accustomed to working together in other ways. The majority of these settings were psychoanalytically orientated, and the techniques used were based on a psychodynamic model using

229

interpretation and taking account of transference and counter-transference phenomena.

The co-therapy relationship was considered to be very important for a number of reasons: it provided a relationship model not only for the marital couple, but for the family itself; it introduced an additional relationship dimension, since the interaction between the workers became part of the process and was available for use in the interest of the treatment process. Skynner (1976) suggests, for example, that in providing a role model for the family, "mutual trust and the combination of personal spontaneity with attentiveness and responsiveness to the partner . . . mirror closely the relationship necessary for the most satisfying sexual intercourse". It allowed the opportunity for carrying out planned strategies aimed at bringing about change as, for example, when one worker agreed to "take sides" with one or more members of a family in an attempt to restructure a pattern of behaviour; or when the therapists adopted a pre-determined role such as one remaining passive leaving the other to be more dominant. In addition, it not only allowed "hand-holding" for workers who were keen to learn to practice, but also increased the learning opportunity when workers could share their differing perspectives of the family and become aware through their own interactions of relationship aspects projected onto themselves.

B.   Some Disadvantages of Co-therapy: Personal Experiences

Aware of the value of co-therapy and the essentials needed to reach a satisfactory level of working together, many practitioners attempted to set up co-therapy relationships, some of which were highly successful and others of which continued over a prolonged period of time. This was largely my own experience when working in a Child Guidance Clinic with a fairly large staff, most of whom remained in post long enough to allow satisfactory co-relationships to evolve. Despite the apparent advantages of such a situation, the kind of difficulties common to agencies less well-endowed were still experienced. As members of an interdisciplinary team, we were encouraged to form an alliance with more than one member of the team, and although there was apparent freedom in the way in which partners selected a co-worker, nevertheless there were occasions when the unmet demands of a particular worker led to pressure from team members for demands to be met. It was this situation which led to an unfortunate early experience for me.

In the clinic to which I am referring, it was at that time customary for new referrals to be discussed at a staff meeting, and it was at such a meeting that a recently appointed colleague accepted responsibility for the "S" family. She immediately invited me to be her co-worker after the two male staff confirmed that they had no vacancies. My prevarication led to my colleagues' firm request that I should consider helping "J" who as a new member of staff, was eager to learn to practice family therapy. My hesitation was due to a number of factors: I was reluctant to expose myself to somebody I felt I had not yet come to know very well; I was aware that she saw me as "experienced" while I considered myself still to be a beginner; I was in the stages of developing a co-worker relationship with two other members of staff, and did not feel that I was ready to attempt a third. My doubts were overruled and I gave in to the pressure! At this stage, we were not yet sufficiently aware of the importance of preparation, and so my colleague and I met for a very short preliminary discussion before we saw the family, but together we wrote the letter of invitation to them.

(1)   The Family Interview

The family comprised Father: a small, passive man who was frequently out of work because of recurring bouts of sickness for which no physical cause could be found; Mother: a part-time domestic worker who had difficulty in travelling on any form of public transport; and Billy, 14, the youngest of three children. His brother and sister were married and living away from home and had apparently given the parents no cause for concern. Billy on the other hand, was said to be finding it difficult to get to school, the parents describing the scenes in which he lay on the floor "writhing in agony".

My colleague had asked me to "take the lead" with this family, saying that although she had read quite a considerable amount, she had had no opportunity to practise. I was a dilatory reader and felt rather threatened by her theoretical knowledge! However, I liked her enthusiasm and had been impressed by her contribution at a recent case conference. I failed to say anything to her about either of these factors. While we waited for the family to arrive, we talked over the information given by the referrer and speculated about the symptom and its relevance to the family, and as the clinic was using a psychodynamic model of working, we focussed on the emotional tie between Mother and Billy, and were curious about his early history. During the early part of the session my colleague, whom I will refer to as AB, remained very quiet and passive and left the running to me as we had agreed. The session moved slowly with Mother insisting on giving a graphic description of Billy's symptomatic behaviour while I attempted to explore what might have precipitated the symptom; Father shared Mother's extreme anxiety that Billy was "*really* ill". After about half an hour, my silent colleague sprang to life and began to be quite active in making suggestions about how Billy should be got back to school, directing Father to carry these out and insisting that his florid behaviour should be ignored. Mother's anxious reactions were ignored; and so was I! The session ended in this flurry of activity between my colleague and Father, while Mother shed a few tears looking appealingly in my direction. I could only look back helplessly. There was no time immediately available to discuss what had happened, only time for AB to comment "that was interesting", and for me to acknowledge, with a multiplicity of feelings, that indeed it was.

An hour later the mother telephoned, asked for me, and complained about the task her husband had agreed to do. She tried to make me her ally reminding me that I had indicated that I was aware of her anxiety and I was too close to the experience to be able to think rationally. I found myself torn between supporting my colleague's strategy and empathizing with the mother's distress. Later, despite the efforts we made to discuss what had happened and to try and agree a way of working in which both of us would feel comfortable, the tension we brought to the next session transmitted itself to the family in such a way that they failed further appointments and asked to be transferred to another agency. I was later to discover that this experience was more commonplace than I had known it to be, and that others, like AB and myself, were sometimes able to use it constructively. In our case we sought the help of a colleague, and made time to talk about the experience in some depth, airing and sharing the positive and negative aspects of the contribution we had each made in such a way that we felt the relationship was enriched, and were able to continue to do some rewarding work together.

C.   Agency Disadvantages of Co-therapy

When difficulties could be resolved satisfactorily, co-therapy was an obviously advantageous method of working. Circumstances sometimes meant, however, that this was not so easy to achieve. Discussion at a depth that often becomes necessary if two people are to reach a degree of compatibility for successful co-therapy to take place, not only needs time and space, but also requires that the workers are likely to be able to continue to develop their skills together by remaining in the same agency over a long enough period of time. Too often, particularly in Departments of Social Service, where there appeared to be a more frequent turnover of staff, co-therapy relationships tended to end with the termination of a worker's term of employment before the full potential of the therapeutic pair had been realized, leaving one frustrated worker feeling ambivalent about starting again to develop another co-worker relationship.

In speaking with social workers, I learned that it was often because of this kind of experience that they had decided against practising family therapy until they could either find work in an agency where they believed there would be less likelihood of staff mobility, or until they had successfully negotiated a co-therapy relationship with a colleague who was aware of what was needed and prepared to commit themselves to an agreed period of working together. Others took steps to approach workers in another agency in an attempt to find a solution, one example of this being the work undertaken when both the Probation Department and the Social Services Department had responsibility for one or more members of a family. This method of working made extra demands on the workers since each was accountable to their own service, and additional meetings which included senior management were often necessary.

In the clinic where I was practising, we began to invite the agency worker who had referred the family, to become the co-therapist with the member of the clinic staff who had accepted the responsibility for the referral: a method also used by many other clinics. This brought other problems:

(1) The workers were not always clear about management responsibility.

(2) The "hidden agendas" of the referrer: "please take this difficult family off my hands", and of the clinic worker: "I'll only take this family if I can work with them", were not recognized or acknowledged!

Again the varying levels of expertise between the workers, or the unrealistic expectations of one about the other was not discovered until they attempted to practice together. This latter situation was often intensified by the fact that the two workers may have been of different disciplines, each having unaired fantasies about the role of the other. In addition, practical considerations such as finding time together when both could be free to meet, and where to do so in order that travelling time was not too onerous, often led to a reluctance to continue.

Despite these difficulties, however, the motivation of many practitioners to learn family therapy techniques played a large part in the efforts made to overcome them, with benefit not only to the workers, but also to the agencies whom they represented, for the need to improve inter-agency collaboration became evident.

As skills developed, so it seemed did the level of expectations rise. Some of the difficulties which might have been ignored or tolerated in the early stages seemed to assume greater importance, and when they could not be overcome, they led to the breakdown of the co-therapy relationship. Similarly, if one of the pair developed at a faster pace than the other, frustration again led to an end of the partnership leading one or both therapists to seek alternative workers with whom to pair. It was out of this shifting and changing that some of the more lasting co-therapy relationships emerged and grew from strength to strength.

Dowling (1980) has carried out a detailed study in which she explores clinical issues regarding co-therapy as a method of therapeutic intervention. She found that

> the therapists were consistent in their personal style of intervention . . . behaved in a similar manner with different therapists and different families — expressed that they would want similar characteristics in a co-therapist regardless of the type of family.

Reference is also made to the need for empirical study into the value of co-therapy as compared to single therapist intervention.

III.   ASPECTS OF THE CO-THERAPY RELATIONSHIP

A.   Personal Qualities Necessary

The fact that co-therapy is still widely practised is an acknowledgement that it has value despite the continuation of some of the problems experienced in the early stages. Many of those who have written about family therapy have commented about the co-therapy relationship; Boszormenyi-Nagy and Spark (1973) are of the opinion that

> an unusual amount of flexibility and creativity are required on the part of both co-workers who should have empathy, compassion and trust, and in addition a capacity for complementarity.

They also suggest that ideally the couple should be heterosexual. This poses problems for agencies where the majority of the staff are female: a not unusual situation in this country, although my impression is that there has been a change in recent years. On the other hand when working with the psycho-dynamic model, the co-therapists may be experienced as heterosexual by family members, investing them with feminine and masculine characteristics. In making reference to this, Dowling (1980) points out the importance of the therapist's awareness of this phenomenon.

Walrond Skinner (1976) lists the most important criteria of choice of partner as

> one with whom one will feel comfortable in sharing and exchanging ideas, feelings and problems as these are experienced both within the treatment situation with the family, and within the co-therapy relationship itself.

By committing themselves to working together over a prolonged period of time, some therapists have achieved a complementarity which has enabled them to work with the most seriously disturbed families. Complementarity can be seen as a counter-balancing of therapeutic input, and may be achieved by, for example, one worker being supportive while the other is more confronting. In an article describing a method for working with schizophrenic families, Mueller, McGoldrick and Orfanides (1976) speak about the need for co-therapy being prompted by the power of such families in keeping their boundaries rigidly closed to outsiders. The co-therapists adopt structured roles: the male supporting the males and setting limits for the females and vice versa, and this is said to greatly facilitate the task of keeping the family engaged whilst working for change. Furthermore, it is claimed that it is extremely difficult for a lone therapist to maintain the required balance between support and confrontation in families who are disorganized yet rigid.

B. Co-therapy with Disadvantaged Families

One of my own experiences is of working with a high percentage of families with a history of severe deprivation (physical, material and emotional) and I found that the heavy demands made by such families became more tolerable when there was a co-therapist to share the task. One particular male colleague and I, able to work together over a long period of time, developed a method whereby we would take it in turns to manage a particularly noisy and disruptive situation, such as that of a family expressing very angry feelings and making demands for action. The "J" family are an example of this as can be seen from the following short excerpt:

Husband: (in loud voice and gesticulating wildly) You get into my guts, stop telling such lies — you're a downright liar — take no notice of her, Miss, she wants you to believe her . . .

Wife: (at the same time and in equally loud voice and sobbing) Stop him, Miss, he's telling lies — how can you sit there and say such things — don't believe him, Miss . . .

My co-therapist and I learned that if one of us stayed "out of the fray", as it were, by remaining less engaged while the other was more active in making comments, clarifying what was being said or demonstrating by non-verbal behaviour that he or she was intent on listening and prepared to speak, then the inactive partner could wait for the moment when the intensity had begun to diminish and then "move in" to focus on one particular aspect he or she considered would be amenable to more coherent discussion. Minuchin *et al.* (1966) give a very good description of this approach:

> Whenever one therapist is involved in interaction with a family, the co-therapist's field of observation includes the therapist, not just the family alone. He learns to watch specifically for the ways in which the family organises his partner into behaving along lines which do not permit family change . . .

In the incident referred to above, I had been making such comments as "I can see you are both very angry with each other", or "it must be difficult to hear each other when you believe that what you are hearing is all lies", and "I hear you both saying that you are worried about whether we will be taking sides . . .", to little or no effect. My almost silent colleague eventually spoke quietly yet with a firm voice addressing himself to me:

> Win, I don't think we will be able to begin to help Mr and Mrs J until they can stop talking together and begin to listen to each other. Could you tell us, Mr J, more about the incident you've just been describing so that we can understand it from your point of view, and then we can hear how Mrs J felt about it.

When, at times, we had not used this technique but had both chosen to be active, we had found it difficult to see "the wood for the trees", and shared the family's exhaustion at the end of the episode.

An additional factor which had to be managed when working with families were the children, often equally deprived, who themselves made constant demands on the therapists. In such circumstances, our strategy was sometimes to decide that one would give attention to the children and attempt to get them to settle down, while the other focussed solely on the parents. It then became possible to bring adults and children together in a discussion when the therapists took the side of either the parents or the children. Nowadays one would ask the parents to settle the children.

C. Making Co-therapy Work

It is evident that the requirements necessary for a co-therapy relationship to reach this level makes heavy demands on the workers; time for talking together before and after each session with a family in order to be open to each other's difficulties, to respect each other's limitations, to recognize and value each other's strengths, and to develop a degree of mutual trust that will safeguard against a family's attempts to split or scapegoat. Frequent and regular communication of this kind can lead to growth for the therapists, both personally and professionally.

It is difficult to know at what stage my colleagues and I began to consider the possibility of practising without a co-worker. In our frequent discussions about this we shared similar doubts and anxieties. Concern centred around such areas as the difficulty for a lone worker in dealing with feelings of extreme helplessness and despair being projected by more than one member of a family; what would be lost by not having a partner who could be used as a "sounding board", and who, having been present, provided the opportunity for detailed discussion of the family and its problems. It was apparent that many of the needs inherent in the concern being expressed were in the nature of having available a kind of "hand-holder", and although there was in addition the recognition of many of the positive aspects of pairing already referred to, when the prospect of working without a co-therapist was being aired, the argument against change was more generally linked with doubts about being able to manage.

Another factor which was frequently referred to as justification for co-therapy was the suggestion that the risk of being "sucked in" to the family pathology was such that a co-worker was essential to "pull one out" before one went "completely under", and although this seemed to imply that family therapy was fraught with potential dangers, there was often more than a grain of truth in the possibility of this taking place, particularly in families where individual boundaries were very diffuse. Having recognized this phenomenon, some co-therapists adopted a way of working in which one of the workers deliberately allowed himself/herself to become involved to a point where it became apparent that he or she was displaying signs of having got caught into the emotional level of family interaction, at which stage the partner would intervene to extricate him. This is a particular feature of Whitaker's work (Napier and Whitaker, 1978).

(1) The "G" Family: Case Example

The following example of work carried out by myself and a male colleague demonstrates some of the points I have been making. My colleague and I had paired on many occasions, and were very comfortable in the way we worked together. Our co-therapy relationship was the result of spending time together before and after each family meeting when we would explore in some depth our separate experiences of the session and discuss areas of disagreement looking critically at each other's contribution. From prior information we were aware of the fact that the "G" family were likely to be somewhat chaotic, the parents having recently re-married following a divorce some years previously. The referrer also told us that during the period of the divorce, when Mr G lived with an unmarried brother, he had returned to his wife and children for most weekends. Mrs G had taken care of many of his material needs, washing his clothes and cooking some of his meals. They had had an annual holiday together as a family, and were sometimes joined in this by Mr G's brother. The children had remained with their mother, but had also spent time with their father. They were referred because Peter, the oldest son aged 13, was not only having difficult in getting to school, but also in mixing with children of his own age. Both he and John, aged 11, were unaccustomed to leaving the house to play with other children because the parents considered their neighbours were "too rough". Any social event had to involve the whole family, so for example, the parents had located a pub with a beer garden so that Peter and John could always accompany them when they went out for a drink together. Likewise, visits to the cinema were always made *en famille.*

My colleague, "C", and I agreed that we would want to try and establish some boundaries between adults and children in the first session, but speculated that this might not be easy. So we planned that we would attempt to find some areas of disagreement between parents and children and then "take sides" in so far as he would join with the children while I would ally myself with the adults. We also agreed that alternatively if disagreement became difficult to locate, he would join fully in family discussion moving freely between all family members while I would maintain a distance and be ready to extricate him when I thought he was becoming too enmeshed.

"C" began the session engaging the family in talking about the problem with which they had come, and then he was active in getting them to describe their family life and relationships and the "togetherness" indicated in the referral became apparent. I remained passive while this was taking place, observing how "C" was joining with the family by showing keen interest in their description of their life together, commenting upon their closeness in such a way that they elaborated upon the detail and I became increasingly aware of the feelings of suffocation being engendered. At this point I commented quite brusquely, for I was beginning to fear that C might not heed me,

> C, I can't agree with you that this family are as close and loving as you seem to think they are, because I find myself wondering whether Mr G might sometimes like to take his wife out alone for a couple of hours without the children. I thought he gave some indication of this when he spoke of looking forward to the day when he could take Mrs G out for a meal. [He had commented that he wasn't able to afford to take all the family out to eat together.]

Mrs G immediately began to deny this, but the look her husband gave me confirmed that I had struck a chord to which he could respond although he needed some support from "C", who now joined me in exploring this possibility before he felt able to do so.

Before the end of the session, we had also been able to establish some boundary between parents and children. This became possible when the boys talked of playing football at school, whereupon C engaged them in "football talk" while I explored interests that the parents had enjoyed together before the birth of Peter. I learned that they had been keen cyclists, but had discontinued this activity when Mrs G became pregnant and were waiting for the boys to be "a little older" before they started cycling together as a family. During this part of the session we changed the seating, C placing himself between the boys and the parents, while I sat opposite to him with the parents on my right; thus we created a physical boundary between parents and children. These moves were established with comparative ease which was, I believe, entirely due to the way in which C had initially allowed himself to be drawn into the family.

IV.   DEVELOPMENTS IN CO-THERAPY

A.   Co-therapy with a Difference

Reference is made at the beginning of this chapter to the changes that took place during the 1970s when many family therapists, accustomed to working from an analytic understanding, became interested in systems theory, and in particular in the structural approach which demanded new skills and techniques. These changes appeared to give an impetus to the move away from co-therapy in which the two workers stayed together with the family group and towards the situation of having one's partner and sometimes partners, behind a one-way screen. It is possible that the increased activity demanded by the new techniques led to difficulties in working with a colleague in the same room largely because of the uncertainty of being able to ascertain that the colleague was sharing the reasons for the moves being made. Working with the feeling content of the family inter-action allowed space for co-workers to become aware of the direction in which the process was moving, as for example, when two therapists were attempting to explore how a family *felt* about a particular piece of behaviour, each could move in and out of the discussion and so on: sometimes active, sometimes passive, but generally staying with the feeling level being explored.

If, on the other hand, these same workers were focussing on the *process* of the communication rather than the *content*, and aiming at effecting some change in this within the session, confusion might well arise unless both were clear about the direction of the change; in addition the authority required to elicit change could become diminished. One example of this was when a therapist, aware that a wife was disqualifying her husband, attempted not only to recognize this, but also to get the couple to interact in a different way in the "here and now"; the intervention needed to be made quickly and firmly, and allowed no time for the workers to discover whether they were in agreement. In other words, it seems that working to effect change in the "here and now" gives no opportunity for co-therapists to communicate about possible strategies without losing the necessary authority unless they can discuss the situation away from the family.

B.   The Advantages of "Distance"

The distance created by the one-way screen is particularly helpful in allowing the therapist working with the family to remain "in charge" as it were, while at the same time having available the comments, understanding, suggestions and criticisms of his co-workers, who, at this distance are often able to see more clearly how the family are interacting with the safeguard of not becoming involved in the emotional aspects of the situation. I consider that when a co-worker behind the screen makes live interventions by, for example, entering the room, he or she can correctly be called co-therapist, and many of the strengths and weaknesses already discussed can be equally appropriate. For example, when a therapist is working alone, the question of "where does the authority lie?" may be problematic unless the co-worker, in making interventions, is careful to avoid undermining or disqualifying the therapist. When co-workers remain together throughout the session, areas of disagreement can be talked about in the presence of the family, giving the opportunity for "modelling" a way of dealing with differences of opinion. Although this may also happen when the co-worker intervenes from behind the screen, unless handled skilfully, the impact runs the risk of removing the authority from the therapist.

This way of working does not mean that the workers have to be constantly in agreement; on the contrary, they may choose to employ a strategy of disagreement although the family is not made aware that this is an agreed decision. Papp (1978) gives a detailed account of a family who were helped by this method, and has developed the notion of the "group" behind the screen: a sort of Greek chorus commenting on the action.

V. CONCLUSION

Co-therapy is considered as a part of the developmental process of Family Therapy practice. It is suggested that it was widely used in the early stages as a method by which therapists could support and help each other while learning to work with families. It was seen to have particular advantages in psychodynamic work in so far as modelling, complementarity and mirroring were concerned, although success was to a great extent dependent on the quality of the relationship between the co-therapists.

The introduction of Systems Theory and consequent development of new skills and techniques appears to have led to therapists choosing to work alone more frequently, although the co-worker(s) may continue to be part of the process behind a one-way screen. The need for ongoing research with particular reference to the value of co-therapy as compared to lone therapy intervention is recognized.

REFERENCES

Boszormenyi-Nagy, I. and Spark, G. M. (1973). "Invisible Loyalties", Harper & Row, New York.

Dowling, E. (1980). Co-therapy: A clinical researcher's view. In "Family and Marital Psychotherapy", (S. Walrond-Skinner, ed.), Routledge & Kegan Paul, London.

Hannum, J. W. (1980). Some co-therapy techniques with families. Family Process, 19, 161-168.

Minuchin, S., Montalvo, B., Cuerney, B., Rosman, B. and Schumer, F. (1966). "Families of the Slums", Basic Books, New York.

Mueller, P., McGoldrick, M. and Orfanides, M. (1976). A Method of Co-therapy for Schizophrenic Families. Family Process, 15, 179-191.

Napier, A. Y. and Whitaker, C. (1978). "The Family Crucible", Harper & Row, New York.

Papp, P. (1978). The family that had all the answers. *In* "Family Therapy: Full Length Case Studies", (P. Papp, ed.), Gardner, New York.

Skynner, A. C. R. (1976). "One Flesh, Separate Persons", Constable, London.

Walrond-Skinner, S. (1976). "Family Therapy", Routledge & Kegan Paul, London.

Chapter 12

Going Back to your own Family

S. Lieberman

I. INTRODUCTION

In this chapter I shall present reasoned arguments to persuade you to use your family of origin as a personal resource in your work. Your experiences in your own family of origin should already have taught you a great deal about the structure, transgenerational influences and resistances which are universally found. Further work with your family can provide added knowledge, skill and personal growth.

Going back to your own family of origin to study it and change your relationships within it is a novel and controversial act. Its novelty stems from its rarity as a prescribed part of training. English family therapists have yet to adopt this procedure within their training programme. It is a rarely described, taught or written technique. Going back to your own family is controversial in that it raises the spectre of confidentiality, personal insight and growth, and involvement of "innocent" bystanders (the therapist's family members) on the road to becoming a family therapist.

A search of the literature reveals a paucity of material which discusses the issue of going back to one's own family of origin. The seminal article was published anonymously (1972) at first, and later published by Bowen (1974). But the original airing of the issue, "Differentiation of a Self in One's Own Family", was presented in 1967 to a family therapy research conference following the breakthrough in Bowen's efforts to work with his own family. Bowen believed that

> the family therapist usually has the same problems in his own family that are present in families he sees professionally and that he has a responsibility to define himself in his own family if he is to function adequately in his professional work.

His attempt to differentiate himself from his parental and extended family was guided by his theoretical postulates of family functioning (Bowen, 1976). Differentiation for him meant being able to "maintain emotional objectivity while in the midst of an emotional system in turmoil, yet at the same time actively relate to key people in the system". I have summarized all of his theoretical concepts elsewhere (Lieberman, 1980), but it is necessary to understand his techniques for working with families in order to grasp why he did what he did with his own family.

II. APPLICATION OF BOWEN'S TECHNIQUES

The three main techniques are detriangling, reversal of emotional cut-off, and increasing the differentiation of self.

A. Detriangling

In detriangling, the therapist investigates a particular family triad. He excludes the most vulnerable individual, whether child or parent from further sessions, and arranges to meet with the remaining family members. The therapist then sits back and awaits triangling moves. When they come, they are resisted and explored by the therapist. The end result is an alteration in the needs of the family members to emotionally bring in (triangle) vulnerable family members which will generalize to the family environment.

B. The Reversal of Emotional Cut-off

This requires only one family member in therapeutic sessions. Bowen coaches individual family members, not necessarily the identified patient, to re-establish relationships with relatives who were emotionally cut off so as to reverse the process. Once in contact, he coaches them to establish a new type of relationship based on "solid selves" rather than "pseudo-selves".*

C. Increasing the Differentiation of a Self

This describes the method by which Bowen attempts to raise the level of differentiation for his patients. He asks individual patients to work with their family of origin so as to continually detriangle themselves from the family. The result of this manoeuvre is meant to be an increased level of

---

* *Editor's note:* Although this term is in common usage by the Bowen Group, it is both distinct from, and overlaps with other writings about "true" and "false" self from a psychoanalytic perspective (see Balint, 1968; Guntrip, 1968; Rycroft, 1968; Winnicott, 1971; Lomas, 1973). There are at least three distinct uses both of *Ego* and of *Self* in the Psychoanalytic and Family Therapy literature. Bowen appears to derive the terms from the American psychoanalytic writings at a time when Hartman (1965) and others were defining the Ego as an adaptive mechanism, very similar to the error-control cybernetic model. "Self", on the other hand has usually been defined experientially in "who I am" terms. The "false self" is the character played by an individual in life-events while the "true self" refers to the individual's authentic experience of him- or herself if and when it can be realized. In contrast, Bowen's "solid self" refers to the level of differentiation, viz. it defines a level of ability to perform certain behavioural and interpersonal tasks which is fixed at a certain point in development, and is relatively uninfluenced by context. "Pseudo-self" on the other hand, is a definition of performance which varies according to the anxiety and relationship context. For further development of these concepts, see Bowen (1966) and Kerr (1981).

self-differentiation.[†] This technique is especially useful when faced with adults emotionally arrested in their adolescent stage of development. While differentiating a self, the individual establishes a new responsibility for himself as he is coached to make his own therapeutic manoeuvres. Bowen, after beginning therapy with adults individually or in marital or family therapy, sends his adult patients home to visit their family of origin, supervising them in their differentiating struggles.

All of the above techniques are used in Bowen's work with his own family. After an account of his family background and history, he details preliminary work which consisted of person-to-person communications over a period of 12 years. These attempts were supposed to enable him to develop independent personal relationships with members of his extended family (reversing emotional cut-off). He hoped he would then be able to break the existing family triangles and prevent himself from fusing into his family's emotional system. This strategy alone proved unsuccessful. "Action is required when words fail to detriangle in emotional systems." Bowen set up a situation in which he precipitated a confrontation between himself, his brother and his mother. His mother would often relate stories about his younger brother to him, while his brother avoided him entirely. Bowen wrote down many of these stories in a letter sent to his brother and primed many of his relatives in various ways for his next visit to the family home. A 2-hour personal discussion with his brother and his brother's wife resulted which was full of fire and thunder while his wife, his mother and his father hovered in the background. During this trying period, Bowen reports that he was able to stay completely outside of his family's emotional system (differentiating a self).

His success and its resultant effect upon him led Bowen to begin coaching his trainee family therapists to achieve a similar goal in their families of origin. He claims that

> Those who had been most successful with their families developed unusual skill and flexibility as family psychotherapists. They were adept at avoiding intense emotional entanglements with families in their practice and they could work comfortably with upset and distraught families.

III.   FURTHER DEVELOPMENTS

Although Bowen's presentation predates all other existing written material on this subject, in 1968 there appeared the first published article (Framo, 1968) by a

---

[†] *Editor's note:* The concept of self-differentiation has been elsewhere clarified by the author (Lieberman, 1981, p.340):

> The concept of differentiation is defined rather tortuously by Bowen. Those individuals with high levels of differentiation of self are emotionally and intellectually integrated with intellectual control maintained. Individuals with low levels of differentiation of self are said to have emotional and intellectual fusion. Here, the control of the self is muddled so that the individual's reactions are liable to be determined by the relationship (family) system and develop a pseudo-self, a concept similar to Winnicott's false self (Winnicott, 1965).

family therapist devoted entirely to the impact of one's family of origin on families in therapy and vice versa. Framo starts from the premise that treating families "revives the specters of one's own past family life" as well as the "subtle suffusing effects on the therapist's current personal family relationships". The remainder of the article he describes as "a kind of self-indulgent labour of love and pain", in which he anecdotally catalogues and compares statements from various family therapy sessions followed by his own personal reflections or vicarious participations. It is a curiously moving paper which Framo later described as his favourite (Framo, 1976). He maintains that a "critical but unnoticed ingredient in all family and marital therapies is the presence of the ghosts of the therapist's own family".

In 1970, there appeared the first of many articles later to be published using Bowen's techniques and theory to describe work with the therapist's own family (Friedman, 1970). Friedman indicates that his goal was to obtain change in his extended family, and that his most potent tools were verbal and behavioural reversal. Specifically, he used himself as an antitherapist in his family "by *not* helping precisely where because of my professional expertise I could have been most helpful". He closely follows the Bowen model of re-establishing individual relationships with each family member and altering those relationships systematically.

In 1972, a systematic attempt to describe both the work on one's own family and the task of the supervisor of such work was published (Guerin and Fogarty, 1972). Guerin first gives a detailed description of a three-generation geneogram which is a starting point for a trainee's work on his own family. This blueprint or map of family relatedness plays a central role in the planning of work with the family. Existing frequency of contact and physical location of each family member are determined, and then the existing family triangles are explored. He reports that 25% of his trainees actually take on the project of working with their own families, all of whom found it personally and professionally helpful. The goal of the project is described as the differentiation of the self from others in the family.

Ideally, the planning and accomplishment of such work is guided by a trained supervisor (who has undergone a similar experience). But Fogarty describes such supervision as a battle for the mind of trainee therapists, as if it were a seduction of the trainee into a new way of thinking. Wooing trainees away from psychoanalytic viewpoints has less relevance in England* and detracts from the real work of supervision as it can occur with a willing and motivated therapist-trainee. Fogarty traces the reluctant path of a trainee from supervision of a case to supervision of the trainee's work with his family; a path which ends in failure

---

* *Editor's note:* The statement is relevant in terms of the different development of both Psycho-analytic and Family Therapy thinking in England, from that in the USA and parts of Europe. The object relations views of an individual (see Winnicott, 1971; Balint, 1968; Guntrip, 1968) have been more readily applied to a family context than the classical psychoanalytic approaches more prevalent in the USA. At the same time, the process of the development of Family Therapy in Britain took a different course, which at least initially meant that theoretical polemics were less relevant (see Cooklin, 1978).

to convert his young disciple. He concludes that family systems cannot be truly understood without personal application of the theory. Ferber's critique of this article is discussed in the section on a family training analysis.

Three further articles detail the intimacies of family therapists using Bowen's approach to working with their families of origin (Colon, 1973; Anon, 1973; Anon, 1974). Finally, two papers which deal with the importance of the family of origin as a resource in therapy (Framo, 1976; Carter and Orfanides, 1976) also touch on the importance of the family of origin of the therapist. It is noted that all of the above work is American in origin. The first presentation of work using a similar approach in England was the presentation of work with my own family to the Family and Marital Course of the Institute of Group Analysis on 21 January, 1975.

IV. A FAMILY THERAPIST'S TRAINING ANALYSIS

In another work (Lieberman, 1980) I have attempted to explore a model for a family training analysis. The necessary and sufficient components of such an analysis would include:

(a) Providing opportunities for insight and self-understanding,
(b) Increasing the empathic skills of the therapist,
(c) Providing an apprenticeship experience,
(d) Teaching a model for working with families,
(e) Providing experiential input through work with the therapist's own family members,
(f) Providing a therapeutic experience where necessary for the trainee and his family.

Insight and self-understanding have been traditional goals of training analyses for psychoanalysts and group analysts for many years. Insight is valued for its ability to warn therapists of their own compulsive and destructive helping behaviour. Insight into one's own family dynamics and relationships would result in similar protection for our client families. Although such insight may be obtained serendipitously, through a do-it-yourself process (such as Freud's self-analysis) or other haphazard means, the family training analysis would be an organized and supervised experience within a training programme for family therapists.

Accurate empathy is an established and important primary therapeutic quality (Truax and Carkhuff, 1967). Research has shown that training programmes can and should aim to increase the abilities of a therapist in this dimension. Empathy refers to the ability to detect another person's emotional state without interfering in it. It has been enhanced by specifically teaching individual therapists to detect feeling states in patients, peers, and standardized audiotapes. Accurate empathy is one of the qualities in therapists which behavioural therapists value (Marks, 1976) as well as family therapists (Minuchin, 1978; Bowen, 1974; Lieberman, 1980). Understanding of one's own family members would provide valuable empathic training in the following way. Family members who are most likely to arouse sympathy, hostility or other emotional reactions provide an ideal testing ground for the development of accurate empathy as defined above. For example, a family therapy trainee was unable to work effectively with a client-family due to the hostility of the father. Work with his own father enabled him to gain the necessary empathy to side with the client father in subsequent sessions. Previously his hostility towards his own father prevented him from being able to feel accurately what the position of his client father was.

An apprenticeship training provides the opportunity for a trainee to work closely with a skilled therapist. The advantages of such an arrangement include exposure to the expertise, and guidance through the literature and the various techniques of family therapy. Family therapy skills are partially intangible and defy concise definition. The art of family therapy is best learned through observation and tuition by experienced practitioners. A family therapy training analysis which links a skilled therapist with a trainee who is investigating his own family of origin can provide a close working relationship which is otherwise unavailable. Given adequate safeguards in the choice of competent trainers, an experienced therapist should be able to provide satisfactory personal tuition in the art of family therapy.

The training analysis will also provide a model for working with families. The trainee, by going back to his family would be learning a model of intervention of use to his clients. Not only would he learn the finer details of the process, he would be intimately aware of the problems involved, having experienced them himself. This experiential input should prove emotionally useful for the trainee when involved in client family sessions.

The model has been described in much greater detail elsewhere (Lieberman, 1980). Briefly, the supervisor-trainee dyad mirrors the therapist-client family relationship. Both involve the exploration of history through use of the geneogram. Both require analysis of the resulting family information. Both provide a rationale for setting tasks which real family members would then complete outside the sessions. The model can be used conjointly or singly with the individual family members.

One final useful outcome of the family training analysis is deeply personal. Individual and group training analyses have often been therapeutic in their effect on trainees, and this effectiveness has enhanced the use of the particular form of therapy by the therapist. The family training analysis might also become a therapeutic experience for the trainee and his family of origin as well as his current nuclear family. This experience might provide certain trainees with confidence in family therapy's effectiveness while rescuing the trainee and his family from their own pain and suffering.

V. FAMILY ANALYSIS: A PERSONAL ACCOUNT

My own search for identity as a family member and as a family therapist has been published (Lieberman, 1980). Since doing that work and speaking and writing about it, I have attempted to internalize the work which I did with my own family and to integrate it with theories of family intervention. The following account presents my work with my own family members tabulated with my retrospective comments in three different theoretical frameworks (see Table I).

Presentation of my own work with my family has raised the important issue of confidentiality and the involvement of innocent family bystanders in what is actually an attempt to change them by changing oneself. That is, although they have of course participated in the maintenance of the family patterns, they may not have asked for any change or played any part in the contract between trainee and supervisor/therapist. Bowen's defence of his work is that no one is an innocent bystander in a family, and that the change attempted is that of the therapist only. This "naïve" position ignores the primary system theory postulate that change in any part of a system affects the whole. The intent of a person may be to change himself, but his alteration is never encapsulated. This is true of individual and group therapy as well as family therapy.

VI. THE PLACE OF WORKING WITH THE THERAPIST'S OWN FAMILY

Perhaps a more honest statement would be an admission that working with your own family of origin changes relationships and may be helpful to some member but harmful to others. Bowen cautions that resistance will be created in family members if you tell them what you are up to. This secrecy of motivation may be viewed by some as dishonesty, trickery and manipulation. There are no independent accounts from family members on the receiving end of this type of approach, nor have negative results been published. Caution with any new and powerful technique is wise since its limitations are often determined after its successes have been reported.

Ferber (1972) presents a reasoned critique of working on one's own family. This critical evaluation is worth reading before any family therapist embarks on a journey through his family. Ferber begins by comparing the family training analysis to a ritual indoctrination so that the trainee may become the special sort of man in his culture that his role as a family therapist requires of him.

> Working with one's family is a ritual journey that one must undertake if one is to return with the grail of extraordinary competence as a family therapist.

His tongue-in-cheek critique continues with a description of the process of work between the supervisor (the master) and the trainee (apprentice) as set out below.

(a) The master establishes a relationship with someone who may benefit from working on their own family.

(b) The master tells the apprentice anecdotes about the master's family.

(c) The master produces postulate I: "Self-control is the only sure posture".

(d) The master produces a parable of his work with his own family.

Table I

Family Systems	(Bowen) Theory[1]	Structural Theory[2]	Transgenerational Theory[3]
Construction and analysis of your own family system	1. Discover relevant triangles. 2. Uncover evidence of fusion. 3. Determine levels of differentiation. 4. Determine presence of emotional cut-off.	1. How enmeshed is your family? 2. What are your family boundaries? 3. How overprotective is your family? 4. How rigid (resistant to change)? 5. What evidence of conflict avoidance?	1. What evidence of family collision? 2. What bonds exist based on family constellations and sibling position? 3. What are the timings of losses and gains in the family system? 4. What secrets exist between family members? 5. What replacements have occurred in the family system?
Set goals and work for change in your family system	1. Reverse emotional cut-offs. 2. Detriangle yourself. 3. Differentiate yourself by taking the "I" position. 4. Resist fusion.	1. Challenge the status quo. 2. Seek constructive conflict. 3. Stop overprotection. 4. Avoid enmeshment.	1. Uncover secrets. 2. Cross generational boundaries. 3. Share unmourned losses. 4. Absorb and reconcile family cultural differences.
Successful Conclusion	"To be with family members without fusing with them"	"To be able to work in high affective moments create and maintain, and be comfortable with moments of high intensity without being drawn in to 'help'".	"To provide a personal growth experience and insight while providing also a personal experience of working within changing a family system".

In 1970, during my first three months of training in Psychiatry, I used geneograms on my patients. Their usefulness led me to an awareness of my uneasiness about my own position within my family of origin.

I constructed a geneogram of my family and found there were gaps in my own knowledge which I felt impelled to fill. During the following year, I searched for the missing data.

I wished to develop character sketches of relatives who had not previously seemed important, either due to distance or death. I was interested in discovering family secrets. Lastly, I sought information about the effects of significant life events upon my relatives. I thought of it as a search for my roots.

When my parents decided to visit my home in Boston, I prepared myself for their visit by organizing a list of questions in my mind. On their arrival I

Recognition of my fusion with mother, emotional cut-off from father, eldest brother and extended family. Taking the "I" position in the presence of older family members was unsuccessful. Many triangles but especially the oedipal one.

First goal was to reverse emotional cut-offs.

Detriangling moves

I recognized my use of conflict avoidance with all family members. Father's rigidity and mother's overprotectiveness were noted. I was part of an enmeshed family system.

I decided to challenge the status quo by avoiding enmeshment and seeking information which might lead to constructive conflict.

Here I challenge the status quo

I probed, clarified and questioned,

I involved myself in a search for my own identity and roots. I wondered what transgenerational influences moulded me into the person I had become. I used my family geneogram as a blueprint.

I sought data about death and illnesses in my extended family. Secrets and the boundaries they created, reactions to lost sibling positions, bonds and family cultural differences were to be sought.

I sought to cross generational boundaries by uncovering secrets

---

[1] See Bowen, 1976.
[2] See Minuchin, 1978.
[3] See Lieberman, 1980.

Family Systems	(Bowen) Theory	Structural Approach	Transgenerational Approach
approached each of them separately. I asked specific questions about their life history and mine which were a mystery to me. For example, I asked my father to share his feelings and thoughts about our move from Chicago (1951) when he first separated from his family of origin.		by speaking separately to my parents.	signalling to my parents that I had crossed the boundary between childhood and adulthood. Family secrets reserved for the elder generation could be shared. The collision of their family backgrounds was broached.
I asked my mother about her own mother's illness and death.			
Much of my probing produced embarrassed silence or hesitant vague replies. Many of their answers awakened my dormant memories. My parents sidestepped some questions leaving me puzzled about many details,	Challenging fusion	A small measure of constructive confrontation as I avoid enmeshment and reject attempts to protect me.	
but as I left my parents at the airport, I was seized by a pang of mixed grief and joy which brought tears to my eyes. My mother felt similarly on the plane. Weeks passed in which a feeling of freedom and sadness mingled, preventing full concentration.	Response to small permanent increase in level of differentiation.	The feeling of release from a trap with less rigidity and overprotectiveness.	A change in family bonding occurred.
I wrote letters and telephoned my geographically scattered relatives. Separate letters to my	Further reversal of cut-off through letters etc.	Exploration of family boundaries.	I sought to alter my family bonding by sharing new feelings and ideas.

parents requested detailed histories of their lives.

My mother responded swiftly with a 9-page letter. She began with a list of her medical illnesses during my childhood which had required that I board with uncles and aunts. She wrote of her siblings' lives and characters, adding facts about two deceased siblings of whom I was unaware. She included secrets about her father's disreputable behaviour. (He was a powerful family figure.)

Her overprotective stance was greatly altered.

Transgenerational influences were revealed.

Sharing of secrets and knowledge that showed me the origin of family collisions and pattern.

The deprivation and hardship she described during her first year of life reduced me to tears. It contrasted starkly with the relative luxury of my life and increased my compassion for her. Some of my anger and resentment abated. Buried feelings of loss surfaced when I read of my dead maternal grandmother's life in Russia and France.

Solidifying the gains made in my level of differentiation.

Recognition of an unrelinquished bond.

I next contacted my mother's eldest brother asking for his memories of life in Europe and Chicago before my mother's birth.

A detriangling move with my mother which also reversed emotional cut-off with my uncle.

I challenged the status quo by establishing my right to contact my uncle without going through my parents. Inviting conflict.

This move let me create another generational boundary.

His reply came after he wrote

My mother's family's secrecy revealed.

Family Systems	(Bowen) Theory	Structural Approach	Transgenerational Approach
my mother. He wanted to know what she had written before he answered my letter.			
I sent a copy of my mother's letter to him and again asked for his help. Finally I spoke to him on the phone. He disagreed with some of my mother's letter and told me a great deal which he was unwilling to commit to paper.	Further detriangulation, also aiding differentiation.	A constructive conflict developed which also led to avoidance of enmeshment.	More secrets were revealed. Another boundary crossed. I altered my place in mother's family of origin.
I next sent copies of all letters to my brothers. I asked them for their memories and their reactions to me. My letter to my younger brother also contained my usual advice about his career.	Further detriangulation and reversal of emotional cut-off from my siblings.	Writing about feelings challenged my siblings.	Sharing secrets. Altering bonds. Changing family patterns.
He replied bluntly with confrontative honesty which was new. I had felt protective towards him while his reply showed emotional maturity beyond mine.	Recognition by my brother of my new level of differentiation allowed him to take the "I" position with me.	No conflict avoidance here anymore!	
My father failed to reply to my letters. I resolved to visit him and continue my work. In March, 1972 I stayed with him for 2 weeks. I brought the family album out and my father spoke freely about his family.	Emotional cut-off remained.	Enmeshed and rigid I had to force a conflict.	More gentle work of exploration. We spoke and shared more. Losses and cultural differences were revealed.
I visited my maternal grandmother's grave and spoke to my	Limited reversal of cut-off noted.		
	Reversal of cut-off and		

Narrative	Therapeutic move	Outcome	Interpretation
grandfather about his turbulent life. I felt free and easy with my parents. On my return to Boston a letter arrived from my father.	detriangling move between him, my mother and myself.	Enmeshment was minimal.	The letter signals a change in our relationship.
Two stories explain influences which moulded him. One illustrates the value of being a good neighbour. The other tells of my father hitting a neighbour's son. He fled in fear when the boy fell to the ground. This story was an explanation of my father's repressed temper.	Further reversal of cut-off. Some differentiation.	Status quo change some conflict resolved.	Much greater understanding of transgenerational influences and family patterns.
I obtained other information from my father's sister when she visited Boston. I learned that my father was the second born in his family. My father carried the name of the eldest who had died in his first year. Also, his family moved from Poland to America after the death of a brother during the war.	Detriangling move with my aunt. Reversal of cut-off.	I was becoming known as a family member who faced conflict and needed no protection.	Information from my aunt which was later shared with my father. Uncovering secrets and crossing generational boundaries.
Two years after starting work with my family, the wedding of a cousin became an opportunity to visit my extended family. My intention was to experience the impact of a large extended family while revisiting the city of my childhood. I hoped to test my new position	A test of my new level of differentiation by being fully engulfed by my extended family.		The large extended family group would test my new position in the family. Family cultural differences and patterns would be evident.

Family Systems	(Bowen) Theory	Structural Approach	Transgenerational Approach
within the extended family. I set as a major goal the viewing of family cine films which dated from 1948-56. Deaths in the family had prevented them from being shown. I found there was great resistance. Each relative said they wouldn't be upset but refused out of concern for someone else. Finally, after asking all of them and receiving their individual approval, I negotiated an occasion for the films to be shown. I also visited old neighbours, taped conversations with many relatives and filmed many of my extended family. I considered my work completed to my satisfaction.	Extensive detriangulation allowed me to work in contact with my family members without fusing with them. able to negotiate a new event	I created a new family structure. Unhealthy overprotectiveness was challenged. In the moments of high affective intensity I was able to negotiate a new event without being drawn in as a compulsive helper.	My success led to a feeling of elation and satisfaction. I maintained my new position within the generational hierarchy of my extended family. My work gave me confidence in dealing with my nuclear family, provided me with resources and understanding which have proved valuable in my clinical work and provided awareness of the fears and problems involved attempting to alter human relationships.

(e) The apprentice learns how to do similar work:

    (1) Identify problem areas in your family.

    (2) Go back and develop relationships with every family member.

    (3) Don't change their behaviour; change yours.

    (4) Open up closed topics.

    (5) Become close to those who are distant and vice-versa.

(f) Deal with problems in step 5 by backing off, rethinkng and re-entering when control is established.

The resulting therapist is described by Ferber as a "lone wolf", training people in the tradition of self-sufficiency and self-control in relationships.

That this end-point is not universally sought is a clear indication that the supervised family training analysis must have proper feedback between the therapist, supervisor and family members as a responsible approach to working with one's own family.

Ferber (1972) has described other ways to work on or with one's own family. These include the presentation of one's family at group seminars either through discussion, audiotape or videotape presentations of structured or unstructured interviews, personal appearances of family members or role-playing of family members. He has himself role-played his family network, shown videotapes and home movies of his relatives, brought his family in for an interview together behind a one-way screen and gone back to various of his family members a la Bowen.*

Throughout the discussions of the use of one's family of origin as a resource, the prime emphasis must be "who is this person; where is he going as a family therapist; and how if at all might he change his position in his family system to further his development as both a person and a family therapist".

REFERENCES

Anonymous (1972). Towards the Differentiation of a Self in One's own Family. *In* "Family Interaction: A Dialogue Between Family Researchers and Family Therapists", (J. L. Framo, ed.), Springer, New York.

Anonymous (1973). A Family Therapist's Own Family. *The Family*, **1**, 26-32.

Anonymous (1974). Taking a Giant Step: First Moves Back into My Family. *In* Georgetown Family Symposium Papers II (1977), (J. E. Lovia and L. McClenathan, eds), George University Press, Georgetown, Virginia.

Bowen, M. (1974). Towards the Differentiation of a Self in One's Own Family of Origin. *In* "Georgetown Family Symposium Papers I", (F. Andrew and J. Lorio, eds), Georgetown University Press.

Editor's note:

    How this development of the therapist as a person will in fact influence his competence as a therapist will depend also on the model of therapy he or she is using, and his or her level of experience in that model. However, the reader of this volume will be able to take the relevant issues raised in other chapters and consider the development of their own competence in the light of this chapter (see also particularly by Byng-Hall in this volume).

Bowen, M. (1976). Theory in the Practice of Psychotherapy. *In* "Family Therapy: Theory and Practice", (P. Guerim, ed.), Gardner Press, New York.

Colon, F. (1973). In Search of One's Past: An Identity Trip. *Family Process,* **12,** 429-38.

Ferber, A. (1972). Follow the Paths with Heart. *International Journal of Psychiatry,* **10,** 23-33.

Framo, J. L. (1968). My Families, My Family. *Voices,* **4,** 18-27.

Framo, J. L. (1976). Family of Origin as a Therapeutic Resource for Adults in Marital and Family Therapy: You can and should go home again. *Family Process,* **15.**

Friedman, E. H. (1971). The Birthday Party: An Experiment in Obtaining Change in One's Own Extended Family. *Family Process,* **10,** 345-359.

Guerin, P. and Fogarty, T. F. (1972). The Family Therapist's Own Family. *International Journal of Psychiatry,* **10,** 6-50.

Lieberman, S. (1980). "Transgenerational Family Therapy", Croom Helm, London.

Marks, I. (1976). Behavioural Psychotherapy. *British Journal of Hospital Medicine,* p.253.

Minuchin, S., Rosman, B. and Baker, L. (1978). "Psychosomatic Families", Harvard University Press, London.

Truax, C. B. and Carkhuff, R. R. (1957). "Toward Effective Counselling and Psychotherapy", Aldine, Chicago.

EDITOR'S REFERENCES

Balint, M. (1968). "The Basic Fault", Tavistock, London.

Bowen, M. (1966). The Use of Family Theory in Clinical Practice. *Comprehensive Psychiatry,* **7,** 345-374.

Cooklin, A. (1978). Family Therapy in the British Concept. *Family Process,* **17,** 99-105.

Guntrip, H. (1968). "Schizoid Phenomena Object Relations and the Self", Hogarth Press, London.

Hartmann, H. (1964). "Essays on Ego Psychology", International Universities Press, New York.

Kerr, M. (1981). Family Systems Theory and Therapy. *In* "Handbook of Family Therapy", (A. S. Gurman and D. Kniskern, eds), Brunner/Mazel, New York.

Lieberman, S. (1981). The Extended Family School of Family Therapy. *In* "Developments in Family Therapy", (Walrond-Skinner, ed.), Routledge & Kegan Paul, London.

Lomas, P. (1973). "True and False Experience", Allen Lane, London.

Rycroft, C. (1968). "A Critical Dictionary of Psychoanalysis", Nelson, London.

Winnicott, D. W. (1971). "Playing and Reality", Tavistock, London.

Chapter 13

The Treatment of Marital and Sexual Problems
A Behavioural Approach

M. Crowe

I. INTRODUCTION

Behavioural marital and sexual therapy can be said to have been launched as a specialist area in 1969-1970, when Stuart (1969) and Liberman (1970) published their seminal papers on marital therapy, and Masters and Johnson (1970) published their now famous textbook on Human Sexual Inadequacy. The twelve years since that time have seen various developments in the two fields, which have brought to attention both the strengths and the limitations of the behavioural approach.

Recent accounts of behavioural marital therapy are given by Jacobson (1981) and by O'Leary and Turkewicz (1978), and both have tended to emphasize a kind of "package" of therapy including the various aspects of reciprocity, negotiation and communication training described below: but for the purpose of simplicity, I will be separating the two approaches in this chapter, and dealing in a third section with approaches to sexual dysfunction. However, this should not be taken as an indication that one should carry out the various types of therapy exclusively of each other. Indeed in most cases, they can be combined to deal with different aspects of the problem simultaneously.

A. Characteristics of Behavioural Approaches in General

Behavioural approaches in general have certain characteristics which distinguish them from dynamic and other forms of psychotherapy. They are characterized by

(1) Observation of behaviour as the raw material for interventions
(2) A concentration on problems complained of, as the goal for therapeutic endeavours
(3) A general reliance on principles of learning
(4) A general tendency to directiveness in interventions
(5) An empirical approach to innovation
(6) A preference for short-term, problem solving involvement and
(7) A commitment to objective evaluation of efficacy

B.   Behavioural Approaches with the Family

Behavioural approaches are distinguished from dynamic and more traditional family systems-orientated approaches in the following ways:
  (1) They are not concerned with fantasy-life, with historical origins of problems, or with any metaphorical aspects of communication.
  (2) They use facts rather than feelings or intuition on the part of the therapist as criteria for intervention.
  (3) They are not concerned with the acquisition of insight.
  (4) They are not designed to produce "growth", although this may occur as a side-effect of improved interaction.
  (5) In assessing progress, the client's and therapist's feelings are given less weight than objective behaviour change.

More recent family systems-orientated approaches, however, have more in common with behavioural approaches. For instance in structural therapy as in behavioural therapy, actual observed behaviour in the treatment session is often the starting-point for therapeutic intervention. In strategic therapy, task-setting shares the directiveness of behavioural work. However, each of these approaches uses the therapist's understanding of the "system" (often based on quite marked speculation on motives and underlying emotions) in framing tasks, and thus depart from the reliance on objective behavioural observation.

Those aspects of behavioural marital therapy which are shared with almost all forms of family and marital therapy include definition of the initial referral, the acceptance by the couple of the interactional nature of the problem, an assessment of the history of the problem and the formation of a therapeutic alliance. These principles might be termed the basic underpinning of the treatment of a case. Problems can arise if inexperienced therapists simply attempt to apply the methods detailed here as if from a recipe book without consideration of the infrastructure of the problem.

II.   ELEMENTS OF A BEHAVIOURAL APPROACH

A.   Referral

Often the referral letter will talk of marital or relationship problems and ask the therapist to see the couple, but in less favourable referrals, there is a tendency for the referring agent to say something like "Mrs G has been depressed for many years, and her long-suffering husband is now saying that he finds this difficult to endure, and is thinking of separation". In the latter case, a good deal of groundwork will have to be done in order to re-align the couple's thinking from the medical to the interactional perspective.

B.   Assessment and First Session

It is important to take a reasonably full history of the marriage, including its strengths and weaknesses. A good question to ask is "What brought you together in the first place?", and this will often lead to discussion of the residual positive attractions holding the couple together in spite of their present difficulties. In addition, an assessment should be made of the couple's willingness to stay together and work on the problem: difficulties may arise if one partner is seriously contemplating divorce, or having an affair, and the other is desperate to remain married. Their willingness to change is another important factor to be assessed in this initial stage. My own preference is to give couples in most cases the benefit of the doubt and to take them on for therapy, bearing in mind some of the factors mentioned above in the form of private reservations on the likely outcome.

C. Making a Therapeutic Alliance

As part of the first session, it is necessary to achieve sufficient co-operation from both partners to begin working on the relationship. It is therefore necessary to make both partners feel that the therapist understands what each wants of the therapy, and he should therefore make every effort to empathize with both partners in the first session.

Having achieved this (and it may be necessary to repeat the exercise from time to time during therapy), another necessary exercise is to shift the couple's thinking from the behaviour disorder/illness model to the interactional model. This may not be achieved quickly, and with some very rigid couples it may be necessary to "accommodate" to their way of thinking for quite some time before being able to work on changing the relationship. For example, a woman with a husband who was partially impotent was most unwilling to concede at the beginning of treatment that the marital relationship could possibly contribute to the problem. She was asked to enter the treatment situation "to help him with his problem", and was soon co-operating well in behavioural therapy.

D. Principles of Task Setting

Tasks in BMT should be essentially interactional in nature, having either something for each partner to do, some gain for each partner to achieve, or at least the necessity for one partner to praise or appreciate what the other partner has done. Tasks should always be simple and practicable (see below under reciprocity negotiation) and goals for the couples to reach between sessions should be well within their reach.

III. BEHAVIOURAL APPROACHES TO MARITAL AND SEXUAL PROBLEMS

These may be divided into three types:
  (a) *reciprocity negotiation* (also known as operant interpersonal or contract therapy),
  (b) *communication training* and
  (c) *sexual skills training combined with anxiety reduction.*

The three types of approach are not mutually exclusive, and can indeed be combined, not only with each other, but other approaches based on cognitive or systems considerations.

IV. RECIPROCITY NEGOTIATION

A. Introduction

This was the initial approach in the field, as described by Stuart (1969). The fundamental principle here is the hypothesis of Thibault and Kelley (1959) that in social interactions the participants are always striving to achieve maximum "rewards" for minimum "costs". Stuart's oversimplified view of marriage and marital problems is as follows:

(1) Of all the possible alternatives for habitual interaction between marriage partners, *the existing one is the most rewarding and the least costly in terms of effort.* Thus, if a man spends many hours in his study working in the evenings, that activity is by definition more rewarding than talking to his wife or doing chores around the house. If, in the same relationship, the wife spends most of her interaction time with her husband complaining about his solitary habits, that to her must be a relatively more rewarding behaviour than any alternative. This concept has a respectable pedigree from the literature of operant conditioning, in the so-called Premack principle, which states that behaviour frequently and spontaneously carried out must be rewarding, and the opportunity to carry out this behaviour can be used as a reinforcer to encourage an increase in a more infrequent piece of behaviour.

(2) Most married people expect a *fairly equal sharing of rewards and costs (or duties) between the partners.*

(3) In unsuccessful or problematic marriages, *this sharing has either reached a very low level, or is unequal.* Some workers have postulated a "balance-sheet" concept of marital interaction in which couples who are well adjusted can accept a negative piece of behaviour from the partner in the expectation that it will soon be outweighed by the more frequent positive behaviour which is expected to occur. In problematic marriages, such positive behaviour is infrequent, and the occurrence of a negative piece of behaviour elicits from the partner an instant complaint, leading to a vicious circle of negative interaction. Thus, in unsuccessful marriages, each partner has great difficulty in persuading the other to do what he or she wants. In the face of this difficulty, each partner resorts to negative control, the implication being "if you stop doing what I'm complaining of, I will stop complaining." However, it is a poor method of control because the partner who is complained of is unlikely to comply, and therefore a kind of escalation of complaint can occur on both sides, with one partner or other usually "leaving the field" by sulking, depression, leaving the room or initiating physical violence which leads the other to seek shelter. Some couples seem to have developed this escalation of complaint to a fine art, as in those marriages in which the major element of interaction is blaming, complaining, threats and

negative reinforcement (cf. Dicks' "symmetrical marriages" and Edward Albee's *Who's afraid of Virginia Woolf?*)

In the face of this situation, the prescription of Stuart, Lieberman and others is very simple. The therapist takes an approach based on the premise that instead of using punishment ("I am hurting you because you hurt me") or negative reinforcement ("When you stop doing what I object to, I will stop hurting you") the couple should use positive reinforcement ("If you do what I want, I will try to please you.") The approach may be dismissed as naïve or excessively optimistic, but outcome studies detailed in a later section have shown it to be more effective than control procedures.

B. Basic Principles of Reciprocity Negotiation

The principles for the therapist to remember are few and simple:
(1) *Tasks for one partner* arise from stated wishes for changed behaviour by the other partner.
(2) If they express no wishes, but only complaints about each other's behaviour, these should be *translated by the therapist into wishes for positive behaviour.*
(3) Such behaviour should be:
   (a) *specific rather than general,*
   (b) *repeatable rather than once-and-for-all,*
   (c) *positive rather than negative,*
   (d) *acceptable to both rather than unrealistic.*
(4) If no wishes for positive behaviour can be extracted from the complaints, the therapist must devise a task which *substitutes a positive piece of behaviour which is incompatible with the negative behaviour complained of.*

By these simple principles, some 50% of marital problems can be significantly improved.

One or two examples will illustrate the approach. A husband may want his wife to show more affection. That is a positive goal, is repeatable and may be acceptable to both partners. However as stated thus, it is too non-specific. The wife has to know exactly how and when to show affection. The agreed task may be: "Kissing me when I go out in the morning and come home in the evenings", or "having a cuddle in bed before we go to sleep". The husband will judge whether it is being carried out.

A wife may want her husband to stop going out to the pub so often. That is a negative, repeatable but rather over-general goal. The task would have to be designed to be positive and incompatible with outings to the pub. A suitable compromise, acceptable to both parties, might be to arrange for the husband to go out to the pub only or two nights per week, and to arrange to do something involving the wife on the other nights (which might be to stay home with some cans of beer, or to go out as a couple). The new task is positive, specific, repeatable, and (if properly negotiated by the therapist) acceptable to both parties.

Another possible task for a wife whose husband objects to her nagging could be to "listen to what my husband says for a few minutes without criticizing". A husband who leaves too many chores for his wife to do could be asked to "spend half an hour between 8 and 9 p.m. helping with the washing up and clearing away". This last task has the advantage that the couple would be thrown together during the washing-up period; lack of time to talk together is often a complaint.

The examples above may seem naïve and irrelevant to the major underlying conflicts experienced by the couple. However, experience with the method shows that often the minimal improvement in relationship achieved by the use of reciprocity negotiation (probably the first such improvement achieved by the couple for many months) improves the whole atmosphere to the extent that more major conflict areas can be tackled.

C.   Reciprocity Negotiation: Case Example

(1)   A Combined Marital and Sexual Problem

This couple presented with a combined marital and sexual problem which they both saw as predominantly sexual in nature. The husband, aged 37, was in his second marriage, and he had in fact terminated the first marriage as a direct result of the present relationship. His wife, seven years younger, had not been married before; indeed he had been her first sexual partner. The problem was that, although the couple were having intercourse twice weekly, with mutual orgasm, the wife almost invariably refused sex and had to be persuaded into it, with more or less bitter arguments. The husband would have preferred to have intercourse more often, and could not understand his wife's "frigidity", especially as she enjoyed sex so much when it occurred. Six months before, the wife had taken a mild overdose of tablets because of continual tension in the marriage.

It appeared that there was a communication problem in that the husband was an eloquent and persuasive talker with an arts degree, whereas the wife was a quiet but competent woman who had little to say and a rather poor self-image. A straightforward explanatory approach was tried, explaining the power differences in the marriage and the way that I could see sex being used as a defensive weapon by the wife. This produced no improvement, and in the second session I suggested that if sex took place twice a week in any case, it would be better to create a timetable for themselves; they agreed to this. Every Thursday and Saturday they agreed would be the husband's days, and the wife would comply in any sexual activity he suggested. However, Sunday, Tuesday, Wednesday and Friday would be the wife's days, and on those days it would be the wife who decided absolutely what the couple did together: she thought that this would probably be cuddling and expressions of affection but not actual intercourse. Monday was left open because both were often unavailable on Mondays.

At the next session, both reported a great improvement. They had enjoyed sex on two days a week (with some interchange of days which had been amicably arranged), and the wife had greatly appreciated the lack of pressure on her days. There had been one dispute, over whether the husband had the right to insist what dress she should wear on his days, but this was settled in her favour without much negotiation. The improvement continued, and in the next session the wife requested that, as it seemed that I had created an unfair division of days, it would be best if Monday (the spare evening) could be designated another of his days, and it transpired that in the previous two weeks sex had been occurring on average three times a week. This increase in the husband's days was arranged, and although I was doubtful of the necessity for continuing the strict rota any longer, both said that it had transformed their marriage and requested for it to be continued indefinitely.

In the last session (the fourth), things were again going very well, with further improvements in their sexual satisfaction, and a considerable increase in harmony in the marriage. The remaining problem the husband defined as their lack of truly intimate communication leading to growth in the marriage: "We really should have no secret thoughts or opinions". While the wife agreed to this, I noticed considerable hesitation in her voice, and suggested that such growth, while desirable, should proceed at the pace of the slower member. Both agreed to work towards it, but recognized the need for the husband to avoid putting on pressure, a pitfall he had learned to avoid in the sexual area. At the follow-up of two months, they reported by telephone that the marriage remained very satisfactory, with continued improvement in sex and communication and no further depression on the wife's part.

The tasks suggested for this couple were in one sense behavioural, in that they ensured that both partners began to get what they wanted out of the relationship. However, the main task also had strategic respects, in that it took sexual relationships out of the area in which the partners were waging an undeclared power struggle, and enabled them to communicate freely in the secure knowledge that the rights of each were being respected.

(2) Extending from Reciprocity Negotiation

This case illustrates some of the points above, but the interventions were not exclusively "reciprocity negotiation" ones.

The couple were referred with a marital and sexual problem. The husband (aged 33) had developed a revulsion against sex with his wife (aged 27), and they also complained that the wife was irritable, depressed and unreasonable, while the husband was "shut in" and unemotional. The husband's parents were divorced, and his mother was described as manipulative, but the wife's family were unremarkable. The couple were professional ballroom dancers who worked together, and had decided at this stage not to have children.

The treatment began with some relaxation and sensate focus (see section on sex therapy), but it soon appeared that there were no technical sexual problems, and the main issue was to change the husband's motivation, which had prevented him in the first three weeks from initiating any sexual or petting activity. When asked what they wanted of each other, the wife said she wanted her husband to take initiatives and be assertive in daily life as well as in sex, and the husband said he wanted his wife to be less assertive, and more of a "little wife". These were specified as the husband initiating some kind of physical (non-sexual) contact each day, and the wife approaching him in a seductive rather than demanding way sexually.

The relationship improved considerably at this stage, and they succeeded in having intercourse once, but the husband did not ejaculate. They reported that the husband had become more assertive, and the wife more "soft and womanly".

A considerable amount of work was done on their communication at this point, and the husband expressed his resentment of the wife criticizing his function as host at a Christmas party: "He should have refilled the glasses more often". She objected to his paying too much attention and respect to his mother and neglecting his wife. I suggested at this point (not strictly behaviourally) that the wife should exaggerate her criticism of him by giving him points out of ten (as in a competition) for his public "performance". I also pointed out how the divided loyalty between wife and mother helped the husband not to be entirely committed to his wife, and that that seemed to be as he preferred it to be.

The relationship continued to improve, as did their dancing and teaching, but sex remained very infrequent, until following a session in which I expressed pessimism and wondered whether it would end in divorce, after a discussion with her mother-in-law, the wife decided to become a more conventional wife (see above) and to cook her husband breakfast each morning. The husband responded by reducing his masturbation and initiating sexual activity as a couple more often. When last seen, they had returned from a successful European tour and holiday, during which sexual intercourse had taken place three times each week, although this frequency had reduced on return. Their final suggestions were to take regular short holidays together, to interrupt their gruelling work routine (husband's idea) and to buy a new double bed (wife's suggestion).

In spite of some non-negotiating interventions, I feel that the main thrust of this therapy, and especially the wife's change of behaviour towards the end, was related closely to reciprocity negotiation.

V. COMMUNICATION TRAINING

A. Introduction

This approach was originated almost as early as Stuart's and Lieberman's Reciprocity Negotiation. For instance, Patterson and Hops (1972) described the training of couples in improving their negotiation patterns, substituting positive and constructive requests for negative and destructive criticism. A full description of the communication technique, which was written for the benefit of clients, but is extremely readable and useful for therapists, is "A Couple's Guide to Communication" by Gottman *et al.* (1976).

The approach shares with Reciprocity Negotiation the rather naïve idea that both partners wish to have a good and peaceful relationship, with logical and matter-of-fact communication, and that the only reason that this doesn't happen is that they are inefficient communicators. While the idea is clearly over-simplified, it does at least give the couple the "benefit of the doubt", and puts the therapist in a relatively unassailable position as someone who is on the side of good relationships and is seeing the best in both partners.

The therapist in this approach asks the couple to talk to each other, and is therefore doing a similar thing to what Minuchin (1974) describes as "de-centering". This is a particularly difficult role to play, especially for therapists who like to be active negotiators, but it is vital to the success of the method to be able to insist that the partners speak only to each other, and that neither of them involves the therapist in conversation until the therapist is ready to intervene with a comment or a re-phrase of what has been said.

B. Examples of Destructive Communications

When the couple talk to each other, it is almost inevitable that one or other will make a comment that intrudes on the sensitivities of the other. Such comments may be of many types, for instance

(1) *Destructive criticism:* ("You're a real coward", or "You really like to hurt me").

(2) *Generalizations* which often amount to character assassination: ("You're always showing me up", or "That's typical of your immature attitude").

(3) *Mind-reading, or imputing destructive motives:* ("You say you're trying to help, but I know it's just to humiliate me").

(4) *Bringing up the past* (often combined with generalization): ("I've suffered this for 16 years and you're still doing it", or "I'll never forgive you for what you said to my mother").

(5) *Putting oneself in the right and partner in the wrong:* ("I've never started a row in the whole of our marriage", or "All I want is peace, and look at the way you treat me").

(6) *Using logical argument as a weapon:* ("All you have to do is to stop over-reacting", or "Be reasonable, can't you see that this is the only way?").

(7) *Raising the voice:* (a ploy that can easily be overlooked)

(8) *Using the sting in the tail:* ("You've stopped criticizing me, but now you've gone silent and that's worse", or "You are trying now, but why couldn't you have done so 5 years ago?")

C. Interventions to Reduce Destructive Communications

This is a small sample of all the possible variety of ways in which couples can play on each other's sensitivities. In intervening in this kind of conversation, the therapist has to be able to stop the action without causing offence, and that is an art which has to be learned by trial and error. After stopping the action, it is important to say something which will enable the partners to get the same message across, but without the problem which emerged in the communication. Thus the therapist may have to point out the error in communication, while at the same time emphasizing the speaker's good intentions. This could take the form of asking the speaker to re-phrase what was said, or suggesting a new form of words more acceptable to the listener. Ideally, some teaching would also be included to help the speaker learn the principles of avoiding the same error in future discussions.

Here are some examples of the kind of feedback which can be given, both in terms of teaching of principles, and the actual suggestions for phraseology:

(1) *Use expression of one's own feelings* instead of imputing feelings to the other partner: ("You really like to hurt me" becomes "I felt very sad to hear you say that."). This example has three improvements: the speaker's feelings are expressed, no imputation of intent is made on the speaker's side, and the sentence applies to a specific and not a general situation.

(2) *Use specific examples:* ("You're always showing me up" becomes "I felt really embarrassed when you spoke about me to George last Friday").

(3) *Avoid mind-reading:* (Partners are requested to ask about motives rather than to insist that they know better than the other partner what he is thinking).

(4) *Stick to the point:* (this can mean not bringing up the past, and not generalizing to similar instances).

(5) Replace logical arguments with *expressions of one's own emotions:* ("All you have to do is to stop over-reacting" becomes "It makes me feel hurt when you raise your voice").

(6) Therapist can point to *non-verbal aspects* such as *body posture* or *eye contact* as something that raises sensitivities.

(7) Partners should be encouraged to *take responsibility for their own actions:* ("You always make me angry and then I get violent," becomes "I can't seem to control my temper.")

(8) Often *monologues* kill communication, and these can be politely discouraged, with a clear message that short-sharp comments are more desirable (note the phrasing of this sentence, with emphasis on the desirability of one rather than the undesirability of the other).

D.   Communication Training: Case Example

This case, as the previous one reported, is not "pure" in its illustration of the communication training approach, but contains enough features of it to be of interest here.

(1) Presentation
The couple presented via another therapist, who had been treating them for the wife's problem of anorgasmia. This had been partially reversed, but she was still unable to achieve orgasm except with a vibrator. However, a more serious problem was that she seemed to be showing an obsessional jealousy of her husband's previous sexual partners.

He was 70 and his wife, 58. It was his third marriage (he was divorced from his first wife due to her infidelity, and from his second wife when she became chronically psychotic) and her second marriage (she had been widowed some years earlier). When the couple first got together, they lived in the village where the husband (then divorced) had been having an affair with a single woman living nearby, and after the marriage, this woman had made a good deal of trouble for the couple, with anonymous telephone calls, etc. This had coincided with the husband experiencing a short episode of impotence for which the wife was very helpful and considerate, but when she complained of not experiencing an orgasm, he replied "Well, none of the others have ever complained". This the wife found intolerable, especially in view of the behaviour of the neighbour, but she could never elicit an apology from the husband, and at the time of therapy, six years later, their communication was characterized by continual complaints by the wife of his previous insensitivity and lack of support, and stone-wall defence by the husband.

(2) Interventions

From the beginning, I asked the wife to write down many of her thoughts instead of bottling them up or talking to her husband about them, and this she did assiduously: I have some sixty typed sheets of her thoughts on the file. However, the pattern was still the same in their interaction, although a bit softer than before. I was very aware of the wife's great tendency to go into monologues, and I asked her to try and leave gaps every minute or so, until she received a reply from her husband. He was then able to reply, but I also had to ask her to avoid interrupting him and let him finish what he had to say. He said that although he knew sex was a sensitive subject, he wanted to say that in spite of the anorgasmia, sex with her was the best he had experienced. When she interrupted to say that he should have told her that 6 years before, I tried to impress on her that he should be rewarded and not punished for statements like that.

In spite of all the improvements, however, the wife was not satisfied with his account of the past, and needed reassurance about that period. The husband got as far as to say "I'm deeply distressed that you were so hurt at that time, but of course I had no intention of hurting you". I asked him to reword this so as to leave her with the reassurance at the end instead of the sting-in-the-tail (she tended to respond to his defensiveness instead of his apology). He did so, by simply reversing the order: "I had no intention of hurting you, but I'm deeply distressed that you were so hurt," and this proved much more acceptable to her, while being something that he could say sincerely.

On another occasion, she began talking about another couple, saying "I don't suppose she has any worries about her sexual relationship". He replied "That's a ridiculous thing to say", which made her very angry. Asked to replay his answer, he said, "It was rather imaginative of you, but I do understand", which she found partially acceptable. He then produced the most satisfactory answer: "I'm sorry that you haven't been satisfied sexually in the way you want". All along, I was careful to ensure acceptability on both sides for what was said, and after a traumatic session in which the husband rebelled and said it was 90% her fault, to the wife's great dismay and anger, they continued their progress until, at the end of therapy (12 sessions over 9 months), they were having a peaceful and less argumentative relationship, with few accusations from her and not much defence from him. The sexual relationship was as before, but both were accepting the use of the vibrator and reducing their unrealistic demands.

VI. ADVANTAGES AND DISADVANTAGES OF BMT

The above account and case examples have, I hope, provided an understandable and usable framework for practising BMT. The approach has many advantages and some possible disadvantages, which will be outlined here.

A. Advantages of BMT

The advantages are mainly related to its simplicity, its objectivity, its effectiveness and its clarity of goals.

(1) Simplicity
The approach *is simple to learn and put across to couples in treatment.* This particularly applies to the reciprocity negotiation approach, and in many couples, especially for the inexperienced therapist, this is a satisfactory way of initiating small but worthwhile changes in interaction. The communication training approach is more complicated, but can be introduced piecemeal while continuing to work with reciprocity.

(2) Objectivity
The approach *is based on objective criteria,* those of behaviour which may be observed by others besides the therapist, so that consensus of observation does not depend, as in more speculative systemic approaches, on agreement as to the underlying hypotheses used in therapy. Most outcome studies in the field use simple client-evaluation of improvement, or evaluation by independent assessor of improvement. An implication of this is that, in a broad sense, "the customer is right", and one cannot make statements such as "they say that interaction is worse, but that's just their resistance."

(3) Effectiveness
The approaches are of *proven effectiveness* as shown by the numerous controlled trials mentioned in a later section. This fact also highlights the susceptibility of the behavioural approaches to relatively uncomplicated assessment of effectiveness, an advantage which is not shared by the theoretically more complicated approaches such as strategic or dynamic family and marital therapy.

(4) Goal Directedness
The directive and goal-orientated nature of the BMT approach makes it highly compatible with the approaches to sexual dysfunction outlined in the next section. Since 60% of cases of sexual dysfunction appear to be associated with major marital problems, a marital therapy which combines easily with sexual therapy is an invaluable adjunct to the other techniques designed to improve sexual interaction as such.

B.   Disadvantages of BMT

Obviously, the above advantages are not an unequivocal recommendation for Behavioural Marital Therapy and there are disadvantages.

(1)   Over-simplistic
Behavioural Marital Therapy has been accused by Gurman and Knudson (1978) of being *over-simplistic*, and even Jacobson (1981) has not claimed that the perspective of reinforcement and positive communication can explain all the depths and subtlety of human interaction. Undoubtedly the BMT approach is over-simplistic, but it does not claim to be anything else: only to isolate the more easily manipulated factors for alteration, and to alter them successfully.

(2)   Motivation can be poor
Poor motivation on one side or the other can indeed sabotage BMT, as when the agreed goals in reciprocity negotiation are not adhered to. This situation can result when either both partners appear to find the status quo more acceptable than the apparent risk involved in change which entails trust in the other partner: or when one partner is clearly in favour of improvement and the other is not willing to commit himself/herself to change. This last situation can arise, especially in the cases where there is an apparent psychiatric condition in one partner. I have been impressed in my experience of marital therapy that, while psychiatric illness does not render therapy impossible, it does increase the "rigidity" shown by the couple, and as such makes change, especially that induced by simple means, less likely to be achieved.

(3)   Undermined by Conflict
Real internal or external conflict can render treatment less easy. *Internal conflicts* are those such as poor self-image or ambivalence about relationships, and are likely to be found in partners who would in other settings be said to suffer from personality disorder. In such couples, like those with psychiatric problems as such, simple resolution of conflict is likely to make only a small difference to the severe interpersonal problems. *External conflict* may be of many types, but one type commonly found is when one partner overtly wishes to terminate the marriage or cohabitation, and the other is keen to remain together. Such couples are perhaps more in need of "separation counselling", which leaves to them the decision of whether to separate, but concentrates on other issues such as deciding on trial separations, on reducing excessive closeness, etc.

(4)   Ignoring Historical Issues
It is also objected, by Gurman amongst others, that BMT *ignores historical issues* such as relationship with families of origin, especially with the couple's parents. This is broadly true, and the only defence of this omission is that it seems in many cases to be possible to achieve satisfactory and *lasting* solutions (see below on outcome) without delving into painful areas such as parental influence.

VI. SEXUAL DYSFUNCTION AS A PRESENTING PROBLEM

A. Introduction

Cases of sexual dysfunction naturally divide themselves into two types, namely those with a technical problem ("I feel sexy but I can't have an erection", "I can't achieve an orgasm in sexual intercourse", or "I can't relax sufficiently to allow penetration"), and those with a more complicated relationship difficulty ("Somehow I just don't fancy my wife", or "I can't bear him to touch me, but I could be aroused by other men"). Analysis of cases presenting at a sexual dysfunction clinic (Crowe *et al.*, 1977) showed that cases of the second type outnumbered those of the first by about 3:2. Both have a sexual problem as defined, but the second type need considerable help with the relationship as well as with the sexual function as such.

Since the publication of *Human Sexual Inadequacy* by Masters and Johnson (1970) a great deal has been learned about the treatment of sexual dysfunction, both from a behavioural viewpoint (Bancroft and Coles, 1976; Annon, 1978; Crowe, 1978; Jehu, 1979; Heiman and Lo Piccolo, 1981) and from a more eclectic approach (Kaplan, 1974). In this section I shall be dealing mainly with behavioural approaches and mainly with couple therapy, although in practice the

Table I.   Classification of sexual dysfunction

Problems presenting in the male partner:
Erectile impotence (primary: no successful intercourse ever)
Erectile impotence (secondary: successful intercourse in the past)
Premature ejaculation (may be associated with impotence after some years)
Retarded ejaculation (if totally absent may be called anorgasmia: prognosis better if
    ejaculation is possible in masturbation)
Retrograde ejaculation (orgasm present, but ejaculation occurs into bladder)
Painful ejaculation
Anaesthetic ejaculation (usually accompanied by hypochondriacal attitudes)

Problems presenting in the female partner:
Anorgasmia (total orgasm never experienced)
Anorgasmia (secondary: orgasm experienced in the past)
Anorgasmia (situational: orgasm achieved by manual or other stimulation but not in full
    intercourse)
Vaginismus (involuntary muscular resistance to penetration)
Dyspareunia (superficial: pain experienced in vulva and vagina)
Dyspareunia (deep: pain experienced in pelvis and abdomen)

Problems presenting in either or both partners:
Low sex-drive or reduced libido
Incompatible sex drives
Fear or phobia of sex
Dislike or refusal of sex

---

number of single people consulting therapists for impotence and other sexual dysfunctions appears to be increasing.

It would not be possible to discuss the treatment of sexual dysfunction without reference to the classification of types of problem and some of the contributory causes. These are given in Table I (classification), Table II (physical causes) and Tables III and IV (non-physical causes). In some conditions (e.g. premature ejaculation and anorgasmia), physical causes are very rare, and one may safely assume that the problem is, for the purposes of treatment, psychogenic. In other conditions, especially secondary impotence and dyspareunia, contributing factors of a physical nature are not unusual and should be investigated before proceeding with therapy. However, even in the most obviously "physical" cases such as impotence caused by diabetic neuropathy or multiple sclerosis, there is often an element of anxiety or marital communication disturbance which can be treated by psychological means with some success (see case No. 1, p.277).

As with marital therapy, there is a good deal of connection between the apparent aetiological factors and the therapeutic interventions used. Thus, in cases where marital communication seems reasonably good and the problem seems mainly related to anxiety, the therapeutic thrust will be towards anxiety reduction, and vice versa in cases of poor marital communication and low

Table II. Physical factors predisposing to sexual dysfunction.

1. Endocrine: (a) oral contraception (?)
              (b) castration (accidents or surgery)
              (c) pituitary tumours, etc.
2. Neurological causes of impotence:
              (a) multiple sclerosis
              (b) spinal diseases and injury
              (c) diabetes with autonomic neuropathy
              (d) nerve compression (disc prolapse)
3. Vascular causes of impotence:
              (a) fistula joining corpora cavernosa and spongiosum
4. Pharmacological causes of impotence, delayed ejaculation and anorgasmia
              (a) anti-depressants
              (b) tranquillizers and hypnotics
              (c) anti-hypertensives and diuretics
              (d) most drugs of addiction (loss of libido)
              (e) alcohol (liver and nerve damage, loss of libido and other more general effects.)
5. Pelvic and vaginal causes of dyspareunia:
              (a) tumours and cysts
              (b) salpingitis and other infections
              (c) vaginitis (monilia, trichomonas, or post-menopausal)
              (d) herpes genitalis
6. Any debilitating physical illness, causing loss of libido.

Table III.   Individual non-physical determinants of sexual dysfunction.

Sexual attitudes (parental influences)
Level of sex drive
Experience of sex (ignorance)
Sexual deviations
Traumatic sexual events (rape, etc.)
Quality of self-image
Ageing
Psychiatric illness of all sorts
Anxiety and life stress
Performance anxiety (often in both partners)

Table IV.   Relationship factors contributing to sexual dysfunction.

1. *Distance and closeness*
    (a) excessive politeness and consideration
    (b) continual symmetrical hostility
    (c) disparate needs (jealousy or constant nagging)

2. *Power relationships*
    (a) threats and violence
    (b) withholding sex as a power gambit

3. *Excessive dependency and protection*
    (a) the "patient" and the therapeutic spouse
    (b) the "parent" and the "irresponsible child"

anxiety. The course of treatment may change from session to session, and the improvement of marital communication may reveal that, even in the presence of good communication, some interference with function is resulting from anxiety, and needs appropriate treatment.

It will be seen from Tables II to IV that there are many possible causative factors in any case of dysfunction, and the need for flexibility in approach should be obvious. In particular, it is often necessary to do simultaneous therapy on improving marital relationships and dealing with the more technical aspects of sexual function. However, it is also useful to have a framework of therapy in mind, and at least in the early stages, the approach modified from Masters and Johnson (1970) is still a very valuable standby.

B.   An Approach to Sexual Dysfunction

(1) History taking
This is usually done seeing each partner separately, to elicit in a non-threatening way some of the factors contributing to the problem (Tables II and III).

In addition it is useful in the early conjoint sessions to enquire about marital history and stresses.

(2) Physical Examination

This is not necessary in all cases, but is especially useful in cases of secondary impotence to exclude physical causes (including testing for sugar in the urine, testicular pain sensation and reflexes). In cases of dyspareunia, consultation with a gynaecologist or experienced general practitioner is advisable to exclude physical disease. In cases of vaginismus, manual examination of the female partner can demonstrate the muscle tension which slowly relaxes: the male partner can insert his fingers afterwards as a prelude to the homework exercises in which he helps to produce relaxation in the vaginal muscles in the same way.

(3) Conjoint Interviews

All those subsequent to the history-taking are conjoint (or "round-table" in Masters and Johnson's phrase), and many general therapeutic measures are used. A good deal of *education* goes on, especially in shy and inexperienced couples. Permission-giving is another important facet: many people are obsessed with the "right way" of having sex, and need reassurance that their own preferred way is probably the best for them. The use of *humour* is extremely helpful: it provides for many couples a face-saving way of achieving change in attitudes, and removes some of the deadening seriousness with which some couples view their problem. *Empathy* is of course important, though it can be dangerous to "understand" one point of view too well, thus making an enemy of the other partner. Sometimes a *challenge* is necessary, as when couples make slow or negligible progress in treatment. All the *marital therapy* techniques mentioned in earlier sections can be extremely useful in dealing with relationship issues. *Bringing out of emotions* can be very beneficial, especially in couples who are inhibited in this area: a good approach is to ask them to make "I" statements about their immediate gut-feelings (Stanley, 1981).

(4) Relaxation

Although not supported by research findings, our experience is that many couples with sexual dysfunction find relaxation helpful (see Jacobson, 1981). Progressive relaxation of different muscle groups, preceded by tensing the muscles, moving systematically up the body from the feet, is accompanied by deep, slow breathing and mental imagery of something like a white flower. Particular attention is paid to the pelvic muscles, as relaxation and contraction of these (Kegel exercises) (Kegel, 1952) is helpful in many forms of dysfunction. Almost all couples in our clinic are given relaxation instructions in the early stages of therapy.

(5) Sensate Focus Techniques

These are a series of exercises practised by the couple at home, between sessions, often with the help of written instructions. The term "sensate focus" was introduced by Masters and Johnson (1970), but techniques have varied a good deal in the intervening 11 years. There is a ban on intercourse and on any touching of genital areas, of breasts or nipples. The couple should ensure that they are warm and comfortable (this may entail special heating of the bedroom during the English winter), and should undress and stroke or caress each other's bodies alternately, using body lotion or oil on the hands if desired. The emphasis is on physical communication through the hands of the active partner and the body of the recipient, and the couple are asked to use very little verbal communication. What they do say should be confined to reporting emotional states ("I feel good", "I feel sad" etc.), and to asking for a change in techniques (as before, this should be phrased as a positive request, such as "Could you press a little harder?", or "I'd rather you touched me on the leg just now"). The absence of the necessity for sexual intercourse often acts as a powerful anxiety-reducer, and may enable the dysfunctional partner to enjoy physical contact for the first time for months or years.

Not all couples are given sensate focus instructions. Some are not ready for it, as their marital relationship is too full of tension or hostility to make it likely that they will co-operate, and even if they do so, the technique is likely to be sabotaged. Others do not seem to need it, and may go straight on to the techniques to reduce premature ejaculation or vaginismus. Still others have "tried it all before" in therapy at other centres, and it would be counter-productive to attempt the same routine as before. However, for those who do co-operate and find the technique anxiety-reducing, it can be a very helpful step in the reversal of their dysfunction.

(6) Self-focussing

For many people, mostly women, who are afraid of their genital areas, who have been indoctrinated against touching themselves sexually, or have simply never experimented, it can be very helpful to encourage them to explore their own anatomy and responsiveness. The use of a hand-mirror can be included as part of the homework task, and it is often helpful to suggest this as an individual exercise, perhaps during a bath. As a later stage in self-focussing, both for men and women, the use of a vibrator can be recommended, which may be either a mains-operated body vibratory massager, or a milder battery-operated vibrator. Many women, in particular, can easily achieve orgasm with a vibrator when this is impossible using other means, and many experience their first climax in this way.

(7) Teasing Techniques

Particularly in cases of impotence and anorgasmia, the transition to mutual genital contact is a rather tricky one, and there is often a complaint at the session following this stage that introducing contact with the genital area reduced sexual excitement rather than increased it. It is particularly helpful here to recommend that the couple do not try to aim directly for an orgasm or for a hard erection: instead they should stimulate each other intermittently, with breaks or pauses whenever a partial erection or some sexual excitement is achieved. Apart from reducing "performance anxiety" in such cases, the pauses also act as a reassurance that it is possible to regain an erection or sexual excitement once it is lost, and this can be a very important factor in increasing confidence.

(8) Oral Sex

Oral stimulation can be recommended at this stage (but not imposed on couples who object to it) as a good transition between manual or vibrator stimulation and full intercourse.

(9) Control of Ejaculation

Control can best be achieved by the stop-start technique first introduced by Semans (1956). The squeeze technique of Masters and Johnson is similar in effect, but harder to teach and therefore less practicable. In the stop-start technique, the male partner is asked, as part of his homework, to stimulate his penis to erection and then to masturbate as if to produce an ejaculation. At the point when inevitability of ejaculation is about to be reached, he is asked to stop touching himself and allow the urge to go off, and to leave about 30 seconds before beginning stimulation again. This activity can be repeated several times, and we suggest carrying on for fifteen minutes before finally ejaculating. The next step is to carry out the same sequence using body oil on the hand (to increase sensitivity and make control more difficult). The man is then asked to carry out the same sequence, with his partner providing the stimulation, first with a dry hand and then an oily hand. Eventually control can be achieved by stopping and starting in the same way in oral sex and in full intercourse. The need to use the stop-start technique eventually diminishes as greater control is achieved.

(10) Ejaculation Failure

Where ejaculation is retarded or does not take place at all, the approach is somewhat similar to that for premature ejaculation, but the emphasis is on what Masters and Johnson called *super-stimulation*. In self-stimulation, in mutual genital stimulation and finally in intercourse, the emphasis is on short but intensive bursts of very rapid thrusting with pauses for rest: in the early stages the use of body-oil on the hand is recommended, to provide a more rapid and stimulating action. The use of vibrators is sometimes very helpful for these patients.

(11) Vaginismus

The use of *dilators* or *finger dilation* is recommended. It is almost always possible to examine the women vaginally using one finger, and the homework following this examination usually entails the insertion by male or female partner of one, then two or three fingers into the vagina very slowly and carefully. Graded dilators can be used in a similar way, and eventual penetration with the erect penis usually follows the use of three fingers or the largest dilator (No.6.) preferably with very little interval so that the vaginal muscles do not have time to contract following the withdrawal of the dilator or fingers.

(12) Use of Different Positions

In the processes of moving from genital teasing or the other special techniques to full intercourse, it is often a good idea to suggest a different position. The woman-above position is a very good one for many problems. If impotence is present, or ejaculation has to be controlled, these can both become problematic at the time of penetration, and it is easier in both situations for the man to be lying on his back, and for either him or his partner to be stimulating the penis just before penetration, which takes place with the female partner kneeling over him and penetrating in that position.

In cases of anorgasmia, a very good position is the one called the "feel free" position. The woman lies on her back with her knees raised, and the man lies on his side facing her with his legs bent under the arch made by her legs. The penis is in a good position for penetration, but both partners are comfortable if they want to go on with intercourse for a long time; also both partners have their hands free for access to the clitoris to stimulate this during intercourse. They can also use a vibrator at the same time as having full intercourse, and this may be a very valuable transitional stage to successful intercourse.

Other positions can help by providing variety of psychological stimulation, and getting away from the conventional position, associated as it is with failure and the expectation of failure.

(13) Psychological Stimulation

Psychological stimulation can be provided in several ways, and can be an adjunct to therapy both in those with a low sex drive (male or female), and in those who have problems where deviant sexual urges are interfering with hetero-sexual drives towards the partner. In such cases, it may be helpful to suggest regular reading of mild pornography (Forum, Playboy, etc.), to go to explicitly sexual films in the cinema, or to orchestrate their sexual experience as a couple to include particular objects or activities (lights, fur, silk, feathers, mild degrees of bondage or domination, etc.). Whatever is agreed must be acceptable to both partners, but there is no doubt from research (Gillan and Gillan, 1976) that such stimulation can increase the frequency and enjoyment of sexual interaction.

In the cases where there is a deviant competing urge, the possibility of mastur-batory re-training may be considered, in which masturbation begins with the deviant fantasy and the patient switches to heterosexual fantasies at the point of orgasm.

(14) Desensitization

This and similar anxiety reduction techniques can be used where there is a clearly phobic element to the sexual dysfunction, as in cases where the imminence of sexual activity causes an acute panic attack. Many workers in the past (e.g. O'Gorman, 1975; Friedman, 1971) have relied primarily on desensitization for sexual dysfunction problems in general, but most thera-pists would now favour the general conjoint approach outlined in the above sections.

(15)   The Time Scale of Therapy
The time scale is usually brief, i.e. weekly or fortnightly visits to the clinic over a period of 3-6 months; maximum of perhaps 10-12 visits. The initial visit is usually about 2½ hours in duration, but subsequent visits average about 45 minutes. In some couples, however, particularly those with low sex drive, non-consumation, or primary impotence, a *slower time scale*, with perhaps 15-20 visits spread over 18 months, may be preferable. In those cases, the problem may be to motivate the couple to interact sexually often enough to make therapy worthwhile, and other approaches such as regular letters from the couple to the therapist reporting activities between sessions can improve progress.

C.   Case Examples (Sexual Dysfunction)

(1)   Secondary Impotence with Diabetes and some Undeclared Marital Problems
The couple, who had one son, were both in their 40s, and presented with the problem of secondary impotence in the husband, which had been present about 3 years, and which was accompanied by a high sex drive on his part. The impotence had begun following his hospitalization for diabetes, and he was being treated with insulin for this, with good control. On examination, there was no evidence of neuropathy, and in particular his deep testicular pain sensation was preserved. There were some rather bitter arguments between husband and wife, which mainly centred on their sexual relationship. Both were musicians, but the wife was the more talented, and in other ways she was better than her husband: more intelligent and more competent socially: their friends were mostly hers before they were his. The husband was excessively tense and lacking in poise at interview, and his wife tended to be the spokesman and dominate the discussion, in a very natural and unassertive way.

Treatment began as usual with sensate focus and relaxation, and she ensured that the rules were kept during the first week, despite his wish to "go further" when he began to have good erections. It emerged in this second interview that the wife had very ambivalent feelings about sexual intercourse: she refused to be examined physically, and at first refused the genital sensate focus (manual genital stimulation). The therapist firmly took the husband's side on this occasion, saying that his wife must not be allowed to dominate him, and telling the wife that for the sake of her marriage she must sometimes give in to his wishes. On the third visit, they had made further progress, the husband had had good erections, and the wife had participated in genital sensate focus despite her misgivings. The therapist underlined the importance of the wife taking her husband's opinions and wishes seriously, and suggested to the husband that before coming to decisions about things involving the two of them, he should consult his wife. They were given instructions for penetration in the female superior position, and at the next visit they were having mutually satisfying sexual intercourse quite frequently.

During the next 3 months there were no appointments made, and at their follow-up appointment they reported that all was going well. They had had a setback to their sexual relationship 6 weeks before, when the husband had again lost his erection. However, they had recognized the problem, and had dealt with it by going back to non-genital sensate focus; within a week they had progressed again to having normal intercourse. There was an alteration in their interaction at the interview: the wife took less command of the situation and allowed the husband to be the spokesman on many occasions. At further follow-up 6 months after treatment, all the improvements were maintained.

(2) Primary Impotence and Non-consummation

The couple, in their early 30s, were referred by another clinic where they had had 3½ years of weekly marital therapy from a dynamic standpoint, with no improvement of the presenting problem of non-consummation, but with the acquisition of a good deal of self-understanding. They had been married 7 years, and were both technically virgins: the husband was a quiet and insecure professional translator, and the wife was a tense and active schoolteacher with a tendency to talk for both partners, and to take the initiative in discussing the problem at home. The husband masturbated approximately weekly, as did the wife, but when they attempted foreplay his erection was insufficient to penetrate, and the mutual sex play only rarely resulted in an orgasm for the wife: in any case, this activity had taken place less than once a month in recent times.

Both were keen to improve the situation, and followed the instructions for relaxation and sensate focus, with some sexual excitement on both sides. However, from the third visit onwards, some problems were obvious: they had had no time to practise genital teasing, both were feeling depressed, they had had some major rows and long periods of non-communication, and his masturbation was causing her to feel resentful. Some friendly fighting was suggested, which would hopefully improve their physical interaction and lead to more obvious sexual interaction. They responded well to this at first, and broke the leg of their bed, while he experienced some more sexual excitement, but they did not progress beyond mutual masturbation. Another period of inactivity followed, in which he became obsessed with physical fitness and began using a bullworker. In an attempt to undercut the couple's dependency on me and their passivity, I expressed impotence, and said that their problem was too strong for my limited abilities. Their next visit (the tenth), they reported that on the wife's return from playing badminton, he had met her in the kitchen, been excited by her flushed face and short white skirt, undressed her and achieved penetration for the first time, but without ejaculating. They continued to improve at a very slow pace with visits spaced perhaps a month or two apart, and at the time of writing, they are having regular weekly sexual activity with penetration and climaxes for her, but ejaculation still does not take place intra-vaginally, and they are contemplating AIH as a means of achieving pregnancy.

(3) Phobia of Intercourse in the Female Partner

This couple, in their early 50s, were referred from a sexual dysfunction clinic some 100 miles away, with a history of having had no sexual contact for some years. They presented as a very co-operative couple, the wife being a part-time hairdresser and the husband a British Rail driver. The wife reported that every time sex might be expected, she would become highly anxious to the point of breathless panic, and that although she could hold her husband's hand and they shared a bed, she could never allow him to touch any other part of her body. This situation had obtained for 16 years, and before that time she had passively accepted sex, discouraging foreplay and suffering in silence despite her panic, until eventually she had told her husband of her fears, whereupon he resolved not to trouble her any further for sex.

They were not ready for sensate focus, and so I embarked upon a very slow form of systematic desensitization, using her approach to his body as the first measure, and encouraging her both in the session and for homework to touch his leg and thigh, first through his trousers and then unclothed. A breakthrough occurred when she was able to touch his penis, albeit with much panic and some fears at first, and gradually he was able to touch her body (at first legs and arms, and later breasts and genital area) without her feeling panicky. Mutual orgasms were experienced in petting, which for her was a revelation, and led to a period euphoria in which she kept talking to her customers about sexual matters (a most uncharacteristic reaction). Over the next couple of sessions (Nos. 9 and 10), successful intercourse took place, the first time that they had both enjoyed this activity, and follow-up showed continued success both sexually and maritally.

D. Limitations of the Behavioural Approach to Sexual Dysfunction

As in the previous section describing behavioural marital therapy, it is clear that some cases of sexual dysfunction are more complicated and difficult to treat than others. Particular factors which have been shown to have an adverse effect on progress are the presence of severe marital problems and the co-existence of *psychiatric symptomatology* (Crowe *et al.*, 1977). Other features showing a more unfavourable prognosis are *poor motivation, internal or external conflicts* (see above) or *personality disorders* associated with impulsiveness and unpredictability. In cases of *alcohol abuse* associated with impotence, the prognosis depends on the ability of the patient to reduce alcohol intake, and this is of course not the easiest of tasks even in uncomplicated alcoholism. In cases where *depression* is a feature associated with sexual dysfunction, there is often a dilemma between improving the depression (and with it perhaps the libido) by antidepressant medication and the known propensity for many anti-depressants to reduce the ability to obtain erection in the male and orgasm in the female. In some cases where there are *organic factors* (e.g. diabetes or multiple sclerosis), progress can still be made by psychologically-orientated behavioural treatment, but the ultimate end-point of treatment is likely to be less favourable (e.g. partial erection and some need for prolonged sex-play or the use of vibrators) than in the uncomplicated case.

E. Alternative Courses of Action in cases where the Behavioural Approach is unsuccessful, in both Sexual and Marital Problems

It may be asked, in view of the limitations shown by both behavioural marital therapy and behavioural treatments in sexual dysfunction, whether other forms of intervention, such as dynamic, structural or strategic, would not achieve good results in precisely those cases for which the behavioural approach is of limited use, i.e. couples with psychiatric problems, personality disorders, alcoholic abuse, poor motivation, etc. In clinical practice, I tend to use a somewhat hierarchical system in this area. Initially I try to use a behavioural approach, either reciprocity negotiation or direct treatment of the Masters and Johnson type, as these are the simplest approaches, and involve a situation of complete frankness and overt helpfulness on the part of the therapist. If difficulties arise, I tend to involve a communication training, which also takes the couple into my confidence, but which involves a more dictatorial style, bringing in overt criticism of interactional style, and active side-taking on the part of the therapist.

Both of the above types of approach are, as shown in the section on research, of proven effectiveness in significant proportions of couples presenting with problems. However in more disturbed couples with motivational problems, clinical impressions suggest that the direct approaches are not so effective, and the next hierarchical step is to move to a structural approach, which has many features in common with communication training, but takes into account other factors such as boundaries, alliances and power within the relationship. A further step along the hierarchical ladder is to move to a strategic approach, in which tasks are set which take the therapist even further away from the "teaching" role and may include "prescribing the symptom" or directing the couple to fight or create tension in the marriage. I will not go into detail on either of these treatment approaches, but further reading could include Haley (1977), Minuchin (1974) and Sluzki (1978).

A word of caution is needed, however, in advocating the move to structural or strategic approaches in cases of unsuccessful behavioural therapy. These approaches require much skill and adequate understanding of systems concepts, and in any case, they have not been subjected to the same rigorous outcome research as the behavioural approaches. But the future of marital therapy, with more far-reaching outcome studies on structural and strategic approaches, and with more accurate identification of problems suitable for each approach, may reverse the situation.

VIII. OUTCOME STUDIES

This is not the place for an exhaustive review of outcome research in behavioural marital and sexual therapy. Numerous studies have now shown that both reciprocity negotiation and communication training are superior to no treatment in improving marital relationships (Azrin, 1973; Liberman *et al.*, 1976; Baucom,

1981; Hahlweg et al., 1981). One or two studies have included extra comparisons: Crowe (1978) showed that a package of treatment including reciprocity negotiation and some Masters and Johnson techniques was significantly superior to a control approach involving non-directive interventions, but that an interpretative systems-orientated approach was intermediate, and not significantly different from either BMT or the control group. These differences held up to 18 months' follow-up, and in this period, the interpretative approach showed some late increase in effectiveness compared with the control group. Emmelkamp et al. (1981), in three separate studies, showed that couples treated with a BMT approach and couples treated with a systems theory interpretative approach both improved significantly more than waiting-list couples. At follow-up of one month, there was a slight relapse in the systems theory-treated couples, but the BMT couples had maintained their improvement.

Bögner and Zielenbach-Coenen (1981) found that those couples given BMT in 15 weekly sessions, showed less extensive changes than couples given the same number of sessions given in two blocks with a five week gap in which there were brief telephone contacts with the couples (the "booster" treatment).

Jacobson (1978a) showed, in a single case design using multiple baseline measures, that six couples with severe marital distress significantly improved their marital interaction through the introduction of problem-solving therapy on one conflict area at a time. In another study, Jacobson (1978b) showed that couples treated in two behaviourally orientated treatment approaches involving problem-solving and communication training, performed significantly better on a behavioural post-test than control couples given non-directive interventions or untreated control couples. However, on marital satisfaction, all three treated groups including the non-directive group improved more than the untreated control couples.

In the area of sexual dysfunction, a large number of anecdotal studies are reported, but few controlled trials. Mathews et al. (1976) found, in a well controlled study, no differences in outcome between (1) Masters and Johnson therapy with two therapists, (2) Masters and Johnson therapy with one therapist, (3) systematic desensitization and (4) "postal" therapy with Masters and Johnson instructions and minimal therapist contact.

Everaerd (1977) found no significant advantage in conjoint therapy using a Masters and Johnson approach compared with systematic desensitization. Arentewicz (1978) found that there were no significant differences between one vs two therapists or intensive vs spaced treatment in sex therapy. Riley and Riley (1978) found that significantly more women presenting with primary anorgasmia became orgasmic in coitus with a programme involving the use of a vibrator, compared with a sensate focus and supportive approach, Kockoff (1976) found that, of patients previously treated with desensitization for impotence, a significant proportion of the unimproved patients benefited from a subsequent Masters and Johnson approach. In the previously quoted study by Crowe (1978), couples treated by Masters and Johnson and other behavioural approaches improved their sexual adjustment significantly more than couples treated with the control non-directive approach. Crowe et al. (1981) showed, similarly to

Mathews *et al.* (1976), that Masters and Johnson therapy was equal to contract marital therapy in the treatment of impotence and anorgasmia, and again that two therapists obtained no better results than one.

IX. CONCLUSIONS

In the eleven or twelve years since its inauguration, behavioural marital and sexual therapy has established a firm place in the range of techniques available to therapists. The approaches are easy to learn and to apply, although some general marital/family therapy skills are required, such as empathizing with each partner and focussing on the interaction. Reciprocity negotiation and communication training have been shown in numerous trials to be effective treatments for moderately disturbed couples, although in seriously disturbed or "psychiatric" couples, these techniques may not be clearly superior to alternative systems or dynamic approaches. In sexual dysfunction, marital therapy is an important component, but specific techniques are undoubtedly effective, especially in such conditions as vaginismus and premature ejaculation. All the approaches mentioned are best learned in supervised practice, and in all of them, the simplest interactional behaviours are used as the basis for change, with the undoubted advantage of such change being objectively assessed and, in many cases, quantified.

REFERENCES

Annon, J. S. (1978). "The Behavioural Treatment of Sexual Problems. Vols. 1 & 2", Harper & Row, New York.

Arentewicz, G. (1978). "Partner therapy with sexual dysfunctions: final report on a controlled study with 202 couples. Paper presented at III International Congress of Medical Sexology, Rome.

Azrin, N. H., Naster, B. J. and Jones, R. (1973). Reciprocity Counselling: a rapid learning-based procedure for marital counselling. *B.Res. & Th.* **11**, 365-382.

Bancroft, J. H. J. and Coles, L. (1976). Three Years' Experience in a Sexual Problems Clinic. *British Medical Journal* (**i**), 1575-1577.

Baucom, D. (1981). A Comparison of Behavioural Contracting and Problem-Solving Communications—Training in Behavioural Therapy. A controlled outcome investigation. Paper presented at international BMT conference, Tegernsee, W. Germany.

Bögner, I. and Zielenbach-Coenen, H. (1981). On maintaining change in behavioural marital therapy. Paper presented at international BMT conference, Tegernsee, W. Germany.

Crowe, M. J. (1978). Conjoint Marital Therapy: a controlled outcome study. *Psychological Medicine* **8**, 623-636.

Crowe, M. J., Czechowicz, H. and Gillan, P. (1977). The Treatment of Sexual Dysfunction: a report of 75 cases. Presentation at VI World Congress of Psychiatry, Honolulu.

Crowe, M. J., Gillan, P. and Golombok, S. (1981). Form and Content in the Conjoint Treatment of Sexual Dysfunction. A controlled study. *Beh. Res. and Therapy,* **19**, 47-54.

Dicks, H. V. (1967). "Marital Tensions", Routledge, London.

Emmelkamp, P., van der Helm, M., MacGillavry, D. and van Zanten, B. (1981). Marital Therapy with Clinically Distressed Couples: a comparative evaluation of system-theoretic, contingency contracting and communication skills approaches. Paper presented at international BMT conference, Tegernsee, W. Germany.

Everaerd, W. (1977). Comparative studies of short-term treatment methods for sexual inadequacies. *In* "Progress in Sexology", (W. Germond and C. C. Wheeler, eds), Plenum Press, New York and London.

Friedman, D. (1968). The treatment of impotence by Brietal relaxation therapy. *Beh. Res. & Therapy,* **6,** 257–261.

Gillan, P. and Gillan, R. (1976). "Sex Therapy Today", Open Books, London.

Gottman, J., Notarius, C., Gonso, J. and Markman, H. (1976). "A Couple's Guide to Communication", Research Press, Champaign, Illinois.

Gurman, A. S. and Knudson, R. M. (1978). Behavioural Marriage Therapy I. A Psycho-dynamic-Systems Analysis and Critique. *Fam.Process,* **17,** 121–138.

Hahlweg, K., Schindler, L. and Revensdorf, D. (1981). The Treatment of Marital Distress, Formats, Modalities and Prediction. Paper presented to international BMT conference, Tegernsee, W. Germany.

Haley, J. (1976). "Problem-solving therapy", Jossey-Bass, San Francisco.

Heiman, J. R., Lo Piccolo, L. and Lo Piccolo, J. (1981). The Treatment of Sexual Dysfunction. *In* "Handbook of Family Therapy", (A. S. Gurman and D. P. Kniskern, eds), Brunner/Mazel, New York.

Jacobson, E. (1938). "Progressive Relaxation", University of Chicago Press, Chicago.

Jacobson, N. S. (1978a). Problem solving and contingency contracting in the treatment of marital discord. *J. Consulting and Clinical Psychol.* **45,** 92–100.

Jacobson, N. S. (1978b). Increasing Positive Behaviour in Severely Distressed Marital Relationships: The Effects of Problem-Solving Training. *Behav.Ther.* **10,** 311–326.

Jacobson, N. S. (1981). Behavioural Marital Therapy. *In* "Handbook of Family Therapy", (A. S. Gurman and D. P. Kniskern, eds), Brunner/Mazel, New York.

Jehu, D. (1979). "Sexual Dysfunctions", John Wiley, Chichester.

Kaplan, H. (1974). "The New Sex Therapy", Brunner/Mazel, New York.

Kegel, A. H. (1952). Sexual function of the pubo-coccygeus musde. *Western J. of Surgery, Obstetrics & Gynaecology,* **60,** 521–524.

Liberman, R. (1970). Behavioural approaches in family and couple therapy. *American Journal of Orthopsychiatry.* **40,** 106.

Liberman, R. P., Levine, J., Wheeler, E., Sanders, N. and Wallace, C. J. (1976). Marital Therapy in Groups: a comparative evaluation of behavioural and interactional formats. *Acta.Psychiat.Scand.,* Suppl.266.

Masters, W. H. and Johnson, V. E. (1970). "Human Sexual Inadequacy", Churchill, London.

Matthews, A., Bancroft, J. *et al.* (1976). The Behavioural treatment of sexual inadequacy: a comparative study. *Beh.Res. & Ther.* **14,** 427–436.

Minuchin, S. (1974). "Families and Family Therapy", Tavistock Publications, London.

O'Gorman, E., Macallister, H., Quinn, J. T., Graham, P. J. and Harbison, J. J. M. (1975). Treatment of frigidity by group desensitization. *In* "Progress in Behaviour Therapy", (J. S. Brengelmann, ed.), Springer Verlag, Berlin.

O'Leary, K. D. and Turkewitz, H. (1978). Marital Therapy from a Behavioural Per-spective: *In* Marriage and Marital Therapy", (T. J. Paolino and B. S. McCrady, eds), Brunner/Mazel, New York.

Patterson, G. R. and Hops, H. (1972). Coercion, a game for two: Intervention techniques for marital conflict. *In* "The experimental analysis of social behaviour", (R. E. Ulrich and P. Mountjoy, eds), Appleton, New York.

Riley, A. and Riley, E. (1978). A controlled study to evaluate directed masturbation in the management of primary orgasmic failure in women. *Brit.J. Psychiat.* **133**, 404-409.

Semans, J. H. (1956). Premature ejaculation. *Southern Medical Journal,* **49**, 353-7.

Sluzki, C. E. (1978). Marital Therapy from a Systems Theory Perspective. *In* "Marriage and Marital Therapy", (T. J. Paolino and B. S. McCrady, eds), Brunner/Mazel, New York.

Stanley, E. (1981). Principles of Managing Sexual Problems. *Brit.Med.J.* **282**, 1200-1202.

Stuart, R. B. (1969). Operant-interpersonal treatment for marital discord. *Journal of Consulting and Clinical Psychology,* **33**, 675-682.

Thibaut, J. W. and Kelley, H. H. (1959). "The social psychology of groups", Wiley, New York.

INDEX*

---

*This index refers to Volumes 1 and 2, and is duplicated in both volumes.